The Other Side of the Hill
Behind the scenes stories of Parliament Hill

Dr. Don Nixon

Cover photograph credits.

Front cover: This handsome fellow, with his eyes shut for the camera, is 'Fluffy,' one of the cats of Parliament Hill. Photographed by the author.

Back cover: Detail from "The Parliament buildings in Ottawa the morning after the Great Fire of 1916. Ottawa, Canada." From The New York Times, Feb. 13, 1916 issue. Photographer: unknown. http://commons.wikimedia.org/wiki/File:Parliament_after_fire_NYT_Feb_1916.jpg.

Copyright © 2012 Don Nixon

All rights reserved. The use of any part of this publication reproduced, transmitted in any form or by any means, electronic, mechanical, photocopying, recording, or otherwise, or stored in a retrieval system, without the prior consent of the author is an infringement of the copyright law.

Published by Don Nixon Consulting Inc., 158 Jericho Road, RR #2, Carleton Place, Ontario, Canada K7C 3P2

Third Edition 2012

ISBN 978-1-105-40882-3

Dedication

This book is dedicated to Mr. Herbert Wilfred HERRIDGE (Independent C.C.F; Kootenay West, B.C.). I never met him, but I think Mr. Herridge had a special fondness for the other side of the hill. As you get into the book you will see what I mean.

Acknowledgements

First of all, I want to thank my wife for her support and patience during the two years it took to write the book. My routine was to spend all morning on the computer and then two or three hours again at night, and I did this almost every day for two solid years. Naturally this took time away from chores around the house, and the job-jar never seemed to go down.

One morning, while I was making my breakfast to take up to the computer, I told Jan that I had just completed a really nice story about the cornerstone of the Peace Tower.

"You're probably wondering what can be said about a cornerstone," I said.

"And I'm sure you're going to tell me all about it."

"No, you're going to have to buy the book, and if you do I'll split the royalties with you."

"I shouldn't have to buy it," she told me. "I've had to put up with this whole shebang for two years!" It's been quite a shebang all right.

I also want to thank Lowell Green, Doug Pickard, Chris Borgal, Terry Sauve (without the é), Bobby Watt, and Frank Foran for telling me their stories of Parliament Hill; all those who provided ideas and suggestions after reading my first draft, but especially Valerie Ladouceur and Lyndsie Selwyn for their detailed review and comments; and Jean Hammell for her excellent work on the final. Thanks also to Graham Beveridge, who suggested I try internet publishing.

Lastly, thanks to Brian Caines and Klaus Gerken (see Chapter 34) for putting a link to my book on the Cats of Parliament Hill Mailing List and the Cats of Parliament Hill Blog.

Contents

Introduction

Part 1
Before it was Parliament Hill

Chapter 1: When it was a Complete Wilderness / 1

In this chapter, we first turn the clock way back and see what Parliament Hill and downtown Ottawa looked like 12,000 years ago. Today 'The Hill' is high and dry, but back then everything was underwater, at the bottom of an inland sea called the Champlain Sea. After this we turn the clock ahead and look at our National Capital 200 years ago when it was a complete wilderness.

Chapter 2: When it was a Military Base / 11

In 1826 Colonel By arrived to build the Rideau Canal. As part of the construction of the Canal, Col. By built a military base on Parliament Hill, but in those days it was called Barrack Hill, not Parliament Hill. In this chapter, we will learn what Barrack Hill was like from the recollections of Thomas Ritchie, Mr. White, George R. Blyth, James Stevenson, William H. Cluff, Mr. H.P. Hill, and George C. Holland. These men grew up in Bytown and used to play on Barrack Hill when they were boys. So, of course, they knew it well.

Part 2
The Victorian Era

Chapter 3: The Project from Hell, Part 1 / 33

Today a visit to Parliament Hill is a 'must see' for millions of tourists each year. The buildings are so quaint and beautiful it is hard to believe that the project to build them back in the 1860's was a complete failure, but it was. In this and the next two chapters, we will learn why. In this chapter we will look at the early stages of the project and will see that it was here that the foundations for disaster were laid - although no one knew it at the time.

Chapter 4: The Project from Hell, Part 2 / 57

Here we look at the 'fun and games' during the tender/award period and get a glimpse at the politicians behind the scenes pulling the strings so their favourite contractors got the job.

Chapter 5: The project from Hell, Part 3 / 65

In this chapter, we relate the sad story of construction and see why, half way through, all work ground to a halt for almost a year for a parliamentary inquiry. Almost everybody, except the contractors, got fired.

Chapter 6: The story of the Nepean Sandstone / 77

Believe it or not, originally the Parliament Buildings were going to be a drab, grey limestone, like the walls of the Rideau Canal - how dreary that would have looked! In this chapter, we learn how the change to Nepean sandstone came about. With the passage of time, Nepean sandstone develops that rich, warm patina for which the Parliament Buildings are now so famous.

Chapter 7: Time Travel / 81

What would it be like to hop in a time machine and go back to 1867, the year of Confederation, and see what Parliament Hill looked like to our great-great-grandparents? In this chapter, we will do just that and see what everything looked like when the buildings were brand-spanking new, and the grounds were a mess of mud.

Chapter 8: Lovers' Walk / 93

In this chapter, we follow the history of Lovers' Walk, "a charming promenade hidden on the side of the rock on which the Parliament Buildings stand," from its beginnings to its closure just before the Second World

War. This chapter recounts Mr. Herridge's unsuccessful efforts to have Lovers' Walk reinstated.

CHAPTER 9: THE OLD CLOCK TOWER / 103

In the Victorian Era, a trip up the winding spiral staircase of the clock tower was just as much a treat as a trip up the Peace Tower is today.

CHAPTER 10: GUN TIME / 111

This is the story of the noonday gun, a nine pound muzzle-loading ship's canon on Parliament Hill that was used on Parliament Hill as a kind of timepiece. For more than a century, almost never missing a day, it announced with a tremendous 'boom!' that could be heard all over Ottawa that it was 12 o'clock noon, 'gun time.'

CHAPTER 11: THE BAR THE POLITICIANS DIDN'T WANT TO ADMIT WAS THERE / 119

Everybody knew there was a bar in the basement of the Parliament Building except - it seems - the politicians.

CHAPTER 12: THE DIRTY TRICK PLAYED ON SIR WILFRID / 121

Most Prime Ministers would be proud to have a tower on the West Block named after them, but not Sir Wilfrid Laurier. He was not at all happy that his name was attached to this particular tower. You will find out all about it in this chapter, which also has other stories of the West Block, such as how opium was once burned in the West Block furnaces.

CHAPTER 13: WHAT DID IT SMELL LIKE IN THE OLD PARLIAMENT BUILDINGS? / 129

Of course there was no environmental legislation back in the Victorian era. However, if there had been, what do you think would have happened if a health inspector had been called in by a disgruntled employee to look at the condition of the heating, ventilating, air conditioning, sanitation and drinking water in the Parliament Buildings? Here's a hint: he would have shut the buildings down!

Part 3
The Fire – Who Dunnit?

Chapter 14: A Blow-by-Blow Description of the Fire that Destroyed the Old Parliament Building / 147

The Centre Block we have today is not the original one. There used to be another one in the same spot, but it burned down in a horrible fire the night of February 3, 1916. In this chapter we get an overview of the fire.

Chapter 15: The Story of the Two Young Ladies who Died Because They Went Back for Their Furs / 153

When we were children in school we were taught in fire drills that when the alarm sounds you leave the building right away – you don't go back. Unfortunately, two ladies died because they did not follow this rule and went back for their fur coats.

Chapter 16: How the Fire Started / 157

The fire did not start like a normal fire. In the next chapter we will look at whether it was an accident, or not, but first we need to look at the fire when it was very young, in its first two or three minutes. Can you imagine that? A whole chapter on just three minutes!

Chapter 17: Who Dunnit? / 165

There are three theories. It could have been (as Prime Minister Borden maintained in his memoirs) caused by a careless smoker. It also might have been an electrical fire. However, 1916 was right in the middle of World War I, which was from 1914 to 1918, and many believed the fire was deliberately set by a German saboteur. All the evidence is presented, and you can be the judge.

CHAPTER 18: WHY THE OLD PARLIAMENT BUILDING WAS NOT RESTORED / 185

Originally, the plan was to rebuild the old Parliament Building however for reasons that will be explained the Government decided not to, building instead today's Centre Block.

PART 4
MODERN DAY PARLIAMENT HILL

CHAPTER 19: CONSTRUCTION OF THE CENTRE BLOCK / 191

A history of the construction.

CHAPTER 20: PEACE TOWER / 197

A collection of little known stories of what must surely be the most recognizable symbol of Canada.

CHAPTER 21: THE INAUGURATION OF THE CARILLON (IT WAS NOT WILLIAM LYON MACKENZIE KING'S BEST DAY.) / 225

The carillon was played for the very first time on Canada Day, 1927. This account is from Prime Minister William Lyon Mackenzie King's perspective – his day started off badly when his butler got trapped in the elevator, and it went downhill from there. He didn't like the carillon when he first heard it played later that day.

CHAPTER 22: THOMAS RITCHIE DONATES A SUNDIAL / 231

In this chapter, we learn about the sundial on Parliament Hill that was donated by Thomas Ritchie. Thomas was born on Parliament Hill in his family's home, which was very near where the Peace Tower is today.

CHAPTER 23: RATS AND ROACHES AND BATS, OH MY! / 233

The story of 'Freddy the Rat' and other creepy-crawly things that used to share the Parliament Buildings with our politicians back in the 1940's.

CHAPTER 24: DEMOLITION OF THE LIBRARY / 239

The 1950's and 60's were terrible decades for heritage buildings. If everything on Parliament Hill that was supposed to have been demolished had been demolished, it would not look at all like it does today. The Library of Parliament was the first building Public Works wanted torn down, and it was thanks to Gordon Robertson, a civil servant, and Prime Minister Louis St.-Laurent that it was not.

CHAPTER 25: DEMOLITION OF THE WEST BLOCK / 243

If this plan had gone ahead, the West Block would have been knocked down and a new building (patterned something after the Centre Block) would have been built in its place. Fortunately the government of Prime Minister Diefenbaker squashed the whole idea, and that is why we still have the West Block today.

CHAPTER 26: DEMOLITION OF THE OLD SUPREME COURT BUILDING / 255

Today there are three buildings on Parliament Hill (the Centre Block and the East and West Blocks), but there used to be a fourth, a wonderful old building down by the end of Bank Street. Sadly it was bull-dozed down in 1955 and turned into a parking lot that is still there today. We have the story here.

CHAPTER 27: DEMOLITION OF THE ABOMINABLE, OLD, WORN-OUT, UNPAINTED, SHABBY LOOKOUT / 261

This is how George Hees, one of our politicians in the 1950's, referred to the summer pavilion. This chapter explains why it was demolished when all that was needed was a few coats of paint.

CHAPTER 28: DEMOLITION OF THE CENTENNIAL FLAME / 265

We also came very close to losing the Centennial Flame. In this chapter we learn why the decision to demolish the Centennial Flame at the end of 1967 was reversed at the very last minute.

PART 5
MY OWN TIMES ON THE HILL

CHAPTER 29: THE STATUES ON PARLIAMENT HILL / 271

This chapter describes how some of the early statues on Parliament Hill were made; what they looked like when they were new; how sulphur fumes from coal-burning factories and plants caused them to corrode; and how we went about conserving them.

CHAPTER 30: THE X-RATED STORY OF QUEEN VICTORIA'S LION / 291

This whole chapter is devoted to the story of the big male lion at the base of the Queen Victoria statue. The lion is missing a 'little something' between his hind legs. If you are a sensitive male you had better skip to the next chapter.

CHAPTER 31: MASONRY CONSERVATION 101 / 301

The Canadian climate has taken a terrible toll on the Parliament Buildings. This chapter is like an introductory college or university course on masonry conservation. It explains in simple language why masonry walls deteriorate and how we went about conserving them.

CHAPTER 32: ALL I KNOW ABOUT COPPER ROOFS / 315

This chapter discusses a collection of off-beat information about the famous copper roofs of the Parliament Buildings: why they turn green; how long it takes; how in the old days workers used to use urine to make them turn that lovely shade of green faster; where the idea to make souvenirs out of the copper roof of the Centre Block came from, and many other stories.

CHAPTER 33: TIME CAPSULES / 327

There are probably hundreds of time capsules buried on Parliament Hill. I will tell you about the time capsules I am aware of, and describe where they are, what they look like, and what is inside them.

CHAPTER 34: THE CATS / 335

I call this is my big, block-buster ending. Many people have heard about René Chartrand, the cat man of Parliament Hill. Some people know that before him there was Irène Desormeaux, the cat lady of Parliament Hill. But no one knows that before her was another cat man, Sgt. Lorne Hull, and that before him was the first cat lady, Mrs. Robina Mabbs.

BIBLIOGRAPHY / 353

END NOTES / 379

INTRODUCTION

My background is engineering. I received a bachelor's degree in civil engineering from Carleton University in 1970, a master's degree in structural engineering from the same university in 1972, and a PhD from the University of Alberta in 1979. I worked in the private sector for several years and then at Public Works and Government Services Canada for 29 years before retiring in 2006. My last 19 years were spent working as a project manager on Parliament Hill. Since then I have worked as a consultant, specializing in the conservation of the Parliament Buildings.

While I was with the Department, I was lucky enough to have managed some really interesting projects: the emergency and urgent stabilization of chimneys, towers, turrets and other rooftop masonry on the Centre, East and West Blocks; the conservation of the Peace Tower; the conservation of the entire front of the Centre Block, which we called the south façade; the conservation of all of the statues on Parliament Hill; the conservation of the War Memorial; making the Queen Elizabeth statue on the east side of the Centre Block; installing the *Evolution of Life* series of stone carvings in the House of Commons Chamber, and many, many more. My point is that if I had worked as an engineer in the private sector I'd have been lucky to have had, in my whole career, just one nationally significant project. But in the Parliamentary Precinct I've had many. It was a great place to work.

One of the things I really enjoyed about my job was giving tours. (This must have come under the 'related duties' part of my job description.) I started in the early 1990's, and continued giving them every summer up to my retirement in 2006. I gave them to new staff as part of their orientation, and to staff who had been around for a while but who spent all of their time working inside the office, like administration, finance and other staff. During Public Service Week I even gave tours to employees from our main office across the river. The tour was very popular, and seemed to appeal to a wide range of people. Over time it came to be called *Don Nixon's Tour of Parliament Hill*.

Over the years I've learned many behind-the-scenes stories about Parliament Hill (it's surprising what you hear when you've been around for a while) and I would tell them during my tours. Everyone liked them and at the end of each tour someone would always come up to me and say, "Don, you should write a book."

I usually just shrugged it off, but one day I was telling my mother a story – I think it was about the chronogram in the cornerstone of the Peace Tower. "Don," my mother said, "what an interesting story - you should write a book!" I thought about it, and after a while decided that I would. So I'd like to thank everyone who has taken *Don Nixon's Tour of Parliament Hill* and who came up to me afterwards and said I should write a book, but I'd especially like to thank my mother. If she hadn't told me to, this book would not have been written.

I should tell you what my stories are not about. They are not about my projects, although I do mention some of them from time to time. They are not about the politicians either, although some of them figure into the stories as secondary characters. And they are certainly not about the mysterious inner workings of the government bureaucracy! This book is definitely not a tell-all exposé!

They are just stories about the buildings and grounds that, when arranged chronologically, form a behind-the-scenes history of Parliament Hill. You know how, in a newspaper, you have news stories, and sports stories and then something called human-interest stories? Well my stories are human-interest stories, but they are all about Parliament Hill.

Some of them are main-stream history. I've included them for completeness and because some of you may not have heard them before. Some stories I discovered while researching old newspapers, books and magazines. These stories would have been well-known at the time, of course, but today are not, even to the experts. Some of my stories are original and appear in print here for the very first time.

Two of my stories, *The Project from Hell* and *Masonry Conservation 101* are a little different from the others. While the book is intended for the layman, these two stories are a little technical and would perhaps be of most interest to young project managers, architects, engineers and construction workers, especially those working on heritage buildings. If you find them tough going they can be skimmed, or skipped entirely.

I enjoyed my time on Parliament Hill tremendously, but I want to make it clear that I no longer work for Public Works and Government Services Canada. I am retired. The stories, views and opinions presented in this book are my own, not those of the Department of Public Works and Government Services Canada.

I hope you enjoy this book. If you do, please recommend it to two friends, and ask them to recommend it to two friends if they like it, and so on, and so on. Who knows? Maybe it will go viral!

Don Nixon, 2012

PART 1

BEFORE IT WAS PARLIAMENT HILL

Chapter 1: When it was a Complete Wilderness

The hill crowned with its ancient trees,
Who's foliage rustled in the breeze
For centuries, all branching wide,
Standing untouched on every side;
A spot where the Algonquin magi
*May have reclined sub tegmine fagi**

William Pittman Lett, 1874[1]

*Sub tegmine fagi is a Latin phrase meaning 'under the beech-tree's shelter.' Before the arrival of the European settlers Parliament Hill must have been a beech tree ridge, covered in huge beech trees.

12,000 Years Ago

When I was giving tours on Parliament Hill I used to tell my group that they were going to learn a lot - and you are too!

We usually met at the Centennial Flame, and I always started my tour with a bit of trivia.

"What," I would ask, "do you think Parliament Hill looked like, say, 12,000 years ago?"

Usually there was someone who knew the correct answer and said, "It was covered in water."

"You're right," I would reply. "If this was an exam I'd give you 100 percent!"

This whole area was once covered in glaciers three to four kilometers high, and over time the heavy weight compressed the ground until it was well below sea level. About thirteen thousand years ago the last of the ice melted and when it did the Atlantic Ocean flooded in, creating the Champlain Sea. This sea covered much of the St. Lawrence and Ottawa River valleys and modern-day Lake Champlain. Quebec City, Montreal and Ottawa were completely underwater. The western shore of the sea was about 30 km west of Ottawa.[2]

The steep limestone cliffs and upper plateau of Parliament Hill existed back then, of course, but it was part of the sea bed, completely under water. It has been estimated that the sea was about 235 metres above modern sea level. Today the flag on top of the Peace Tower is 170 metres above sea level, so if the Parliament Buildings had existed back then the water would have been about 65 metres higher than that. It's hard to imagine tourists in the Peace Tower looking out at fish swimming around in lazy circles and maybe at a big beluga whale bumping its blunt snout into the window and blowing bubbles at them!

With the immense weight of the ice gone the ground began to rebound, but this process (called 'isostatic rebound') is very slow, taking several thousand years. As the ground rose, the sea began to slowly drain back to the ocean.

Ten thousand years ago, the ancient Ottawa River, fed by glacial lakes in northern Ontario, the Prairie Provinces, and the upper Great Lakes, was much wider and deeper than it is today. It emptied into the Champlain Sea, which was at the time to the east of Ottawa, carrying sediment ranging from sand and gravel to silt. The sand and gravel (being heavier) were deposited in shallow water, and the lighter clays and silts remained in suspension and were carried further into the sea and deposited in deeper water. As high ground, Parliament Hill may have once had a thin till cover over the bedrock, but probably little to no clays which would have settled to lower areas in the sea.

A huge sand delta was created at the mouth of the river over Ottawa. The ancestral river evolved as it adjusted to the receding sea, and several times it shifted into new channels - sometimes eroding sand, sometimes depositing it. Today the remains of this large delta appear as patches of sand. Scientists call them 'erosional fluvial terraces,' and some are as high as 220 metres above modern sea level. One of them is right on Parliament Hill, although very few people know about it.

In the early 1990's, I was project manager for the equestrian statue of Queen Elizabeth II, which is on the east side of the Centre Block. When we were doing the archaeological investigation for the statue's base (an archaeological investigation is required under the Canadian Environmental Assessment Act as well as other government acts and policies) my archaeologist discovered about 50 cm below the grass another 50 cm of sand right down to bedrock; wonderful white beach sand. I thought it was brought in after the great fire of February 3, 1916 for landscaping and told my archaeologist so. However, he said that it was native to the site, caused by the recession of the Champlain Sea. He could tell because the artifacts from the Barracks Hill and early Parliament Hill years were above the sand. If the sand had been dumped here after the fire the artifacts would have been below.

Further proof that everything used to be underwater can be seen in fossilized seashells that can be found in abundance in sand deposits all around Ottawa and the surrounding countryside. In 1948, workers dug up the fossilized skeleton of a whale in a sand pit that used to be located at the corners of what are now Hunt Club and River Roads. This attracted the attention of newspaper reporters[3] and scientists from the Geological Survey who came and took it back to their laboratory. They said that from its blunt skull it probably belonged to a white or a beluga whale, similar to those found in Hudson Bay and the Gulf of St. Lawrence.

Terry Sauve worked in the same building as I did. As it happens his dad, Roger Sauve, used to be a truck driver with Roy Braseau Cartage. Roger was at the sand pit the day that Pete, the shovel operator, found the whale. Roger was there to get his dump truck filled up with sand to take over to a construction project at the East Block on Parliament Hill when they found it. I won't tell you now what they asked Terry's dad to do when he got to the East Block to help make the new copper roof they had put on go green faster, but I will later (see the story THEY USED TO DO WHAT? in Chapter 32).

Over time the glacial lakes disappeared, and the size of the Ottawa River reduced. Eight thousand years ago the countryside around Parliament Hill looked much like it does today except, of course, everything was covered in a vast primeval forest.

200 YEARS AGO

"Ok," I would say to my group, "now let's go forward in time a little. What do you think Parliament Hill looked like 200 years ago?"

There was usually someone who would say it was a military post built by Colonel By when he was constructing the Rideau Canal.

"Almost correct," I would say, "but not quite. If this was an exam I would give you...maybe...70 percent." Then, remembering I gave 100% to the other person, I'd add, "That's not a bad mark!"

But this was a trick question because two hundred years ago was before Col. By arrived and built Barrack Hill (Barrack Hill is what it was called before it was Parliament Hill. You'll learn *a lot* more about Barrack Hill in the next chapter.)

Now, I'm writing this story in 2008 so two hundred years ago was 1808. In 1808 there was a small town across the river in Gatineau, founded in 1800 by Philemon Wright who came up from Woburn, which is near Boston, Massachusetts. However, it wasn't called Gatineau in those days; it was Wright's Village or Wrightsville, renamed Hull in 1875. Today the population is mostly French Canadian but back then it consisted almost entirely of Americans.[4]

The Ottawa side of the river was thick, primeval forest. James Corbett, who was Col. By's clerk-of-the works on the Rideau Canal, wrote: "The Banks of the River Ottawa upon which Bytown [the old name for Ottawa] is built were a complete wilderness...the undisputed domain of the Wandering Indian...."[5]

What would someday be Canada's National Capital was then nothing but forest, swamp, brushwood and beaver meadows. F. Gertrude Kenny said that LeBreton Flats was dwarf cedar, juniper and brush.[6] William Pittman Lett tells us that Ashburnham Hill (the old name for the part of Ottawa where Gloucester, Nepean and Lisgar Streets meet Bronson Avenue[7]) was beech and hemlock; Parliament Hill was a beech ridge; the south side of Rideau Street down to Laurier was a hemlock ridge; the north side of Rideau up to Cathcart Street was a cedar swamp with giant pines here and there; and north of Cathcart it was a beech ridge varied by large hemlocks.[8,9]

Today we think of Parliament Hill as being north of Wellington Street, and of course, politically speaking, it is. But as anybody who has ever walked up Metcalfe Street knows, Canada's most famous hill geographically starts around Queen Street where the ground starts to rise.

The bottom of the hill was swampy, extending from what is now Queen Street down to about Laurier, and from Bank over to Nicholas.[10] A creek ran along Queen Street, emptying over the steep at the rear of where the National Arts Centre would someday be, into a beaver pond near the eastern end of the swamp.[11,12] The beavers kept a dam on its northern side and the creek flowed from an outlet north to George Street, then east along George, diagonally down to York, east to King Edward and then north along King Edward Avenue until it was lost in a huge, mosquito-infested cedar swamp that covered most of Lower Town.[13]

The countryside was full of wolves, bear, deer, wild duck, plover,[14] squirrels, pigeons, ruffled grouse, black ducks, teal and snipe.[15]

The first settler on the Ottawa side was Jehiel Collins, also an American, who arrived in 1809 and built a landing, log cabin, and store at what is now Le Breton Flats but was then called Collins' Landing. Later his clerk, Caleb Bellows, married his daughter, took over the business, and Collins' Landing became known as Bellows' Landing.

In 1818 a group of soldiers and their families arrived. They had been given land at what would become the town of Richmond. At this time, there were two other homesteaders at the Landing besides Bellows; there was Isaac Firth, who operated a tavern at the Landing, and Ralph Smith with his family.[16,17] The soldiers and their families remained at Bellows' Landing that summer and over the winter. They cut a road some 30 kilometres through the forest to where their new settlement would be and after erecting log cabins moved into their new homes. After that, Bellows' landing was known as the Richmond Landing. The road they cut through the bush is still there; it's called the Richmond Road. It's not the fastest way to get to Richmond, but once you're out in the country it's very pretty.[18]

In 1816, lumber shanties began to appear in what would become Lower Town.[19]

In 1817, John Burrows Honey acquired 200 acres of property bounded by Bronson Avenue on the west, Waller Street on the east, Laurier Avenue on the south, and on the north side it extended two-thirds of the way into present-day Wellington Street. Honey built a log cabin near the corner of Lyon and Wellington and started farming.

In 1821, Nicholas Sparks, who had been working for Philemon Wright, left his employ and bought John Burrows Honey's land, along with the cabin and furnishings, for £95. In those days one pound was equal to about four dollars, so to buy what amounted to the downtown core of Ottawa cost him all of $380!

Sparks began farming but he found it hard going because the land was nothing but rock, sand and swamp. His friends laughed at him for wasting his money on such a foolish purchase. Sparks didn't know it at the time, but in a few years Col. By would arrive to build the canal and to provide accommodation for the men working on it. He would build a small town (Bytown) that would lay almost entirely on Sparks' property. After the arrival of Col. By, Sparks changed careers, getting into real estate, and it made him rich beyond his wildest dreams! The land that cost £95 in 1821 was valued at upwards of £40,000 in 1849,[20] and by the early 1850's it was estimated at £200,000.[21] Today who knows how much it is worth!

> He knew not then, that 'twas not mould
> he turne'd up, and tilled, but gold.
>
> – William Pittman Lett, 1874[22]

Sparks soon became famous for his land purchase, and a legend quickly grew over how it came about. Captain Henry A. Murray heard the story when he was passing through Bytown in the early 1850's,[23] and it was first published in the September 1861 issue of *Harpers Magazine* in an excellent article titled The Capital of the Canadas, by M.J. Hickey.[24]

According to Hickey, Wright owned large tracts of land on the north side of the river, and even though the south side was not as good for farming, being mostly rock, sand and swamp, he had secured a large quantity of land there also. Nicholas Sparks worked for Wright as an ox teamster and, the story goes, had gone several years without pay. When it came time for Wright to settle his accounts he found that he was in debt to Sparks for some two hundred dollars. Unfortunately, Wright didn't have the money to pay him. All he had was land, and offered him a parcel across the river. Sparks looked it over and thought perhaps he might be able to do something up near the falls, but to the south of those limestone cliffs it was nothing but rock, sand and swamp. So Wright said, "I'll tell you what I'll do besides, Sparks, I'll give you a yoke of oxen, and I'm sure in spite of what they all say you'll get on well." The deal was settled.

Of course, we know Sparks bought his land from John Burrows Honey for £95 so this legend is not true; it's just a story. Nontheless, it's a story that's been passed down through the generations and Lauren Moline, Philemon Wright's great-great-great-great-granddaughter, says it is still being told in her family. "He is said to have acquired the debt through a poker game," she says, "but who knows, the story has passed through a number of generations!!"[25]

If the Parliament Buildings had existed 12,000 years ago, the Peace Tower would have been completely underwater. Can you imagine tourists looking out at this view? Photograph by the author.

When it was a Complete Wilderness 9

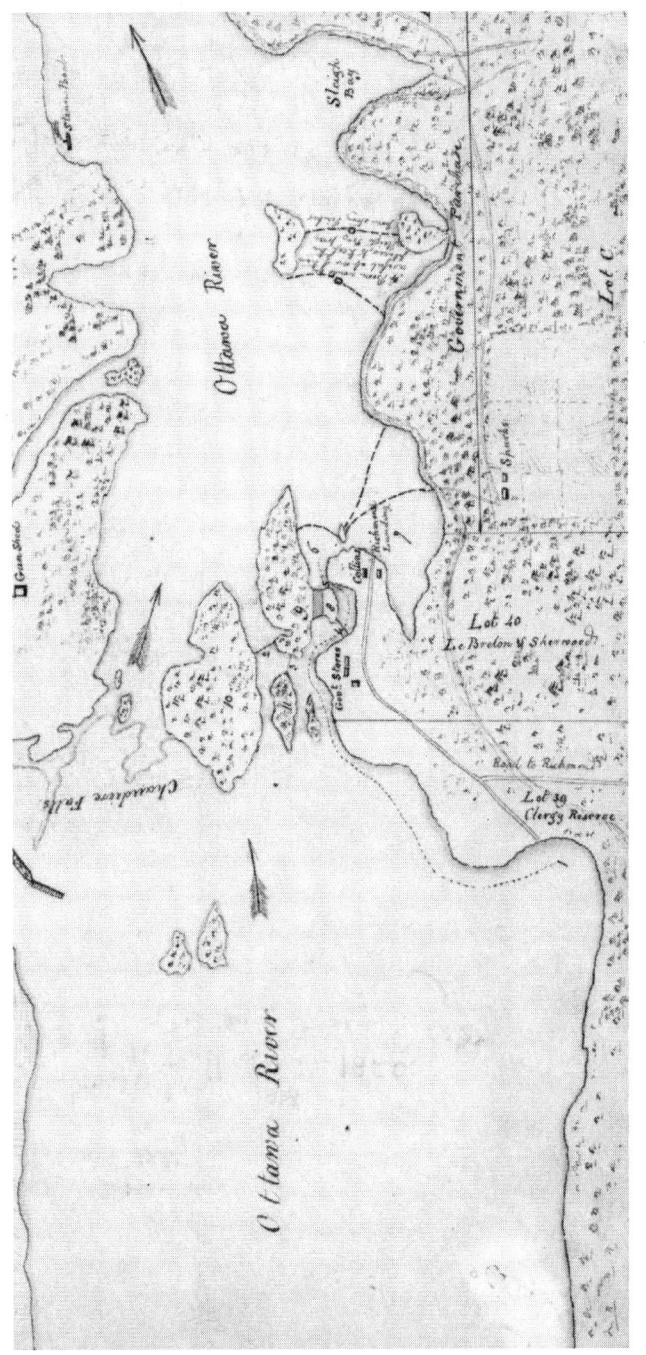

Detail based on "Sketch of both banks of the Ottawa River and the Chaudière Falls, from P. Wright's house to the Steamboat Ferry on the North side & showing Gov't Stores, Richmond Landing and the Road, the Clergy Reserve, the Lebreton & Sherwood property, the Government purchase and Spark's House on the South side," manuscript by G. Elliot, 1825. Sleigh Bay is today the entrance to the Rideau Canal and Parliament Hill is the tree-covered promontory on its left in the photograph. Credit: Library and Archives Canada/NMC 3163/ Call No. H12/440/Ottawa/ [1825]

Chapter 2: When it was a Military Base

In 1834 there were a number of buildings on the hill. All were one story high and built of stone. Two of the largest had been burned down previous to this date. These all stood on or very near the site of the main building. A cedar picket fence ran across from east to west, just in a line with the front of the parliament buildings. At each end there was a gate and a turnstile. The grounds in the enclosure were nicely kept and as level as they are at present. The grounds outside were very uneven with stumps here and there, and reaching away down towards Queen Street. Some privileged cows pastured on the grounds around the hill. Then, as now, the walk around was the favorite walk on a summer evening.[26]

George R. Blyth, speaking of Barrack Hill in 1925

The Early Owners of Parliament Hill

In 1802 the British Government granted Jacob Carman about 600 acres of land in return for the services of his father who had fought in the Revolutionary War. This land, bounded by the Ottawa River and Murray Street on the north, the Rideau River on the east, Wellington and Rideau Streets on the south and Bronson Avenue on the west, included the site of today's Parliament Buildings.

In 1812 Jacob Carman sold it to Thomas Fraser for £12 Halifax currency (about $48 dollars). In 1823, Thos. Fraser's son, Hugh Fraser, sold 415 acres of it (containing Parliament Hill) to the Earl of Dalhousie for £750. In 1826 Dalhousie gave it over to Col. By for the canal.[27]

The Arrival of Col. By

James Corbett worked with Col. By on the Rideau Canal project as clerk of the works. "In the early part of the year 1826," he wrote, "Lt. Colonel By of the Royal Engineers was sent to Canada to construct the Works of the Rideau Canal which were commenced on the 21 September 1826, and the first Steam Boat passed through the Canal on the 29 May 1832. Up to the year 1827, the Banks of the River Ottawa upon which Bytown is built were a complete wilderness and in the month of March in that year the first tree was cut for the purpose of clearing the forest, where the town now stands."[28]

When Col. By arrived, a temporary headquarters was established across the river. Corbett explained, "The village of Hull on the opposite bank of the River had been built about 13 years previous to the first settlement of Bytown, and on the Rideau Canal being commenced the only accommodation that could be procured in the vicinity for the officers and Persons employed on the Works was at Hull where some comfortable houses had been erected."[29]

The entrance for the canal was chosen at Sleigh Bay, renamed Entrance Bay.[30] The headquarters at Hull included a temporary commissariat, a key department in every construction project back then. In the British Government, the commissariat department was responsible for providing food and fuel for the soldiers, forage for the horses, and was also responsible for preparing tenders and awarding construction contracts.[31]

It is from Matthew Connell that we learn that the first building constructed on Parliament Hill was a log cabin. Mr. Connell came to work on the Rideau Canal in 1827 as an officer in the commissariat department under Assistant Commissary General Colin Miller. When he arrived, he was initially stationed at Hull, but soon a small clearing was made, and a log cabin was built about where the Parliament Buildings stand. Mr. Connell and other commissariat staff who were assigned to the canal were transferred there from Hull. They worked out of this log building until August 1827, when the stone commissariat building down by the locks was completed and then they moved into it.[32]

The log cabin on Parliament Hill is long gone, but the stone commissariat is still there. It is in its original location down by the locks, and is now the Bytown Museum. This is the oldest building in Ottawa.

Part of the work of constructing the Rideau Canal was done by two companies of the Royal Sappers and Miners, so Col. By had to find them accommodation. As the *Perth Independent Examiner* reported in 1830, "This gave rise to the erection of three large and commodious barracks upon the ground reserved betwixt Upper and Lower Bytown – substantial stone buildings, with fanciful and expensive roofs, upon the high ground overlooking the mouth of the canal and the Ottawa River." [33] The barracks were 33 metres long, 21 metres wide and built of rubble stone. Each had a lovely verandah that wrapped around all four sides. Inside were sixteen rooms on the ground floor and a garret.[34]

Today the Centre Block faces south, towards Wellington Street, but when they built the barracks they turned them around, so that the front doors faced the other way.[35] Can you guess why? The men didn't clear all the trees on top of Barrack Hill (as it was called) right away. In the early days a few were left standing around the barracks.[36] Looking through them from their front verandahs the soldiers had the most wonderful view of the sweeping river, the thundering falls, the green forest and the hazy mountains in the distance beyond.

THE BULGE

In 1827 Col. By collaborated with Nicholas Sparks to build the portion of Wellington Street to the west of Bank Street. Sparks donated 20 metres from the northern edge of his property and Col. By added 10 metres from the government purchase for a total road width of 30 metres.[37] In other words, while today the stone and wrought iron Wellington Street Wall marks the southern extent of Parliament Hill, the original southern extent of the Government Purchase, and of Barracks Hill, was on a line one-third of the distance into present day Wellington Street.

In the same year Col. By expropriated a large chunk of Sparks' land below Barrack Hill and fenced it in with a big cedar log fence. The fence started at the corner of Bank and Wellington, curving in a south-easterly direction until it reached Queen Street. From there, it went east to Metcalfe Street, then northeast past the old cemetery (more about this later) to the Sapper's Bridge in a shape called the bulge.

Of course, I'm using these modern-day street names to describe the shape of the bulge; there were no streets between Bank and the canal at the time. In fact, it was mostly swamp.

Sparks was not at all happy that his land had been stolen and he began a long, drawn-out legal battle to get it back. In 1846, he won his lawsuit against the government, and the southern line of Barrack Hill went back to its original location (about one-third of the way into Wellington Street).

In 1923, Mr. H.P. Hill wondered what the development of Ottawa would have been like if Sparks had not won his lawsuit, and the Government had retained the land down to Queen Street. "It is a matter now of regret," he said, "that it was not so retained as it would have provided such a magnificent site for all the Government buildings."[38]

In 1847, the town expropriated the ten-metre strip of land across Barrack Hill and extended Wellington Street in a straight line from Bank Street over to the Sapper's Bridge.

The government objected, and in 1849 extended their fence into the northern third of Wellington Street. Later that year, the government relented and moved their fence back to the north side of Wellington, about where the Wellington Street Wall is on the south side of Parliament Hill today.[39]

RECOLLECTIONS OF BARRACK HILL

The following description of Barrack Hill is pieced together from maps,[40] the recollections of Thomas Ritchie,[41,42] Mr. White,[43] George R. Blyth,[44] James Stevenson,[45] William H. Cluff,[46] Mr. H.P. Hill,[47] and George C. Holland[48] as well as other references.

Thomas Ritchie was born on Barrack Hill on January 4, 1838. His father, Sergeant Robert Ritchie was Barrack Master.

His home, along with his father's office and store, stood very near where the Peace Tower is today.[49,50]

Mr. White also lived on Barrack Hill. His home was in the eastern Soldier's Barracks, near where the Senate Chamber is. Mr. White always said that the best view down the Ottawa River and over Lower Town was from their very own window on the north side of the Barracks.

James Stevenson didn't live on Barrack Hill, but he was a resident of Bytown and was the first agent of the Bank of Montreal. The other men were also residents of Bytown and so,of course, they all knew the lay-out of Barrack Hill very well.

BARRACK HILL PROPER

"The Barracks were occupied by one or two companies of Imperial troops," said William H. Cluff, "with all the ram-roddy appearance of the then British soldier, including that instrument of torture, a heavy stiff leather stock."[51]

Barrack Hill proper, where the buildings stood, was separated from the remainder of the grounds by a fence, or stockade, of cedar posts about 3.6 metres high, sharpened at the upper end. Mr. Blyth said it was just in a line[52] with the front of the Parliament Buildings and at each end there was a gate and a turnstile.

The main gate was at the eastern end. To the right of the gate, protected by the same type of stockade, was the fuel yard. Mr. White said it had a heavy cedar plank door and a large padlock that was opened by a key about 100 mm long and 25 mm thick.[53] He didn't know why such precautions were taken around the fuel yard, but it may have been that they kept other things in there from time to time besides firewood.

Sentries mounted guard outside the stockade. Mr. Hill remembered, "To my youthful eyes they were a race of giants, in their old-fashioned uniforms and tall headgear. In all seasons, summer and winter storm and shine, they mounted guard, their only protection from the inclemency of the weather being a sentry box which stood near where the noon-day gun is located now." This was in 1923, when the gun was on the east side of the Centre Block.) "They must have been sturdy men," he went on, "to wear their heavy caps and stiff, uncomfortable stocks in the tropical summer weather."[54]

If you walked through the eastern gate, the guardhouse, which contained three sturdy cells,[55] was the first building on your left. "Just about where the Sir John Macdonald monument now is," said Mr. White. "The guard house reached from about the head of the east-side steps to the north of the monument."[56]

Bytown didn't have a jail, so the guardhouse was used for civilians as well as soldiers. Local miscreants were kept there under the watchful eye of a civilian constable (because the military didn't want to get involved in civilian matters) until they could be walked up to the closest courthouse, which was in Perth, 80 kilometres away. Presumably the accompanying jailer rode his horse.[57]

There used to be three stone barracks, but on the afternoon of January 5, 1832 a fire broke out in the kitchen of the centre barrack. Lt. Frome of the Royal Engineers, who was dressing for dinner when the fire started, escaped safely but managed to save only a small money box. Within minutes the building was reduced to ruins, with just the stone walls and chimneys standing.[58] The western barrack burned down shortly after but was later rebuilt. In the 1860's it was used as a site office when the Parliament and Departmental Buildings were being constructed.

From the guardhouse, a fence went north to one of the cookhouses, and from the cookhouse it continued in a straight line to meet the eastern barrack. Then the fence went west, from the eastern barrack over to the bar and store, and from there to the stone walls of the centre barracks (which, as mentioned before, were in ruins from the fire). It then turned south and (with one small zigzag) connected back to the stockade, creating a fenced enclosure.

Inside the enclosure, near where the Peace Tower is, were another cookhouse, the Barrack Sergeant's quarters where Mr. Ritchie was born, the Barrack Store and a garden. There were also two privies, one near each end of the southern side of the enclosure.

Outside the enclosure (but still behind the stockade that ran from east to west across the hill) were the ruins of the western barrack and a stable for the horses.

"The grounds in the enclosure," said Mr. Blyth, "were nicely kept and as level as they are at present." On a fair summer day, the soldiers enjoyed playing cricket, and it is said they used to place the wicket about where the Speaker of the Senate's chair is.[59] A sundial stood exactly where the sundial is located on Parliament Hill today.

The officer's quarters, a two-story stone building, was north of the West Block and was protected by its own stockade.[60]

The soldiers tried to sink wells at two different locations. They dug down eight metres through solid limestone bedrock, but both wells came up dry. In the end, they had to resort to bringing water up from the river in casks on a handcart. Once they got the cart up the hill, the water was poured into storage tanks, one near the barracks and the other over by the officers' quarters. It took four or five men several hours each day and it was hard, hard work.[61, 62]

THE GROUNDS

The main entrance to Barrack Hill was a large white gate at Elgin Street, which was kept open during the day but always closed at night. There was also a gate at Bank Street, and another at the Sapper's Bridge. These gates were always kept closed and locked, Mr. Stevenson said, but there were stiles next to these gates that allowed people to get up and over the fence. There were also sentry boxes at various points along the fence and sentries at night.

Unlike Barrack Hill proper, the grounds, also called *The Commons*, were very rough and uneven, with stumps of large beech trees here and there, and quite a few boulders. Horses and cows belonging to the military officers were allowed to graze on what grass there was. Can you imagine cows grazing on the front lawn of the Parliament Buildings today and maybe wandering up to the Centennial Flame for a drink when they got thirsty?

The soldiers planted vegetable gardens here and there where they spent their spare time hoeing, weeding and watering. There was a large garden in the enclosed area behind the stockade and another over near the officer's quarters. Mr. White remembered these gardens where, he says, the soldiers grew potatoes and 'garden truck.'[63]

A number of foot paths cut across the grounds. One, which cut straight across between the gates at Bank Street and Sapper's Bridge, was used as a shortcut between upper and lower towns. Of this, Mr. Stevenson said, "The foot-path, fondly remembered and associated with pleasant evening strolls and genial intercourse with kindred spirits, has been converted into a splendid street commemorating the heroic name of Wellington." Other paths went up to Barrack Hill proper and over to the officers' quarters.

The grounds were accessible at all times; however horse riding, carts and carriages were not allowed. It was a favorite place to spend a few quiet hours on a warm summer evening, strolling along the paths, and people enjoyed it then as much as they do now.

BREWERY BAY

The Fraser boarding school, run by three daughters of a Lanark Minister (name unknown), was a boarding school for girls in the 1850's located at the northwest corner of Sparks and Elgin.[64] On nice evenings in the summer, the girls would spend several hours on the hill - always, of course, chaperoned by one of the Fraser sisters. Some of them studied, others did fancy work (sewing), while others liked to watch the colorfully dressed lumbermen assembling the square timber rafts down in the bay behind the Officers' quarters, and hear them sing.[65]

Over the winter, the lumbermen cut down giant pine trees in the forest, scored and hewed them into square timber, tied them together into rafts and floated them down the Ottawa River to the markets at Quebec City. Toward the end of May, the rafts would begin to reach the Deschênes Rapids, which are upstream of the Chaudière Falls. Here they were broken into cribs and run down the rapids, through the slides and then floated over to quiet water where they were reassembled.

The lumbermen could choose from a number of bays in which to do their work. Rafting bay, the first bay on the right just past the slides was a good one, and there were others. But the men especially liked Brewery Bay at the end of Bank Street. Not only was the water nice and calm, but there was a brewery there where they could buy a nice cold beer. Assembling cribs was hot work!

> *And Michael Burke, who kept a still –*
> *And made beer down below the hill*
> *Where malt and hops together came,*
> *And gave the "Brewery Hill" its name –*
> *That hill with pathway to the right,*
> *Where Bank Street ends upon the height.*
> *And many a barrel of his beer*
> *Went down, the Irish heart to cheer.*
>
> *- William Pittman Lett, 1874*[66]

Early maps[67] show the path at the end of Bank Street. It curved to the right as it went down Brewery Hill, and went past Michael Burke's brewery, past Brewery Landing, and ended at Drummond's Wharf Landing which was on the edge of the water to the north of where the West Block is today. Sadly, Brewery Bay and Brewery Hill don't exist anymore. Brewery Bay was filled up with landfill in the 1920's and 30's and made into a government parking lot called the pit parking. Just before I retired, I managed a very big archaeological project in this area, and my archaeologists told me they thought the remnants of Michael Burke's brewery might well still be there, buried under tons of landfill. (Historian Harry J. Walker places Michael Burke's brewery up on Wellington Street,[68] but this is incorrect.)

Anyway, six men were allowed per crib, and a raft contained from 50 to 150 cribs. The men started as soon as possible after daylight and finished about 8 or 9 o'clock at night so it was a very long day! The cribs were tied together with a kind of rope made from birch saplings. The saplings were about 4 to 8 metres long, but no more than 40 mm in diameter at the bottom. They were cut in the forest around Bytown, tied up in bundles of 12 and brought in by wagon to the lumbermen. They were twisted until they split into long fibers. The fibers were quite pliable, and this is the rope that was used.[69] One of the cribs, called the cookery, was tied together extra well. It had a large fireplace in the centre, built on about half a metre of sand and ashes that was kept in place with timbers.

William H. Cluff, who as we shall see later in this chapter was very rambunctious and daring as a young boy, must have got himself invited onto cookeries more than once. "The fire was built in the centre," he said, "and over it was a stick set in two crotches some 6 feet above the fire, on which the pots for cooking hung; around the fire the bread was baked in chauldrons (iron kettles) by heating the sand and burying the chauldrons in it, and at nearly all times it was SOME bread, and the tea was strong enough to float an iron wedge, while the fried-cakes or crockshinolls were very fine. I can speak from experience on this subject." [70]

The girls from the Fraser Boarding School and William H. Cluff were not the only ones who liked to watch the lumbermen work. It was a favorite pastime of everyone in Bytown, especially in spring time when the water was high and the river was filled with rafts, and Barrack Hill was the best place to do it.

The whole operation took about a week for each raft, and when the raft was finished the lumbermen were on their way again, usually leaving about 5 o'clock in the afternoon for the next breaking up point which was at Grenville, 100 kilometres downstream. The men lived on the raft until it reached Quebec, sleeping in little board cabins scattered about.

Mr. Cluff said, "It was a pretty sight, a small flag on each sleeping cabin, a flag with the owners' trade mark floating from a tall pole on the cookery, every man at his post with his 24 foot sweep or oar duly poised, so it could be brought into operation at a motion from the foreman who was in the centre of the raft. After rowing out from the bay in which the raft was put together and getting well into the current of the stream, it was allowed to float down stream and the oars were used to keep it straight and prevent mishaps."[71]

WILLIAM H. CLUFF'S WILD SLEIGH RIDE[72,73]

William Cluff was famous for being the only boy in history crazy enough to sleigh down the Barrack Hill. This would have been in the year 1850, or maybe 1852. There were many hills around Bytown that made for good sleighing. Dr. Hill's hill on Wellington Street was a good one, and the path down Brewery Hill to Drummond's Wharf Landing was another.

The path down Brewery Hill was steep enough, but one day William was standing there with his sleigh, just looking around, and got the idea of going up to about where the West Block is now and starting off from there, sleighing straight down Barrack Hill. He spied a route that was pretty clear of trees, and he climbed up to the top, got on his sleigh (which, by the way, he had made himself with tools out of his father's carpenter box) and took off!

But he had forgotten that the path, which he would have to cross at right angles, was built up on the river side from 2 to 4 metres high and in winter the snow made the bank even higher. He shot down, sped across the path and up the bank, sailing through the air. When he landed it was about 3 metres away. The snow that day was crusty, and when he landed the runners of his sled broke through the crust and the sled came to an abrupt stop. But William continued, sliding and tumbling another 15 metres down the steep hill. When he finally stopped and was able to collect his senses, he found that the skin on the right side of his face was about all gone, and his right ear almost torn off. Fortunately, he didn't have any broken bones. He said he felt awful, but he got his sleigh, hobbled home, and never tried to sleigh down the Barrack Hill again.

William Cluff was lucky. A few years earlier, on the morning of August 31, 1847 a grown man named Greene was found at the foot of Barrack Hill dangerously hurt. He had left Lower Town to help fight a fire at Mr. T.M. Blasdell's Foundry and Blacksmith's shop over on Wellington Street. It being very dark, he must have fallen over the edge. He died a few days later.[74]

Target Practice

The troops used to practice with their smooth bore Brown Bess rifles on a flat piece of rock a little over the level of the river where Kent Street, if extended, would reach. From here they would fire at a target back at the base of Barrack Hill and William H. Cluff tells us their shooting at about 200 metres was excellent "The picking up of shattered lead from the bullets expended afforded great fun to us boys," he said.[75]

So, if future archaeologists digging on the hillside below the West Block ever find shattered lead bullets that look like they might have come from smooth bore Brown Bess rifles, we will know how they got there. They will be the bullets that William Cluff and his friends didn't find when they were out there looking!

The Graveyards

The road wound round the Barrack Hill,
By the old Graveyard, calm and still;
It would have sounded snobbish, very,
To call it then a Cemetery.

- *William Pittman Lett, 1874*[76]

Up to 1828, there were no graveyards in Bytown. The dead were taken over to Wright's Town to be buried.[77] But in 1828, swamp fever, a type of malaria, broke out among the canal workers and spread throughout the town. So many died that year that Col. By had a half acre spot at the southern end of Barrack Hill fenced off and made into two graveyards side-by-side, one for Protestants, the other for Catholics.

The fencing around the graveyards was very sturdy, just like the stockade fencing up on Barrack Hill. Cedar logs about 3 metres high were sharpened at the upper end and spiked to longitudinal pieces, and about 60 cm from the ground, and 60 cm from the top, bands of strap iron were spiked to the upright posts.[78]

The graveyards were in a natural sand deposit (this was the sand from the Champlain Sea). While sand makes for easy digging, a definite plus for the grave diggers, it has its drawbacks.

In 1843 a man who identified himself only as 'Mator' complained to the *Bytown Gazette* of a horrible stench. "Having had constant occasion, during the last two or three years," he said, "to pass and re-pass the Barrack Hill, my attention, in common with that of many others, has frequently been arrested by the existence of a floating vapor, (especially in the evenings, and early in the morning) and which, at times, would spread itself over the entire surface of the government ground, but generally assumed a more or less fixed position at the south eastern extremity of the enclosure."[79] After a little investigation, Mator discovered it was "the corrupting body of a fellow mortal, and over whom another was placed, and which last was only covered by two feet of loose sand." In 1845, two years after this horrible incident, the cemetery was moved to Lower Town, north of Rideau Street, and in 1872 the Beechwood and Notre Dame Cemeteries were established.[80]

The Barrack Hill cemetery was located on the south side of where Sparks Street is today, between Elgin and Metcalfe. In the late 1840's and early 50's, when Mrs. Symmes was a young girl, she attended the Fraser Boarding School, which being at the northwest corner of Sparks and Elgin, was quite near. But according to Mrs. Symmes the presence of the abandoned graveyard did not frighten the girls in the least.[81]

Since the graveyards were right in the middle of what would become downtown Ottawa, some people may wonder if, over the years, anybody has ever come across any bones. The answer, unfortunately, is yes because - although the cemetery was moved in 1845 - they didn't move all the remains.

In 1864, when he was ten, Mr. MacCracken was a pupil at the Ottawa Grammar School. This was a wood-frame building that used to be on Metcalfe Street halfway between Queen and Sparks Streets. He said he and other students used to wander through the old cemetery behind the school where they frequently found skulls and bones lying about.[82]

These may have come to the surface because of construction projects in the vicinity. When William H. Cluff (now a grown man and a contractor) was excavating the basement of the A.W. Ault Building on Queen Street, he came across 20 or 30 coffins. "They simply crumbled when touched," he said. "They had been simple plain pine coffins painted black, names were on some of them, formed by the use of brass tacks, and in two cases cut with a knife, in every case where the bones were as carefully as possible taken up to be re-interred the teeth were found white, clean and perfect, not one missing."[83]

Another time, a skull was found when workers were excavating the basement of The Bank of British North America (which used to be on the south side of Sparks Street between Elgin and Metcalfe[84]). The construction workers gave it to the architect, Colonel C.P. Meredith of the firm *Band, Meredith and Burritt*, who took it home and gave it a decent burial in his garden.[85]

THE ROAD AROUND BARRACK HILL

A government road went around the bulge. Mr. Hill said there was nothing more dismal in the world than a stroll in the early days of Bytown from the lower town to the upper town at night. Having to pass the graveyard in the dark was bad enough, but all the area to the south of the road was swamp, filled with hoards of mosquitoes and bullfrogs.

Worst of all, the road was a hang-out for the toughs of Bytown, of which there were many. "The custom in the early days," said Mr. Hill, "was to wait at the corner until a little party gathered together so that one would not have to travel alone down that awful road."[86]

CULTURAL EVENTS

Barrack Hill was also a focal point for cultural events. On February 6 and 7 of 1837, the soldiers put on Bytown's first theatrical performance. A make-shift theatre was set up in one of the barracks, and the play was called *The Village Lawyer*. It was a great success. The audience was delighted and the proceeds of the evening went to help the poor.[87] After that came

The First Floor, The Blue Devils and other plays that did equally well, all the money going to charity.[88]

In the summer, Colonel Hughes, the commanding officer, allowed the band from the 24th Regiment to practice outdoors for several hours every night when the weather was good. This attracted large crowds of spectators who clearly enjoyed the fine music, and who showed their appreciation with frequent rounds of applause.[89]

Barrack Hill's Final Days

In 1853, the regular soldiers were recalled and replaced with twenty-five retired soldiers on pension. This 'pensioner scheme' as it was called had been introduced in 1851 as a cost savings measure where retired soldiers were used to maintain a light guard to act as reserves in case of sudden attack. After the Rideau Canal was transferred to the United Provinces of Canada in 1856, all of the pensioners except for one were discharged.[90]

The last soldier was Sergeant Robert Ritchie, who married Ann Martin, and whose son Thomas was born in their home on Barrack Hill. Sergeant Ritchie and his family remained there until 1857,[91] or 1858,[92] when he too was recalled.

William H. Cluff remembered Sergt. Ritchie as "a kindly gentleman if there ever was one, a Christian in whom there was no guile, who wore his character on his coat sleeve so all might know; a lover of flowers, he pottered about in his garden and on Sundays, after service, when so many people walked up to the Hill nothing seemed to give him more pleasure, after a few kindly words, than to give some of the lads and lassies a posy from his garden."[93]

William Pittman Lett also thought very highly of Sergt. Ritchie:

> *And Sergeant Major Ritchie, there*
> *He stands before my vision, where*
> *In youth I used to see him stand*
> *On Barrack Hill with cane in hand.*
> *For many a year ere death's disaster*
> *He held the post of Barrack Master,*
> *And amongst people who reflected*
> *Most highly always was respected.*
>
> *- William Pittman Lett, 1874*[94]

After Sergt. Ritchie left, Barrack Hill was deserted. With the soldier's cows and horses no longer there to graze, the stunted cedar shrubs and wild grass quickly took over.[95] For the next two or three years the grounds were used for local fairs where farmers exhibited cattle, and the farmers' wives sold wonderful homemade pies, pickles, jams and jellies.[96]

These fairs lasted until December of 1859 when contractors came in and began clearing away the scrub. Barrack Hill was about to become Parliament Hill!

When it was a Military Base 27

"*Entrance of the Rideau Canal, Bytown, Upper Canada (Ottawa)*" watercolor by Henry Francis Ainslie, February, 1839. Barrack Hill can be seen on the right, with its fence of cedar posts about 12 feet high, sharpened at the upper end. The building on the canal edge in the centre is the stone commissary where Matthew Connell worked after transferring from the temporary log cabin commissary on Barrack Hill. Credit: Library and Archives Canada/C-000518/Acc. No. 1955-128-11.

Detail based on "Plan and Elevation of the Barracks and Hospital erected on the Hill right hand or west side of the Canal Valley, Ottawa River," colored manuscript drafted by Lt. Col. By, Commanding Royal Engineers, Rideau Canal, in October of 1827. One of the barracks is on the left; the hospital (later the officer's quarters) on the right. Credit: Library and Archives Canada/NMC 23046/ Call no. H2/450/Ottawa/1827 (Barracks)

When it was a Military Base 29

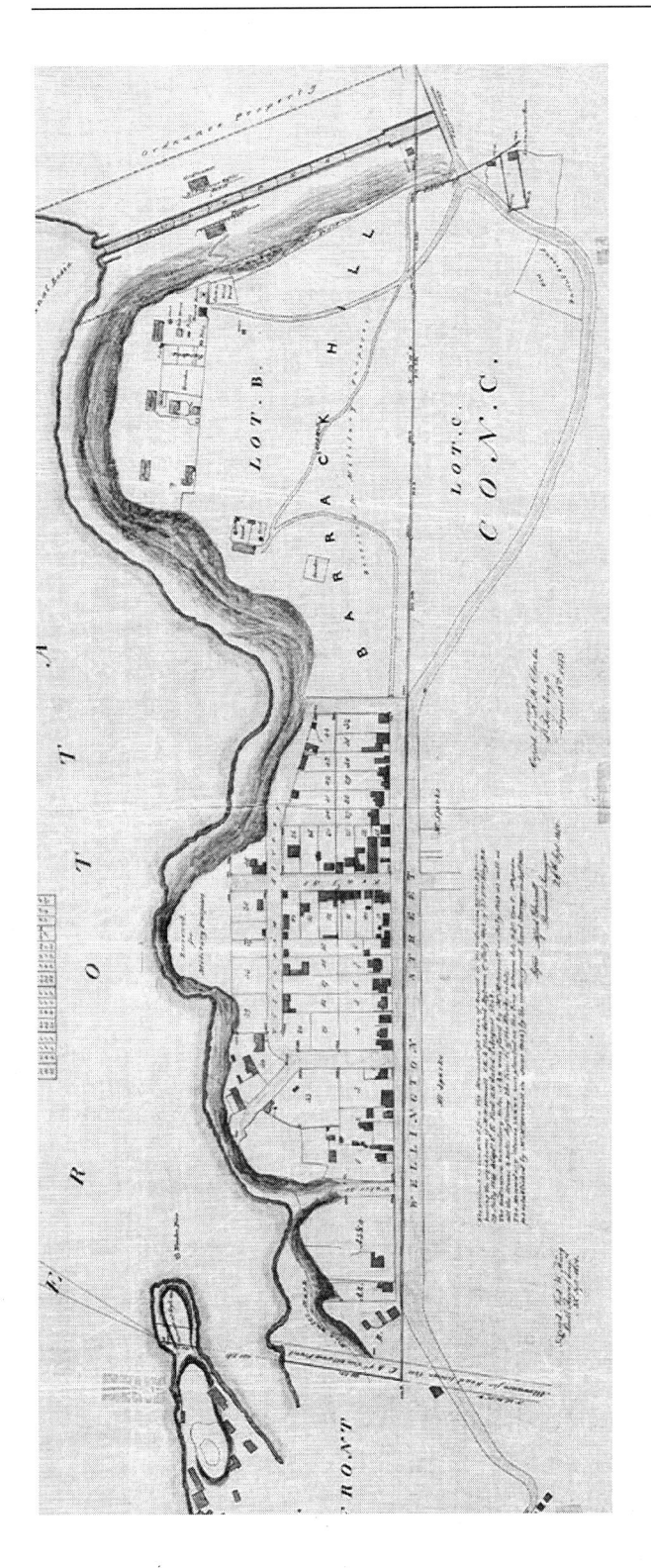

"Plan of Upper Bytown. Plan no. 1, Part Second, 3094, 1845." © Government of Canada. Reproduced with the permission of the Minister of Public Works and Government Services Canada (2011). Source: Library and Archives Canada/Department of Public Works fonds/NMC-122352.

"View of the Chaudière Bridges on the Ottawa River at Bytown (Ottawa)," oil on canvas by Edmund Willoughby Sewell, ca. 1843-1859. This quiet bay where the lumbermen are working is Brewery Bay, named after a brewery on shore owned by Michael Burke. The bay was filled in the 1920's and today is the 'pit parking lot' behind the Confederation Building. Credit: Library and Archives Canada/C-011048/Acc. No. 1991-120-2.

"Wellington Street near Bank Street, Ottawa," watercolor by C.Sedley, painted from the window of Doran's Hotel on Wellington Street ca. 1853. The large white building on Barrack Hill is the officers' quarters, located just north of where the West Block is today. William Cluff made his famous sleigh ride down the cliff starting off perhaps a little to the right of the officers' quarters. Credit: Library and Archives Canada/C-001548/Acc. No. 1992-675-2.

PART 2

THE VICTORIAN ERA

CHAPTER 3: THE PROJECT FROM HELL, PART 1

Haste makes waste.

Anonymous

PLANNING AND DESIGN

Today we have three Parliament Buildings, the Centre Block and the East and West Blocks. However, back in the 1860's there was only one Parliament Building. The original Parliament Building was not the Centre Block we have today, but it was located in the same spot as the Centre Block, with the Library at the back, and a clock tower at the front where the Peace Tower now is. The East and West Blocks were there, but they were not Parliament Buildings. They were Departmental Buildings for civil servants who had previously been spread out at offices in Toronto, Kingston, Ottawa, Montreal and Quebec. In those days the entire civil service of Canada could fit into just these two buildings – how it's grown since then!

There are many ways that the story of building the original Parliament Buildings could be told. History majors might write it one way, architectural historians another. An interesting account could be written from a contractor's perspective, or from a politician's viewpoint. John Q. Public living in Ottawa in the 1860's, reading about it in the newspapers and walking up to Parliament Hill to watch the work might tell it yet another way.

I am writing it from the perspective a project manager who has spent over two decades working on the buildings they built, exploring the attics and towers and all the other out of the way places tourists never get to see. It's strange. When I was researching this story, and reading about it for the very first time, I felt a strange closeness to that project team of so long ago. I felt we were like colleagues, almost.

You may not know this, but the project to build the first Parliament Buildings was a big, big failure. Costs skyrocketed, and half way into construction work was stopped for a year and a half for a Parliamentary Inquiry to see what went wrong. Many mistakes were made.

I'll tell you what I think the really big ones were, and how they might have been avoided. They say hindsight is crystal clear, and it's easy to look back and say what they should have done, but the interesting thing is, given the same circumstances, many of the mistakes they made back then could easily be made again today. This chapter and the next two have many lessons for young project managers today.

The *project from hell* is my name for it. Those on the project team didn't call it that when it started, although they may have later when it got into trouble. To them it was the Public Buildings project (also known as the Government Building project, the Ottawa Buildings project and the Provincial Buildings project). The project included an official residence for the Governor General. However, a new building was never built and in 1867 the Government purchased Rideau Hall instead.[97]

FIRST, WHAT DO WE MEAN BY CANADA?

Well, it's not what we mean today. Our story takes place in the 1850's and the early 1860's. Remembering back to your schooldays, this was before Confederation, which occurred at twelve o'clock noon on July 1, 1867.

At the time of our project British North America consisted of five separate colonies: Newfoundland, Nova Scotia, New Brunswick, Prince Edward Island, and the Province of Canada. Prior to 1840 the Province of Canada had been two separate colonies: Lower Canada (the future Quebec) with its Capital at Quebec City, and Upper Canada (the future Ontario) with its Capital at Toronto. Upper and Lower Canada were also referred to as 'the Canadas.' In 1840, the two Canadas were united to form one colony called the Province of Canada.[98] When we talk about 'Canada' in this story, what we mean is the *Province* of Canada.

Strangely enough, Canada had two Capitals: Quebec City and Toronto. The Government had been trying since 1840, and it was absolutely impossible for them to choose one city or the other (or even some other city) as Capital and stick to it, and so it had been decided that the Capital would alternate every four years between Quebec City and Toronto.

When the project officially started in May 1859, the Capital was at Toronto, but in the summer the Government would be moving back to Quebec City. Moving was always done in the summer because, as everyone knows, the middle of a Canadian winter is not the time to be going anywhere.

In those days, people used pounds and shillings to buy things. Under the revised *Currency Act* of 1854, provincial accounts could use dollars as well as pounds,[99] and although the *Act* was revised in 1857 so that, after January 1 1858 all provincial accounts would be kept in dollars, engineers and architects continued to use both systems for several years afterwards.

When we speak of estimates and cost in this and the next two chapters, conversion to dollars will be done automatically wherever pounds were used originally, using the conversion rate then in effect of £1 = $4.

THE APPROPRIATION

In 1854, Toronto architects Cumberland and Storm prepared preliminary designs of the Public Buildings and estimated their cost at $490,980. However it was more of a 'guess-timate' than an estimate because it did not include all of the costs - heating, ventilation, gas, and water, for example, were missing.

In March of 1856, the House of Assembly needed a better estimate. The task fell to Frederick Preston Rubidge, Public Works' assistant architect and (one of those rare combinations) engineer too. He was told an approximate estimate would be fine, and was even told how to go about it. "The estimates prepared about two years since by Messrs. Cumberland and Storm...will not be a safe guide," wrote Thomas A. Begly, Secretary of Public Works. He went on, "...still, by comparing them with the various estimates for Public Buildings lately acquired by the Department, you will be enabled to furnish estimates sufficiently reliable, and such as will meet the views of the Legislature."[100]

Public Works had recently erected and completed a very extensive building in cut-stone masonry known as the New Court-House in Montreal, but Rubidge thought its cost would be too high owing to changes in plans and delays.

However, the department had on hand fifteen competition plans and estimates for a New Custom House in Quebec, the cost of which varied from a low of 8.3 cents a cubic foot to a high of 15 cents a cubic foot. Striking the average of twelve of these estimates amounted to 10.4 cents, which he rounded down to 10 cents. Rubidge multiplied this average cost by the volumes of the buildings Cumberland and Storm had calculated two years earlier, and after adding allowances for heating, ventilating, gas, water, fixtures, fittings, and fireproofing came up with a total of $1,142,619. Rubidge reported back to Begly with this estimate the next day. This estimate was "as nearly correct as possible, and applicable to the Provincial Edifices proposed to be built" he said.[101]

Unfortunately, Rubidge's estimate was cut back, and on March 24, 1857 the Legislature passed a resolution approving an appropriation of only $900,000.[102]

However, the project team couldn't really do anything yet. Although they had money they didn't know where to erect the buildings. Should the Parliament Buildings be built in Toronto or Quebec City or where?

THE STORY OF HOW THE CAPITAL CAME TO OTTAWA

The cost and expense of moving Parliament, staff, equipment, and files every four years between Quebec City and Toronto was not very popular, and by the time of our story the need for some permanent location was very apparent.

M.J. Hickey wrote in 1861, "Canada was vexed. From Sandwich to Gaspé it was angry. Angry was the country, but mad were the towns. The Houses of Parliament shook with furious declamation. Politicians agreed on many points, but on one they could not agree. Quebec abused Montreal and Montreal abused Quebec. Quebec and Kingston abused both, and Toronto abused them all. It was really a jolly scramble and a lively one!"[103]

Since it had been proved that it was completely impossible for them to choose on their own, the House of Assembly passed a resolution the same day they approved the appropriation to ask the Queen to select "some one place as the permanent Seat of Government in Canada."[104]

Shortly after that, the secretary of the Governor General wrote to the mayors of Toronto, Montreal, Kingston, Ottawa and Quebec asking them to each prepare a paper "setting forth the reasons which may in their opinion favour the claim of that place to be selected by the Queen."[105] On April 17, 1857 she agreed to make the choice.

The case for Ottawa was drafted by the Hon. R.W. Scott, penned by the skilled hand of David Scott (of the Ottawa River works office), signed by John Bower Lewis (mayor) and William Pittman Lett (city clerk) and sent on its way across the Atlantic. On December 31, 1857, to everyone's complete surprise, the Queen chose Ottawa.

We don't know why she did. Several pretty stories floated about. One was that after carefully studying each mayor's submission and examining the most accurate maps of the Canadas ever made, she shut her eyes and placed her finger on the map and said, "Here is the spot."[106]

Now, you would think that once the Queen had made her choice, that would be it, wouldn't you? Well, it wasn't, and the fighting continued. In the Legislature on July 28, 1858 Mr. Duncan moved: "That an humble address be presented to Her Most Gracious Majesty the Queen, to represent that this house most humbly prays Her Majesty to reconsider the selection she has been advised to make, of a future Capital of Canada, and to name Montreal as such future capital."[107]

An amendment declaring, "in the opinion of this House the City of Ottawa ought not to be the permanent seat of Government of this Province" was passed by a vote of 64 to 50.[108] So much for what the Queen wanted!

In January 1859, following a tremendous lobbying effort, it was voted on again. This time the negative vote was reversed. It was close. Only 64 to 59 – but it was good enough.[109] The way was finally cleared for the project to start!

NOTICE TO ARCHITECTS

By May 1859, Public Works had decided to hold a design competition that would be advertised in a *Notice to Architects* in major newspapers all across the Province of Canada.

Rubidge knew they had money problems, but the Commissioner, who was new to the Department, did not. John Rose had just been appointed Commissioner on January 11, so he would only have been in office about three months.[110] He would have been aware that the appropriation was $900,000, of course, but he did not know about Rubidge's 1856 report and its higher cost estimate of $1,142,619. Rubidge sent him a copy of his report on May 3, 1859 adding that the cost would not be less than what he estimated.[111]

At that time the Department was in the process of getting a new Deputy Commissioner (this was Samuel Keefer, a civil engineer with the Department who we will meet shortly). Rubidge spoke to him about cost and gave him a copy of his report too.[112] Rubidge must have hoped Keefer would understand the trouble they were in and get more money, but nothing changed (see box on next page).

So, since $900,000 was all there was, Rubidge set about making it work. "I drew the advertisement at the request of Mr. Rose," he said, "and it contemplated rigid economy not ornate, but plain...."[113]

The architects had to be given a budget to work with, of course, but how much? It could not be all $900,000 because the appropriation was based on architectural estimates, not actual construction costs, and some money had to be set aside for contingencies and risk.

> *Keefer's 1st mistake. He didn't think the Government was serious about the $900,000.*
>
> *"I never supposed the appropriation would complete the buildings for this reason," he testified at the inquiry later. "Before I came into this office, the Assistant Engineer and Architect of the Department had furnished me an estimate...that to complete the buildings would cost £285,656 [$1,142,619], and the appropriation of £225,000 [$900,000] being less than this, and as I never yet knew an architect or engineer's estimate but was exceeded in the actual construction of the work, I therefore concluded that the appropriation was only so much towards the buildings."**
>
> *Unfortunately he was wrong. What he should have done was to discuss Rubidge's concerns with the Commissioner and (the two of them being the new kids on the block, so to speak), try to get more money. If they couldn't, they couldn't, but at least they would have tried.*
>
> **Province of Canada, Report of the Commission Appointed to Inquire Into Matters Connected With the Public Buildings at Ottawa. Quebec: Hunter, Rose & Co., 1863, Testimony of Samuel Keefer, September 5, 1862.*

At first Rubidge thought he would tell the architects they had only $480,000 for the three buildings on Parliament Hill, about half of the appropriation.[114] But he decided this was really not enough (you have to be practical, after all!) and increased it to $300,000 for the Parliament building and $240,000 for both Departmental Buildings (see Table 1). This would definitely force the architects to design cheaply - if they stuck to it that is.

But what does this budget mean in terms of quality? Can you build a nice looking Parliament Building for $300,000? Now, lack of money does not automatically mean lack of quality. My own experience is that architects can sometimes do amazing things with very little money. But, roughly speaking, the more money you have, the higher the level of quality you can afford.

Table 1. The project budget in May 1859

	Cost
For the Parliament Building	$300,000
For the Departmental Buildings	$240,000
For the Governor General's Residence	$100,000
Other work, contingencies and risk	$260,000
Appropriation	*$900,000*

We have seen that twelve different architects tried designing the New Custom House in Quebec, and that their costs varied between 8.3 to 15 cents a cubic foot. None of the twelve architects was able to design it cheaper than 8.3 cents a cubic foot.

Using these costs and doing exactly the same calculations Rubidge did in 1854 and adding the same allowances he did for heating, etc. we get the range of estimates for the Parliament Building shown in Table 2. (Rubidge shows all his calculations in his report, so this is not difficult to do.)

This means that if these same twelve architects competed for the Parliament Building, and designed to the same level of quality as they did on the New Custom House in Quebec City, we could expect their costs to be somewhere between $410,840 and $739,512.

As it turned, out the New Custom House in Quebec was a very nice building. William Thomas, a Toronto architect, won the competition and for many years the New Court House, with its Doric portico, was the most beautiful building in Quebec City. By co-incidence the contractor was one Thomas McGreevy, whom we shall meet shortly.[115]

Table 2. A range of estimates for the Parliament Building

	Estimate
Most expensive (15 cents)	$739,512
Rubidge's estimate (10 cents)	$493,008
Least expensive (8.3 cents)	$410,840
Budget given to the Architects for the Parliament Building	$300,000

But $300,000 is well below this cost range, so the quality of the Parliament Building would have to be lower (much lower) than the Custom House in Quebec. The problem was the appropriation, said Thomas Fuller. "If the appropriation first made was all that was intended for the Public Buildings, it did not warrant their undertaking at all."[116]

Be that as it may, the *Notice to Architects*, dated May 7, 1859 was signed by John Rose in Toronto and appeared in the newspapers two days later.

"My first knowledge of the Parliament Buildings," said Fuller "was derived from a notice to architects, from the Department of Public Works, dated the 7th of May, 1859. From seeing that notice I with my partner, Mr. Jones, determined to compete for the designs."[117]

MR. VANKOUGHNET AND MR. SHERWOOD

As we have seen, there were many politicians who didn't like the idea of the Capital being at Ottawa. In May of 1859 the Government was in Toronto, and one of the honorable members, a Mr. De Blaquière, said he did not believe the Government would ever go to Ottawa. Mr. Vankoughnet, the Commissioner of Crown Lands, said he was wrong. "You will see - the foundation stone will be laid within two months."[118]

Mr. Vankoughnet may have been exaggerating a little, but not by much. An early start at construction was politically important because, once big money was being spent, it would be difficult for Mr. De Blaquière or anyone else to lobby for Ottawa to be 'unselected.' Remember, the vote for Ottawa had been very close!

Mr. Vankoughnet and Mr. Sherwood, another member of the government, wanted construction by fall of 1859 and were piling the pressure on Public Works to make this happen.[119]

Fall usually begins near the last week of September, so this meant holding the architectural competition, evaluating the submissions, awarding the architectural contracts, doing all the design, all the tender documents, tendering, awarding, mobilizing and starting construction...all in five months! This is an impossible schedule today and, as events would show, it was impossible back then too.

SAMUEL KEEFER BECOMES DEPUTY COMMISSIONER

On May 9, 1859 Samuel Keefer was appointed Deputy Commissioner of Public Works. Although he was a Deputy Commissioner (today he would be called a Deputy Minister), he was very hands-on, directing the architects and doing many of the day-to-day tasks that I used to do as an ordinary project manager.

The first thing he did was to look over, revise, and approve the amount of accommodation required.[120] He edited the statement of accommodation to tell the architects, among other things, that the buildings were to be arranged around a quadrangle that would later become the famous front lawn of the Parliament Buildings.[121] This brilliant landscaping concept, the famous 'quadrangle open on the south side,' was thought up by an engineer. (*Ahem!*)

Keefer probably got this idea in his first day or two on the job. His obituary in the January-December 1890 transactions of the Canadian Society of Civil Engineers reads, "The arrangement of the detached blocks, forming the Parliament Buildings and departmental offices, upon three sides of a square, is due to him, and no little of the effect of this splendid pile upon a magnificent site is due to his disposition."[122]

Although Barrack Hill seemed to be the obvious location for the Parliament and Departmental Buildings, it was not decided on until May 21, 1859 when Keefer was in Ottawa with the Governor General and a portion of his Council to look at different sites. "We visited Barrack Hill, the Major Hill, and Ashburnham Hill, a place to the west of this", he said. "There seemed to be no difference of opinion about Barrack Hill being the place for these buildings."[123]

THE EVALUATION

The competition closed on August 1, 1859.[124] Fourteen architects competed for the Parliament Building, and six for the Departmental Buildings. "I took the plans to the Parliament Buildings in Toronto, where there was room, and had them extended on the walls where they could be seen and properly examined, and where the public had access to them," Keefer said.[125]

On August 12, he sent Rubidge to get John Morris, who was then employed as clerk of the works in the construction of the University buildings in Toronto, to make cost estimates[126]

The method they used was an approximate one called 'cubing the buildings,' the same one that Rubidge used in 1856. With this method, the interior volume of the building is calculated from the basement to the roof and then it is multiplied by a unit cost. They used '6d' (this means 6 pence or 10 cents) a cubic foot, which Keefer thought was the actual cost of the University of Toronto. "I found they were all within the estimate in this rough way, except the Parliament Building, which I estimated at £90,000 [$360,000]. I learnt afterwards from Mr. Morris, that the University cost 7½d [12½ cents] a foot, but I did not know this at the time."[127]

The evaluations were done by Keefer and Rubidge using a point system. The designs were rated in ten different categories. Keefer and Rubidge evaluated the designs individually, giving between 0 and 10 points for each category, for a maximum score of 100.

Unfortunately, Keefer didn't follow the rules. While Rubidge considered all the designs, Keefer rated only the three he thought would win.

The architects had been instructed not to sign their drawings (to ensure impartiality) but to identify themselves with a secret motto instead. Keefer and Rubidge both agreed that the winner for the Departmental Buildings was *Stat nomen in umbra* (this is the Latin motto chosen by the architects Stent and Laver, which means *the name stands in the shadow*). However they didn't agree on the Parliament Building. Keefer chose *Semper paratus* (the motto of Fuller and Jones, which means *always prepared*), while Rubidge chose *Stat nomen in umbra* for this building too.

The main reason Rubidge didn't choose the same architect as Keefer for the Parliament Building was cost. Rubidge had given it zero out of ten, while Keefer had given it a nine.

"I did not think they were the style the advertisement called for," Rubidge later said of his zero score. "I considered the Parliament Building could not be built for the appropriation. I thought the Departmental buildings might be built for the sum appropriated for them."[128]

Alexander Mackenzie, who in 1873 would become our second Prime Minister, was a builder before he entered politics, and in 1859 he bid on these buildings. "I consider the mode of cubing buildings of this class not a correct mode," he said. "It may do very well for common buildings. The proper and reasonable precaution was to have got the architects or some competent persons to make out quantities of the work, and to apply the ordinary values to these quantities and thus establish the value of the building. If this had been done, it would have appeared that the appropriation did not warrant this extent of building."[129]

When Keefer submitted his report on August 25, the Governor General asked some very difficult questions, like why not disqualify every architect whose design exceeded the budget and choose from those remaining? And why couldn't he and Rubidge agree on the architect for the Parliament Building?

Keefer solved this problem by getting rid of Rubidge so he wouldn't be around to answer questions: "...the exigencies of Public service have rendered it necessary that Mr. Rubidge should return to Quebec to attend to the works in progress there"[130] was how he explained it to the Governor General.

With Rubidge out of the way Keefer was able to work on the G.G. and on August 27 an Order in Council was passed awarding the Parliament Buildings to *Semper paratus* and the Departmental Buildings to *Stat nomen in umbra*.

Keefer's 2nd mistake. Before any architects were selected the costs of their designs should have been estimated more accurately.

The method of "cubing the buildings" was much too crude. Keefer should have had the architects provide the quantities of work with their designs, supplying detailed calculations of volumes of brick, stone, etc., and had Mr. Morris and Rubidge check them over and put fair prices on them. Alexander Mackenzie said that if this had been done, it would have appeared that the appropriation did not warrant this extent of building.

How different Parliament Hill would look today if these architects were not chosen because their designs were too expensive! The world would never have known Fuller and Jones' masterpiece; we would not have their beautiful Library of Parliament today; and the East and West Blocks - at least in their present forms - would not exist.

THE PUBLIC EXHIBITION

In the first week of September 1859 the people of Toronto were treated to a public exhibition of the designs which were still on the walls where Keefer had hung them. Keefer was on hand to greet people and explain the designs. He especially liked showing them a very pretty, nicely colored drawing of the Parliament Building. It showed a perspective view from the position of someone standing over near the West Block. The day was beautiful, the sun was shining, the birds were singing, and groups of people were strolling about. After explaining how beautiful a design it was he liked to point out "the Governor General in the act of alighting from his carriage, and the dragoons a-riding up behind him."[131]

The newspaper reporter from the *Leader* must have been very impressed. "And if, as we are assured, it can be constructed for $300,000, we shall have obtained a noble structure, an ornament to the capital, and a credit to the Province."[132]

However, *Pro Bono Publico*, probably an architect himself, was not impressed. He wrote a letter to the *Daily Globe* and, perhaps poking fun at the rules of the design competition, signed the letter with this motto (it means 'for the public good').

Pro Bono sniffed his nose at the *Leader*. "A noble structure indeed," he scoffed, "and not on a diminutive scale either, but covering an area of nearly three acres of ground, the lowest portion of it being about 40 feet high, and at the back – devoted to library purposes – even 90 feet high; a front (with its seven towers, the central one of which is to be 180 feet high), and all for $300,000. Build it, certainly, for even with all its defects, it is worth the price. But, joking apart, I have no hesitation in saying, with numerous architects and builders of this city who have examined the plans, that to carry out this design in its integrity would cost a sum not less than $800,000."[133] Actually, as we will see in Chapter 3, it would cost $2.8 million.

Quality-Time-Cost

Project managers think of a project in terms of scope, time and cost. Scope includes quality, but it also includes all the other project requirements. For example, should the buildings be fireproofed? Should every room have a sink and a tap with clean running water? What about the washrooms? Should they have those new, flushable toilets, etc.? But in order to simplify the discussion, we will consider just quality, time and cost.

A project that is done better, faster, and cheaper is a great success. However, this doesn't happen very often, and most project managers are happy if they can deliver the quality they were supposed to, on time and on budget. If they deliver two out of three it may still not be too bad; one out of three is not very good; and zero out of three is, well, let's say very bad.

Which of quality-time-cost do you think is most important? Well, it depends on who you ask. If you were to ask Keefer to place the three in order of importance, he would probably say it was time-quality-cost. To him, time was most important because of the pressure he was under to go fast, but he definitely had a vision of what Parliament Hill should look like, and quality must have been a close second. Cost would have been third because, as we have seen, he thought the appropriation was just a start.

For the architects, it was probably quality-time-cost (architects putting quality first is quite understandable) and for Mr. Vankoughnet and Mr. Sherwood it was time-time-time (time for them was in first, second and third places).

Keefer was stuck in the middle, like all project managers, trying to get all three and keep everyone happy. Unfortunately, he couldn't, and when the wheels fell off the wagon halfway into construction, and the project ground to a halt, to the Commissioners of the Inquiry what was important was cost-cost-cost.

Nobody knew it yet, but the project was already in big trouble. The problem was that the quality was way too high; there was not enough time; and not enough money. As any project manager knows, this is not a good way to start.

GO FASTER!

On September 8, 1859, before the architects were even hired, before there was anything to bid on, Keefer tendered the construction contracts. "This early notice was given that there might be no delay in letting the contracts, and was done at the insistence of the Hon. Mr. Vankoughnet, and Mr. Sherwood, two members of the Government," Keefer explained.[134] "I was pressed to go on with the work in the fall of 1859."[135]

THE ARCHITECTS ARE HIRED

After Fuller and Jones put in their designs, the first they heard back from the Department was a letter of September 3, 1859 from the Assistant Secretary of the Province, telling them that they were the winner for the Parliament Buildings, but that their plans needed further work and would not be adopted unless they were altered so as to be made satisfactory to the Government. If they wanted the work, they would have to go to Public Works' offices in Quebec to discuss the changes required.

Fuller and Jones arrived at Quebec on September 5, met with Keefer, and after several discussions over three days they received their letter of award. The letter described the modifications required, and requested them to have plans and specifications ready for the approval of the Department by October 10, 1859 and to be ready to show the contractors on October 15.

"I remonstrated with Mr. Keefer about the shortness of the time between then and the 15th October, to do all the work mentioned in the letter," said Fuller, "but he urged the necessity of letting the work that year, and I was induced to undertake to do it the best way I could during the given time." [136]

Stent and Laver went to Quebec September 8 and on the 9th they had their interview with Keefer. At this meeting Keefer instructed them to alter their plans, so that instead of retaining their block shape, with courts in the middle, the Departmental Buildings became 'L' shaped.[137] This design change by Keefer allowed great capacity for future expansion. Over the years both buildings have been added to and today are once again block shaped with interior courtyards.

WORK ON THE DRAWINGS AND SPECS

At Keefer's request, Fuller and Jones returned to Toronto by way of Ottawa, to see the site of the buildings, and got back to Toronto on September 10. From that time until October 11, they worked on the plans.

It was during this time that Keefer first began to worry about cost. "When the contract plans were preparing", he said, "I felt afraid that when we came to carry the designs out, good *bona fide* tenders would show they would cost more than had been allowed, and in order to keep within the sum mentioned in the notice the plans were drawn as cheaply as possible. Wooden floors were put in, and several things which I do not now remember...."[138]

NO TIME TO LOCATE BEDROCK

Between May 21 and June 6 1859, James Slater, an engineer with Public Works, surveyed Barrack Hill and prepared plans that showed ground elevations on a 50 foot grid.[139] For some reason these plans sat on somebody's shelf and were never given to the architects.

When Fuller was in Ottawa on September 8 he saw that the ground was not level, but as the particular locations for the building had not been decided, and he did not know about Mr. Slater's plan, he assumed for his drawings that the ground was level (he had to show something for the contractors to bid on). He called Keefer's attention to this on October 11, and Keefer agreed. Bedrock was assumed at two feet under this assumed ground line.[140] Similar assumptions for ground and bedrock were also made for the Departmental Building.

Keefer said, "There was not time to exhibit the actual one, and it was arranged with my consent that the assumed line should be exhibited. I knew there would be extra work in the foundations, but I had no idea how much. The plans were got up in such a hurried manner...."[141]

> Keefer's 3rd mistake. He should have had bedrock investigated. Keefer blamed it on lack of time. Rubidge testified, "I do not see that it would have hindered them materially in making their plans and specifications, if they had been requested to furnish the Department with the block plans of the buildings, and not to make the sections for the foundations or specify them, until the sites had been fixed, and the foundations tested. There was time to do all, if it had been determined to do it."*
>
> *Province of Canada, Report of the Commission Appointed to Inquire Into Matters Connected With the Public Buildings at Ottawa. Quebec: Hunter, Rose & Co., 1863, Testimony of Frederick Preston Rubidge, September 9, 1862.

NO TIME TO INCLUDE HEATING AND VENTILATION

On October 7, 1859, Keefer telegraphed Fuller saying that he would be in Toronto on Monday evening, and to get the specifications translated into French, and have copies ready to send to Quebec. Fuller said this was impossible. "It would have been impossible to have prepared the plans in time, shewing [sic] the system of heating and ventilating...."[142]

Keefer went to Toronto and on October 11, and after several consultations, it was decided to leave the heating and ventilation system out of the architectural plans and specifications.[143] The next day, Keefer sent Stent and Laver a telegram saying the same thing. "The heating of the buildings may be left out of the specification, and made a separate contract."[144] "I was pressed to go on with the work in the fall of 1859," he said. "If we had waited to adjust the heating and ventilating to these buildings, we could not, in my opinion, have commenced the work in 1859."[145]

The idea was to tender the heating and ventilating separately to firms who specialized in designing and constructing these systems, and coordinate their work on site with the contractors who were working on the buildings. This approach is called 'construction management' today and is often used to save time on modern office buildings. For example, it allows excavation of the basement and construction of the foundation to begin while parts of the building higher up are still being designed. It works when the higher parts don't affect the lower parts.

However it didn't work on this project because, as we shall see, the design of the heating and ventilating system required the building contractors to do an enormous amount of extra work that the heating and ventilating contractor could not do. There were excavations for the boiler houses and air ducts, the masonry in them, the construction of the smoke and air shafts, and the ventilating flues, all of which had to be done as costly extras by the building contractors.

Alexander Mackenzie said, "I think it was imprudent to contract for the Parliament Buildings until the plans for heating and ventilating had been matured and incorporated with the plans of the buildings; there seemed to have been undue haste in all the preliminary preparations." [146]

PLANS AND SPECIFICATIONS FOR THE BUILDINGS ARE READY

The plans and specifications were translated and ready for the contractors, without showing actual bedrock and without showing heating and ventilating, between October 15 and 30 1859.[147] The completion date given in the specifications – February 1, 1862 for the Departmental Buildings, and July 1, 1862 for the Parliament Building – gave the contractors only a little more than two years.[148]

Keefer's 4th mistake. He should have kept the heating and ventilating in the architect's contracts.

Rubidge testified, "There was provision made for heating and ventilating in the original designs, which should have been sufficient under the limited appropriation, till the Legislature provided another system." *

**Province of Canada, Report of the Commission Appointed to Inquire Into Matters Connected With the Public Buildings at Ottawa. Quebec: Hunter, Rose & Co., 1863, Testimony of Frederick Preston Rubidge, September 9, 1862.*

"Mr. Samuel Keefer," photographed by Helen Sherwood, Topley Studio, ca. 1850-1880. Although he was Deputy Commissioner of Public Works, he did many of the day-to-day tasks on the project that today would be done by a project manager or project leader. Credit: Library and Archives Canada/C-021683/Acc. No. 1941-088 NPC.

"First prize winner in the competition for the design of the Parliament Buildings. Front view. Architects, Fuller and Jones." The day is beautiful, the sun is shining, the birds are singing, groups of people are strolling about and the Governor General can be seen in the act of alighting from his carriage with the dragoons a-riding up behind him. Credit: Library of Parliament collection / Library and Archives Canada / PA-187219.

The Project from Hell, Part 1 55

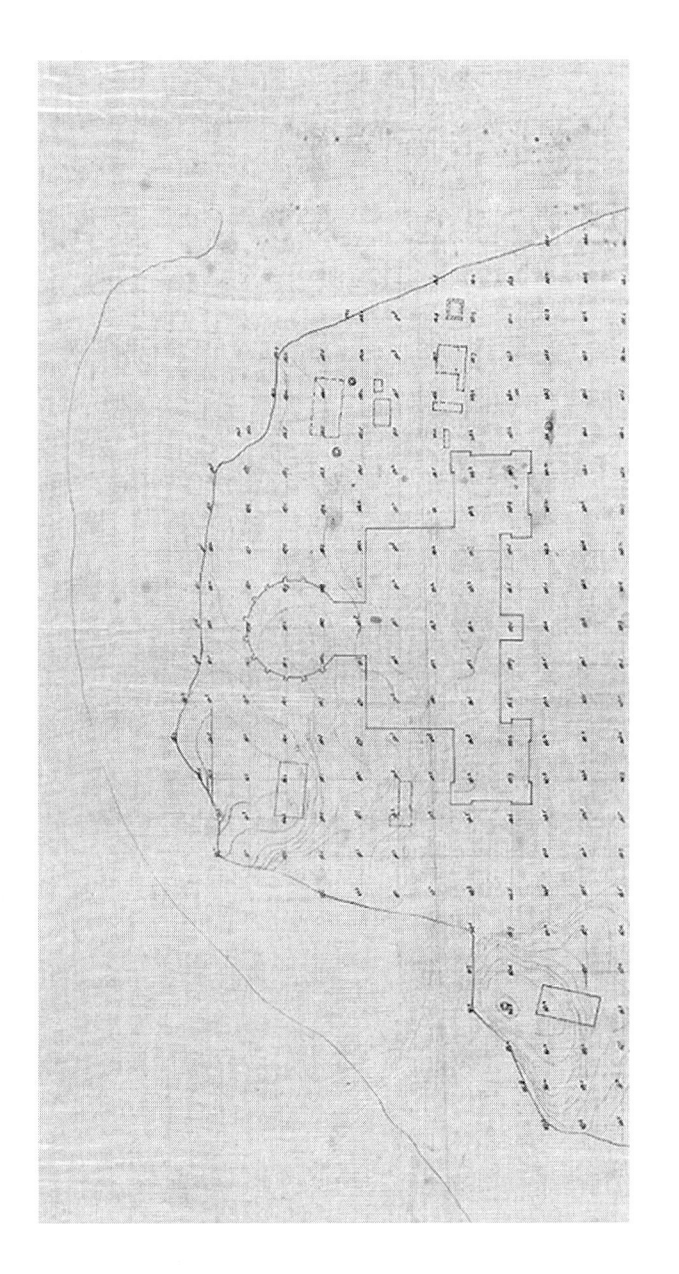

Detail based on "Grounds, Parliament Buildings, Ottawa. [Plan of Barrack Hill, showing elevations.]" This is Mr. Slater's map on a fifty foot grid that was drawn in June 1859. The building outlines were added around January 1860 when their locations were approved. Note the old Barrack Hill structures also drawn on the plan. © Government of Canada. Reproduced with the permission of the Minister of Public Works and Government Services Canada (2011). Source: Library and Archives Canada/Department of Public Works fonds/NMC-118810.

Chapter 4: The Project from Hell, Part 2

When the plans and specifications were finished they were as perfect as plans usually are, and would enable contractors to estimate their quantities fairly.[149]

Thomas Fuller, 1862

TENDER AND AWARD

Tenders closed at noon on November 15, 1859, and were sent unopened to the Executive Council where they were opened. Afterwards, they were returned to the Department of Public Works for a report.

In his report of November 17, Keefer listed the seven lowest tenders for each contract.[150] On the next page, we see that the low bidder for both contracts was Mr. Peters, Thomas McGreevy was second lowest for the Parliament Building and Jones, Haycock & Co. came in fourth for the Departmental Buildings. Keefer also indicated that a tender had been received from Thomas McGreevy for the whole work of $579,000. This was $61,900 off McGreevy's separate tenders, and exactly equal to the sum of Mr. Peter's two bids – a tie for first place![151] Interestingly, although Alexander Mackenzie bid, he was not in the seven lowest.

SOME BACKGROUND ON THOMAS McGREEVY

Mr. McGreevy was a politician as well as a contractor. In the fall of 1857, he ran for election as municipal councilor in Quebec City and won. As a councilor he became close friends with the mayor of Quebec City, Hector-Louis Langevin, who was also a

Table 3. The seven lowest tenders

	Parl't. Bldg.
Charles Peters, Quebec	$346,000
Thomas McGreevy, Quebec	$361,900
David Glass, London	$379,000
F.X. Berlinguet, Quebec	$399,810
Jones, Haycock & Co., Port Hope	$434,500
James Stewart & Vo., Kingston	$450,000
John Gibson & Co., Toronto	$460,000
The Architect's estimate	$492,000

	Dept'l. Bldg.
Charles Peters, Quebec	$233,000
Brown & Watson, Montreal	$238,400
John Gibson & Co., Toronto	$249,000
Jones, Haycock & Co., Port Hope	$251,000
F.X. Berlinguet, Quebec	$273,900
Thomas McGreevy, Quebec	$279,000
Alexander Manning & Co., Toronto	$290,000
The Architect's estimate	$288,000

member of the Legislative Assembly. The Langevin Building, directly across from from Parliament Hill today, is named after him. Through Langevin, McGreevy met and became friends with Joseph-Édouard Cauchon, another member of the Government, who became Commissioner of Public Works in 1861.[152] According to the *Daily Globe,* he was also a good friend of Mr. Baby, another politician.[153]

McGreevy was well-connected, and he knew it.

NOT EQUAL IN ALL RESPECTS

Although Mr. Peters' and Mr. McGreevy's tenders were for the same amount, they were not equal in all respects. Mr. Peters' tender had the required *schedule of prices* attached, while Mr. McGreevy's tender did not. Also, Mr. McGreevy's tender was ambiguous with respect to fireproofing.

A schedule of prices was a section at the end of the bid listing all the different types of work in the project. Schedules were prepared by the architects, with empty spaces left for the contractors to fill in their prices. When completed, they formed part of the contract.

For example, in 1859 digging in earth, clay or gravel and wheeling or leveling within 50 metres was 21 cents a cubic metre; a laborer was paid 80 cents a day; a cart, horse and driver $1.50 a day; a wagon, team and driver $2.70; Nepean sandstone facing on the Parliament Buildings cost 52 cents a square metre; two coats of stain and varnish typically cost 11 cents a square metre and so on.[154]

The schedule listed all the different types of work required, and the prices multiplied by the quantities in the project had to equal the contractor's bid. Schedules were used for calculating monthly payments, and also the cost of extra or additional work.[155]

FUN 'N GAMES

On November 22, Mr. McGreevy's tender for the Parliament and Departmental Buildings was accepted by an Order in

Council, but he was directed to prepare a schedule of prices and to clarify his bid regarding fireproofing.

McGreevy confirmed that fireproofing was included. He also sent in a schedule except that he didn't sign it, and his prices didn't add up to his bid. If monthly payments were made on the basis of his schedule, the whole contract would be paid before the work was half done.

It was at this time that we first hear about a 'secret deal' that was made with Mr. McGreevy. McGreevy refused to put in another schedule because, he said, Keefer had made an agreement with him that extra and additional work would be paid at fair value, not using the prices in the schedule. "It was between Mr. Keefer and me that the agreement was made that the schedule of prices should not be applied to extra or additional work, before the contract was signed."[156]

Then the finger-pointing started. Keefer said later at the inquiry that it was the Commissioner who made the agreement, not him. "I now say distinctly that the arrangement made between Mr. McGreevy and the Commissioner was, that extra and additional work, not included in the contract, was to be paid for at fair wages, and that the schedule of prices was to apply only to the contract work for progress estimates...."[157]

The Commissioner said that he had made no such agreement. "I may have expressed an opinion to him or the Deputy Commissioner that if there was extra work it should be paid for at a fair price. I cannot say, however, that I have any distinct recollection of saying this."[158]

Keefer went even further and said the Government itself was aware of the arrangement. "Not only has the interpretation which I have put on the contract, been acted upon all along with the full knowledge of the Commissioner, but also with the knowledge of the Government."[159]

Whoever it was, it was unfair to the other bidders. Alexander Mackenzie said, "It was distinctly intimated, that no tender would be received which was not accompanied by a schedule of prices.... I say the schedule I put in with my tender represented in detail the bulk sum of my tender, and also the prices I expected to be paid for extra and additional work."[160]

How They Solved the Problem

"From conferring with him [Mr. McGreevy]," Keefer said, "I saw it was utterly hopeless to expect from him a schedule which would be satisfactory, and I directed the architects to prepare one, so as to be applicable to his tender, and they did so."[161]

The way the architects did this was fair enough given the circumstances. They used three tenders which they thought to be fair prices for the work, and comparing the average with McGreevy's lump sum they estimated his tender to be about 35% too low. Taking the average prices in the three schedules, they made a new schedule which they reduced by the same 35%. This schedule was attached to the contract, and McGreevy agreed to it for monthly payments, but he still did not agree to it for extra and additional work.

The Departmental Building contract

On December 1, 1859 McGreevy wrote the following letter to John Rose:[162]

Quebec, December 1, 1959

> *Sir,*
> *In order to secure the speedy erection of the Government Buildings at Ottawa; if the Government accedes, let the Departmental Buildings be given to Messrs. Jones & Co., of Upper Canada.*
>
> *I have the honor to be,*
> *Sir,*
> *Your Most Obedient Servant,*
>
> *(Signed)*
> *THOS. R. McGREEVY*

McGreevy's suggestion about splitting the contract was approved by an Order in Council on December 5, and on December 7 the two contracts were signed without a remark or protest of any kind by the contractors even though the headings on the schedules plainly said they were to be used for calculating extra and additional work. And why was this? It was because the clause in the contract that dealt with extra and additional work had been carefully rewritten by the law office so that it did not say that the schedule was to be used — even though it was attached, and even though by its title it said that it was supposed to be used. Instead, the contract itself (which takes precedence over the attachments in case of conflicts) said that extra and additional work was to be paid at fair and reasonable rates, as Mr. MGreevy wanted.

But why would Mr. McGreevy give away the Departmental Buildings? Was he just a nice guy, helping the Government make the work go faster? Also, if his contract was going to be split, why would the Departmental Buildings go to Jones, Haycock & Co., who came in fourth in the tender, instead of Mr. Peters who came in first?

According to the *Daily Globe* it was all planned from the beginning. "Without any apparent cause, Mr. McGreevy surrendered the departmental buildings to Messrs. Jones, Haycock & Co., of Port Hope, with whom were connected Mr. Burton, then member for East Durham, and a supporter of the Ministry. They, of course, inherited all Mr. McGreevy's advantages in the shape of extra work, and did not fail to do their part at the general election. Their money flowed freely in many counties, and proved successful in some."[163]

WHAT ALEXANDER MACKENZIE SAID ABOUT MCGREEVY'S BID

"I did tender for all of the public buildings at Ottawa, and the Governor's residence", Alexander Mackenzie said. "I spent about a month, assisted by six others, in examining the plans, and making out estimates for these buildings. I had two plumbers, three carpenters and two masons with me. I made a careful estimate of quantities, and I tendered to build the Parliament building and the Departmental buildings for the sum of

$801,500.... I considered Mr. McGreevy's contract too low. My own was as low as it could possibly have been done for in my judgment."[164]

Mr. McGreevy and Messrs. Jones & Co. had just contracted to build these buildings for $579,000. They would need a lot of extras to make a profit, and as events turned out they got them.

CHAPTER 5: THE PROJECT FROM HELL, PART 3

Messrs. Fuller & Jones were the successful architects, and although the design was considered by many as too costly, responsible contractors were found who tendered within the government vote. Upon examination, however, of the spot selected for the erection, formerly known as the Barrack Hill, it was found from the inequality of the ground, that immense excavations were necessary, which made in solid rock added enormously to the original cost, and could not have been foreseen by builders nor architects. The government finding no provision for this work in the grant, and fearing it would cost a large portion of the original sum voted, stopped works, and for some considerable time there was no progress.[165]

Hand Book to the Parliamentary and Departmental Buildings, 1867

CONSTRUCTION

On December 20, 1859 the first sod was turned by Commissioner Rose and Deputy Commissioner Keefer.[166,167] The first day of winter is the winter solstice, which in Canada is December 21. Therefore, strictly speaking, it was still fall on December 20. In this way of looking at it, Keefer met the deadline imposed on him by Mssrs. Vankoughnet and Sherwood by one day.

Soon afterwards, workers began to clear the site. In 1859, Martin Daly was a young boy of 11 living at Old Chelsea. He remembered visiting Ottawa for the first time with his father, and seeing the workers clearing the scrub cedar bushes off Barrack Hill so that the excavations for the Parliament Buildings could be started. Years later, he could remember that day so well that he could even tell you where they had dinner – it was at Barrett's Hotel on the market. The meal was excellent and it only cost 25 cents each.[168]

The heating and ventilation system package was tendered on November 14, 1859. Five bids were received, and on January 28 the contract was awarded to Mr. Charles Garth of Montreal.

In January, a decision was made to turn the eastern Departmental Building around to take advantage of a downward slope in the bedrock, thereby saving money in rock excavation. The long side that now faces the Parliamentary lawn was originally intended to face Wellington Street.[169]

By mid-February 1860, carpenters', blacksmiths', and stonecutters' shops were built, and the western barrack from the Barrack Hill days was turned into a site office for the project teams; one side for the Parliament Building and the other for the Departmental Building. Five or six stone quarries were being worked in the area, providing stone for the construction. Four or five hundred men and two hundred teams of horses were working hard and making good progress despite the cold weather.[170]

A notice from an Ottawa newspaper dated May 1, 1860 offered guided tours of the work. "Persons desiring admission to view the Government Buildings may obtain necessary cards upon application to the architects Messrs. Fuller and Jones on Sparks Street, or Messrs. Stent and Laver on Wellington Street." To encourage out-of-towners, those within 10 miles of Ottawa could only visit the buildings on the 12 and 25 of each month, but those at a greater distance were admitted every day except Sunday.[171]

All of the excavation was done in that first year, and do you know where the thousands of loads of earth and stone were dumped? It was in the swamp and depressed area below the old road that used to go around the Barrack Hill.[172]

The excavations for the foundations took a lot more digging than expected. At the Parliament Building, they had to dig from two to fifteen feet deeper than the assumed line for bedrock shown on the plans, and at the Departmental Buildings nine feet deeper. However, it was the excavations for the heating and ventilation system that were absolutely enormous. The fresh-air duct for the eastern Departmental Building was 117 metres long, for the western Departmental Building 127 metres long and for the Parliament Building 120 metres long; enormous trenches cut into solid limestone bedrock.

At the West Block, for example, it was 7.6 metres deep, 4.6 metres wide at the bottom and 6.7 metres wide at the top, and in this was built a structure of solid masonry. There were three levels. At the top (the first level) there were two air ducts. There were three air ducts on the second level, and on the third there was a sewer.[173]

The boiler house in the Parliament Building was 26 by 24 metres, the one in the eastern Departmental Building 13 by 9 metres, and in the western Departmental Building 12 by 12 metres.

All of this was extra work for Mr. McGreevy and for Mssrs. Jones, Haycock and Co., and was done without any estimates being made or approvals obtained.[174] "In November the excavations were far advanced, and attracted my notice," Keefer said. "I thought there was going to be an immense amount of unauthorized extra work."[175]

The cornerstone was a crystallized, almost translucent white marble from the Portage du Fort quarry in Pontiac County, Quebec about 100 km northwest of Ottawa. Use of this particular stone was the idea of Dr. Van Cortland (also spelled Van Cortlandt, van Cortlandt, and Van Courtland), one of Bytown's first citizens. He was a very odd and eccentric man and in addition to being a medical doctor, was also an amateur mineralogist, geologist, botanist and archaeologist.[176, 177, 178] Upon its arrival, the big block of stone was paraded up and down the streets. The wagon halted at Dr. Van Cortland's house, and everyone gave him three hearty cheers of appreciation![179]

The lettering in the cornerstone read:

This cornerstone of the building
intended to receive
The Legislature of Canada
was laid by
ALBERT EDWARD PRINCE OF WALES
on the First day of September
MDCCCLX

The cornerstone was laid at 11 o'clock on September 1, 1860 by His Royal Highness, Edward Albert, Prince of Wales. After the mortar was spread and the stone lowered, Mr. Morris applied the plumb, Samuel Keefer the level and the Prince of Wales announced the stone "fairly and duly laid."[180]

The architects had no role to play in the ceremony and just sat there in the audience, fuming that the honor of applying the plumb had been given to Mr. Morris. Fuller complained about it, without success.[181] After the ceremony, bullocks and sheep were roasted whole over fires and everybody ate their fill.[182]

Later, a bronze plaque in the shape of a six-pointed star was placed on top of the cornerstone, and after the mortar was spread around it the stone on top was placed down, sandwiching the plaque in-between. The plaque, which is now mounted on the wall in the Hall of Honour of the Centre Block, has quite a story attached to it — see THE MISSING PLAQUE THAT ALMOST BECAME SOMEONE'S COFFEE TABLE in Chapter 24.

Unfortunately, either McGreevy or Jones, Haycock & Co. (we don't know which one) began to treat their workers unfairly. In December 1860, the men who were cutting and shaping stone for the buildings had to take a big pay cut if they wanted to keep their jobs over the winter. One stone cutter said, "I will state here that the wages given to first class stone cutters in the summer season was $1.75 per day, and that the same class of men are now reduced in their wages to $1.00."[183] Problems with the stonemasons continued, and whenever they did the men reacted by going on strike. In 1863, the Stonemasons Association posted a handbill proclaiming "There have been more strikes on this Parliament Building than on any other job on this continent...."[184]

In May 1861, the cost estimate was $1^2/_3$ million dollars. Keefer tried to put a positive spin on it: "The Houses of Parliament in England, covering 4½ acres of ground, were estimated to cost 3½ million dollars, but the actual expenditure was 14 million dollars. The extra cost connected with the heating and ventilating alone cost upwards of one million dollars. The Houses of Parliament and Public Offices at Ottawa cover 3¾ acres of ground; and if they can be completed for $1^2/_3$ millions of dollars, the cost for the large amount of accommodation provided cannot be considered excessive."[185]

In June 1861, Mr. Rose resigned as Commissioner but retained his seat. He was replaced by Joseph-Édouard Cauchon (who, it will be remembered, was Mr. McGreevy's friend). Within three months, and without discussing it with Keefer or anybody else, he agreed to the contractors' claims for more money and paid them. "When I came into the Department," he said, "I did not consult Mr. Keefer, the Deputy Commissioner, for I had no confidence in him."[186]

After Mr. Cauchon made these payments, there was no money left in the appropriation. On September 27, he stopped the project throwing some 1,700 men out of work.[187] At this time, the outside walls of the buildings were generally built up to the level of the main cornices.

The Government tried to blame everything on Mr. Rose, who denied all responsibility.[188] Alexander Mackenzie, now no longer a builder but Leader of the Opposition, moved for an inquiry into the Public Buildings. He quoted facts and figures and showed the enormous prices that were paid for extra work, in many cases double, in some cases four times and in others even seven times those in the schedule of prices.[189]

On June 21, 1862, a Royal Commission was appointed, and they submitted their report on January 29, 1863. They found many things done wrong, and Keefer took the brunt of their criticisms.

On April 18, 1863 new contracts were signed with the original contractors. After a delay of one and a half years, work started again. Although the commissioners recommended all the architects get new contracts, Public Works fired the lot of them. However, Thomas Fuller was re-hired, along with Charles Baillargé, as joint architects for all three buildings. In their day-to-day work, Fuller concentrated on the Parliament Building and Baillargé on the Departmental Buildings.

After being fired, Chilion Jones of the firm Fuller and Jones, and his wife Eliza Maria Jones (Harvey), returned to their home on the outskirts of Brockville and started to raise a family. Eliza went on to become famous as a scientific farmer, cattle breeder, producer of exceptionally fine butter, author and speaker.

Chilion, it seems, left architecture completely. He wasn't interested in farming, and his wife managed the whole thing on her own while he lived in nearby Gananoque managing his brother's shovel factory.[190]

Stent and Laver were extremely bitter about being fired. They refused to leave and a year later could still be seen wandering around the construction site giving orders to anyone who would listen.[191, 192]

Nonetheless, the work progressed well. On August 15, 1864 George Brown wrote a famous and often quoted letter to Sir John A. Macdonald saying "The buildings are magnificent; the style, the extent, the site, the workmanship are all surpassingly fine. But they are just 500 years in advance of the time.... To say the truth, there is nothing in London, Paris, or Washington approaching to it."[193]

In 1864, Samuel Keefer was fired too.[194] As Maurice Laframboise (the new Commissioner) put it, Mr. Keefer did not fulfill the duties of his office to his satisfaction.[195]

By 1865, work on the roads and grounds was underway. By October the Departmental Buildings were completed and ready for move-in.

In February 1866, Public Works asked Baillairgé to gather proof of corruption that they could use in the arbitration of claims from the first contracts. This was the end of Baillairgé. Langevin, Cauchon and McGreevy worked behind the scenes to concoct false charges against him, and before the incriminating evidence could be put together they got him fired for "gross dereliction of duty."[196]

Parliament had its first session in the new Parliament Building on June 8, 1866. George C. Holland, who was a Senate reporter for almost half a century, was there that day. "The public buildings," he said, "stood in isolated majesty on Parliament Hill, forming three sides of a square, the south side of which was framed with a cedar log fence. The square itself was striking only for its ugliness. The stunted cedar shrubs and sickly wild grass which, prior to the erection of the buildings, partially covered the shallow soil, had disappeared and the debris inseparable from the work of construction had been only partially removed."[197]

Here is some Parliament Building trivia: the completed buildings had more than 10 acres of plastering, 1,200 doors and windows, 20 kilometres of cornices and many thousands of square metres of masonry, cut-stone work and carvings.[198]

In March 1867, all of the contractors' claims were settled. By May, Thomas Fuller's services were no longer required, and he was dismissed. That year he designed a lovely house for Mr. McGreevy at sixty-nine Rue d'Auteuil, in Quebec City. He built the house using the same grey type of Ohio sandstone he used on the Parliament Building.[199] The house is still there today, but the grey sandstone has weathered to a lovely buff color.

By the time of Confederation on July 1, 1867, the buildings were what we today call 'substantially complete.' So far, $2,723,981.58 had been spent with the roof of the main tower and the library (estimated at $185,000), fencing, landscaping and roads still to be done.[200] Doing the math, at substantial completion it was 3 times over the appropriation of $900,000 (not counting the G.G.'s residence) and 5 years late.

The tower roof was completed in 1873, and the library in 1876. The final cost was $3,032,792 ($1,750,720 for the Parliament Building, main tower and library, and $1,282,072 for the Departmental Buildings.)[201]

BACK TO OTTAWA BEING THE CAPITAL...

Lieutenant-Colonel C.P. Meredith (this is the same Colonel C.P. Meredith, of the firm of *Band, Meredith and Burritt* who buried the skull in his garden) said it was frequently stated that "it would be impossible for the Government to remain here and that the Parliament Buildings would be sold to a religious order."[202] Many people felt this way. This is why the cornerstone said the building was only *intended* to receive the Legislature.

You can still read this on the cornerstone of the Centre Block today, although the letters are rather faded. This is the original cornerstone, recovered after the fire of February 3, 1916 and re-used with these new words added:

Relaid
By his brother
ARTHUR DUKE OF CONNAUGHT
on the First Day of September
MDCCCCXVI [203]

Thomas Fuller's Carving

There is a stone carving of Thomas Fuller on the front of the Centre Block, three stories up and about three metres west of the Peace Tower. This carving was done by the builders of the Centre Block to honor this fine architect.

The head on the carving is Thomas Fuller's, but his body is some kind of four-legged animal with claws and a long, curvy tail. The scientific or medical term for this fanciful beast is chimera (pronounced ki-mer-ah). You might be surprised to learn that chimeras actually exist. For example, a geep is a sheep-goat chimera. The first geep was created under laboratory conditions in 1984 by fusing a sheep embryo with a goat embryo.[204] But it doesn't look strange. Not like the chimera of Thomas Fuller.

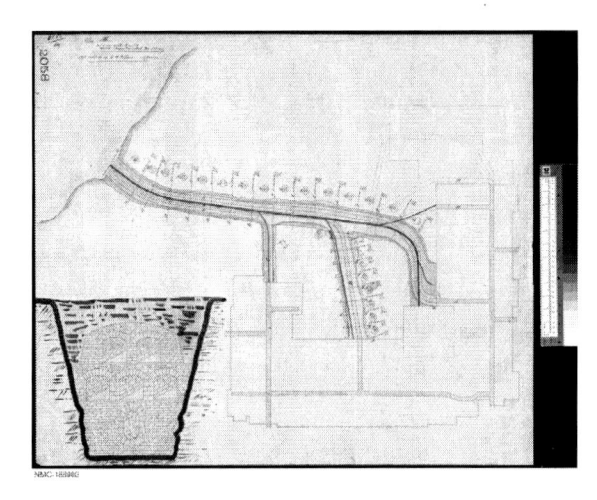

"West Block, Parliament Buildings, Ottawa, Departmental Buildings. Plan M, Drain and ducts." © *Government of Canada. Reproduced with the permission of the Minister of Public Works and Government Services Canada (2011). Source: Library and Archives Canada/Department of Public Works fonds/NMC-188980.*

"Parliament Buildings under construction." Photograph of the eastern Departmental Building in the summer of 1865, before move-in. Workers have just completed the famous face in the main tower. If you look closely you will see the two eyes, the nose and the mouth as if it is saying "Boo!" We don't know if the face was put in accidentally or on purpose but my guess is on purpose! Credit: William Notman/Library and Archives Canada/C-10074/Acc. No. 1980-023 NPC.

74 *The Other Side of the Hill*

C-010978

"Feu-de-joie, Ottawa, Ont." Celebration of Victoria Day, May 24, 1868. Note the youngsters sitting on top of the rickety old wood fence propped up along Wellington Street. Credit: William James Topley/ Library and Archives Canada/ C-010978/Acc. No. 1936-270 NPC

"Thomas Fuller." Fuller was 36 when he bid on the Parliament Building. This photograph was taken in June of 1889, some 30 years later when he was Chief Architect for Public Works. Credit: William James Topley/Library and Archives Canada/ PA-116162/Acc. No. 1936-270 NPC

This carving of Thomas Fuller is on today's Centre Block three windows up just to the left of the Peace Tower. The face is an excellent likeness. The stone carver got Fuller's fleshy chin and mutton-chop whiskers exactly!

Chapter 6: The Story of the Nepean Sandstone

When I was here in December, 1859, I saw some nice looking stone lying about the ground on the Barrack Hill, said to have been brought in as specimens of stone in the neighborhood. It was the kind of stone we wished to use, and which Mr. Morris had not found except at a distance out of reach. On enquiry, it was found to have come from a quarry of Mr. Augustus Keefer, about 10 or 11 miles distant; as soon as it was examined it met with general approval, and Messrs. Fuller & Jones and Messrs. Stent & Laver suggested its use."

Samuel Keefer, 1862[205]

Nepean sandstone makes up most of the Parliament Buildings. J. D. Edgar (Speaker of the House of Commons from 1896 to 1899) said of this stone that, "Its coloring is varied and beautiful, and grows in richness under the hand of time."[206]

Speaker Edgar would have been surprised to learn that originally a rather dull looking limestone was going to have been used instead. If it had, the color of the Parliament Buildings would have been something like the grey sides of the Rideau Canal.

On September 9, 1859 Samuel Keefer asked John Morris, the clerk of the works, to investigate and see what kinds of stone were available in the vicinity of Ottawa. Although Nepean sandstone was known to exist in the area he didn't see any. Morris recommended limestone, which Keefer agreed to, and this was passed on to the architects.

Nobody was really happy about using limestone, but it was the best they could do in the time they had. Fuller said, "That this limestone would make sound and durable work if the stones were carefully selected, there can be no doubt," he said, "but the color being grey the general effect would be, in any style, somber."[207]

In 1858, the year before he was given this task, Morris was in Toronto working as clerk of the works on the University Buildings, so he may not have been aware of a story in the *Ottawa Banner* of April 22 where Dr. Van Cortland called public attention to the existence of a quarry of compact sandstone on Lot 24, 2nd Concession Templeton about four miles away, and said if the stone was carefully selected quite free from iron stains that it would be in demand for the new Parliament Buildings.[208]

In November 1859, Van Cortland gave a lecture on building stones and showed some beautiful specimens of sandstone from Nepean, Templeton, Pembroke, and the Calumet.[209] It may have been that Fuller attended this lecture and started thinking about sandstone because it was about that time, after the pressure of preparing the tender documents was over, that he started looking for a different stone.

On January 27, 1860 Fuller wrote to Keefer:

> *We have been most anxious to find some other stone lighter in color and of equal durability, and have for some months been making enquiries and obtaining specimens of the sandstone in the neighborhood; and as those from the rocks at Napean [sic] and Templeton appeared to us the most suitable, we have personally inspected them both....*
>
> *The effect produced by the varied tints of Templeton stone for quoins &c., the Napean [sic] stone for the rubble facing, and the Ohio stone for the dressings of windows and doors &c., would be very pleasing and would add far more to the appearance of the building than could be produced by an outlay of ten times the amount in ornamentation by moldings, carvings, &c.*[210]

On February 28, 1860 Keefer recommended these changes to the Commissioner. As supporting documentation, he attached Fuller and Jones' report, a letter from Stent and Laver, a report from John Morris on cost and durability, and a letter from Sir William Logan, the Provincial Geologist who wrote, "one of the characteristics of this stone, besides its power of resisting atmospheric influence, is its capability of enduring great heat without injury. If an edifice built of it were destroyed by fire, the walls would still continue sound, and the renewal of the woodwork is all that would be required to re-establish it."[211] He didn't know it then, but the fire resistance of the stone would be given a very practical test on the night of February 3, 1916.

However, the Commissioner saw no reason for the change, which was merely a matter of taste, he said, and besides there wasn't enough money. However, he was over-ruled, and by an Order in Council on June 2, 1860 the change was approved.[212]

At first, they got the Nepean stone from a quarry about 16 or 17 kilometres away belonging to Augustus Keefer, Mr. Bishop and Mr. Wilson, but the owners got into difficulty and this quarry had to be closed.

The contractors then opened quarries of their own, about four kilometres further from the city. The stone was as good, but the bedding was not, and the stone required more work.[213] Thomas Stent said, "The stone there [in the first quarry] was in beds, and easily broken square, but the stone from the next quarry did not rise in beds, required to be blasted, and broken with plug and feather, and had to be worked on the beds and joints; I now think it was worth fifty cents [a square foot] over and above the value of the limestone."[214]

Chapter 7: Time Travel

I pressed the lever over to its extreme position. The night came like the turning out of a lamp, and in another moment came to-morrow. The laboratory grew faint and hazy, then fainter and ever fainter. To-morrow night came black, then day again, night again, day again, faster and faster still. An eddying murmur filled my ears, and a strange, dumb confusedness descended on my mind.

"The Time Machine" by H. G. Wells (1895)

WE saw that by 1867, the year of Confederation, that the Parliament Buildings were substantially complete. What do you think it would be like if we could take a time machine back to that time? What would it be like if we were to sit in the public galleries looking down on the Chamber of the House of Commons on November 6, 1867, when the Parliament of the new Dominion of Canada sat there for the very first time?[215]

Let's pretend we have a machine that is exactly like the one in H.G. Wells' 1895 classic *The Time Machine*, and that it is all set up on the front lawn of Parliament Hill, gassed up and ready to go. We have to start our voyage from Parliament Hill because, as everyone knows, time machines don't fly through the air like an airplane. They just fly backwards or forwards through time, staying at the same spot. So climb in, sit down and buckle up. (Remember, safety first!)

According to H.G. Wells flying one of these things is not difficult. Here is one little white lever, and here is another. If you push forward on this lever it sends the machine into the future; and if you pull back on that one it sends the machine into the past. There are four dials on the dashboard that show when you are. The first dial records days, the second thousands of days, then millions of days, and the last thousands of millions. The trick is to pull back on the lever that sends you backwards in time, and then, when you think the time is right, to push it forward, but slowly so that you come to a gradual stop. It's not good to jerk. Ok...ready? Grab the lever and give it a try!

What an expert you are! The machine shudders and shakes at first, but then glides smoothly to a stop. When we get out and look around, it is still Parliament Hill all right, but what we see is not at all like what we left.

Along the southern boundary, where today we have the beautiful stone and wrought iron Wellington Street Wall, there is just an ugly solid board cedar fence. It is taller than a man and goes all the way from Elgin Street to Bank. It has only two entrances, one at Elgin and the other at Metcalfe.[216] The fence is not in good repair, and on the Wellington Street side it has been braced every few metres to keep it upright.[217]

The buildings themselves are magnificent, but they are standing on absolutely bare ground! There is no landscaping of any kind: no grass, no statues, no beds of red and yellow tulips, no lamps, nothing! The square, which will someday be the famous parliamentary front lawn, is dirt and stones roughly graded to the level of the Departmental Buildings. However, there has not been much grading carried out anywhere else, and there is still a lot of construction debris lying about in the dirt.[218]

The central walkway is made of boards, and wooden stairs at the end lead up to a wide terrace in front of the main tower of the Parliament Building. Diagonal paths, shortcuts, have been trampled out across the square. (These paths are still visible today if you look down on the lawn from the top of the Peace Tower.)

A continuous horse and carriage road has been made all around the square. On the east and west sides, it inclines gently to the north for a distance and then rises more steeply up to the terrace. On the south side, it has been extended along the fronts of the East and West Blocks. Boardwalks have also been built along both sides of these roads.

The East and West Blocks (which, in 1867 are Departmental Buildings, not Parliament Buildings) are for the most part two stories high because most of the first floor, or basement, is below grade. The eastern Departmental Building is shaped like the letter L, with the long part of the L facing the square and the base of the L facing Wellington Street. Inside are the Governor General's office, the Privy Council, the Minister of Justice, the Minister of the Miltia, the Secretary of State, the Finance and Audit Offices, the Registrar, the Receiver General, the Secretary of State for the Provinces, the Customs and the Inland Revenue Departments.

The western Departmental Building is also L shaped but the L is reversed, with the base going to the left instead of the right. Also, the height of the L is only about half its base. Inside are Public Works, the Post Office, the Adjutant General and Militia Departments, Marine and Fisheries, the Bureau of Agriculture, and the Patent Department's model room.

The Parliament Building to the north is three stories high, the first being an above-ground basement. The ground floor is one storey up, and above that is the first floor. The main tower rises about 48 metres above the terrace. The clock and bell are not yet installed and work on the crown, which will increase its height by another 30 metres, has not started.

The roofs of the buildings are not that beautiful apple-green copper we have today; in fact, they are not copper at all. They are slate; horizontal bands of purple and green slate from the State of Vermont.

Along the top of the roofs, where they meet the skyline, is a knee-high ornamental cresting, or fence, made of wrought iron with hammered flowers and leaves. Long, spear-like 'terminals' (nowadays we call them finials) also of wrought iron, stick up from the peaks of dormers, towers and turrets. The crestings and terminals on all three buildings are painted deep blue, with the prominent points gilt.

The stonework is all brand-new and clean looking, the overall impression being creamy-white. The 1867 Hand Book to the Parliamentary and Departmental Buildings says:

> *The plain surface is faced with cream-colored sandstone of the Potsdam formation, obtained from Napean [sic], a few miles from Ottawa. The spandrils of the arches, and the spaces between window-arches and the sills of the upper windows, are filled up with a quaint description of stone-work, composed of stones of irregular size, shape and color, very neatly set together. These with the Potsdam red sandstone employed in forming the arches over the windows, afford a pleasant variety of color and effect, and contrast with the general masses of light coloured sandstone, of which the body of the work is composed.*[219]

As we walk up the walkway, we can see on the western Departmental Building that quaint description of stone-work. It is in the sunken panels in-between the second and third storey windows, made with different coloured stones, all cut at funny, odd angles. John Page, Public Works' chief engineer in 1867, calls this random work,[220] and in the 1990's my good friend Marcel Joanisse, Public Works' Chief Heritage Stone Mason, called it "that crazy stonework."[221]

The overall effect is much more colourful than it is today. The purple and green bands of the slate roofs, the deep blue wrought iron finials and crestings with their gilded tips, the grey Templetone stone, the red relieving arches over the windows and doors and the colourful random work make a stunning contrast against the creamy-white of the walls. Even the mortar between the stones is coloured!

Behind the western Departmental Building is a little stone building. It is the officers' quarters from the Barrack Hill days, but in 1867 it is being used for government offices.[222]

Going up the stairs to the terrace in front of the main tower, we turn to the left and follow the road around to the back of the Parliament Building. The road dead-ends; it goes along the side of the building and then just stops. It doesn't loop around the library as it does now. Construction on the library stopped several years ago and the walls are only up to about the underside of the large windows.

Walking across the compacted soil to the edge of the cliff (thank goodness it hasn't been raining or this would all be mud!) we see that then, as now, the best view of the surrounding countryside is from behind the library. The river, the islands, the rapids upriver and the green forests and purple hills in the distance are all fine, but it is the boiling, churning Chaudière Falls, with its booms and slides that immediately grabs our attention.

It is not at all like the Chaudière Falls of today which are tame in comparison because of the dams that have been built. In 1826 John MacTaggart, who was clerk of the works for the Rideau Canal, told of a cow that one morning fell over the falls and he said she didn't show up again until she reached Fox Point, about 16 kilometres away. When they got her out of the water she wouldn't stop bawling, but he said she was not badly hurt and lived for years after.[223]

There is a small island at the foot of the cliff, opposite the old Brewery Hill at the end of Bank Street in Upper Town. For many years, this island was known for its beautiful lone pine tree. It was an Ottawa landmark that everybody knew. William Pittman Lett said that it flourished until about about 1865, but then some "atrocious vandal" took a boat and rowed out in the middle of the night and cut it down for firewood.[224]

But let's return now and take a look inside the Parliament Building. It's too bad it's the summer recess because we won't get a chance to see the Hon. Members at work.

The entrance to the Parliament Building is at the main tower. The arches of the tower, with their deeply cut moldings, carvings and clusters of polished marble columns from Arnprior, open into a groined porch large enough for a horse and carriage to pass through. Over the wide door is an elaborate stone carving of the Royal Arms.

Passing through this door we enter a vestibule. As it is today, the Senate is to the east side of the building and the House of Commons is to the west. We stop and look around. In the wall behind us, on both sides of the doorway we have just come through, are large, ornamental windows of cut glass. Straight ahead, on the far wall, are five tracery windows with quarry lights that open onto the central court to ensure ample daylight. Below these windows is a grand staircase and in front of the stairs a line of six columns. Their shafts are polished marble from Arnprior, and their carved capitals, which John Page says with characteristic understatement are "believed to possess considerable artistic merit,"[225] are sandstone. The molded arches over them are also sandstone.

The first few steps lead up to a platform, from which flights lead left and right to large, circular landings on the ground, or main, floor. The stairs are of blue Ohio sandstone and are constructed with hanging steps. Both the stairs and the landings have ornamental stone balustrades.

The floor of the vestibule is Portland cement,[226] but the Parliament Building is still a work in progress, and before the end of the year the floor will be paved with decorative tiles.[227] The ceiling is pine, fine sunk paneled work with tooth enrichment, oiled and varnished.

We cross the vestibule and proceed up the staircase, keeping to the left. From the circular landing we take another flight of stairs up to the Public Gallery overlooking the House of Commons Chamber.

The Public Gallery is first come, first served. Although it is sometimes called the Gentlemen's Gallery,[228] in fact it is for both ladies and gentlemen. There is, however, a special gallery reserved for ladies only.[229]

The galleries are capable of seating 1,000 people in all. The Public Gallery is the whole of the north gallery and the northern two-fifths of the east gallery. The southern three-fifths of the east gallery are for Senators. The south gallery is the one for Ladies, spoken of earlier, and the southern part of the west gallery is for guests of the Speaker. The remainder of the west gallery is for reporters. Reporters also have the lower gallery over the Speaker's chair.

Senator Charles Bishop always thought this lower gallery was rather spindly. "It never collapsed", he said, "but the support seemed none to strong and one felt as if it were liable to crash at any time with possibly calamitous consequence."[230]

The Chamber is 25 metres by 14 metres, with a 14 metre high ceiling and desks for 194 Members. The Speaker's chair, which is of a temporary character, is not on the north wall where the Speaker's Chair is in the Centre Block today. It is in the centre of the west side, facing east "in the direction from which the wise men once came."[231]

When the Chamber was designed there were 130 members: 65 from Upper Canada and 65 from Lower Canada. According to an 1893 newspaper article, the Speaker's chair was originally at the north end, and the rows of seats ran lengthwise along the east and west sides, with the floor of the House running lengthwise down the middle.[232]

The British North America Act, signed by Queen Victoria on March 29, 1867 but not proclaimed until July 1, 1867, joined together three of the former Colonies – the Province of Canada, Nova Scotia and New Brunswick – into the new Dominion of Canada, consisting of the four Provinces of Ontario, Quebec, Nova Scotia and New Brunswick, with Ottawa as its Capital.[233] With Confederation, the number of Members would be increased by the addition of new provinces and increased representation in the old ones. There would be 194 Members, and it would be simply too crowded.

The problem was solved by moving the Speaker's chair to the west side. The Members' desks were arranged along the width, seven rows on the north side and seven on the south side. The two front rows were on the floor of the House, but the others were on platforms that rose seven inches with each row; the last row was about three feet over the floor. It was found that the new arrangement was better than the old. Not only did it allow more seating, but it is much better for hearing.[234]

The Chamber is surrounded by large marble pilasters carrying clusters of marble columns with carved capitals which, in turn, support pointed arches that reach nearly to the ceiling. The piers and arches are a light grayish marble from Portage du Fort, while the columns are dark marble from Arnprior.

The ceiling is deeply molded pine framework filled in with ground glass and sunlight just pours in through the skylights above. In the east, west and north walls are large windows with mullions and tracery of sandstone, and the inside sashes are richly ornamented stained glass windows of the most brilliant colors filled with the Royal, Provincial and other coats of arms and heraldic devices. At night the Chamber is lit by gas jets that reflect off the glass ceiling.[235] It is a truly beautiful room.

Today, tours of the Centre Block always end with a trip up to the top of the Peace Tower, but we couldn't do this in 1867 because the main tower of the Parliament Building was not finished. Only the masonry was, and the crown on the roof with the observation deck at the top was not completed until 1873. After 1873, everyone who could manage it always climbed the 287 steps up to the top (there was no elevator in those days!), and they all agreed the view was the best to be had anywhere.

"South West view of Parliament Buildings (Centre Block) and portion of Eastern Block - Departmental Buildings." In 1867 John Page said, *"All the Buildings are constructed in what may be termed the Pointed Gothic style of architecture, and from the bold, broken outline they present – their numerous towers, high pitched, variegated slate roofs, pierced by dormers and surmounted by ornamental wrought iron cresting and terminals, together with the quaintness of the carved figures, combine to produce an imposing and picturesque effect."* [236] *Photograph circa 1868. Credit: Samuel McLaughlin / Library and Archives Canada / C-018369/Acc. No. 1964-144 NPC*

90   *The Other Side of the Hill*

This looks like the Peace Tower entrance to today's Centre Block, but it's not — it's the entrance at the tower of the original Parliament Building! Credit: William James Topley/Library and Archives Canada/PA-008902/Acc. No. 1936-270 NPC

"(Parliament Buildings) Vestibule of the old Centre Block." This is the view from the circular landing on the House of Commons' side. The arched doorway across the vestibule leads to the lobby in front of the Senate Chamber. Behind us is a similar arched doorway to the lobby in front of the House of Commons Chamber. To our left (off camera) are the stairs that will take us up to the Public Gallery. This photograph was taken in 1878. Credit: William James Topley/Library and Archives Canada/PA-012409/Acc. No. 1936-270 NPC

"(Parliament Buildings) Interior view of House of Commons." This photograph was taken from the north-east corner of the public gallery looking south east. Note the soft glow of light coming through the glass ceiling and the stained glass windows, the galleries, the marble pilasters, columns and arches, the Speaker's chair facing east, and the paired desks for the Members of Parliament. Above and behind the Speaker's chair was the gallery for reporters that, to Senator Bishop, appeared like it could collapse at any time. Credit: William James Topley/Library and Archives Canada/C-014582/Acc. No. 1933-223 NPC

Chapter 8: Lovers' Walk

When we were teenagers your aunt and I would go to Parliament Hill with Vivian Sparks and a group of other friends, and the first thing we would do when we got there was run behind the Parliament Buildings and take the stairs down to the Lovers' Lane. It was wonderful! It was just like being in the country except you were right in the middle of the city!

Vivian Nixon, 2011

According to historian Lucien Brault, the Minister of Public Works, William McDougall, went down to inspect a ventilation shaft opening below the north edge of the hill during construction of the Parliament Building, and among the trees he saw a pretty little path made by the rafts men as a shortcut to their lodgings in Lower Town. Then and there he decided to have it made into a walkway.[237]

Brault's view that it was at first a foot-path in the Barrack Hill days is supported by a verse from William Pittman Letts' *Recollections of Bytown and its Old Inhabitants*:

> *A forest path across the hill*
> *To Bank Street led – the place was still;*
> *No noisy vehicle passed there,*
> *The dwellers of the wood to scare.*

> *- William Pittman Lett, 1874*[238]

There were many paths on top of Barracks Hill, but since all of the trees had been cut down it would take a hard stretch of the imagination to describe any of them as a forest path. William

Pittman Lett is probably describing the path that McDougall liked so much.

However, it may have been someone else, not the rafts men, who made it. William Cluff said the rafts men stayed on the raft until the job was done. They didn't sleep in their lodgings in Lower Town. "One crib on the raft was for cooking purposes," he said, "as the men all lived on the raft until they delivered it in the proper cove in Quebec. They slept in little board cabins scattered about on the raft."[239]

While we may not know for sure who made the path, we do know that the walk itself was constructed in 1869. F.P. Rubidge, who was now the Chief Architect of Public Works, described in his Annual Report for 1870 what they had built the previous year.

> *A pleasant retired foot walk has been cut and embanked along the almost perpendicular face of Barrack Hill, winding through the natural brushwood.*[240]

Years later William Lyon Mackenzie King said, "The walk which we have around Parliament hill, the walk that runs around the hill from Elgin street to Bank street, is, I believe, the result of work that was provided one year for the unemployed from the Mackenzie administration during the hard times of 1874 to 1878, and it has been of service to the country ever since."[241] King had his dates wrong, and whether it was work for the unemployed, or not, we don't know.

In 1871, only two years after it was constructed, Charles Roger wrote about it in his book *Ottawa Past and Present*:

> *Around the face of the rock, fronting the river, on which the buildings stand, a curiously devised path has been made, with rustic seats, fountains, and every convenience for loungers.*[242]

In the *Illustrated Guide to the House of Commons and Senate of Canada* of 1879 it was described like this:

> *The Lovers walk*
> *A charming promenade hidden on the side of the rock on which the Parliament Buildings stand. This road which is over a quarter of a mile in lenght [sic] is wide and kept in good order, seats are placed here and there for the convenience of persons who want to enjoy a solitary rest. From that place the tourist has a splendid view of the Ottawa river, in all its grandeur including the Chaudière Falls in the distance.*"[243]

Unfortunately, Lovers' Walk soon became a favourite hangout for the toughs of Ottawa. On August 25, 1879, Mr. T. Mackay wrote to the Department of Public Works complaining that the walk was "a meeting place for blackguards" and requested that the Dominion Police "see that fellows conduct themselves accordingly."[244] Two Dominion Police officers were permanently assigned to patrol the walkway and to watch the fresh air intakes at the top of the hill to keep anyone from getting inside[245]

On June 28, 1898, the *Globe* reported an extraordinary runaway. George Howe's handsome driving mare, Mayflower, was was tied on Sparks Street and, for some reason taking fright, broke her bridle and dashed up to Parliament Hill. On the way, the carriage was demolished and the mare, running at top speed, jumped the high hedge at the Lovers' Walk, tumbling down the hill almost to the water's edge. Mr. Howe took her to the veterinarian's where she was treated for bad cuts on her legs.[246]

William Lyon Mackenzie King was, of course, our tenth prime minister, but when he came to Ottawa in July, 1900 it was not as a politician but as a public servant. He was Deputy Minister of the newly formed Department of Labor.

After getting off the train, he took a streetcar into town and on the way in had a chance to look at what would become his new home. He was not impressed. "The business part of the town is small & like that of a provincial town, not interesting but tiresome...& has all the non-attraction of a small town" he wrote in his diary that night.[247] However, he liked Parliament Hill, and he liked the Lovers' Walk. A few weeks later his parents came for a visit. "I came in about 5.20 & took father and mother for a walk around the Lovers' lane by the Parlmt. Bldgs. which is extremely pretty."[248]

In 1904, a public washroom was built.[249] The building is still there today; it is the small shed with the slightly arch-shaped roof on the escarpment behind the Queen Victoria statue, just next to the cat colony.

Lovers' Walk was a favourite spot for politicians, staff and other people who worked on Parliament Hill, especially as the buildings were not air-conditioned. Even today, the top three floors of the Centre Block do not have air conditioning, just portable units that are stored in the winter and dragged out each summer. Prime Ministers Macdonald, Laurier, Borden and King all took pleasure in walking along Lovers' Walk and getting away, however briefly, from their stifling hot offices and the pressures of their Prime Ministerial duties.[250, 251]

In May of 1921, Mackenzie King, when he was Leader of the Opposition, was trying to memorize a two-hour speech. "Went over parts of it in my thought," he wrote in his diary, "then went to the club for a hurried bit of lunch, after which I walked around the Lovers' Walk, going over the speech in my mind, found I had the essential points pretty clear." He must have memorized it well, because he was given a splendid ovation from his side of the House when he gave the speech later that afternoon.[252]

In 1930, a man was fined for carving his and his girl's initials on a bench. *The Citizen* took the position that it is the inalienable right of men to carve their sweetheart's name into the benches provided they are in love and provided they are less than thirty years of age. Before thirty, *The Citizen* explained, a man in love is a poet; after thirty he is an ass. In this case the man was in his forties.[253]

For Tom Reid (Lib; New Westminster, British Columbia), it was a favourite place to play his bagpipes, flooding the grounds with the strains of tunes like *Flowers of the Forest*. In 1931, while thus occupied, he was threatened by a Mountie who said that if he didn't stop he would be jailed. However, Mr. Reid knew his rights, and he stood his ground and said to the Commissioner of the R.C.M.P. that if he tried to arrest him for playing his pipes, he would have to take full responsibility for any riot that might occur.[254]

The walk was always closed in the winter because it wasn't safe. In 1933, eleven-year-old Ford Carruthers, accompanied by another boy, climbed over the locked iron gate, and got to a point just above the Rideau Canal locks. He accidentally slipped on the ice and fell over 20 metres down the steep slope. His fall was stopped when he hit a large tree, breaking his left thigh.[255] Ford's father tried to sue the government for the doctor's bill, but was not successful.[256]

In 1937 a newspaper said the walk was "not what it used to be 25 or 30 years ago."[257] In 1939 Prime Minister King vetoed the expenditure of $5,000 for the maintenance because the war had started.[258] In 1940, the walk was closed and Public Works put up signs saying: *Closed – Dangerous.*

Mr. Joseph Enoil MICHAUD (Liberal; Restigouche-Madawaska, N.B.), acting Minister of Public Works, explained in 1942: "I understand that a couple of years ago part of the ground along these walks fell away and it has not been found possible to repair that, and there would be danger if persons were allowed to frequent these lonely places."[259]

Once it was closed, Lovers' Walk went into disrepair very quickly. Rain washed soil down the steep slopes, and muddy piles of dirt and debris collected on the pathway. Trees uprooted and fell. Retaining walls tipped. Rainwater that had soaked into cracks and open joints in the stonework froze in winter and cracked the walls apart. Big pieces of concrete and stone tumbled down the escarpment, iron pipe railings broke, and entire sections of walkway disappeared.

In 1945, Prime Minister King asked Public Works if it was possible for the walk to be reopened, but he was told it would cost thousands of dollars and that the department felt unjustified in doing this until after the war.[260] *Ottawa Citizen* Reporter James Oasler used to picket with a large sign saying 'Government Unfair to Lovers.'[261]

Excerpt from the House of Commons Debates
July 18, 1960, p. 6458

Mr. Herbert Wilfred HERRIDGE (Independent C.C.F; Kootenay West, B.C.): ...I would much prefer to see the money spent on restoring and renovating what is known as lovers' lane. I have walked around the back of the building –
Some Hon. MEMBERS: Oh.
Mr. HERRIDGE: Mind you, I have only been there because I wanted to see the beauty and do some botanizing. I would suggest there is such a wonderful opportunity for landscaping right from the Rideau Canal round to the Supreme Court building and that something should be done to give the public an opportunity to enjoy this fine scene and walk overlooking the river. As it is, this wonderful river walk is denied to members of the House of Commons and the Senate, as well as to residents of Ottawa and visitors to the city. I would urge the minister to give instructions for the repair and renovation of what is known as lovers' walk, behind the parliament buildings.
An Hon. MEMBER: Why?
Mr. Herridge: So that it's natural beauty and advantages may be enjoyed by all.

Excerpt from the House of Commons Debates
July 20, 1960, p. 6605-6606

Mr. David James WALKER (Prog. Cons.; Rosedale, Ont.; Minister of Public Works): ...the lovers' walk was ordered closed many years ago by the former government. As a matter of fact I think the late Right Hon. W. L. Mackenzie King himself confirmed that closing and he himself was a very romantic person in his conception of nature. He himself suggested that it should be closed, and the Royal Canadian Mounted Police have insisted all along that it should remain closed because it is extremely dangerous.
Mr. John Whitney PICKERSGILL (Lib.; Bonavista--Twillingate, Nfld. and Lab.): To whom?
Mr. WALKER: I mean dangerous, not in the way in which the hon. member for Kootenay west is thinking -

Some Hon. MEMBERS: Oh, oh.

Mr. WALKER: *- but dangerous to life and limb. Anybody that goes out there is apt to have a serious accident; I mean a physical accident.*

Some Hon. MEMBERS : Oh, oh.

Mr. WALKER: *You are apt to slip and fall. Just recently, as a matter of fact, a man was very badly hurt.*[262]

Excerpt from the House of Commons Debates
July 21, 1960, p. 6691

Mr. HERRIDGE: *I made a suggestion during the discussion of the administration item that what is known as lovers' walk should be restored. I did so after conversations with a number of Ottawa citizens and civil servants. Since making the suggestion in the House I have received a number of letters from people who are very interested in this proposal. I want to say this was a serious suggestion. I have reached an age where the romantic aspects of the walk are strictly academic. I am sure the minister will understand that.*

In reply the minister stated the estimated cost of the restoration was $300,000. I have made inquiries since and while I do not question that figure, I found out that, I think it was in 1939, the walk was maintained for about $5,000 a year. Whatever the amount might be, there is 50 acres of beautiful parkland going to waste right next to the Ottawa river. In 1939, the then prime minister vetoed the expenditure of $5,000 for the maintenance because the war had commenced. I find there is great interest in this walk. Seriously speaking, it is a lovely area very close to the parliament buildings, and I think it is a shame that in the capital city of Ottawa, this area should be neglected. I suggest that the minister have a survey made of the situation to see what it actually would cost to restore the walk. I am not suggesting it is necessary to build stone walls in many places and other extensive works. If the stone steps were satisfactory, the rest of the walk could be made safe by shoring along the bank without a lot of these stone walls. As I said, I suggest a survey be made and a sort of progressive restoration of this beautiful park be undertaken.

Mr. WALKER: *In connection with the lovers' walk, I shall not make any more comment except to say that I would be glad to study the feasibility of my hon. friend's suggestion.*

Mr. Richard Albert BELL (Prog. Cons.; Carleton, Ont.): On the ground?

Mr. WALKER: I will leave the external work to the hon. member for Kootenay West.

A year later, Mr. Herridge asked Mr. Walker what he had found out. Mr. Walker replied that both the R.C.M.P. and the National Capital Commission were firm that Lovers' Walk should remain closed.[263] The question came up again in 1966[264] and in 1972[265] with the same result. Lovers' Walk has remained closed ever since.

Lovers' Walk 101

PA-034227

"Lover's Walk showing Stairway." The steep slopes made annual maintenance necessary right from the start. In the winter of 1878 a horse and sleigh hauling stone for repairs crashed down the slope to the ice below. Happily the horse was uninjured.[266] This photograph was taken in the 1920's. Credit: Canada. Dept. of Interior / Library and Archives Canada / PA-034227 / Acc. No. 1936-271 NPC

Maintenance was cut at the start of World War II. Without maintenance the condition of Lovers' Walk became worse and over time large sections disappeared completely, tumbling down the escarpment. Parts still exist today, but they are in complete ruin. This photograph was taken just below the cat colony. The opening of the ventilation shaft at the top of the stairway may have been the one McDougall saw. Photographed by the author in 2006.

Chapter 9: The Old Clock Tower

It is one of the best time-keepers.[267]

Mr. J. J. Radford,* speaking of the tower clock, circa 1879

*Mr. Radford was the DPW man in charge of the clock.

In official publications, the clock tower in front of the Parliament Building was called the Victoria Tower.[268] However ordinary people didn't call it that. To them it was just the old clock tower.

The clock tower stood slightly behind where the Peace Tower is today. Its back face was in line with the front face of the Parliament Building, whereas today the Peace Tower stands somewhat in front of the Centre Block, separated by a three-story 'link' (as we call it) that has the elevator lobby and the hallway to the Memorial Chamber.

John Page described the tower in considerable detail in his 1867 report.[269] He said that it was about 9 metres square, not including the large buttresses at each corner. It rose to a height of 47.5 metres above the surface of the terrace. Over its height, it was divided into five unequal spaces by horizontal bands of stone called belt courses.

The first belt course had large molded arches on the south, east and west faces, which were decorated with moldings, carvings, and ranges of marble columns. Inside the carriage porch, above the entrance, was a large stone carving of the Royal Arms.

The second belt course had three arched windows and two niches of the same size on the south, east and west faces. The room inside the tower is shown on the first floor plans as a caucus room, but John Page said it could be used for committee rooms and other purposes as well.

The third belt was divided into two areas, each of which had three deeply sunk, molded, arched and weathered panels on the three sides.

Up to this height, the north wall of the tower was part of the building, but above this the tower projected above the roof line.

Each of the four sides of the fourth and largest space had two deeply-weathered, molded, enriched, and ornamentally perforated belfry windows.

In the fifth space, the tower was finished off by a temporary roof with clustered columns and pinnacles on the four corners. Between them, on all four sides, were pointed gables and in the gables were circular openings for the clock, which was not yet installed. The gables and pinnacles were enriched with 'crockets' (stone carvings that look like a curled leaf).

John Page said, "From its mass, and the variety of light and shade produced by its deeply recessed windows, projecting buttresses, and the characteristic ornaments of the style, it presents a very imposing appearance." [270]

The crown, which was made of wood, was completed in 1873 and increased the height to 77.7 metres.[271] It was not quite as tall as the Mackenzie Tower of the West Block, which was built a few years later and which is 83 metres high, or today's Peace Tower which is 90 metres.

Then, as now, tours of the Parliament Building always ended with a trip up to the top of the tower. From the ground there were 287 steps to the observation gallery, which was surrounded by a tall iron fence to prevent accidents. Looking through the railings the tourist could see a great distance and had a wonderful birds-eye view of downtown Ottawa, the river and the surrounding countryside.[272]

According to the 1879 *Illustrated Guide to the House of Commons and Senate of Canada* Parliament approved an appropriation of $7,000 for the clock in 1875.[273] This booklet described the clock in considerable detail. Although technical terms such as 'three leg gravity escapement' and 'two seconds compensated pendulum' may have been understood by readers back then, their meanings today are understood only by horological historians. Nevertheless, here is what it said:

> *This clock was manufactured by M.F. Dent & Co. 33 Cockspur Street, London, England and the mechanism was put up by Geo. Sutherland of Ottawa. It is an eight day clock with Dennissons' three leg gravity escapement and two seconds compensated pendulum. The length of the pendulum is 14 feet and its weight is 500 lbs. It has a remontir train to move the hands every half minute. It is driven by weights of 500 lbs. for the time portion and 700 lbs. for striking power. It strikes every hour with a 50 lb. weight on a bell of one ton weight situated about 60 feet below the mechanism. This bell was manufactured by Meneely and Kimbury, Troy, New York, U.S. 1875. The dials, four in number are made of black slate 1½ [inches] thick with gilt figures and they are 8 feet diameter.*

The Peace Tower has four lightning rods mounted on the spires at the very top of the green roof, one at each corner. But in the 1800's none of the buildings had them and there were several lightning strikes during a fierce electrical storm in the summer of 1895.

Excerpt from the House of Commons Debates
June 13, 1895, p. 2573

Mr. George Elliott CASEY (Lib.; Elgin West, Ont.): Before the orders of the day are called, I would like to direct the attention of the House, and especially of the hon. Minister of Public Works, to the injury done this morning by lightning to one of the buildings on these grounds. The fact, as reported to me, is that the lightning also struck this block in which the Houses of Parliament are situated; it appears that the current was felt and played pranks in several of the rooms. I may say, in parentheses, that I believe some of the committees were slightly electrified this forenoon by lightning or otherwise. But, speaking seriously, the fact has been demonstrated that these buildings, in spite of their national character and public usefulness, are liable to be struck by lightning as well as other buildings. The startling fact appears also to be demonstrated that these buildings are not protected by lightning rods; and I would call the attention of the Minister of Public Works to the advisability and necessity of having lightning rods placed upon them for the protection of the lives of the people who are obliged to remain within them, as well as of the public property. I hope it is not too late in the day to argue that lightning rods are a necessity. When the buildings are struck, the large amount of iron in the floor joists and in the walls appears to become saturated with electricity which escapes by way of the electric light, telegraph and telephone wires. I believe that the iron in the buildings has been relied on too much to carry off the lightning. It appears that it is not sufficient, and something ought to be done to increase the protection of these buildings.*

There was a powerful electric light at the top of the tower that shone at night whenever the House was in Session. Of this, Speaker Edgar said in 1898:

> *Over the town and over the great basin of the Ottawa Valley this beacon flames out the signal to farm and hamlet, for twenty miles around, that the representatives of the people are keeping their weary vigils. It may be that it brings to the mind of many a citizen the thought that, after all, the life of an M.P. is not a happy one, and that the honours are dearly bought at the price of absence from home, and of many sleepless nights.*[274]

At the very top was the flag. The Red Ensign flew from the tower from Confederation up until 1904, when it was replaced by the Union Jack.

Excerpt from the House of Commons Debates
March 17, 1904, p. 220

Mr. Joseph Henri Napoléon BOURASSA (Lib.; Labelle, Que.): Mr. Speaker, before the Orders of the Day are called I would like to have an explanation from the government in regard to a small incident to which some newspapers and people have attached some importance. I noticed on the day of the opening of parliament as well as today, which is St. Patrick's day, that the Canadian flag which used to be put up on the tower of the parliament building has been replaced by a Union Jack. I would like to know why the old flag that has been used in Canada ever since confederation should be laid aside.

Rt. Hon. Sir WILFRID LAURIER (Lib.; Drummond-Arthabaska, Que.; Prime Minister): I am sorry to say that I cannot satisfy to-day the rather fastidious curiosity of my hon. friend, but I will make inquiry and try to give him an explanation upon another day.

Mr. BOURASSA. Perhaps the British Empire League has something to do with it.

Hon. JAMES SUTHERLAND (Lib.; Oxford North, Ont.; Minister of Public Works): I may explain to the hon. gentleman (Mr. Bourassa) that the flag hitherto flown on the parliament building has been what is known as the Canadian Merchant Marine flag. It is not the national flag in any other sense. The national flag, as we understand it for this purpose, is the Union Jack. Many complaints have reached the department on previous occasions that the flag floating over the parliament buildings was not the authorized flag for that purpose, and when we were buying a new flag the one which we bought, in accordance with the custom of Canada and of all portions of the empire throughout the world, was the one authorized for the purpose.

Mr. BOURASSA. I know that the red ensign is the merchant marine flag but I know it has always been used in this country –

Hon. Mr. SUTHERLAND. Not at all.

Mr. BOURASSA. – as being the special colonial flag to which we have added the escutcheon of confederation. It has always been used on the building.

"Centre Block, Parliament Buildings." The 'crown' (that portion of the tower from the clock up) was made of wood and was completed in 1873. The clock was installed three years later. Credit: William James Topley/Library and Archives Canada/PA-009260/Acc. No. 1936-270 NPC

The Old Clock Tower 109

"Scene from Main Tower of Parliament Building, c 1885-1898." Credit: Topley Studio / Library and Archives Canada / PA-008390/Acc. No. 1936-270 NPC

> THIS BELL WAS TAKEN FROM THE RUINS
> OF THE CLOCK TOWER DESTROYED BY FIRE
> FEBRUARY 3, 1916
> "THE FIRE RAGED FIERCELY FOR HOURS.
> THE MAIN TOWER WAS NOT TOUCHED UNTIL
> ABOUT 11 P.M., AND ONE OF THE MOST PATHETIC
> INCIDENTS OF THE NIGHT, WHICH MOVED THE
> SPECTATORS, WAS THE STRIKING OF THE MID-
> NIGHT HOUR BY THE OLD TOWER CLOCK. THERE
> SEEMED ALMOST A HUMAN TOUCH AS ITS FAMILIAR
> TONES BOOMED OUT FROM THE MASS OF FLAMES."
> FROM THE 1916 REPORT OF THE
> DEPUTY MINISTER OF PUBLIC WORKS

The tower served the country well right up until the very end, when on the night of February 3, 1916 it was destroyed by fire. The bell was rescued from the ashes and is today behind the library with this plaque. On this plaque it is called the clock tower, the main tower, and the old tower, but nowhere the Victoria Tower. This is perhaps the most poignant evidence that to ordinary people it was just the tower.

Chapter 10: Gun Time

And the gun! How many thousands of people since the seventies have listened for its noon-hour blast! To those civil servants who went at twelve o'clock the gun was a bosom friend. To those who went at one o'clock it was an incident – an indication that an hour must elapse before they could satisfy the cravings of the inner man. To the mechanics on the outside jobs around town who could hear the gun, what a pleasant sound it had. And the clerks in the stores would cock an ear for the staccato crack of the gun. To them also it had a pleasant sound. Thousands upon thousands of watches have been corrected or hand spiked because of the noon-hour declaration of the gun. It has been a great old gun – everybody's friend.

Canadian Illustrated News, June 8, 1872

The tradition of the noonday gun, or cannon, began in 1869 when the Hon. Mr. Campbell was Postmaster General. In those days, there was no such thing as Standard Time (it would be another ten years before it was invented by the Canadian engineer Sanford Fleming). Everybody had pocket watches, but because nobody knew what the correct time was, their watches seldom agreed.

Mr. Campbell came up with the idea of a noonday gun fired from Parliament Hill when it was exactly 12 o'clock. When they heard the *Boom!* everybody in Ottawa would know the correct time and could then 'handspike' their watches. This was before the days of stem-winders, and people set the correct time by using their watch key to handspike, or set, the time.[275,276]

Knowing the correct time was especially important for Mr. Campbell and his Post Office employees because, of course, the mail had to be on time.

On March 6, 1869, Sir John A. Macdonald signed an Order in Council that authorized the purchase of the gun and the start of the new time service. The gun was purchased from the British garrison for $250.45 and was shipped from Montreal, arriving in Ottawa on April 14.

On March 18, 1869 *The Ottawa Times* wrote, "The Post Office Department has arranged for direct telegraphic communication between the Montreal Observatory and the West Block. In a few days the correct time will be given by the firing of a cannon near the Parliament Buildings."[277]

The gun and the carriage were made in Arsenal, England. The barrel is marked with George III of England and was made on February 28, 1807. The gun carriage is stamped 4-1-15, so it was made on either January 4 or April 1 of 1815; most think the former. It is a nine pound muzzle loader and saw battle in the Crimean War, which was from 1854 to 1856.[278, 279, 280, 281]

Now here's a question for you. How do you think the noon gun man knew when to fire? Do you think he used his pocket watch? He couldn't use the tower clock because in 1869 the clock wasn't there. There were just the circular openings in the masonry. The tower clock wasn't installed until 1876.

Here is what he did. The correct time was calculated by an astronomer at the McGill observatory in Montreal from the position of the sun, taking into account that it would reach the meridian at Ottawa a little later than at Montreal.[282] At exactly noon Ottawa time, a signal was telegraphed to the West Block,[283] and from there it was sent along electrical wires into a small cabin beside the gun. The signal released a small metal ball that dropped to the floor. When the noon gun man saw the ball drop, he fired.[284] Now, wasn't that clever!

SAMUEL GREENFIELD, THE FIRST NOON GUN MAN (1869 TO 1905)

Samuel Greenfield fired the gun from 1869 until three years before his death in 1908. He was an employee of the Post Office Department and was appointed by Mr. Campbell because he had been in the Royal Artillery for many years.[285]

On April 26, 1869, at exactly 12 o'clock when the sun was exactly overhead, the cannon boomed across Ottawa for the very first time.[286] There was no ceremony, no ribbon cutting, no flag raising, no press release, no special invitations, no speeches. Although a newspaper article about the gun being used as a timepiece had appeared a month earlier (see the quote at the top of this Chapter), many people didn't know what the sound meant and thought it was just someone blasting rock.

After the firing, a colonel of the imperial regiment wrote an angry letter to Mr. Campbell demanding to know why the gun had been shot without his permission. The colonel said he was in charge of all military operations in Ottawa, and since firing a cannon was obviously a military operation it should be the garrison, not the Post Office, that did the firing. However, Mr. Campbell was able to explain to the colonel that the gun was being used as a timepiece so that the mail would be on time. It was not being used to defend the city in any way, shape or form, so its firing remained with the Post Office.[287]

At first, the gun was located north of the East Block. For a brief period of time, it was moved over to the west side of the Library, overlooking the Chaudière Falls. However, it had only been there a short time when complaints came from the Governor General's office in Rideau Hall. They couldn't hear the gun because it was pointed away from them, so it was moved back.[288]

About 1905, Mr. Greenfield's failing health forced him to retire, and the responsibility for firing was given to Mr. Snowden, who became the second noon gun man.[289] During the transition, Mr. Greenfield's son Robert fired the gun for a short while.[290]

ERNEST SNOWDON, THE SECOND NOON GUN MAN (1905 TO 1944)

Mr. Snowdon's experience with guns came from being a member of the Soo Rifles in Toronto. He came to Ottawa from Aurora in 1900, and for a while worked at the Ottawa Dairy. He joined the Post Office as a letter carrier in 1903[291] and to earn a little extra money helped out Mr. Greenfield. Mr. Snowdon fired the gun for the first time on April 4, 1904.[292]

The gun was moved to Major's Hill Park in 1916, shortly after the fire burned down the Parliament Building.[293] By this time, clocks told the right time and the gun was not as useful as it had once been. Also, the noise was bothering some of the politicians and the vibrations set off by the cannon were causing busts in the Centre Block to shake on their pedestals.[294]

Here is a description of Mr. Snowdon's routine for firing.[295] He usually arrived at Major's Hill Park about ten minutes early. In the summer, groups of tourists would already be standing around, waiting, cameras at the ready and they would ask him all kinds of questions like, "how old is the gun?" and "where did it come from?" and "how long had he been firing it?" Mr. Snowdon always had the answers, and never tired of telling them. This was in the summer, but in the winter he was generally alone.

He first removed the padlock from the muzzle and took out the cast iron plug using a special key. Then he removed the padlock from the touch-hole and took off the cap there. At about 5 minutes to twelve he went into his storehouse and came out with a pound-and-a-quarter bag of black powder. He placed the bag into the barrel and then rammed it home. After that, he fitted a percussion cap on the detonator, attached the lanyard, which was a short length of rope with a hook on it, and then he waited.

He didn't trust the Peace Tower clock. Instead, he used his own watch, which he knew to be accurate to the second because he set it on his way to the Park using the clock in the Langevin Building, which was controlled by the Dominion Observatory. When it got to a half minute before noon he concentrated on the second hand ticking around the dial and an instant before it reached the twelve, he yanked. The cannon went off with a deafening roar, and a tongue of flame three, maybe four metres long and a huge cloud of smoke shot out of the barrel! Cameras flashed, and tourists oohed and aahed and clapped their hands at the spectacle. Mr. Snowdon just smiled.

The sound could generally be heard as far as Aylmer, 12 kilometres away; but when the wind was blowing right it could even be heard at Navan, which was 30 kilometres away.[296] After firing, Mr. Snowdon brushed off the barrel, checked it for cracks, and then put the plug and the cap back on.

Mr. Snowdon fired the gun 365 days of the year. Most of the time it was at noon, but on Sundays, Christmas, New Year's Day, Thanksgiving Day and Good Friday it was at ten o'clock. It was fired early on Sundays so it wouldn't disturb the nearby churches, and it also allowed Mr. Snowdon to attend services.[297] Mr. Snowdon retired from the Post Office in 1934, but kept firing until 1944.[298]

WILLIAM. J. DAVIS, THE THIRD NOON GUN MAN (1944 TO 1966)

Mr. Davis worked for the Federal District Commission, which in 1959 became the National Capital Commission. He had been around the gun since 1928 when he would sometimes stand in for Mr. Snowdon.[299]

In 1944 when he took over from Mr. Snowdon, it was no longer the Post Office but the Federal District Commission that had responsibility for the gun.[300] Mr. Davis was given the appointment of 'Noon Gun Man' by an Order in Council on July 26, 1944. At first he was paid only 50 cents a day,[301] but by 1959 his salary had almost tripled to $1.30,[302] and by 1963 it was $1.61.[303]

Mr. Davis used a worn-out old pocket watch that his son found in the mud in the summer of 1941. It still kept good time, and every day at 11 o'clock he checked it with the Dominion Observatory time signal to be sure. Like Mr. Snowdon before him, he didn't trust the Peace Tower clock. "You won't catch me using that thing," he said. "Why, one night a couple of years ago she struck 232 times."[304]

If the gun misfired (or 'hang fired,' which is the technical term), he tried again. If it didn't work twice in a row he stopped, because then he knew something was wrong.[305]

When Mr. Davis retired in 1958, he was kept on by Public Works[306] which by now had responsibility for the gun. That year when they went to order more detonating caps, they found that the caps, which had stopped being made in 1918, were no longer available. This almost ended the tradition because, without the caps, the gun wouldn't fire.

Strangely enough, it was a television show that saved the day. One night, the man in Public Works in charge of purchasing the caps was watching a cops and robber show on T.V. When he saw the bad guys using dynamite to blow up the bridge, he got the idea of asking blasting experts for help. They told him the gun could be adapted to use modern blasting equipment and suggested the detonating caps be replaced by 'squibs' – these are little caps used for testing blasting machines. The idea worked.[307]

Public Works borrowed a replacement gun from the army while the noon day gun was in the shop being worked on. When it came back the noise was just as loud. The same amount of black powder was used, but it was a lot cheaper to fire. If they had to order custom-made detonating caps, they would have paid $9.80 each; each squib costs only pennies.[308]

There haven't been many accidents in the history of the gun. The most serious was in 1961 when a 14 year old boy stepped in front of the gun exactly when it went off. He was knocked to the ground, his coat caught fire, his face was covered with blood, he became deaf in one ear, and he was badly burned.[309]

On Friday, January 28, 1966 Mr. Davis arrived at the usual time but was completely flabbergasted to find the barrel gone! Just the barrel; the four wheels were still there.[310] Mr. Davis called that day 'Black Friday.'

It turned out that the barrel, which weighed three tons, was carried away by some University of Ottawa students as a winter carnival prank. Someone tipped off the RCMP, who found it the same day beside the Minto Skating Club. Public Works sent some men over with a crane truck and got it back.[311]

Mr. Davis, getting on in years, fired the gun for the last time on March 24, 1966.[312] Claude Lafleur, another Public Works employee, carried on until a replacement could be found.[313]

FIRINGS STOPPED, STARTED AND STOPPED AGAIN

At some point between 1966 and 1991, the National Capital Commission got back jurisdiction of the gun and continued the tradition of the noon firing. Then, on April 1, 1991, without any public announcement, the 122 year tradition was stopped, and the gun was silenced.[314] It was simply a matter of cost. It was $26,000 a year, the NCC said, and too expensive to keep up. They said they had talked to Canada Post and National Defense about sharing the cost, but they weren't interested. So, for the first time in its history, the daily firing stopped.

Then, on May 6, 1992,[315] and just in time for the official opening of Canada's 125th birthday celebrations, the House of Commons Speaker John Fraser brought the noon day gun back to Parliament Hill. This time it was put on the Victoria Lookout just below the Queen Victoria statue.[316] Six women and four men were chosen from among the House of Commons' Post Office messengers. They were trained in the history and tradition of the gun by the acting Curator of the House of Commons, and on how to fire it by two Parks Canada staff from the Halifax Citadel.

The ten messengers were divided into five groups of two, each group working for one week at a time. Their additional pay was $10.00 a day (substantially more than the $1.61 a day Mr. Snowdon was paid twenty-nine years earlier). They fired the gun for the first time on June 18, 1992.[317,318]

Firing continued five days a week, Mondays through Fridays, for a few years but after a while it was stopped, again because of cost. In 2000, the former head of the NCC, Jean Pigott, tried to revive the tradition. Tourists loved it, she said.[319] However, she was unsuccessful. The gun was never fired again and in 2010 it was moved to the Museum of Civilization.

118 *The Other Side of the Hill*

"Noon Day Gun at Parliament Hill. c 1882." Look at how long the blast of smoke is! To the left is the cabin that contained the timing apparatus and the small figure below the vertical puff of smoke at the touch hole is Mr. Greenfield. Credit: Topley Studio / Library and Archives Canada / PA-008384 / Acc. No. 1936-270 NPC

Chapter 11: The Bar the Politicians didn't want to Admit was There

It was possible also to travel from the Senate bar to the Commons' bar and vice versa by slithering through a hole in the region of the furnaces. Sometimes it was prudent to pass that way.

Paul Bilkey, 1940[320]

I'll bet you didn't know there was a bar in the old Parliament Building. It was down in the basement, on the House of Commons side.[321] There was also one over on the Senate side, but it was the bar on the Commons' side that caused the problem because it was open to the public. It stayed open late, later than the hotel bars, and when they closed for the night men with nothing better to do just went up to the Parliament Buildings to continue drinking.[322] Afterwards they staggered home to sleep it off. When their wives asked them where they had been, and they answered, "up at the Parliament Building, drinking," you can imagine the problems this would have caused.

By the late 1890's, the temperance movement was cranking up the pressure to dry Parliament Hill and to "remove what is a reproach to Parliament and a stain on our national honor."[323] It worked. On September 16, 1896 the House of Commons bar was closed.[324]

However, Senator Charles Bishop said there was a lot of skepticism about whether it was *really* closed.[325] He told of one member running for re-election who said he didn't know anything about it himself. However, if he was re-elected he would get to the bottom of it.

He was re-elected, and kept his promise. It is said that he went down to look for the bar every day. He was greatly admired for his dedication, and for keeping his election promise so faithfully. However, whether or not he found it, he didn't say.

Excerpt from the House of Commons Debates
April 12, 1916, p. 2833 - 2834

Mr. Edward Walter NESBITT (Lib.; Oxford North, Ont.): Might I suggest that a great deal of room was taken up in the old building with what — I will not call it the bar —

Mr. George Perry GRAHAM (Lib.; Renfrew South, Ontario): Say restaurant.

Mr. NESBITT: I should not call it a drinking room.

Mr. Robert ROGERS (Cons. Winnipeg, Man.): I object to that expression.

Mr. NESBITT: As we passed a prohibition measure the other day, I hope Parliament will set an example to the country by doing away with any room of that kind; we could use the space for rooms.

Mr. ROGERS: In the new building there will be a restaurant where meals will be served for the convenience of hon. members. That is my view, at all events, and I shall be glad to suggest it to the committee. Beyond that, I have no recommendations to make. If my hon. friend has anything to suggest, we shall be glad to hear from him at the committee.

Mr. GRAHAM: There has been no bar there for very many years.

Mr. ROGERS: Quite so. I am surprised that my hon. friend from Oxford (Mr. Nesbitt) should have got the idea that such a thing existed in the old building.

Chapter 12: The Dirty Trick Played on Sir Wilfrid

Sir Wilfrid, when he passes this way, is believed to have spasms of apprehension....[326]

The Globe, 1906

Most of the towers in the West Block don't have names. When I worked on Parliament Hill, we used to refer to them by their locations, as in the southeast tower, for example. But two of the towers do have names. There is the Mackenzie Tower on the west side, named after Alexander Mackenzie our second Prime Minister, and in the middle of the north side there is the Laurier Tower, named after our seventh Prime Minister, Sir Wilfrid Laurier.

However, back in 1906 when the north wing of the West Block was being constructed, the Laurier Tower wasn't called that; it didn't have a name. Then on April 5, 1906 at about ten minutes to noon, without almost any warning at all, the almost-completed tower fell to the ground with a thunderous crash, scattering a jumbled up pile of stone, brick, bent and twisted steel beams, and crumpled-up copper roofing all across the lawn.[327, 328]

Some of the stones landed on the roof of the West Block, crashing out a hole "big enough to drive a horse and cart through."[329] "It all happened in about a second" said a man who was passing. "I saw the building crack and then the whole side bulged out and fell with a crash into a heap."

Several workmen who had been laying copper pans on the roof of the tower had just enough time to jump clear before it fell. Mr. Belledeau, who was working inside the tower, heard a stone fall and raced through a door into the adjacent wing of the West Block. Others escaped into this wing too. Mr. Norrey and Mr. Charlebois, who had been working on the tower roof, were coming down a ladder when they heard that terrible rumble and jumped to safety onto the lower roof of the West Block.[330]

David Ewart, the Chief Architect for Public Works, wasn't talking about it that day. When questioned by a reporter all he would say was:

"Have you seen the place?"

"I have," replied the reporter.

"Then you know more about it than I do, for I haven't seen it yet."[331]

The collapse was discussed that afternoon in Parliament, but a careful reading of the *Debates* for April 5, 1906 shows that the name Laurier Tower was not used. The headline for the story in *The Ottawa Evening Journal,* April 5, 1906 said *The Tower Came Down With a Terrific Crash.* The newspaper called it the tower, not the Laurier Tower. They couldn't call it the Laurier Tower because on April 5 the name didn't exist. It didn't exist until the next day.

Excerpt from the House of Commons Debates
April 6, 1906, p. 1269-1278

Mr. Andrew BRODER (Cons; Dundas, Ont.): There is no expert necessary to see pretty plainly why that building fell.... I took the trouble to get some of the – I don't know what to call it. One will have to be an expert to tell what they call this, mortar or lime or cement.

Mr. Thomas Simpson SPROULE (Cons.; Grey East, Ont.): Sand.

Mr. BRODER: No, filling.

Mr. Charles Smith HYMAN (Lib.; London, Ont; Minister of Public Works): Might I ask the hon. gentleman where he procured the sample he has in his hand?

Mr. BRODER: I went up in the inside of the building – and this is no matter of curiosity, it is a matter of public concern what our buildings are being built with; I went on to the roof and got this sample out of the wall at the top of the fallen part of the tower. There is no bond whatever in it. I will take the liberty of sending the sample over to the hon. gentleman because if he has not seen it before, he should see it now. I understand that the upper part of that wall was built during frosty weather, and apparently there is no bond whatever in the material which is supposed to hold the wall together.... When the frost came out of this so-called mortar, it softened and the building tumbled down. Its fall may be prophetic, because I believe it was called the Laurier tower. We have to come to the conclusion that the government's feet are not of brass, but of clay, because the whole thing is falling down. This is a matter of considerable concern to the other side of the House, surely. I do not think that the contractor could depart from the specifications; but if that is the kind of work the public is getting all over this country from the large expenditure of money by the Department of Public Works, it is a subject should take a very live interest. I suppose no one will admit that more fully than the hon. gentleman himself. I am quite aware that the tramping of soldiers or even the running of a dog over a bridge is sometimes dangerous, even to a strong bridge; but there was no tramping to cause this bridge to fall down. Six men went on the roof to put on the copper, and down she came. There was no wind, no storm; It was a departmental failure, that was the trouble.

[And skipping further along in the debate...]

Mr. Joseph Elijah ARMSTRONG *(Cons.; Lambton East, Ont.):* Mr Speaker, having had considerable experience in building bridges and cement walls, I had the curiosity to investigate the building to which this accident has happened, and I quite agree with my hon. friend from Dundas (Mr. Broder) that it is a very good indication that the present government is dying at the top.

An hon. MEMBER: *We have heard that before.*

[And further on in the Debates...]

Mr. Herbert Sylvester CLEMENTS *(Cons.; Kent West, Ont.):* As I took the occasion of accompanying my hon. friend from Dundas (Mr. Broder) to the top of the Laurier tower in order to gather some of the cement which had been used in that tower, I might take this opportunity of giving my experience.... I have had considerable experience in cement, and one would naturally suppose that in a construction of this kind the specifications must surely have called for cement. *But after examining the top of the tower with my hon. friend from Dundas (Mr. Broder), there appeared to be nothing there but sand, and what surprised me was that the tower should have stood as long as it did.... It has been a fortunate thing for the country that the Laurier tower fell as it did, because it has brought to the attention of this House the fact that there must certainly be a great deal of laxity on the part of the officials of the department.*

[And further still...]

Mr. Melzar AVERY (Cons.; Addington, Ont.): I think we have heard a good many remarks that will be of benefit to the people of this country, especially where we have public works; and I hope that the government, if they still intend to have in this beautiful building a structure called the Laurier Tower, should have a better tower than they started out with.
Mr. Jacques BUREAU (Lib.; Three Rivers and St. Maurice, Que.): Will the hon. gentleman inform us when and where this tower was christened the 'Laurier Tower'?
Mr. George William FOWLER (Cons.; King's, N.B.): No wonder you are ashamed of it.
Mr. AVERY. It is the newspaper press....

From that day on it was always the Laurier Tower, and the opposition did its best to embarrass the government by linking the fall of the Laurier Tower with the fall of the Laurier government. As the *Globe* wrote a few weeks later, "The fall of the tower is the only piece of good fortune that has come to the Ottawa Opposition. They are making the most of it."[332]

An inquiry was held during April and May, 1906 to determine the cause of the collapse.[333] They found the upper stage of the tower was built the previous November and December, when the weather was quite frosty, and the lime mortar in the part below, which had been built in late fall, had not had time to properly set. Simply put, the stonework and mortar froze over the winter, and when it thawed out in the spring, it couldn't hold up the weight, and the whole thing came down. There were other causes too, but freezing of the mortar was the big one.

So, as Mr. Bureau asked, when and where was it christened the Laurier Tower? Mr. Avery's answer "it is the newspaper press" didn't provide much information.

The answer to Mr. Bureau's question remained a secret for many years until 1940 when Paul Bilkey, a newspaper man, told all (or, almost all) in his memoirs.[334] It seems that after the collapse, two unnamed, trouble-making Tory newspaper men had remembered that somewhere, sometime, someone had suggested it be named the Laurier Tower in honor of the Prime Minister. All they did was to start calling it that. Bilkey didn't tell us who they were, and their names are now forever lost in history. "Hence it was," Bilkey said, "that although the tower had not stuck, the name did."[335]

OTHER STORIES ABOUT THE WEST BLOCK

A similar scandal could easily have happened when the Mackenzie Tower of the West Block extension was being built in 1876, thirty years earlier. On September 1, 1877 a stone weighing three thousand pounds fell from the tower and broke through the roof of the West Block. A number of men inside narrowly escaped being crushed to death.[336]

* * *

Sir John A. Macdonald, then Leader of the Opposition, was known for making wild and reckless statements. He said that not only was the extension ugly, but it was so badly put up it would probably have to be taken down again.[337] The tip of the Mackenzie tower, he said, looked like a cowbell.[338]

* * *

Fire broke out in the West Block at 4:15 p.m. on Thursday, February 11, 1897. Mr. Davy, a civil engineer in the Public Works Department on the third floor, was the first to spot it.[339] It was running beneath the attic floor near the southwest corner of the building, and he could see the flames coming up beside the steam pipes near the elevator. He and some others unwound the hose on the wall and turned on the hydrant, but the water only dribbled out because of poor water pressure and the condition of the old hose. Probably as much water leaked out through the holes in the hose as came out through the nozzle.

When the city fire brigade arrived, they found all of the hydrants on the hill were frozen. After a half hour of thawing out, they started to work, but only small streams of water came out.

At 5:30 p.m. a pump belonging to the Chaudière lumbermen was hooked up to a hydrant on Wellington Street, and this provided the first good stream to the firemen. Ottawa's big fire engine, *The Conqueror*, was hooked up to a hydrant on Sparks Street and provided a magnificent stream.

Up to 6 o'clock, the fire remained in the same area, but no headway could be made. A crowd of about 1,000 people were gathered outside, but many didn't think it would amount to much and went home to dinner.

By 7:30 p.m. the fire had spread, consuming the old timber underneath the slate mansard roof, to the middle of the south side. By this time, the south west tower was a flaming torch, and the fire was so bright that the glow could be seen as far away as Brockville, 123 kilometres away.

At 8:30 p.m. the Hull fire brigade arrived with their fire engine. By now the crowd had grown to about 5,000.

At 10 o'clock the fire turned the corner and began along the eastern side of the building where exploding chemicals shot colored flames high into the night sky. When it reached the mounted police's storage area, cartridges exploded with great bangs which, combined with the colored flames, looked like a fireworks display.

Although the fire went right up to the extension built in 1876 by Mackenzie, the newer construction proved to be fireproof, and northward progress of the fire was stopped. (So much for Sir John A. Macdonald's remark about how badly built it was!)

Later, the investigation showed that the fire had spread beyond its original area because someone had cut an opening into the fire wall to make a doorway in the attic. This destroyed the fire protection the solid wall would have provided.

Also, a wooden spiral staircase had been built from the attic down to the 3rd floor, and flames had started to travel down these stairs to the office of Public Works. The newspapers reported that it was the Minister himself, the Honorable Israël Tarte, who turned a hose on these flames thereby saving the lower stories from burning too.[340]

* * *

Did you know that Canada Customs used to be in the West Block and opium that was seized was destroyed in the West Block furnace? On April 4, 1911 the *Globe* reported $55,000 worth of opium had been seized at ports in British Colombia. This amount of drug would take about two days to burn. Workers put the drug into $25 dollar cans of sheet copper and then tossed them into the furnace. Unfortunately, one of the men, in poking his shovel around in the fire, accidentally broke open a tin and the fumes that rose up from the hot shovel affected him so much that he had to be dragged outside to recover.[341]

The building behind Sir Wilfrid Laurier on the Canadian five dollar bill is the West Block, but curiously the tower behind him is not the Laurier Tower. The tower on the bill is on the east side of the building facing the front lawn; the Laurier Tower is at the middle of the north side. It is as if Sir Wilfrid does not wish to be associated with the tower that bears his name...now why do you suppose that might be? Photograph by the author.

Chapter 13: What did it smell like in the Old Parliament Buildings?

The Parliament Buildings at Ottawa may surpass our own [the provincial Parliament Building in Toronto] in beauty, but they are a long way behind in light, heating and ventilation. There are smells in the corridors adjoining the Commons Chamber that are fully as old as this fair Dominion. The ventilation of the chamber is a long-standing grievance.[342]

The Globe, June 4, 1895

Architectural historians are interested in what the old Parliament Building *looked* like. I am interested in that too, but I like to dig a bit deeper. What was it *really* like? What did it smell like? Was the air nice and fresh? Were our hard-working politicians toasty-warm in the winter, and nice and cool in the summer? What were the washrooms like? Was the general condition of sanitation good? What about the drinking water? Was it ice-cold and sweet-tasting? These are the kinds of thing we will be looking into in this chapter.

Of course we know that environmental legislation didn't exist back then, but what if it did? Suppose an employee working inside the Parliament Building in the Victorian Era made a complaint, and a health inspector was called in to investigate. What do you think he would find?

Description of Typical Rooms

John Page gives a complete description of every room in the old Parliament Building, including the Speakers' Chambers, committee rooms, etc.[343] We will take a peek inside the office of an ordinary, hard-working Member of Parliament.

All their rooms had double windows, the lower halves of which could be opened to provide fresh air and cooling. They were also furnished inside with Venetian blinds to keep out the sun. There were heat registers in each room. Each room also had a fireplace, with a pointed arch, molded chimney-piece, and a hearth of sandstone. The fillings around the grates and mantle-pieces were grayish-blue polished Arnprior marble. The floors of the rooms were tongue and groove pine. The 'skirtings' (baseboards) were also of pine, chamfered and grooved into the floors. The doors and ceilings were also pine; beautiful molded and sunk paneled work. The woodwork was all oiled and varnished, giving it a rich and very fine appearance. In rooms with plastered ceilings, there were cornices suitable to the size of each room. Most of the rooms had stands with marble tops and wash-basins. These were provided with silver-plated taps.

A Description of the Heating and Ventilating System:[344]

In summer, fresh air was brought in by opening windows, but of course this was not possible in the Chambers, which were located in the interior of the Parliament Building.

In winter, the Parliament Building was heated by steam produced from six boilers under the central courtyard. The boiler room was huge, and was excavated deeper than the other areas of the basement.[345] The attic, the vestibule at the main entrance and some of the rooms in the clock tower were heated by steam radiators, but most rooms, including the Chambers, used a method called the vault system.

With the vault system, fresh air was drawn into the building through long air ducts (five opened onto the brow of the hill on the sides and back; one was in front of the building). They were constructed of 'pick faced' limestone masonry. Some of these openings can be seen today. When you are next to the look-out behind the library, look down to just below the iron fence.

Once inside, the cold air entered a series of warming vaults made of brick walls almost a metre thick running the whole length of the building. These vaults were enormous; in many them a man could walk upright.[346] Inside these vaults were coils of iron pipe carrying hot steam that warmed the cold air. The fresh air from the outside passed around and between the steam pipes, became warmed, and then (because hot air rises) went up through flues into the rooms above.[347]

Every corridor and every room had a register to admit, limit or stop the supply of hot air at the pleasure of the Parliamentarian. The air already in the rooms was drawn out through the ventilation towers, which acted like giant chimneys. In this way there would be a constant flow of warm, fresh air throughout.

Special consideration was given to the Chambers and the Library because of their size. Big fans were installed below the floors to draw the air downward. These flues led to the main smoke and ventilation tower. In the centre of this shaft were two big iron smoke pipes to take the smoke from the fires under the boilers. The heat from the smoke pipes warmed the air in the shaft around them, increasing the chimney effect, drawing out more air.

In 1862 Thomas Fuller said: "So far as I am capable of judging, this system of heating and ventilating is the best which could be conceived. I have considered the subject, and believe I am capable of forming a correct opinion upon it."[348]

This time, however, the great man was wrong.

HEATING

Wood was burned at first, before the furnaces were switched over to coal in the early 1870's.[349] In 1866, at the first session in the new Parliament Building, Alexander Mackenzie complained about how much it was going to cost to heat the buildings. He said that he had great doubts whether the country would ever be able to maintain them for he had been told on good authority that it took 70 cords of wood per day to warm the Departmental Buildings in severe weather....[350]

This was a bit of an exaggeration, and the Hon. Mr. Skead corrected him. "...a great deal has been said about the cost of heating the public buildings, and some of the most outrageous stories had gone abroad on the subject, yet while the great portions of them were still open and exposed to the cold, the expenditure of wood was for the three blocks just 16¾ cords per day, or less than $50...."[351]

Tests done after completing the East Block showed that in cold weather it could generally be kept at about ten degrees Centigrade by burning four cords of wood a day.[352]

However, when it was really cold outside, and even though they could light fires in their fireplaces and wear their coats and mittens, the hon. members shivered in those old stone buildings. You might be surprised to hear that today only the roof of the Centre Block is insulated – the stone walls are not. Back then, neither the roof nor the walls were insulated.

VENTILATING

Alexander Mackenzie was also the first to complain about the ventilation. It was so defective, he said in 1866, that a change must be made.[353] He wasn't the last to complain. It had been discussed many times in the House.

Excerpt from the House of Commons Debates
June 6, 1887, p. 786-787

Mr. John CHARLTON (Lib.; Norfolk North, Ontario) moved for:
Copies of all papers and correspondence relating to any proposed change in the mode of ventilating in the House of Commons Chamber.

He said: This subject was under discussion some years ago. At that time the ventilation in the Chamber was wretchedly bad. Some improvements were made. Still, I think that other improvements might be made that would very much improve the sanitary condition of this Chamber. This is a subject which interests every member of the House, and that is my excuse for bringing it under consideration. I do it in the hope that some further improvement may be secured in the ventilation of the

Chamber. The necessity for that is not as apparent, fortunately, as it is in the winter season, because we can open the windows and get a supply of fresh air in that way which we are otherwise unable to secure. But in the winter old members of the House are aware that the atmosphere of the Chamber is very injurious to health. I find myself, after a few days, that the effect of the atmosphere in this Chamber is very deleterious. Headache, stupidity almost –

Some hon. MEMBERS: *Oh, no.*

Sir John Alexander MACDONALD (Lib.-Cons.; Kingston, Ontario): *Oh, no, that is impossible.*

Mr. CHARLTON: *The mental barometer goes down, and the amount of mental force, in the case of a member who sits in the Chamber habitually till midnight or after, gradually diminishes. The system by which we are supplied with air is a bad one. We have running from this building to the face of the cliff a number of sewers, through which the air is conducted to the fans, and so brought into this Chamber. I call them sewers, though they are not used for the purpose of sewers. They do not, I believe, convey any offensive matter from the building to the outside; but the air is brought through these subterranean passages which are damp and moldy, and which are liable to be foul. Dead dogs and cats may be in them for ought I know, and I think the mode of bringing the air into this Chamber is radically defective and deleterious to health, and cannot be otherwise....*

On April 12, 1889 Sir Richard John Cartwright (Cons.; Lennox, Ontario) said over the last few weeks the air had been getting gradually worse. Mr. Charlton said it was because the air still came in through the ducts at the edge of the cliff. "No matter what air is brought into the Chamber it will, as long as that system lasts, be something like the air we get in cellars and sepulchers."

Mr. Louis Henry Davies (Lib.; Queen's County, P.E.I.) suggested the corridor windows be left open but Mr. James McMullen (Lib.; Wellington North, Ont.) said this wouldn't work. "It is perfectly impossible for us to expect this Chamber to be pure," he commented, "when there is so much corruption in it."[354]

Air Conditioning

Excerpt from the House of Commons Debates
July 4, 1905, p. 8694-8696

Mr. George TAYLOR (Cons.; Leeds South, Ont.): I regret the Minister of Public Works is not in his place, but I see the Minister of Agriculture, who is the father of the cold storage system, and if the Minister of Public Works does not act, the Minister of Agriculture might take steps to obtain some better arrangement than that which now exists for cooling the air in this chamber. The Prime Minister has just referred to the fact that during the present session four members have been called away; the only wonder is that the number is not greater. In this chamber last night there were eighty degrees of heat, and when you came in from the outside, where you were breathing fresh air, the foul air here struck you at the door. It is the duty of the government to at once correct this. Surely some arrangement can be devised whereby this chamber can be made healthy; the windows ought to be removed on such a day as this and the fresh air allowed to come in. We should have fresh air introduced through pipes filled with ice so that it may be cooled. Just now the temperature here is 75, while outside it is 70. Under this very room there are five or six furnaces kept going day and night for the purpose of supplying hot water; and if it is necessary to have hot water in the building, some arrangement should be made for heating it outside and forcing it through in pipes. We have put up with this state of things long enough. The session of parliament is never going to be got through in cool weather. We commenced on the 11th day of January and here we are in July. I never expect to see a session over again before six or seven months, and it is time the government did something to preserve the health of the members who are obliged to attend their public duties here.

Hon. George Eulas FOSTER (Cons.; King's, N.B.): I do not think any words can be too strong to impress this matter upon the minds of those who have it in charge. Ever since I have been in the House this has been a constant complaint, and nothing efficient has ever been done to provide a remedy. It is not too much to say that a man either of very rugged health or of delicate physique takes his life in his hands when he attends the sessions of parliament in this chamber regularly afternoon and night. A man midway between the very rugged and those of a very slender type seem to get through much better than the others, but anyhow the place is very unhealthy. That floral tribute on that vacant desk today tells us of the passing away of one of our members. I do not know that directly the foul air in this chamber had anything to do with it, but I do know that the members of this House feel very strongly — I feel so myself very strongly — that when one attends this chamber constantly he takes great risks on living out the term of his natural life. There ought to be something done right away to cool the air in this chamber; and our caretakers, aided by scientific advice, should immediately take up the matter. If necessary they should knock out the sides of the thing one way or the other; better knock out the side of the House and allow fresh air to come in than make us live in this foul atmosphere. The fact that the temperature is higher in this chamber than it is outside is patent to everybody; you cannot come in from the fresh air and enter that corridor without distinguishing the deadly atmosphere. Something ought to be done; and if nothing can be done to this chamber, let us take some of the money we are lavishing in other ways — for instance, on the mint and the museum — and let us make a chamber which will be at least healthy for the people's representatives, whose lives are at stake.

Rt. Hon. Sir WILFRID LAURIER (Lib.; Drummond--Arthabaska, Que.; Prime Minister): My hon. friend (Mr. Foster) has rightly said that this is not a new complaint; he and I have heard it ever since we have been in this House. Something certainly ought to be done at the earliest possible date to remove the grievance to which he has alluded. I shall make it my special duty to call the attention of the Minister of Public Works to this state of affairs, so that he may try any means possible to have it remedied.

Despite Prime Minister Laurier's assurances nothing was done.

SANITATION

The washrooms in the Parliament and Departmental Buildings had flushable toilets called water closets which, when the buildings were being designed in 1859, were still very new.

The first American patent was only in 1857, and in 1860 water closets were shown at the Crystal Palace exhibition in England. The doors had coin operated locks and for one penny people could unlock the door and 'try them out.' This is where the expression 'to spend a penny' comes from. For you younger readers, this means to go to the bathroom.

The water closet stalls in the western Departmental Building were wood, with two-inch tongue and groove divisions between adjacent stalls. Each had a two inch thick, four paneled door with an inside bolt. Inside was a framed seat riser and cover of oak, a cast iron enameled urinal, and a cast iron enameled washing trough with two basins. The water closets were a 'best pan closet apparatus' with blue basin, sunk handle, and all the necessary cranks and handles. Overhead was a cistern, enclosed in a paneled and molded frame that contained the water, ready for the flush. The flow of water to the urinals was kept constant during the day and made to shut off at night.[355]

In the Parliament Building, the water closets were a higher quality of course; a lovely, creamy white Queen's ware, pan closet apparatus. The urinals were slate, sawn and rubbed and then waterproofed by heating the slate and thoroughly saturating it with pure oil.[356]

All of the drains from the toilets and urinals in the western Departmental Building and the west half of the Parliament Building emptied into the Ottawa River a short distance upriver of the Library. The washrooms in the east half of the Parliament Building and those in the East Block emptied downstream.[357]

On June 30, 1886, one of the washrooms on the House of Commons side of the Parliament Building exploded, injuring a workman who happened to be standing nearby. At first, officials tried to deny it happened, but the truth came out the next day. The cause was pent up sewer gas in one of the toilets. "This occurrence," the *Globe* reported, "is generally accepted as a fair exhibition of the extremely bad sanitary condition of the Parliament Buildings."[358]

In 1901, *Saturday Night* said there was no lack of deserving women willing to attack the dirt with pail and scrub-brush, yet there was no branch of the civil service on which the unemployment line was longer.[359]

The Minister of Public Works felt ashamed every time he passed through the corridor, but said it was very hard to get money to scrub down the halls.[360]

In 1911, Mr. Hughes M.P. (Lib.; King's, P.E.I.) stood up in the House and complained: "I would again point out that the sanitary accommodation in this building is in a prehistoric condition, some of the accommodation is not up to the standard of a railway closet."[361]

DRINKING WATER

At first, water was supposed to have been supplied to the Parliament and Departmental Buildings by the City of Ottawa. On July 4, 1859, shortly after the design competition for the Parliament and Departmental Buildings was advertised in the newspapers, Thomas C. Keefer submitted a plan costing $300,000 to the Council of Ottawa. His plan was to build an aqueduct that would take water from above the Chaudière Falls to a huge water tank on Parliament Hill. The water works would be ready by the time it was required for the Public Buildings, and then Parliament Hill and everybody in the city of Ottawa would have fresh, clean water fed by gravity. An application was made to the Provincial Government but the request was rejected.[362]

In 1861, after the City of Ottawa plan failed, Chief Engineer John Page recommended that Public Works take matters into their own hands. After consulting with Fuller and Jones, he suggested that water could be pumped from the river into water tanks in the buildings.

It was decided that the best source of water would be on the river edge at the rear of the Library where "the point stands furthest out into the current and the purest water would most likely be obtained."[363]

An engine-house was built at the base of the cliff on a small surface of flat rock. The side walls were about 4 metres high and the end walls were carried up in gables. The roof was covered with galvanized iron. Inside there were two pumps driven by steam engines, each engine having a separate chimney. One pump was a back-up to ensure the supply of water would not be interrupted if the other shut down. Inside was a receiving well, and all the water drawn into it passed through a filter made of two sheets of finely perforated copper placed 600 mm apart, the space in-between being filled with clean gravel.[364]

From the engine house, a 150 mm diameter water pipe went obliquely up the face of the hill buried in a deep trench. At the top, it curved and went nearly straight to a room in the basement of the north-west tower of the Parliament Building. From here, the pipe continued vertically and emptied into a tank in the roof of this tower. From this tank, the water went to storage tanks in other parts of the Parliament Building as well as the Departmental Buildings. These tanks supplied the kitchen, wash basins, water closets, urinals and boilers as well as fire hydrants.

Do you remember that the raw sewage was dumped into the river upstream of the library? This, of course, drifted down on the current where it was sucked back in again. In 1866 N.F. Belleau, M.P., said, "It was well known to the hon. member that means would have to be taken to purify the water, which now came into the buildings in anything but a fit state to be used."[365]

During this time, the citizens of Ottawa got their water from public wells. There were several about, but one was the 'Frost Well' in Lower Town at the corner of George and Cumberland Streets (it was named after a family who lived on George Street). It was in the middle of the street, and water was drawn out in an old oaken bucket using a hand-crank and chain. It was an open well with a raised wall to prevent anyone from falling in and had a small house built around it for protection. Mr. John Bambrick drank the water from it and said that while nobody ever tested the well for bacteria as far as he knew, the water was always good and no sickness was ever caused by it as far as he could judge.[366]

People could draw their own water, but most bought it from water carriers who delivered it door-to-door in barrels on heavily loaded horse-drawn carts. The water carriers also drove their carts to fires and sold water to the firemen. The *1864 Ottawa Directory* said that at the first alarm of a fire, a hoard of water carts would descend on the scene "whose owners as a class, are not over-scrupulous in their language as expressed to parties standing in their way or to their own hard-worked animals." The article went on: "The men are paid by the barrel at a fire, but barrels often...leak badly and are only half full when they reach the fire."[367]

In an editorial *The Citizen* on July 13, 1868 remarked that "for purposes connected with the fire department it is notoriously deficient, and for other purposes, such as domestic and general sanitary, it is still more deficient."[368]

On August 18, 1868 a boisterous meeting was held in the city hall to discuss building a new waterworks. The place was filled with angry water carriers who of course were against it, and these noisy ones had it all their own way. Nothing was accomplished at the meeting, and a decision to change the system was not going to happen on that day![369]

In 1875, after years of further delays, the city finally built a pumping station, drawing water from the centre of the river above the Chaudière Falls.[370] Parliament Hill was connected up to this system, and the old pumping house at the base of the cliff was abandoned. Its ruins can still be seen today along the pathway at the river's edge, although there is no sign explaining the history of them.

In 1911, defective joints in the intake pipes allowed polluted water to be taken in, which caused a severe outbreak of typhoid, and many people died.[371] Responding quickly, Public Works put in one supply of sterilized drinking water on each floor of the Parliament Building.

Excerpt from the House of Commons Debates
January 27, 1911, p. 2583-2588

Mr. Thomas Simpson SPROULE (Cons.; Grey East, Ont.): It seems to me there is an obligation resting on others as well as on the government. We pay a consideration to the city of Ottawa for the provision they have made to give us water for these buildings. It is natural to assume that that means healthy and pure water, and if nothing is dished up but what is mixed with sewage we are throwing away our money and are very careless with regard to the health of those who come from every part of the country to spend four to six months of the year attending parliament....

Mr. William PUGSLEY (Lib.; City and County of St. John, N.B.; Minister of Public Works): I believe they are doing the best they can in the serious conditions with which they are confronted. Either some other source must be obtained from which the supply of water can be got or else something should be done to sterilize and purify the water contaminated by the sewage which is emptied into the Ottawa River from towns such as Aylmer, Arnprior, Pembroke and Renfrew and others along its banks. The city of Ottawa is doing the best it can. It has engineers endeavoring to find some other source from which water can be obtained. The only thing we can do, in the discharge of our duty, is to sterilize the water and make it as palatable as we can. Our officials are giving their utmost attention to that; and if hon. members will be careful to drink only from the sterilized water, they need not fear any danger.

[And continuing the next day...]

Mr. PUGSLEY: I made a statement last night of what has been done. We have one supply of purified water on each floor.

Mr. James Joseph HUGHES (Lib.; King's, P.E.I.): Why not have it all over the offices?

Mr. PUGSLEY: We are providing for that. We have communicated with the Finance Department with a view of putting that system in each of the blocks....

Mr. George Henry BRADBURY (Cons.; Selkirk, Man.): I am not a scientist, but I venture to say that boiling the water is not a sure preventative of danger. If you boil a pail of sewage, how much better is it than it was before? By boiling it you kill anything alive that is there, but I have grave doubts whether you remove all the danger.

Mr. PUGSLEY: The best physicians say the microbes will be killed.

Mr. BRADBURY: I do not agree with the Minister of Public Works. A few days ago I was laid up, and feared an attack of typhoid. I told my physician who attended me that we were taking the precaution of boiling the water, and he said: "if you boil a pail of sewage, does it make it any purer? You kill anything that is alive, but you do not purify it."

Mr. PUGSLEY: Microbes have life; surely if you kill them you get rid –

Mr. BRADBURY: I would like to see the government have a little life on this question.

Mr. PUGSLEY: We have been trying to kill the microbes.

> Mr. BRADBURY: *I say, in conclusion, that this is no laughing matter, but a very serious one. If the cost is $10,000 or $500,000, to provide pure water for the employees of this government, the honor of the government is at stake, and it ought to be done and done immediately.*

So that was what it was like for our politicians working in the buildings a hundred or so years ago. When we look at heritage photographs of the Parliament Buildings, it's easy to get nostalgic about the old times. Sometimes we wish we could have lived back then, when life was simpler, but it wasn't really simpler, was it?

142 *The Other Side of the Hill*

"Parliament buildings from Major Hill Park, Ottawa." The engine house is at the end of the roadway at the base of the cliff. Digital ID: (digital file from original item) ppmsca 18106 http://hdl.loc.gov/loc.pnp/ppmsca.18106 Reproduction Number: LC-DIG-ppmsca-18106 (digital file from original item) Repository: Library of Congress Prints and Photographs Division Washington, D.C. 20540 USA http://hdl.loc.gov/loc.pnp/pp.print. Copyright 1901 by Detroit Photographic Co.

What did it smell like in the old Parliament Buildings? 143

Detail from "Parliament buildings from Major Hill Park, Ottawa" showing the pump house with its end walls carried up in gables and its two chimneys. A water pipe went obliquely up the hill to the Parliament Building, buried in a deep trench. It is possible that the remains of the pipe may still be there, waiting to be found by archaeologists.

PART 3

THE FIRE – WHO DUNNIT?

Chapter 14: A Blow-by-Blow Description of the Fire that Destroyed the Old Parliament Building

This fire must have spread with lightning rapidity; the heat and flame spread around the corridors of the House of Commons Chamber, and into the roof of the House of Commons and Senate Chambers, which were wide open, the construction of which was a veritable forest of timber. [372]

Fire Chief J.W. Graham, 1916

The fire started at about four minutes to nine on the evening of Thursday, February 3, 1916, in the reading room of the Parliament Building. The alarm rang two minutes later, all over the building. It was a May-Oatway Automatic Fire Alarm System, connected directly with the Ottawa fire station.

In the Chamber they were discussing the marketing of fish, and Mr. Loggie had the floor. At nine o'clock Mr. Stewart, Chief door-keeper of the House of Commons burst into the Chamber and announced there was a terrific fire in the reading room. Here is the official account as taken down by George Simpson, the Hansard reporter:

Excerpt from the House of Commons Debates
February 3, 1916, p. 577-578

Mr. William Stewart LOGGIE (Lib.; Northumberland, N.B.): In my judgment fish are sold at moderate prices all over the Dominion. He says that prices seem unreasonably high, and that this condition mitigates against the end in view, which is to encourage the greater consumption of fish throughout Canada. I shall be very pleased to support the resolution to have this matter discussed before the Marine and Fisheries Committee.

9:00 p.m. At this time Mr. C.R. Stewart, Chief Doorkeeper of the House of Commons, came hurriedly into the Chamber and called out: "There is a big fire in the reading room; everybody get out quickly." The sitting was immediately suspended without formality, and members, officials and visitors in the galleries, fled from the Chamber. Some of them were almost overcome by the rapidly advancing smoke and flames before reaching a place of safety. The fire, which had originated in the reading room, gained momentum with extreme rapidity and was soon beyond control. It continued till the following day, resulting in the almost total destruction of the Parliament buildings, together with the loss of several lives.

Fire Chief Graham reached the scene two or three minutes after the alarm sounded. The Chief happened to be in the station on Laurier Avenue where his automobile was, and he made pretty good time, passing the motor truck from number 6 station. There had been several false alarms from the West Block lately, and coming up Nicholas Street he said to his driver, "I wonder if this is another false alarm?" When they came in view of the building at Elgin Street, the driver said, "This is the real thing this time." They could see the reflection of the fire in the night sky because the roof of the reading room where the fire was burning was glass.

They drove around to the back of the building where the fire was, and could see the red-helmeted, rubber-coated firemen from motor engine 8 already had a stream of water on the fire.

The Chief saw the fire "was bursting out in great shape," and he knew at once it was going to be a serious one.

It was very icy, but he ran as fast as he could to the box located inside the building near the tower entrance and sent in the second alarm. The time recorded for the second alarm was five after nine.[373]

Within minutes the hose companies had twenty streams of water on the fire. The first line laid down was on the west side of the Library, in between the link leading to the Library and the reading room. Chief Graham said the water pressure was "first class – the pressure on the hill was 60 pounds on the hydrant."

Later that night there would be 78 men fighting the fire using 3½ kilometres of hose and 260 metres of ladder.[374]

By ten o'clock, the central portion of the roof had fallen in, and the ventilation towers at the back of the building were like flaming torches. To the crowd outside, it didn't seem as if the streams from the firemen's hoses were having any effect at all.[375]

Khaki-clad soldiers from the 77th Battalion were assigned to crowd control. At first their lines were stretched along the Vaux wall just below the road in front of the main tower, but as the fire became more and more ferocious the crowds were pushed back further onto the lawn.[376]

At a quarter to eleven all the lights in the building went out, making the work of the firemen, police, and those engaged in rescue work all the more dangerous.[377] The problem was a short circuit from the main feeder supplying the new wing. Public Works electrician Frederick A. Wilson had it fixed within ten minutes, and the lights remained on until morning.[378]

Curiously, the fire was spreading westward, even though the wind was to the east that night, and by eleven o'clock the whole of the central and western portions of the building were in flames. The main tower was still up; the beacon light was still burning at the top, and the clock struck the hour as if everything was perfectly normal.[379]

There was a great uproar in front of the Rideau Club when a fire hose burst, sending huge amounts of water spraying in all directions, drenching about fifty people standing nearby.[380]

Shortly after eleven the ring of beacon lights at the crest of the steeple flickered and went out.[381]

At midnight the old clock tried to strike out the hour; it struck nine, ten, eleven, and tried to strike the twelve but couldn't.[382] However, it kept on running, stopping finally at half past twelve.[383] By this time, the crowd had been pushed off the hill completely and was lined up along Wellington Street.[384]

At one o'clock, the main tower was a gigantic torch of flame. Three field kitchens were set up on the hill and served hot coffee and soup to the soldiers and firemen.[385] At 21½ minutes after one o'clock the crown of the main tower, which was built of wood, fell.[386] The *Ottawa Citizen* wrote that it was 21½ minutes after one o'clock "gun time,"[387] referring to the noon-day gun.

Carol Fuller, Thomas Fuller's six year old granddaughter, was in the crowd with her father. "First the roof fell," she said, "then the flag and after that the bell."[388, 389]

Ottawa didn't sleep at all that night. Long after midnight, Sparks Street was jammed with automobiles, street cars, and thousands and thousands of people. The quick lunch places (yes, they called them that back then) did a fine business, and the hotel lobbies were crowded with people who came in to get out of the cold.[390]

The next day, Ottawa was like a military camp. Twelve thousand soldiers of the 77th Regiment stood guard around Parliament Hill; no one was allowed in. Fire engines continued to stream water on the smoldering ruins.

A special force with loaded rifles guarded the East Block.[391] There was a reason. All of Canada's gold supply was kept in its vaults, as well as gold sent over by France and Great Britain for safekeeping during the war. Between 1914 and 1918 more than forty million ounces of gold were weighed there, worth at todays prices some 30 billion dollars! [392]

On Saturday firemen were still pouring water on the smoking ruins and soldiers and policemen continued to guard the grounds.[393]

A Blow by Blow Description 151

"Fire - Parliament Buildings - Ottawa. "Photographed by John Boyd a day or two after the fire. Now that the initial shock was over the question on everybody's mind was, "who did it?" Credit: John Boyd / Library and Archives Canada / RD-000243 / Acc. No. / 1971-120 NPC

Chapter 15: The Story of the Two Young Ladies who Died Because they Went Back for their Furs

Right Hon. Sir Wilfrid LAURIER (Lib.; Drummond--Arthabaska, Que.): "*And what have we to say, Sir, of the loss of those two young ladies....*"

House of Commons Debates, February 4, 1916, p. 578-581

Seven people died in the fire: Bowman Brown Law (Lib.; Yarmouth, N.S.); Alphonse Desjardins (Dominion Policeman); Alphonse Desjardins (Public Works Steamfitter and uncle of the policeman of the same name); Randolph Fanning (Post Office employee); René Laplante (Assistant Clerk of the House of Commons); and Mable Morin and Florence Bray, who were guests of the Speaker and his wife.

All of these deaths were tragic, but the deaths of the two young ladies are especially so because they died for no reason other than they went back for their fur coats. It received a lot of attention in the newspapers and at the inquiry, and because of this we are able to piece together a fairly complete picture of the chain of events.[394]

Florence Bray was the wife of Mr. H.A. Bray of Quebec City, and Mable Morin was the wife of Mr. Louis Morin of St. Joseph-de-Beauce, Quebec. These two ladies, together with Mrs. Dussault, wife of Dr. and Alderman N.A. Dussault of Quebec City, were guests of Mrs. Albert Sévigny, wife of the Speaker of the House of Commons.[395]

They had been visiting for the last several days, staying in the Speaker's apartments, which were at the back of the building on the west side. Back then, the Speakers of both Houses were provided with handsome suites of apartments in the Parliament Building, where they lived with their families while Parliament was in session. Residential apartments were also provided in the building for the Black Rod in the Senate and the Sergeant-at-Arms in the Commons.[396]

When the fire broke out, Mr. Sévigny was in his office on the ground floor of his apartment. Mrs. Sévigny and her three friends were upstairs in the parlor, and the children were asleep in the nursery. Mr. Sévigny heard a banging on his door, and when he opened it Mr. Martin was there and shouted "Fire in the House, get out!"[397]

Mr. Sévigny ran up the stairs. At the top of the stairway, on the left, was a narrow hall and at the far end was the parlor. The Speaker's apartment was very long, about 45 metres.[398] He saw his wife in the parlor – he didn't see her friends, but knew they were there with her. She was a long way away, and he shouted, "Save the children and save yourselves!"[399] When he saw her jump up, he knew that she had understood and thought that her friends would be coming with her.

The bedrooms were to the right. Mr. Sévigny ran to the nursery, and almost immediately his wife arrived.[400] The nursery was practically above the reading room, where the fire was by this time blazing out of control. Mrs. Sévigny told her nurses, Misses Tremblay and Belanger, to wake the children and take them out. One nurse took the younger child. Then the other nurse carried out the other.[401]

As the nurses left to go downstairs, Mrs. Sévigny looked down the hall and saw that Mrs. Morin and Mrs. Bray were still in the parlor. She couldn't see Mrs. Dussault. She ran over to the two ladies, grabbed their skirts and cried, "Follow me!" She managed to pull them to the top of the steps, but they pulled their skirts away from her hands saying, "Wait a minute, let us get our furs."[402] She begged them to come. "Yes, we will," they replied, "but we will go to our room first, we have time."[403]

Mr. A.E. Harman, the Speaker's steward, ran up the stairs and met the nurse with the youngest child as she was coming down. He took the child out of her arms and proceeded back down. Mrs. Sévigny passed him, then the Speaker. When they got to the main hall Mr. Harman handed the little child to Mrs. Sévigny.[404]

Mr. Sévigny shouted to Fred Bingham, his waiter, that the three ladies were still upstairs. Mr. Bingham ran up, and at first he thought they were in the parlor, but they were not. Smoke was everywhere, and he had to break a window to get some fresh air. He didn't know where they were, and he was forced to come back down. "The smoke was too dense – if I had not come down, I would not have come down," he later said. He went up again with Randolph Fanning (who later that night would himself die), but the lights were all out and they could not see what they were doing.[405]

Mrs. Sévigny also tried to go back up, but the smoke was so dense that it drove her back. She had one foot on the step and was half choked; she later remembered Mr. Nickle, M.P. caught her and carried her from the stairs. Her husband then tried to go up, but she caught him by the coat and dragged him back, telling him it was impossible.[406]

Mrs. Sévigny went outside. As she stood on the ice, she suddenly saw Mrs. Dusseault at an upper window, crying for help. "Don't jump!" she cried, "Wait!"[407] Mr. Sévigny was in the dining room and had opened the window. He heard Mrs. Dusseault's cries from the window above, and he also shouted at her to wait for the firemen.

Mr. Harman ran around to the front of the Parliament Building and met the first ladder truck coming up the road by the East Block, and shouted at the driver to go around the Library. By the time the firemen arrived, Mrs. Dussault had climbed out and was sitting on the window sill. The captain of the motor truck got out a net, and the Dominion Police ran with it to her window. She must have fainted and fallen off, because when she landed into the net she was unconscious. She was taken to hospital.[408]

Mr. Sévigny thought that Mrs. Morin and Mrs. Bray had been with Mrs. Dussault. He called to them to jump too, but got no answer. At this point, he assumed they must be dead. He collapsed from grief. Mr. Harman and Mr. Bingham carried him outside.[409]

It was very cold. All Mrs. Sévigny had on was a light house dress, and the children were in their night clothes. They were taken down to the Chateau Laurier along with the nurses, where they were safe. "Oh," she said over and over, "Oh, if those two ladies had only followed me when I tugged at their skirts, instead of returning for their furs, they would have been safe." [410]

Chief Graham sent firemen D'aoust and Shiner up the ladder. "We went into the room," D'aoust said, "and I could not see with smoke, and searched over the room and found we were in the hallway and the flames were coming up the stairway and the carpets were on fire, and we took a stream up and put out the fire and went into the room and that is how we got the women.... One was on the head of the sofa and the other at the end of the sofa."[411]

They brought the two ladies down immediately, but one was dead and the other died a few minutes later. Their hands and wrists were covered with blood. They had tried to escape by breaking the window glass with their fists.[412] The window frames upstairs had been recently painted, and the dried paint had glued the windows stuck so they could not be opened.[413]

Mable Morin, thirty, left a husband and five children, two boys and three girls, the eldest of whom was only eight years old. Florence Bray, who was twenty-seven, left a husband and a three year old boy.[414]

The death of Mrs. Morin is particularly poignant because she had taken ill while visiting. She had planned to return home two days earlier, but had put it off several times. She was going to leave that very morning, but decided to put it off just one more day.[415]

Chapter 16: How the Fire Started

I felt a wave of heat passing up alongside me, as if from a hot air register, and I turned around and almost immediately with my turning I smelt the burning of paper and I stooped down and saw the smoke coming out, and my recollection is that this burning was on the second horizontal part of the desk, of the one behind me – it was well in on the pile of papers.[416]

Samuel Francis Glass, February 10, 1916

A Royal Commission was appointed on February 7, 1916 under commissioners Mr. R.A. Pringle and Judge D.B. MacTavish, with Mr. W.R. Wright, K.C. as counsel. Subpoenas were issued to all persons who would be likely to give evidence as to how the fire started. The inquiry was held at the Ottawa City Hall. The first meeting was on Thursday, February 10. A number of witnesses were examined at the first meeting. The commissioners invited anyone who had knowledge of the fire to contact them. They subsequently held a number of public meetings at which many witnesses were examined.

The commissioners' report was due about the middle of April, 1916. As that date approached, and no report had been submitted, some of the Hon. Members decided to have a little fun at the Minister of Public Works' expense.

Excerpt from the House of Commons Debates
April 12, 1916, p. 2835

Mr. Arthur Bliss COPP (Lib.; Westmorland, N.B.): Has any report been filed by the commission appointed to investigate the cause of the fire in the old building?

Mr. Robert ROGERS (Cons. Winnipeg, Man.; Minister of Public Works): No, I understand the commission is about to report about the middle of this month.

Mr. Edward Walter NESBITT (Cons.; Oxford, Ont.): I understand that the commission has arrived at the conclusion that a fire occurred.

Mr. ROGERS: I would not like to say that, but I hope to have the report in a few days.

Mr. George Perry GRAHAM (Lib.; Renfrew South, Ontario): The report will show that there were indications of a fire.

The Commissioners' report, entitled *Royal Commission Re. Parliament Buildings Fire at Ottawa, February 3, 1916: Report of Commissioners and Evidence*,[417] was submitted on May 15, 1916. This chapter, as well as the other chapters on the fire, is based on the report, newspaper accounts and other references.

THE READING ROOM

As mentioned earlier, the fire started in the reading room. This was a long, rectangular room at the back of the Parliament Building, just in front of the Library. The long dimension was in the east-west direction. The room's ceiling was flat in the centre and sloped on the north and south sides. The sloping part was made of wood paneling, heavily oiled and varnished. The flat part was paneled and filled in with ground glass. This allowed day light to come in through skylights higher up.[418] The floor was a composition of rubber about 12 mm thick.[419]

The room contained six reading desks made of wood, arranged between the door to the House of Commons on the west and the door to the Senate on the east. The desks were also rectangular, but with the long dimension going north-south. Desk A was nearest to the House of Commons, then desk B, and so on over to desk F, which was nearest to the Senate.

These were double desks, meaning people could stand on both sides and read. The major dailies were spread out on the tops. The less frequently read papers from the smaller towns, weeklies, and others were stacked on the shelves below. Each desk had two shelves. The lower shelf was about 300 mm from the floor and the upper one about 150 mm above the lower shelf.

Wooden screens, or partitions, were arranged on each side of the room from which several hundred newspapers hung like laundry draped loosely over a clothes line. A wooden gallery went all around the room, with shelving filled with books.[420] There were about 20,000 volumes - three or four tons of books.[421] Most of the wood was 50 year old white pine, and had been varnished many, many times. It was tinder-dry and ready to go.

THE DRAFT WAS TOWARDS THE CHAMBER

The ventilation system in the reading room consisted of two ventilators in the skylight, both of which were open, and an exhaust fan underneath two gratings in the centre of the floor. Acting on its own, the draught would be inwards, towards the centre of the reading room floor. However, it was overpowered by the larger ventilation system in the House of Commons Chamber. This system consisted of two blower fans about 6 metres above the skylight and two fans down in the boiler room - one a blower, the other an exhaust. The net effect was that the draft in the reading room was west towards the Chamber.[422,423,424]

There was always a draft in the building, more or less,[425] but after the fire started it became very strong. Mr. C.R. Stewart, Chief door-keeper said that it forced the door on the Commons side of the reading room to stay open.[426]

THE FIRST THREE OR FOUR MINUTES

On the evening of Thursday, February 3, probably around a quarter to nine, Mr. Glass[427] (Samuel Francis Glass; Cons.; Middlesex East, Ont.) entered the reading room from the Commons entrance on the west side. Constable Thomas Moore was at his post right outside the door. When Mr. Glass entered the room Mr. Northrup (William Barton Northrup; Cons.; Hastings East, Ont.) was standing on the west side of desk A, two or three papers in from the south end, reading. Mr. Glass walked along this desk to see if there were any London papers on file. When he saw there were none, he passed on to desk B, which had the Ottawa papers. He stopped at the northwest corner of desk B where he began reading. Stanley Scott Spencer, the Assistant Curator, was in one of the small rooms off the reading room marked *Curator of Reading-room,* where they handled their papers.

"They are on fish to-night" said Mr. Glass to Mr. Northrup, and (it being a Thursday) Mr. Northrup joked, "It is not a very appropriate night for fish; they should have waited until Friday."[428]

Mr. Glass was absorbed in reading the Ottawa papers, but heard the door opening and other people passing in and out. Nothing was amiss at this time. Mrs. Verville, wife of Mr. Alphonse Verville, the member for Maisonneuve, arrived and went over to the fourth desk. Sir Thomas White came in and passed behind Mr. Glass, between the two desks, and on to the third desk. "I lifted my head as I saw him at the file opposite to me," Mr. Glass said, "and spoke to him and continued reading." Mr. Northrup left and after reading the papers for a minute or two, Sir Thomas heard Dr. Reid at the House of Commons door who motioned him to come with him to his office, and he left.

Mr. Glass continued reading. "I had been reading only a short part of this paragraph," he said later, "when I felt a wave of heat passing up alongside me, as if from a hot air register, and I turned around and almost immediately with my turning I smelt the burning of paper and I stooped down and saw the smoke coming out, and my recollection is that this burning was on the second horizontal part of the desk [meaning the bottom shelf], of the one behind me – it was well in on the pile of papers." When Mr. Glass was asked about the size of the flame, he said, "It was covering a space of from 15 to 18 inches."[429]

Notice the sequence of events. Several people were in the room, and nothing was amiss for some considerable time – no fire, no smell of smoke, nothing unusual. Then all of a sudden, without any warning, Mr. Glass felt a wave of heat as if it had come from a hot air register, and then he turned, and then he smelled and saw the paper burning.

He put up his hands and called for the curators, thinking they would be around the other desks. No one responded, so he ran to the door on the Commons side and called to the policeman. Constable Moore came in and saw the fire, and then Mr. Glass said, "Where are the fire extinguishers or hose?" Mr. Glass said they had better ring in an alarm. Constable Moore ran out and almost instantaneously there was other help.[430]

When Mr. Spencer heard Constable Moore hollering "fire!" he ran into the reading room. He immediately started to pull away papers from underneath the shelves to try to keep them from catching one to the other.[431] Mr. Stewart was on the other side of the desk removing papers from there.[432]

When Constable Moore ran out, he saw Mr. C.R. Stewart, Chief door-keeper of the House of Commons, standing in the lobby and shouted that there was a fire in the reading-room. He then turned and ran back to the other end of the corridor in the reading room at the Senate side and grabbed the extinguisher off the hook and ran back.[433]

Plain clothes man James Edward Knox ran to the reading room when he heard the noise, and saw Constable Moore arrive with the extinguisher. He said there was very little blaze at that time, only two papers were on fire.[434] Plain clothes man Knox saw Constable Moore turn the extinguisher on, and in trying to reach under, the force of the extinguisher blew the paper apart, and it immediately burst into flame, and the burning papers blew against the newspapers that were hanging loosely, and they caught, and then the fire went very rapidly.[435]

It was at this time that Mr. Glass ran out to notify the Commons, and he had just got out the door and turned to go to the

Chamber when he felt a kind of 'puff out,' like a sudden release of a big volume of dense smoke. Then the corridor became filled with smoke.[436]

Mrs. Verville saw the constable use the extinguisher, and when the flames spread to the wall ("just about half way up the wall – not all the wall,") she ran out the Commons side. The fire was near the door, and she passed very close to the flames.[437]

As she escaped down the hall, Mr. Arthur De Witt (ex-Conservative Member of Parliament from Kings, Nova Scotia) came up dressed in his overcoat and rubbers. He had been in the reading room earlier, between eight thirty and eight forty-five, and was on his way out but wanted to see the papers from Halifax before he left. "I started to go into the reading-room again to see those papers, and when about 10 feet from the swinging doors of the reading-room the flames broke out, the full size of the doorway, and pieces of burning paper were coming through, and the hot air ignited and caught the lockers next to the room, almost instantly."[438]

The ceilings of the corridors were wood. The walls of the corridors on the Commons side were lined with wooden wardrobes, or lockers, where the Members kept their winter coats, hats and galoshes.[439] All the woodwork was heavily varnished, and the floors were shellacked. In addition to being highly flammable, burning varnish and shellac cause a great deal of smoke.[440]

Mr. Stewart and Mr. Spencer stopped pulling out papers and got out when the fire went up over their heads, and the roaring and the draught started, forcing the swinging doors of the reading-room wide open[441] Mr. Spencer said, "When that roar went up, I could not see very well with the smoke. I could not get out by the Commons corridor, and I ran the other way."[442]

It was the heat that forced plain clothes man Knox and Constable Moore to retreat. Constable Moore backed out the Commons door with the extinguisher still on the fire and didn't drop it until halfway down the corridor. They ran around the front corridor and back up to the Senate side and took the hose off the stand in the Senate corridor, turned it on and continued fighting the fire from there.[443]

Meanwhile, in the Chamber it was business as usual. Edgar N. Rhodes, Deputy Speaker of the House of Commons, was sitting in the Speaker's chair. It was nine o'clock exactly, and the fire had been burning only about four minutes.

"Everything was calm and normal in the Chamber," Mr. Rhodes said. "I noticed a slight commotion in the hall and a second after the door opened and Mr. Glass came in and I knew something unusual was up by the expression of his face, so much so that my eyes were riveted on his face. He called out 'Mr. Speaker, the building is on fire!' I do not think the words left his lips before the corridor behind him was filled with thick smoke and sheets of flame were interspersed through these black clouds and the smoke curled into the Chamber immediately behind Mr. Glass. I cannot describe how quickly the Chamber was apparently filled with smoke, but it was very quickly."[444]

Since the House was sitting, the ventilation system in the Chamber was in full operation. When Mr. Glass opened the doors, the powerful fans under the floor drew the smoke and flames into the Chamber. Mr. Stewart described it as "a roaring noise – the corridor seemed to act like a flue with a tremendous draught.... I guess it caught in the members' wardrobes. They were made of pine and everything there was ready to catch." [445]

It has been estimated that the fire traveled along the corridors at a speed of about 50 to 100 centimetres a second. [446]

HOW THEY SAVED THE LIBRARY

There were no fire checks or iron doors in the building with the exception of the iron door to the Library. Mr. M.C. MacCormac, one of the clerks in the Library, went on duty a little before eight. About the time the fire started, he was looking up information for two or three members.

He was just crossing the floor in front of the white marble statue of Queen Victoria when one of the messengers cried out that the reading room was on fire. Mr. MacCormac told him to lock the iron door, which he immediately did.[447] When he slammed the door shut the draft along the hall into the Library that was caused by its big ventilation fans stopped.

James Hunter, Deputy Minister of Public Works, testified that the attic of the House of Commons and the Senate had always been particularly dangerous fire-traps and the previous summer they had fireproofed it. The fireproofing they put in was metal lathing around the wooden beams, and then concrete and plaster.

The result was to delay the progress of the fire to such an extent that the firemen were able to get control of the rear part and save the Library. "I think the work we did last summer saved the Library," he said.[448]

Chapter 17: Who Dunnit?

Three weeks before that fire our men in the German Embassy came to me - I was in our New York office at that time - and told me that that morning the plan for destroying the Ottawa Parliament buildings had been discussed and they were to be fired in three weeks from that date, and on that same day I went to Snowden Marshall, the United States District Attorney for New York, and made that statement to him, coupled with the statement that two or three munitions factories in Canada were to be blown up at the same time. And three weeks to the day after I had made that statement, the Ottawa Parliament Buildings were destroyed, and within forty-eight hours of that time two of your munitions factories were blown up. Now I am not prepared to say that this was anything but a coincidence, but if it was a coincidence, it was one of the most remarkable coincidences in the history of the world.[449]

John R. Rathom in a speech at the
Empire Club of Canada, June 15, 1917

To Official Ottawa the fire was an accident, caused by a careless smoker. Sir Robert Borden, who was Prime Minister at the time of the fire, wrote in his memoirs "We appointed R.A. Pringle, K.C., and Judge D.B. MacTavish commissioners to investigate the origin of the fire but their report threw little light upon the question. There were many wild rumors and conjectures as to the incendiary origin through German enemies but to these I never attached the slightest importance. The Reading-room was sheathed with very inflammable wood which had been many times varnished; some careless person, throwing a lighted match or cigar-butt into the waste-paper basket, had left the room; the flames leaping from the basket quickly reached the wall which was like tinder, and the building was doomed."[450]

Even though it was against the rules, the habit was, whether right or wrong, that members, their friends and even reporters used to smoke in the reading room.[451] There had been a rule about no smoking ever since the fire in the West Block attic in 1898, but it was not enforced.[452] In 1915, Dr. Sproule, then the Speaker of the House of Commons, passed another rule against smoking[453] and five *No Smoking* signs were hung up in the reading room.[454]

However, this didn't stop the members from smoking. Mr. Spencer, Assistant Curator in the reading-room said at the inquiry into the cause of the fire, "As a rule I do not pay any attention to them because if nobody else can't stop them [*sic*] I can't."[455]

Plain clothes man Knox testified, "I might say that this smoking in the reading room has been a regular occurrence, because I was through it often and saw members often and often smoking in this place."[456] Dr. Sproule smiled, "We found it pretty difficult to restrain them."[457]

However, there are a couple of problems with the careless smoker theory. The first is, contrary to what the Prime Minister just said, the fire did not start in a waste-paper basket.

Everyone knows that a lighted match or cigar-butt thrown into a waste paper basket can start a fire, especially if the papers are crumpled and loose. However, from Mr. Glass' testimony at the inquiry we know the fire did not start in a waste paper basket. It was "well in," in the centre of a stack of newspapers lying flat on the lowest shelf of desk A.

Mr. Glass did not think it could have been ashes from a cigar that caused the fire. "It was hardly probable that a man shaking a cigar and dropping ashes would drop it into the centre," he explained, "but it would be possible for a man passing to use a match and then shake it and throw it into the centre – that is quite a possible thing."[458]

When you want to start a campfire, you don't place the kindling directly on a stack of flat newspapers and then lay a match in the centre of the paper. It's not going to light. You first crumple up sheets of newspapers so they will catch fire. It is really very difficult (not impossible, but very difficult) to set fire to a stack of flat newspapers by tossing a lighted match on them. Try it and see, but put the match near the centre of the stack, away from the edges. And remember, safety first! Do this experiment in your fireplace!

However, the Parliament Building fire did not start like a fire started by a match - it seemed to just suddenly flash into existence, with a lot of heat. Mr. Glass said it felt like a wave of heat, as if from a hot air register. If it was caused by a lighted match tossed onto the lower shelf of the desk, it must have been smoldering during at least the ten minutes Mr. Glass was standing there reading, and perhaps as long as half an hour. But smoldering fires give off smoke first and then burst into flame afterwards. If it had been smoking all that time wouldn't it have been detected by smoke or smell first? And yet Mr. Glass said, "I did not detect the fire by the smell of the smoke – it was the heat first. I saw the smoke before smelling it."[459] Does this sound like a smoldering fire to you?

The second problem with the careless smoker theory is that Mr. Glass had been in the reading room for ten minutes before he noticed the fire and said he was not smoking, nor were Mr. Northrup and Sir Thomas White. This was confirmed by Mrs. Verville and Mr. Spencer, the Assistant Curator of the reading room.

Earlier, between eight thirty and a quarter to nine, Arthur De Witt Foster (an ex-Conservative M.P. from Kings, Nova Scotia) passed quickly through to look at the Halifax papers. He did not remember seeing anyone else there, and said that he had not been smoking. During that same time period William Nickle (William Folger Nickle; Cons.; Kingston, Ont.) went in briefly to look at the New York papers. He said that he was alone, and that he was a non-smoker. He said conditions in the room were "absolutely normal." It would have taken a very brave person to admit he was smoking in the reading room that night, but from the corroborating testimony of five or six eye-witnesses, it certainly appears that this was the case, at least in the half hour leading up to the fire.[460] So how else could it have started?

Today we know that many house fires start from defective electrical wiring, and the desks in the reading room had wires running through them for the lights. When asked at the inquiry if defective wiring could have caused the fire, Mr. Thompson, an electrician in the House of Commons, said it was "impossible, utterly impossible." He said that if it was started by the wiring, it would have put the light on the desk out, and they would have had to send for him. [461]

This answer seemed to satisfy the commissioners, but modern-day fire investigators would not have discarded the possibility that it was an electrical fire so quickly. They would have examined the wiring in undamaged areas, looking for danger signs like frayed insulation, arcing and minor burns. [462]

However, the defective wiring theory raises a number of questions. How would an arcing and sparking wire inside the desk cause the top sheet of a stack of newspapers on the shelf to catch fire? Assuming the wire and paper were not touching, of course. Wouldn't it be the desk itself that would catch fire first? And yet all of the eyewitnesses said it was the paper that was burning. No one said it was the desk.

Also, how could a small fire (and it was small at the start) give off such a wave of heat? Mr. Glass said that he was reading at desk B, with his back to desk A where the fire started, and yet he could feel the heat through his trousers "as if from a hot air register." And remember, he was standing across the aisle. Puzzling, isn't it?

Another theory, popular at the time, but today generally considered to be rather far-fetched, is that the fire was deliberately set. The First World War started in 1914, and the fighting stopped in 1918, so the fire in 1916 was right in the middle. Could the fire have been deliberately set by a German agent? In the remainder of this chapter we will examine this theory in considerable detail, looking at new evidence that was not available at the inquiry back in 1916. Then you can decide for yourself if it is far-fetched.

BEHIND-THE-SCENES IN THE GERMAN EMBASSY

The United States did not declare war on Germany until April 6, 1917. In 1916, Germany enjoyed diplomatic (if shaky) relations with America, and had an embassy in Washington located at 1435 Massachusetts Avenue NW.

The building was designed in 1881 by Adolf Cluss and Paul Schulze as a residence for Civil War Major Thomas Ferguson. However, it was altered to suit the requirements of the embassy when they bought it in 1893. It was made of red brick faced with brownstone, and had a porte cochere. The ground floor was offices. One level up on the main floor was a large ballroom with tapestries ornamenting its walls, and heavily-craved black oak furniture upholstered in red damask with gold trim. Off the ballroom were reception and drawing rooms, and in turn these opened into a large drawing room and the dining room. It was an exceptionally handsome place but, unfortunately, was demolished in 1959.[463]

In 1916, Henry Landau was an agent with the British Secret Intelligence Service. Today this is popularly known as MI6, but back then it was MI1, and Landau worked in section c. In 1937, after he had retired, Captain Landau wrote *The Enemy Within: The Inside Story of German Sabotage in America*,[464] exposing in great detail the German sabotage system that operated out of this embassy. Landau knew personally many of the characters involved.[465]

He said the Embassy was staffed by four executives.[466] The Ambassador was Count Johann von Bernstorff. The Military Attaché was a young cavalry officer named Captain Franz von Papen, who would later become Chancellor of Germany. Captain Karl Boy-Ed was the Naval Attaché, and lastly there was Dr. Heinrich F. Albert, the Commercial Attaché or banker of the organization.

According to Landau, before the war these men carried out normal consular and diplomatic business. However, after the declaration of war the British Navy blockaded all of Germany's ports, effectively cutting her off from the west. It was impossible for her to be able to receive food and war supplies from American factories, but her enemies, the British, French and Russians, were perfectly able to do so.

The war had started. It was too late for Germany to send trained espionage agents into America to sabotage the factories and plants and blow up ships leaving American ports bound for

Allied countries. It was also too late for Germany to use her submarines to prevent goods and supplies from reaching the Allies. The task fell to the Embassy, von Papen in particular. His task was to build a spy and sabotage organization in the United States using German reservists and nationals, assisted, when required, by German Consuls and consular representatives.

The structure they set up was like this. Von Papen was responsible for sabotage in the United States and in Canada; Boy-Ed for blowing up or setting fire to ships and ports; and Dr. Albert was responsible for the money. As Ambassador, Count von Bernstorff was to stay out of it as much as possible and keep up appearances.[467]

Over the next two years, incendiary devices or bombs were used on forty-seven ships carrying war supplies to the Allies, and on forty-three American factories causing partial or complete destruction and much loss of life.[468] This averaged three or four attacks each month.

One well-known German incendiary device consisted of small 'scent bottles' filled with feuerwasser (fire water), which consisted of phosphorus dissolved in carbon disulphide or some other solvent. All an enemy agent had to do was to sprinkle a few drops on some papers or rags and then sneak away without being noticed. After the solvent evaporated, the fine grains of phosphorus would suddenly burst into a white hot flame, igniting all flammable material within reach.[469]

In January 1915, the *Providence Journal*, a journal from Providence, Rhode Island with John Revelstoke Rathom as its Editor and General Manager, began writing a series of scoops that exposed the spy and sabotage system.[470, 471]

Von Papen and Boy-Ed's role soon became clear, and on December 4, 1915 President Wilson requested their recall, charging the German Government with conspiracies against the Unites States' neutrality. Von Papen left on December 23, and as he was leaving protested that he had a "clean record." Boy-Ed left a few days later (December 29) and said he would refrain from "refuting all the stories which were told about [him] in the American newspapers."

On January 2, 1916, on the way back to Germany, von Papen's luggage was seized by the British authorities at Falmouth who found cheque books, letters and other incriminating documents inside. The cheque stubs in particular documented payments to known sabotage agents who had already been caught and convicted. When informed of the convictions, von Bernstorff, still playing his role, said "I don't believe it!" After von Papen's and Boy-Ed's departure, sabotage continued under the direction of von Papen's assistants, Wolf von Igel and George von Skal.

Attacks on Canada (see Table 4) were fewer than those in the United States. Of particular interest is the last entry in this table.

John Revelstoke Rathom's scoops and his flamboyant character made him popular as a guest speaker at dinner functions. Unfortunately, he sometimes exaggerated the role he and his newspaper had played in bringing these spies to justice. In 1918, his speeches attracted the attention of the U. S. Department of Justice who accused him of making false statements in regard to his own activities and the activities of the Department of Justice. In order to avoid testifying, Rathom agreed to make a 'secret confession.' This confession was made public in 1920.[472]

It is from this confession that we learn that Rathom's exaggerations were mostly in his speeches. The only thing that was not true about his stories regarding the Ottawa fire (both in his newspaper coverage and in his speeches) was that he had not been truthful about the source of his information. He said that the *Providence Journal*'s sources had provided valuable knowledge on a great many matters. In order to protect these sources, Rathom had suggested other sources which did not actually exist.

In his speech at the Empire Club of Canada, for example, (see excerpt at the start of this chapter) he said, "Three weeks before that fire our men in the German Embassy came to me...." This suggests that the *Providence Journal* had newspaper men working undercover in the Embassy. However, this was not true. The newspaper did not have men in the German Embassy. The source of his information for the Ottawa fire, he said in his confession, was Mr. Means; a Mr. G. B. Means.[473]

Table 4. *Examples of sabotage against Canada, extracted from Captain Henry Landau's book 'The Enemy Within: The Inside Story of German Sabotage in America'* [474]

Date	Sabotage Activities
September, 1914	German agent Horst von der Goltz developed a plan to blow up the Welland Canal, but it was called off because the canal was too well guarded. Later von der Goltz was captured and testified against his accomplices
January 3, 1915	Cipher telegram Number 386 to von Bernstorff: Secret. The General Staff is anxious that vigorous measures should be taken to destroy the Canadian Pacific in several places for the purpose of causing a lengthy interruption of traffic. Captain Boehm who is well known in America and who will shortly return to that country is furnished with expert information on that subject. Acquaint the Military Attaché with the above and furnish the sums required for the enterprise. Zimmermann [475]
February 11, 1915	Reply from von Bernstorff: The carrying out of your telegram, No. 386, for Military Attache was entrusted to a former officer, who has been arrested after [causing] an explosion on the Canadian Pacific Railway. Canada demands his extradition. I request authority to protect him; according to the laws of war, the decision ought presumably to be: Non-extradition, provided that an act of war is proved....
May, 1915	Plans were thwarted to dynamite railway bridges and tunnels in the Canadian Northwest. In December 1917, Franz Schulenberg confessed to the plot.
December 21, 1915	Fred Metzler (Paul Koenig was one of von Papen's sabotage directors and Metzler was his secretary) and Richard Emil Leyendecker confessed to their part in a second attempt to blow up the Welland Canal. Koenig, Leyendecker and a man named "Justice" were indicted by a Federal Grand Jury for the Southern District of New York on December 23, 1915.
February, 1916	**"An incendiary fire was started in Houses of Parliament in Ottawa."** *(Landau's own words)*

Mr. Means

So who was Mr. Means? It turns out that he was none other than Gaston Bullock Means: American detective, spy, trickster, hoodwinker, influence peddler, con man and convict. He was about "six feet tall, weighing 200 lbs.," with a "bullet head, small bright eyes, an ingratiating smile, [and] a round chin under hung with a fat neck."[476]

Mr. Means is quite famous in history, although not for the Parliament Building fire. Searching the internet using the keywords 'Gaston B. Means' gives about 2.5 million hits. He is best known for his 1930 book titled *The Strange Death of President Harding* in which he accused the President's wife of murdering him, and then in 1932 for his role in the Lindbergh baby kidnapping case where, instead of helping arrange for the safe return of the child, he stole the ransom money. Means died in 1938 in Leavenworth, where he had been serving 15 years for grand larceny.[477]

However, it is Mr. Means's early career that interests us the most. In 1910, Gaston Bullock Means (just call me 'Bud'[478]) joined the William J. Burns Detective Agency as an undercover man.[479] In 1914, he left the Agency to work for Captain Boy-Ed who wanted him to work as a German spy to find out what the U.S. was shipping to England.[480] He also worked with other German spies to tie up the building of electric boats in America, the so-called 'mosquito fleet.' Means found that these boats had gun emplacements, and Captain Boy-Ed drew this to the attention of the Neutrality Board at Washington. On another occasion he delivered $1,300,000 which he had received as a cheque to Captain Boy-Ed,[481] from whom we do not know. All of this, of course, was before America entered the war. While it may not have been ethical, it was not treason.

"I was receiving $100 a day for my services," Means said, "and sometimes I would get $1,000 a week."[482] "While I was doing this for Captain Boy-Ed, I did not work for the Burns Detective Agency," he said. "This agency could have made money, but the company was decidedly pro-English."[483]

Understandably, this work was not done out in the open. He did not have an office in the embassy. Mr. Means met with Captain Boy-Ed at the German Club in New York City to exchange information. Another favorite meeting place was the Old Trinity churchyard. On one occasion, he received a lump sum payment of $85,000 and at another time $92,000 for his services to Germany.[484] It was behind a tombstone in this graveyard that Captain Boy-Ed stashed these large amounts of money, to be picked up by Mr. Means later.[485]

After this, Mr. Means worked for the German clients of a private detective agency, but by this time it was under the condition that he reports anything of interest to the United States Government. While thus employed, he discovered a German plot to restore Victoriano Huerta, (the ex-President of Mexico and Germany's friend) and then start a war between Mexico and the United States. Means reported this to Secretary Tumulty on March 8, 1915. Shortly after, Captain Boy-Ed confronted Means and told him a report of the Huerta plot had been made to the American Government. He said there were only five living men who could have reported it, and told Means it must have been him. "I told him I did it," said Means, "and that I had agreed to furnish to the United States Government any information detrimental to it which I discovered." Boy-Ed then told him to go down and see his German clients, which he did, and they immediately fired him.[486] After his firing, Means was employed by some German commercial interests.[487]

Mr. Means' Warning

It was four weeks before the fire, while Mr. Means was working for these German commercial interests, that he heard about a plot to attack Canada's Parliament Building. He said he told Secretary Daniels of the United States Government when and how it was to be done.[488]

Perhaps a week later (three weeks before the fire), he told Mr. Rathom. Rathom did not place much credence in most of what Mr. Means told him (no surprise there!) but nevertheless passed the information on to the Department of Justice. "Every attempt of Mr. Means to get into communication with us," he said, "and every specific and improper activity of his of which the Providence Journal or I ever had any knowledge was made the subject of immediate reference to the Department of Justice."[489]

On that same day, Mr. Rathom met with H. Snowdon Marshall, the Federal District Attorney of New York and A. Bruce Bielaski, Chief of the Bureau of Investigation of the Department of Justice, in Mr. Snowdon's office in New York City. He said he told them that in three weeks the Parliament Building in Ottawa was going to be burned down by the Germans.[490]

Then, exactly three weeks later, the Parliament Building did burn down. The next day *The Providence Journal* prefaced its coverage of the fire with the following statement:

> *The Providence Journal three weeks ago notified the Department of Justice that it had received information directly through employees of the German Embassy that the Parliament House of Ottawa, Rideau Hall, the home of the Governor-General in Ottawa, and large munitions plants in Ontario were to be the next objects of German attack on this continent, in the order named.*
>
> *The Journal furthermore notified the Department of Justice at the same time that the German Embassy had given instructions that the work of destruction in American munitions plants should be temporarily suspended, and that the next move to be made would 'give the people of Canada a few things to think about.'*[491]

The day after the fire, Snowdon Marshall confirmed that he and Rathom had met about three weeks ago, but Mr. Marshall said no specific target was mentioned – he said they were talking about a number of things and his recollection was that Rathom had said "he had notified the Department of Justice that he had information there would be some sort of German attacks on Canada in the course of two weeks."[492]

Was Rathom's version of the warning another example of his story-telling? Here is what Rathom had to say in his confession: "It is my specific recollection that in my conversation with Mr. Marshall, I told him that the Ottawa Parliament Building would be the first object of this attack, although I understand

Mr. Marshall states that he does not remember that any specific place was mentioned."[493]

Mr. Means' warning never reached Ottawa.[494] Snowdon Marshall said that he did not take any action because Rathom had already done all that he himself could have done. He said that he paid no further attention to the matter because it did not concern the Southern District of New York.[495]

INCENDIARY EXPERIMENTS AT THE INQUIRY IN OTTAWA

The Commissioners were well-aware that there were certain chemicals which, when poured on a newspaper, ignited spontaneously after periods varying from a few minutes to more than an hour, and arranged for Edgar Stansfield, Chemist of the Fuel Testing Division of the Mines Branch and his assistant Mr. Carter do a demonstration.

According to a newspaper account,[496] Mr. Stansfield and Mr. Carter first laid out a large sheet of asbestos on the clerk's table in the council chamber. On this they conducted experiments with a lighted cigar, a lighted cigarette, an ordinary match and a chemical solution. After lighting a cigar Mr. Pringle puffed on it rapidly a few times until it was burning well. He then tried several methods to get a folded newspaper in a dish on the table to burn, without success, although he did cause it to smolder. Experiments with a lighted cigarette on papers in another dish gave similar results.

Then Mr. Pringle tried to light folded papers in another dish with a match. These burned slowly at first, and then more rapidly. Mr. Stansfield easily put the fire out.

The chemical solution was poured on folded newspapers in another dish and for a while did nothing but evaporate, giving off fumes that at first were easily smelled in all parts of the room. However, the odor decreased rapidly after the liquid was poured on the paper. After a few minutes, it was such that it would usually escape notice in a well-ventilated room like the reading room. Mr. Stansfield said that other liquids of this nature may be obtainable that are free from odor.[497]

Five, ten minutes passed, and after fifteen minutes with no flames Mr. Stansfield gave the paper a slight wave and it burst into flame. They extinguished the fire, but it was difficult, more so than with the fire started with the match.

After seeing these two fires, Mr. Glass was asked if he saw any difference in the appearance of the flame. He answered "Yes, the appearance of this one is more like it to me, I mean the one started with the chemicals."[498]

Explosions

Fire Chief Graham testified that he distinctly heard explosions. Major Stetham, who was just back from the front, said he heard explosions too, and that they sounded very much like the explosions of Adien shells. The Chief said the first explosion was in the courtyard behind the Speaker's quarters, when the ventilation tower fell. The stones were thrown a considerable distance, and his men had to run to avoid getting hit.[499]

However, David Ewart (a consulting architect at the time of the fire but who had previously been Chief Architect for Public Works) examined the wreckage and saw no indication whatsoever of an explosion. He said the noises could have been the falling of the ventilation tower and the falling of the ceilings. He looked at the stones in the courtyard that the Chief talked about. One stone in particular was a long way from the building. When he was asked how it could have gotten there he examined the stone and found it was the top stone of the chimney.[500]

Security

What about security? The evening of the fire there were seven uniformed policemen on duty and one plain clothes man.[501] There was a policeman at the Senate side of the reading room and on the House of Commons side as well, up to eight thirty, and the latter was there after that.[502] Could a spy just walk into the reading room and pour chemicals on the papers? Wouldn't the police have stopped him?

Colonel E.M. Macdonald, M.P. testified, "Without any reflection upon the police the number of people who were in the habit of coming and going for years around those corridors on political business, unless a man actually looked disreputable, and a person who could not possibly have any right to be there, the policemen would not stop him."[503]

Charles Bowman (editor of the *Ottawa Citizen* between 1915 and 1945) said in his memoirs, "Canada had literally no security organization up to the third year of World War I. Strangers were still free to stroll around in the Parliament Buildings in 1916. They could use the reading room."[504]

According to the evidence at the inquiry, there were several suspicious-looking characters about that night. Col. Macdonald was entering the main door at about twenty five minutes to nine, and he was struck by a man standing on the ledge, on the left door going into the lobby. "I was struck by his appearance and restless manner – I was not thinking of anything in particular, and nothing to attract my attention at all, except by some influence this man struck my attention. He was nervous and his eyes were shifty. When I saw him looking at me, he looked at me very intently, and I said to myself, 'That is a very curious man,' and seemed to be worried about something and I passed on."[505]

The Speaker, Mr. Sévigny, said a stranger came in to see him the Monday before the fire.[506] The fire was on a Thursday and the stranger came on the Monday. He spoke French and said he was from 'La Maison Lafitte,' in Paris, but Mr. Sévigny thought he was German. The man represented himself as a French soldier just back from the war and said he was very anxious to take pictures of the building. The Speaker refused him, saying that in ordinary times he would give him permission, with pleasure, but these were serious times and it was impossible to give that permission.

The man came right to the door of the Speaker's apartments and evidently had no difficulty in passing the guards and reaching the door of his apartment. He came back again Tuesday and perhaps, the Speaker thought, on the Thursday morning too. However, the Dominion Police found out that the photographer was, in fact, just that – a French-speaking photographer from Montreal. He had been at the Parliament Building two years earlier taking photographs, and after questioning him the police were satisfied that he had nothing to do with the fire.[507]

When Mr. Northrup left the reading room the evening of the fire to go home, he stopped at his wardrobe and put on his overcoat and rubbers. On his way out he noticed an altercation between a stranger and the door-keeper at the corridor that leads to the reading room. He was a tall young man, Mr. Northrup said. He had never seen him before and had no idea who he was. Despite the stranger's odd appearance – he was dressed in a plaid or check suit and his overcoat was a grey check of a rather striking color – he had the appearance of a respectable man. Mr. Northrup looked to see how it would work out as he passed, and his impression was that the stranger went on down the corridor towards the reading room. A few moments later, the fire alarm went off.[508]

Charles Bowman told of another suspicious character, a Mr. Babson who, a few weeks before the Parliament Building fire, arrived in Ottawa with his wife and daughter and rented a furnished house in the Glebe.[509] Babson spoke English, but according to a neighbor when he was alone with his family in their back garden they spoke in a 'foreign language.'

One day Babson showed up at Bowman's office at the *Citizen*, wanting to borrow a past issue to read an article titled *A Plea for the Passing of War*. Bowman left his office to get the back issue, and when he returned he caught Babson staring out his window. It overlooked the Holden factory, a busy factory that worked day and night making army uniforms.

Babson thanked him for the paper, and before leaving said he would have come earlier but that he had been out of town. Bowman found out later he had rented a cottage up at the Rideau Lakes – in the middle of winter – to carry out some chemical experiments and wanted to be away from where anyone would be disturbed by an explosion.

Shortly after that day, the Holden factory was burned down. Police said it was arson, and Bowman suspected Babson did it as practice to test out his chemicals before using them on the Parliament Building.

The morning after the Parliament Building fire, Bowman reported his information to the chief of the Dominion police. The Chief did not take him seriously, but listened politely, and even went over and knocked on Babson's door to question him.

However Babson and his family had disappeared without a trace.

A FIRE TWO DAYS EARLIER

Two days earlier there had been another – almost identical - fire in the reading room. Mr. Weichel (Cons., Waterloo North, Ontario) testified, "My friend Lockhead was reading the *Telegraph* and I was reading the *Daily News Record*, when I felt a slight heat about my feet and left knee – I unconsciously put my hand down to feel what was the matter, when I felt more of the heat coming in contact with my hand, when I looked down, and at the same time Colonel Lockhead did, and we saw that one of the country newspapers in one of the lower shelves, about two feet from the floor was slightly burning, on its surface – there was a flame that possibly would not cover any more than your two hands – it was immediately pulled out and thrown on the floor, and we stepped on it and put the fire out...." [510]

The two fires were very similar - both started on a flat stack of newspapers; both were on a shelf under a desk in the reading-room; both flamed up suddenly, without warning; both were detected by a wave of heat first, not smell; and both were in the three week time frame given in Mr. Means' warning. What are we to make of that?

THE INQUIRY'S RECOMMENDATIONS

The commissioners of the inquiry said that they had no proof, but there was a "strong suspicion" of sabotage, especially because no one was smoking in the reading room for some time before the fire. Although they did not have conclusive evidence, they felt strongly that evidence might be obtained at a later date that might establish beyond question whether it was accidental or deliberate. They recommended that their report be treated not as a final report but as an interim report, that the commission be left open, and if they were able to obtain further evidence at a later date that they be allowed to do so.[511] There never was a second report.[512]

WHAT DO YOU THINK?

I think it was deliberate. However, there is no proof. All of the Dominion Police's files on the fire are either missing or lost. There may be information in the British Secret Intelligence Service's files that show what Landau knew (he worked in section MI1c), however all SIS files remain closed.[513]

There might be a smoking gun in the archives in Germany. As indicated earlier, von Papen's luggage that was seized by the British authorities at Falmouth in January of 1916, about the time Mr. Means said he heard about the plot to burn down Canada's Parliament Building, contained cheque books, letters and other incriminating documents. So, detailed records were kept. It would be a great research topic for a student to find out if there is anything there.

For now, though, it's a mystery. Like a judge in court, you will have to look at all the evidence and then decide what best fits the facts, and makes the most sense. The table on the next page might help.

So, what do you think?

Table 5. This may help you decide. Evidence in support of...

Accident	Sabotage
Even though it was against the rules, Members, their friends and even reporters used to smoke in the reading room.	Based on sworn testimony of five or six eye-witnesses, no one was smoking in the reading room in the half hour leading up to the fire.
It is possible that someone may have used a match to light a cigar, shook it out, and then tossed the (supposedly) burned-out match into the middle of the papers on the lower shelf. This could start a fire.	It is historical fact that German agents carried out sabotage in Canada and the United States during the First World War. Proof exists in secret telegrams that were intercepted and decoded by British intelligence agents; seized cheque stubs documenting payments to known saboteurs who had been caught and convicted; and in recorded confessions, court cases, etc.
Faulty wiring was, and still is, a common cause of fire. The lamps on the desks in the reading room had wires running through them. There could have been frayed insulation.	Three weeks before the fire there had been a warning, although there is some dispute over exactly what was said.
	In 1916 security was not what it is today. Strangers could get into the reading room if they looked presentable.
	There were two identical fires within two days in the reading room. They both occurred on papers lying flat on desk shelves. Neither was a smoldering fire — they burst suddenly into flame and were discovered by the heat they gave off, not by smoke or smell.
	Feuerwasser ignites spontaneously, burning with a white hot flame.
	Henry Landau, in 1916 a WW1 agent with the British SIS, stated, "An incendiary fire was started in Houses of Parliament in Ottawa."

Who dunnit? 183

"Gaston B. Means, 3/14/24." Digital ID: (digital file from original) npcc 25463 http://hdl.loc.gov/loc.pnp/npcc.25463. Reproduction Number: LC-DIG-npcc-25463 (digital file from original). Repository: Library of Congress Prints and Photographs Division Washington, D.C. 20540 USA.

Chapter 18: Why the old Parliament Building was not Restored

I see by the discussion that you still have a longing for the old walls. Well so had I but when it was decided to put an extra storey this old wall had to come down.[514]

Senator Watson to Sir Wilfrid Laurier

Initially the plan was to rebuild the old Parliament Building. At an emergency council meeting the day after the fire, it was decided to use the Victoria Museum in Ottawa temporarily. Public Works got it ready in record time. Borden wrote in his memoirs it "was an achievement which reflected great credit upon the Minister of Public Works and his officials. The work was carried on with great vigour from our adjournment on Friday afternoon until Monday when accommodation was available not only for the House and the Senate but for the officials and officers of each House."[515]

Architects John A. Pearson from Toronto and Jean-Omer Marchand from Quebec were appointed by Robert Rogers, Minister of Public Works, to inspect the ruins and prepare plans. P. Lyall & Sons Construction Company was hired to clean up the site.

Pearson and Marchand's report was read to the House on February 17, 1916, and it was good news. The building, they said, represented an asset of $2 million that could be re-used. The walls, although blackened by fire, were still standing. The floors, which were made of concrete, were still solid and were holding the walls in alignment. The masonry, they said, was first class both in materials and workmanship. However, considerable damage was done to the main tower, and the centre of the building, where the reading room and Chambers were, was completely destroyed.[516]

The architects worked long into the night and by March 22 1916, had completed concept plans and sketches. The appearance was the same from the outside, but inside they were able to improve the efficiency of the layout and provide an extra 33 percent accommodation. The cost of rebuilding was estimated at $1,500,000, and it could be ready by autumn of 1917 or the early part of 1918.[517]

This extra accommodation was badly needed. Overcrowding began at the time of Confederation, when the Parliament and Departmental Buildings were only a year old. The Parliament Building was designed for representation from the Province of Canada (Ontario and Quebec), and in 1866 there were only 130 members. With Confederation on July 1, 1867, Nova Scotia and New Brunswick joined Ontario and Quebec to form the new Dominion of Canada, and the number of members increased to 194. It was overcrowded right away.

Seating in the Chamber was solved by moving the Speaker's chair to the west instead of the north side (see Chapter 7), but there was still the question of office space. It became worse as more and more provinces joined. After a fire in the West Block attic in 1897, it had been suggested that another storey be added during the reconstruction of the roof, but the minister decided it would be unwise to do so since "it might change the aspect of the other buildings." Instead, the West Block was rebuilt according to the original plans.[518]

In 1901, a suggestion was made to create extra space by joining the eastern and western blocks to the Parliament Building, creating a single building with an irregular, semi-circular shape. Fortunately, this bad idea did not go ahead because, although considerable extra space would be added, "the result might be to sadly mar the architectural beauty of the legislative and departmental buildings."[519]

However, overcrowding worsened, and by 1916 members were sharing offices with three or four colleagues.[520] While the extra 33 percent accommodation in the restored Centre Block went part way to solving the problem, it was apparent that an additional storey was needed.

On May 14 1916, P. Lyall & Sons were engaged for the rebuilding. A sketch with the additional storey was adopted on May 15, and the next day Pearson and Marchand were retained as architects for its construction.[521]

Placing an extra storey upon the building meant dismantling chimneys and turrets above the roof line and then taking the walls down to good, solid masonry that could carry the additional weight. When workers began dismantling the walls, the architects saw that they were in much worse shape than they had thought. The sandstone facing had de-bonded from its interior backing, leaving gaps big enough to shove your arm in, and the lime in the mortar had washed away leaving only sand to hold the stones together.[522]

Some people think it was the fire that caused this damage, but it wasn't. It was rainwater that had entered the walls through cracks and open joints (see Chapter 31). Nepean sandstone itself is really quite fireproof. Sir William Logan had recommended its use in 1860 because of this characteristic (Chapter 6).

Workers continued dismantling, looking for solid masonry on which they could start building. Down and down they went.

On May 23, J.B. Hunter, Deputy Minister of Public Works, telegrammed Pearson about the manner in which the two shifts of wrecking crews were handling the stone. Pearson didn't reply.[523]

By June the cost of rebuilding had increased to $5 million,[524] and the completion date had slipped to December 1918.[525]

On June 20, Hunter sent a telegram to Pearson again, asking how the stone was being marked so that each piece could be put back in its proper position later. Again Pearson didn't reply.

On June 27, he sent another, demanding to know "what portion of the walls is to be left intact and what portion is...to be taken down carefully for the purpose of reusing."[526]

It wasn't until July 29, after all the walls and floors had been taken down to the ground that the architects sent in their report explaining, after the fact, why everything had to come down.[527]

The amazing thing is that they did this without any approvals or authority whatsoever. As you can imagine, the politicians were furious, and the architects were forced to accept formal, written responsibility. But since the walls were down, the government had no choice but to build a new building.

"Reconstruction of Centre Block, Parliament Buildings." When Thomas Fuller's granddaughter Carol was ten, her father took her to the site when it had been cleared. Eighty years later she still remembered walking up and down the empty lot. "There was nothing," she said, "only the library."[28] Photographed by DPW, August 15, 1916. Credit: Library and Archives Canada / PA-130624 / Acc. No. 1979-140 NPC

PART 4

Modern day Parliament Hill

Chapter 19: Construction of the Centre Block

This afternoon Mr. Pearson, the architect took me over the Houses of Parliament.... The interior of the buildings are very fine, when completed the whole structure will be one of "rare and noble beauty." The Commons Chamber is particularly impressive, most appealing to one's spirit. The building is certainly to have a wholesome effect on the lives of the men & on legislation. It is still far from completion but the picture of it all is easily framed in one's mind. It was a great joy, a real inspiration in going about. I shall be happy when my life is centred there.[529]

William Lyon Mackenzie King, November 22, 1919

In July 1916, negotiations began for the purchase of 16,000 tons of Nepean sandstone. Contracts were signed with seven different quarries, but the Campbell quarry in Nepean supplied most of the stone for the new Centre Block and all of it for the Peace Tower.[530]

A shed was erected directly in front of the Centre Block to cut and prepare the stones. In addition, a shop was built on Sussex Drive where the American Embassy is today. According to the architect John Pearson, these shops were the best of their kind in Canada for the finishing of stone and marble. Many of the buff Ohio and Nepean sandstones were saved from the original building to be recut and used in the construction.[531]

The cornerstone from the old building had been taken from the ruins of the fire and was re-laid at the northeast corner of the new building on September 1, 1916.

On September 29, the construction contract with P. Lyall & Sons was signed.[532] The contractor was paid a percentage of construction costs up to $5 million, which was the cost estimated by the architects in June, but received nothing for costs that exceeded this amount. The contract was back-dated to February 3 so it included all clean-up after the fire. Everything was to be completed by December 31, 1918.

The war made it difficult to obtain men and materials, and the lack of competition caused many tenders to come in high. In 1918, it was the only major project being built by Public Works. New projects were not being approved, and even some of those underway had been cancelled to free up money.[533]

By early 1919, the exterior work, except for the tower, had been completed, with $3,768,080.70 spent. Now that the war was over, unions tried to regain some of the wages lost over the last four years. The combination of strikes and the rising cost of materials caused the cost of construction to rise sharply. By May, 1919, $4,623,532 had been spent; by September $5,340,094; by the end of 1919 the cost had reached $5,980,354; and by the spring of 1920 it was $6,496,555.[534] Between the start of construction in 1916 and summer of 1920, the cost of materials had increased 144% and wages 100%.[535]

The completed Centre Block must have looked a little funny without the Peace Tower, but nevertheless the Fourth Session of the Thirteenth Parliament opened on February 26, 1920.[536]

In April 1920, Pearson's design for a 90 metre high free-standing tower was approved, except for the carillon. The term 'free-standing' means it is free standing from the fourth floor up; below that is connected to the Centre Block by a three story 'link.' Although the carillon was not approved, Pearson was allowed to plan for it and build space so that it could be installed later.[537]

In December of 1921, when the tower was at the half-way point (about to the roof of the Centre Block) Pearson quit because of a dispute over fees. No work was done for the next two years.[538]

He was re-hired in 1924 under a new contract, and by November the contractor had completed the stonework up to the circular openings for the clock faces, leaving only the roof.[539]

On March 2, 1925, the purchase of the bells, clock and carillon was approved.[540] By the end of 1925, the tower was completed, but without the carillon.[541] In May 1927, the carillon bells arrived from England and were installed.[542]

Construction of the Centre Block 193

The final cost of the Centre Block was $12,226,582.32.[543] They were supposed to complete everything for $5 million by December 31, 1918, so the project was a little more than two times over budget and nine years late – not that much different from the 1860's project.

"Parliament Buildings – Construction at rear of Library." The formwork in the foreground is for the foundations. All of the foundation walls in the Centre Block are poured concrete except in the southeast corner of the building where they are made of huge blocks of limestone. There, for some reason, the architects decided to retain the original foundation made by Mr. McGreevy in 1860 and poured a short portion of 1916 concrete foundation wall on top. Note the steam-powered concrete mixer bottom left. Photographer unknown; photographed September 18, 1916. Credit: Library and Archives Canada/PA-180262 / Acc. No. 1979-140 NPC

194　*The Other Side of the Hill*

"Reconstruction of Centre Block Parliament Buildings." *The progress of construction by August 7, 1918. The structure on the front right is the base of the flag pole between the Centre Block and the West Block and the photograph was taken looking towards the south west corner of the Centre Block. Note the masons sitting on swing stages halfway up the building working the masonry. The men in the foreground are working on the steam tunnel. No hard hats, safety boots, or other safety equipment was used in those days. Credit: Library and Archives Canada/ C-38764 / Acc. No. 1966-029 NPC*

Construction of the Centre Block 195

"(Parliament Buildings) Construction of Centre Block." Photographed in 1919. It look's odd without the tower, doesn't it? Credit: William James Topley/Library and Archives Canada/PA-012925 / Acc. No. 1936-270 NPC

196 *The Other Side of the Hill*

"(Construction) Erection of Parliament Buildings, Ottawa, Ont." This photograph shows how the Peace Tower was constructed: a lift of stone on the outside was first put up, and a metre or so behind this was a lift of formwork. Portland cement concrete was poured into the space in-between. Photographed by DPW July 10, 1924. Credit: Canada. Dept. of Public Works / Library and Archives Canada / PA-057518 / Acc. No. 1971-085 NPC.

Chapter 20: Peace Tower

*It will be called [the] Peace Tower.**

The Ottawa Citizen, July 29, 1919 [544]

This is the first time it was called the 'Peace Tower' in the Ottawa Citizen, or in any other newspaper. The Citizen was right that it would be called the Peace Tower, but it would not be for another decade.

The 'Mistake' on the Peace Tower Clock

Before I retired, I used to give tours of Parliament Hill to summer students and staff as part of an orientation to Parliament Hill. (This must have come under the 'related duties' part of my job description.) We always met at the Centennial Flame, and to pass the time while waiting for the entire group to arrive I would give a little quiz:

"Remembering back to your schooldays," I would ask, "what is the Roman numeral for five?"

Somebody would say V.

"Right," I said, "now how about eight?"

VIII would be the answer.

"Right again...and how about four?"

"IV".

"OK, so now take a look at the clock on the Peace Tower and tell me why it's IIII instead of IV! What's going on?"

You need good eyesight to see it, but it really is IIII. Apparently it is a convention among clock and watch makers to use IIII instead of IV, although nobody seems to know why. The majority of tower clocks use IIII but not all. For example, Big Ben uses IV. (Actually, Big Ben is the name of the bell, not the clock, but you know what I mean.)

By the way, IIII is not wrong; it is how four was written when the Romans first invented Roman numerals. In the early days, the Romans used just the additive principle, but some numbers became very long this way and so after a time they included the subtractive principle too. This is how we learned Roman numerals in school.

After I had explained all this, I would ask my group to look at their wristwatches and see if any of them have Roman numerals. In a group of twenty or so there is sure to be someone and his or her watch probably has IIII for the four. This always catches them by surprise because, although they may have been wearing the watch for years, they never noticed it!

How about you? Does your watch have Roman numerals?

How the Peace Tower got its Name

I used to tell my groups that it was called the Victory Tower at the start, because we won the war, and that some years later - perhaps in the early 1930's - it was changed to the Peace Tower. If this was true, it would have indicated a subtle, very pretty change in Canadian thinking; from victory to peace.

However, this is not what happened. A word search of William Lyon Mackenzie King's on-line diaries[545] shows that, at the start, he usually didn't use any name, referring to it simply as the 'tower' or the 'parl. Bldg. tower.' The first time he used a name it was Peace Tower and this occurred in his diary entry for November 29, 1925:

> *Before & after supper Joan and I put in quite three hour over suitable inscriptions for the large bell of the carillon to go in Peace Tower. The one I like best is 'To commemorate the Peace of 1918 and to keep in remembrance the service and sacrifice of Canada in the*

Great War – erected by authority of prlt. – A.D. 1926 – ' with the words 'Glory to God in the Highest, on earth Peace & Good-will to men' – around the rim of the bell at the base.[546]

King used the name Victory Tower only once (on September 27, 1926) but after this, whenever he used a name in his diary, it was always Peace Tower.

A word search of the *Ottawa Citizen* Newspaper shows that up to 1928 half the reporters were using one name and half the other, but that after 1928 use of Victory Tower dropped off quickly, as shown in the graph. The same conclusion is arrived at by considering another newspaper, for example the *Montreal Gazette* which is also on-line.

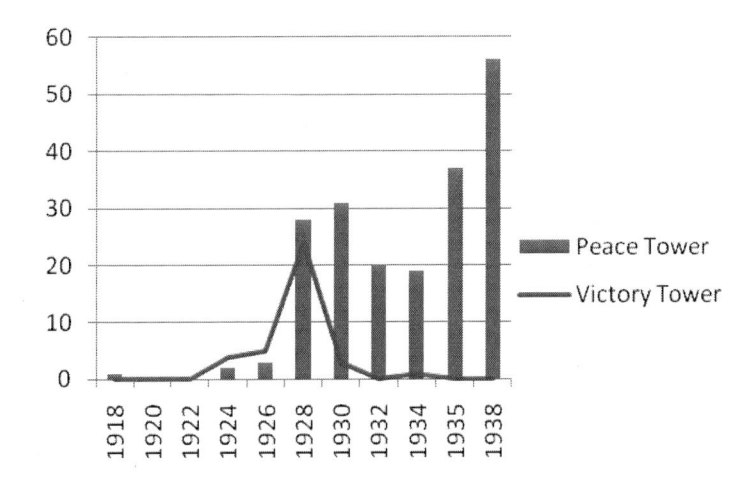

Number of newspaper articles found in a word search of the Ottawa Citizen Newspaper using the key words 'Peace Tower' or 'Tower of Peace' versus 'Victory Tower' or 'Tower of Victory.' By 1930 most people had stopped calling it the Victory Tower.

In 1928 the Government published a small booklet for carillon lovers titled *Carillon – The Peace Tower*, which included interesting and useful information on the carillon, the bells and the summer programmes. It was prepared by the Department of Public Works and sold in book stores everywhere. During the summer recitals of 1928, it was available on Parliament Hill at a cost of ten cents.[547] The popularity of the carillon recitals and the title of this little book may have played a role in people agreeing that it was, indeed, the Peace Tower.

By 1939, it was generally known as the Peace Tower.[548] However, Victory Tower appeared once more in a *Citizen* article in 1941[549] and - for the last time - in 1952.[550]

A surprising thing is that the choice of name was never voted on in Parliament. You would think that naming what must be the most recognizable symbol of Canada all over the world would have at least been debated in the House of Commons, but it wasn't! Canadians just seemed to somehow agree that this was the right name.

A similar sort of thing happened with our two-dollar coin.[551] Many names were suggested when it was introduced back in 1996: the toonie, the doubloonie, the bear-buck, the bearie, the bearly, and the deuce were all proposed, but somehow it was the name toonie that stuck. This was never voted on in Parliament either, but everybody calls it a toonie. If I said something silly like, "I can go into Timmy's with a toonie and come out with a double-double and change," you would know exactly what I mean.

MR. CRERAR

The markings on the Peace Tower clock are bronze, cast at the old Victoria Foundry in Ottawa. The hands of the clock are made of aluminum, for lightness.

The ringing of the Peace Tower's bells is automatic, being controlled by a mechanism that resembles a music box. Clappers driven by a cogged barrel strike the outside of four of the bells each quarter hour to sound the 'Westminster Quarters' melody, and a 254-kilogram clapper strikes the hour upon the big *Bourdon*, the name given to the largest of the bells.[552]

The mechanism was started on July 1, 1927. Not three weeks later, Mr. J. P. Crerar, who lived in the Roxborough Apartments, complained that the playing of the Westminster Quarters melody every quarter hour and the tolling of the big bell every hour was robbing him of a good night's sleep. "Does the carillonneur stay up all night ringing the bells in the Victory Tower to let us know the time? If so, would it not be kind of the Government to let him go to bed at eleven and start again in the morning, when people are going to work?" [553]

When locals were asked by *The Citizen* what they thought of the idea of silencing the bells at night, say between the hours of midnight and seven a.m., most people objected. Merchants along Sparks Street were unanimous in their opposition and said they were far more interested in getting rid of really annoying street noises like honking horns and rattling of street cars. They found the chimes soothing. Mayor Balharrie remarked, "It certainly is pretty early to be getting tired of the chimes." [554]

Anyway, the problem went away. Within the year, Mr. Crerar solved his problem by moving out to a beautiful house on the Aylmer Road.

THE DAY THE STARS AND STRIPES FLEW FROM THE PEACE TOWER

The Union Jack was the first flag to be flown from the Peace Tower and in 1945 it was replaced with the Red Ensign.[555] On February 15, 1965 (Flag Day) the Maple Leaf flew for the very first time.

However, the day I'd like to talk about is February 6, 1976, when it was the Stars and Stripes that flew over Canada.

It was only up for a short time. At 8:50 a.m. the American flag was about a third of the way up the mast, flapping strongly in the wind, and by 9 o'clock it was on its way down. The Maple Leaf was back up by 9:17.

Excerpt from the House of Commons Debates
February 6, 1976

George Harris HEES (Prog. Cons.; Broadview, Ont.): Mr. Speaker, I have a question for the Minister of Public Works, who is responsible for the raising and lowering of the flags on public buildings. Will he advise the House what was the purpose behind the raising of the American flag over the Peace Tower this morning? Was it to show our American neighbors that we really do love them, and is it planned to give the Cuban flag equal time later this day?

Charles Mills DRURY (Lib.; Saint-Antoine--Westmount, Que.; Minister of Public Works): Mr. Speaker. I have not been in communication with the raisers of the flag this morning. I am told they are from the academic community with which perhaps the hon. Member is more familiar than I.

Mr. HEES: You mean I am a little better educated?

An Hon. Member: It doesn't show, George.

Mr. HEES: I am so modest I keep it under a bushel.

Mr. DRURY: Their purpose, Mr. Speaker, in raising the flag has not been made too clear to the Sergeant-at-Arms who has succeeded in collaring them all, according to accounts.

It turns out it was a prank by University of Ottawa student Pierre Guevremont, 22, and some of his friends as part of Carnival Week. We don't know how they did it, but the students got into some out-of-the-way part of the tower about four-thirty the previous afternoon, and stayed there overnight. Guevremont said that they couldn't sleep well because of the Westminster Quarters bells going off every fifteen minutes, but especially because of the big *Bourdon*.

He said that it was just a prank, not a political statement. The Stars and Stripes was actually their second choice. What they really wanted was a pirate flag, the skull and crossbones, but they couldn't find one big enough.[556] It looks small from the ground, but it's amazing how big the flag at the top of the tower really is.

Security guards nabbed the suspects at the top of the tower minutes after the American Flag was spotted, and while some politicians joked about it, it raised serious questions about security.

Excerpt from the House of Commons Debates
February 12, 1976, p. 10876.

James Alexander JEROME, Speaker of the House of Commons:
Before proceeding with the balance of routine proceedings, on Friday last questions were raised, particularly by the right hon. member for Prince Albert (Mr. Diefenbaker), about security implications relating to an incident involving the flag on the Peace Tower. I do not propose to make any further statement in the House, but I do want to assure hon. members that I have received a very thorough and detailed report as a result of an investigation into the incident. I have had an opportunity of discussing that report not only with the House leaders but also with the right hon. gentleman who raised the point of order. The advice I have received has been most helpful and perhaps remarkable for this chamber in that the conclusion we reached and the recommendations we considered were unanimous.

I simply want to assure all hon. members who are interested in the subject that they are welcome to discuss it with me privately. I have the report and the recommendations under review and will continue to keep the matter under very careful study. As I say, it will not be the subject matter of any further comment on the House.

STONE CARVINGS

There are approximately 370 carvings[557] on the Peace Tower. There is a lion, a unicorn, oak leaves, maple leaves, provincial shields, apples, pumpkins, grapevines, sheaves of corn, bundles of wheat, pinecones, sunflowers, shamrocks, thistles, roses, lilies, beavers, inscriptions, World War I soldiers, ugly monsters clinging impossibly to the stonework with their big claws, caricatures, mythical creatures, beasts, grinning dragons, swimming fish, ducks, owls wearing eye-glasses (owls are known for having exceptional eyesight, but not these)...and many more.

The contractor who built the Peace Tower was required to include twenty thousand dollars in his cost for stone carving (remember, this was back in the 1920's) and to hire only the most experienced and skillful carvers.[558] Carving was done either at Public Works' stone shop on Sussex Street, in which case the completed sculpture was lifted up and set into place by the stone masons, or the carvers worked right on the scaffold, chipping and shaping the rough blocks or 'blanks' the masons left in the stonework. In either case, full-size clay models or 'maquettes' had to be made first by skilled modelers to work out elements of composition and detail from which was taken a plaster cast. It is the plaster cast that was shown to the architect, and if it was approved the cast was used as a model for the carving in stone.[559]

Not all of the blanks were carved during construction. Those higher up on the tower were, in order to take advantage of the tall scaffold that surrounded the tower. However, near the ground blanks were left to be carved later by Dominion Stone Carver Cléophas Soucy, and his long-time assistant Coeur de Lion MacCarthy. During the 1930's and 40's these two men, who were modelers as well as carvers, with the help of additional carvers hired on contract, completed many of the carvings in and around the Centre Block and all of the carvings on the outside of the tower. [560,561]

EVERYBODY LOVES STONE CARVINGS

Everybody loves stone carvings. Well, almost everybody. Dave Spence, a Member of Parliament in the 1930's (Cons., Toronto-Parkdale) was one who did not.

On May 8, 1936 he stood up in the House of Commons and complained. "Go into the lobby and look at the carving," he said to the Minister of Public Works. "It is spoiling good stone and is a waste of money. There is nothing artistic about it. It is spoiling good stone." To this the Hon. P.J.A. Cardin (Lib.; Richelieu, Que.; Minister of Public Works) replied, "I might be inclined to agree with the hon. gentleman, but then my taste may not be good."[562, 563]

For this clever put-down I have to say: "Hooray for the Minister!"

BUCKY THE BEAVER

I call the rather crusty looking beaver that sits on the apex of the gable over the main entrance 'Bucky.' That's my name for her. As far as I know, she doesn't have an official one.

In 1920, the architectural drawings for the tower showed it was the British lion that was supposed to go here. The block of stone remained uncarved until 1938, but by this time stone carver Cléophas Soucy and architect Allan Keefer had chosen something a little more Canadian. It was a mother beaver with her nine little kittens. Each kitten represented one of the then nine Canadian Provinces (Newfoundland, our tenth Province, did not join the Dominion until 1949.) The idea of carving a family of beavers was announced in the newspapers in January 1938.[564]

However, by June there was a problem. Some troublesome, nit-picking expert said that a litter of nine kittens was biologically impossible. He said that mother beavers don't have nine kittens; only three or four at most. So, even though a clay maquette of the group had been completed, the whole idea of the beaver family was dropped in favor of scientific accuracy, and the maquette was relegated to a store room in the basement of the Centre Block.[565]

Sometime afterwards, it was decided to carve just the mother beaver, without her little ones. This is Bucky, the beaver we have there now.

THE CHRONOGRAM IN THE CORNERSTONE

This has to be my favorite story. A *chronogram* is a puzzle. The word comes from the Greek *chronos* meaning time and *gramma* meaning letter. The lettering on the cornerstone at the northeast corner of the Peace Tower is a chronogram.

The cornerstone of the Peace Tower, photographed by the author.

This inscription tells us that the cornerstone was laid in the year of victory. Now I want you to pretend that you can't see the 1919 that is carved into the stone below the lettering when you answer this question. Here it is. Thinking back to the history of World War One, what would you say was the year of victory?

Without the 1919 to guide them, most people would answer 1918, but this is not correct. It is true that fighting stopped on November 11, 1918 (the eleventh hour of the eleventh day of the eleventh month), but it was the signing of the Treaty of Versailles the next year, on June 28, 1919 that ended the war and brought about the victory. Therefore, contrary to popular belief the year of victory was 1919, not 1918.

The lettering is a chronogram because the 1919 is there, but it is hidden. Can you see where? And I don't mean at the bottom!

Here is the secret: if you look closely, some of the letters have little square dots carved underneath them. The secret is in those little dots. For example, in the first line which reads "THIS STONE WAS LAID BY" there is a small dot under the I in the word THIS, and three more under the L, I and D in the word LAID. Think of these letters in terms of Roman Numerals,

$$I = 1$$
$$V = 5$$
$$X = 10$$
$$L = 50$$
$$C = 100$$
$$D = 500$$
$$M = 1000$$

These letters add up. 1 + 50 + 1 + 500 = 552.

What, do you think, will be the result if you do this for all five lines and then add up the sums for each line? Right! 1919!

Romans used the letter J instead of I, and V instead of U. Our stone carver took advantage of this and spelled the Latin word OPUS (work) with a V instead of a U. By spelling it this way and placing the last dot under the V he was able to get the mathematics right. Very clever, eh?

But that's not all! After I retired, I consulted back to the department for a while, and I gave my tour to staff at lunch time. It was during one of these tours, when I was asking my group if they would like the solution that they came up with two more!

If you count the number of little dots there are nineteen (this from Steve Wolba) and if you count the number of blocks of information, such as the word THIS, you get another nineteen (this from Shawn Moher). Surely all these hidden nineteens can't be a co-incidence. Our stone carver must have been very clever indeed!

The history of the chronogram is silent up until August 12, 1946 when Tom Reid (this is the same Tom Reid who used to play his bagpipe on Lovers' Walk) stood up in the House of Commons and announced to Mr. Fournier, who was the Minister of Public Works at the time, that they had a big problem.

Excerpt from the House of Commons Debates
August 12, 1946, p. 4672

Mr. Thomas REID (Lib.; New Westminster, B.C.): I should like to draw the attention of the minister to something which I think should be rectified, but first I wish to ask whether any consideration has been given to the completion of the carving of the blank stone in this building. I do not know whether hon. Members have noticed this or not, but as you come in the main entrance from the east you will see a stone bearing these words:

This stone was laid by Edward Prince of Wales, September 1, in this year of victory Finis Coronat OPVS.

Those Latin words mean, "the end crowns the work". Not long ago a visitor asked me what was the year of victory.

Mr. John Ritchie MacNICOL (Cons.; Toronto Northwest, Ont.): 1918

Mr. REID: The hon. Member is wrong, it is 1919. I challenge any hon. Member to go there and try to figure out the little dots under the various letters. I took these down and tried to find out the key, but I could not. Finally I took the matter up with the Clerk of the house and I found that he had the key, I suppose for having been here for such a long time. He told me the first line was 552; the second, 1151; the third, 1; the fourth, 108; and the fifth, 107. If you add them all up together you get 1919. I suppose the architect simply left this riddle to be worked out by future generations. I am going to suggest to the minister that he should have "1919" carved on that stone.

Mr. MacNICOL: Why not 1918?

Mr. REID: The war ended officially in 1919. As I point out, no one would know what it means unless he added up all the dots under the letters and knew what they meant.

Mr. Alphonse FOURNIER (Lib.; Hull, P.Q.; Minister of Public Works): I shall tell my officials to read carefully what the hon. Gentleman has said and, if there is no reason why this work should not be done, then I will give instructions that it be done.

Mr. Fournier consulted his staff, and they must not have seen any difficulty with Mr. Reid's suggestion. By the second week of September, a stone carver could be seen blocking out the figures 1919 and getting ready to begin carving.[566] When you look at the cornerstone today, you will see the 1919 he carved out at the bottom. The font is slightly different from the text above, and the numbers are crisper because it was carved in 1946, whereas the original lettering was carved in 1919.

Personally, I think it is unfortunate the date was added. If I had been working in Public Works in 1946, and Mr. Fournier had asked me what to do, I would have recommended leaving the corner stone alone. The 1919 is already there, I would have said to him. It's hidden in the dots – it's a puzzle, and a darn good one! What's missing is that it has to be explained better.

Unfortunately this was never done very well, even back in 1919 when the corner stone was unveiled.[567] One reporter commented, "Most of us, perhaps, would have to take the dictionary to help us translate them, but nonetheless ILIDDDICLIIIVICIICV means 1919."[568] Actually, it doesn't. Mathematicians will tell you that what this reporter wrote is not even a proper Roman numeral. He obviously did not know the secret, even though he was reporting on it.

THE INSCRIPTIONS ABOVE THE MEMORIAL CHAMBER

Charles Bowman, editor of the *Ottawa Citizen* between 1915 and 1945, was good friends with architect John Pearson who, as we have seen, designed the Peace Tower. "John Pearson cherished the thought that I would someday write the narrative of this national architecture," he wrote in his memoirs. "We would spend time together going over the plans."[569] We might wonder if, back in 1919, Bowman had not also discussed with his friend what the tower might be called, and if Pearson had not said to him, "it will be called Peace Tower" and this is what Bowman printed in his newspaper (see the excerpt from the *Ottawa Citizen* at the start of this chapter). I suspect this is the case, but we don't know.

Anyway, one day Pearson asked Bowman if he would find an inscription to carve into the fireplace in what was then the Press

Gallery's lounge. Bowman found a very nice text from Byron's *Don Juan* –

> FOR WORDS ARE THINGS AND A
> SMALL DROP OF INK,
> FALLING LIKE DEW UPON A
> THOUGHT, PRODUCES
> THAT WHICH MAKES THOUSANDS,
> PERHAPS MILLIONS, THINK. [570]

This verse was so perfect that he asked Bowman if he could find inscriptions to go over the stained glass windows of the Memorial Chamber. At that time (early 1921) these arches, lovely olive-green bands of Wallace Sandstone from the Wallace Quarry in Nova Scotia, were blank.

Bowman tried to find suitable lines from Shakespeare, Milton, Ruskin, and Epictetus but couldn't. Then he went to the Bible and in the Old Testament found these words from Psalm 72, verse 1 to go on the south window:[571]

GIVE THE KING THY JUDGMENTS, O GOD, AND THY RIGHTEOUSNESS UNTO THE KING'S SON.

This verse has a religious meaning, of course, but it can also be understood in terms of modern-day parliament. "The king is synonymous with the sovereign people," Bowman wrote. "As the Canadian people's representatives enter parliament, members and senators, the prayer for judgment and guidance is surely in accord with the will of the nation."[572]

He then asked the Southam brothers, Wilson and Harry Southam, for help. They gave him these words from Proverbs 29, verse 18 for over the west window:

WHERE THERE IS NO VISION THE PEOPLE PERISH.

For over the east window, all three agreed on this line from Psalm 72, verse 8:

HE SHALL HAVE DOMINION FROM SEA TO SEA.

However their choices were causing problems with some of the Hon. Members.

Excerpts from the House of Commons Debates
May 27, 1921, p. 3995 - 3998

Mr. Alexander Kenneth MACLEAN (Lib.; Lunenburg, N.S.):   I could not hear distinctly, but I think my hon. friend from Middlesex (Mr. Ross) asked what letters were being inscribed on the tower. I did not catch the minister's answer.

Mr. Fleming Blanchard McCURDY (Cons.; Shelburne and Queen's, N.S.; Minister of Public Works): Yes, he asked that question and I told him I could not give him the information.

Mr. MACLEAN: Is there any means of finding that out? Because if the inscription should not be placed there this is a good time to stop it.

Mr. McCURDY: Yes, I hope before the committee rises to be able to give my hon. friend the information.

* * *

Mr. McCURDY: In answer to a question asked by hon. member for Middlesex west (Mr. Ross) and the hon. member for Halifax, the words which are being inscribed on the tower, some of which are now visible, are as follows. Facing Wellington Street:

Give the King thy judgments, O God, and thy righteousness unto the King's son.

That is taken from Psalm 72 as, no doubt, my hon. friend will recognize. On one side will appear these words:

Where there is no vision, the people perish.
On the other side:
He shall have Dominion from sea to sea.
Also from Psalm 72.

Mr. MACLEAN: Is that approved by the Parliamentary Committee?

Mr. McCURDY: That detail was not approved by the Parliamentary Committee.

Mr. MACLEAN: *While one is diffident about expressing an opinion in regard to a matter of this kind offhand, it strikes me as being an absurdity; I do not think it will add anything to the beauty of the tower and it is altogether inappropriate.*

* * *

Mr. Charles MARCIL (Lib.; Bonaventure, Que.): *Have these inscriptions been put on the tower?*

Mr. McCURDY: *They are being put on the tower now.*

Mr. MARCIL: *I do not raise any question, but it will be raised some time or another, regarding an inscription in French.*

Mr. McCURDY: *This is a matter that has not come before the Parliamentary Buildings Committee. I knew, half an hour ago, just as much about it as other members of the House. I have made inquiries since, and the intimation which I have is the result of my inquiries. I solicited an expression of opinion from the House and I am getting it now.*

Mr. MARCIL: *The two languages being official, the point will certainly be raised at some time or other, and it might as well be considered now.*

Mr. William Stevens FIELDING (Lib.; Shelburne and Queen's, Nova Scotia): *While I have no objection to the words myself, I can quite understand the point will be raised, and for that reason the hon. gentleman will be well advised not to put any such words on at all. I am not objecting to them; but they would be objected to in other quarters, and we have questions enough of that kind without adding another one.*

Excerpts from the House of Commons Debates
May 28, 1921, p. 4075

Mr. Charles MURPHY (Lib., Russell, Ont.):... *I appeal to the minister, to stop, through his officers, the placing of what, for want of a better term, I may describe as mushy inscriptions on the walls of the rooms within the building, and on the outer wall of the main tower itself. I understand that some reference was made to this subject yesterday afternoon. I did not happen to be in the chamber at the time, but I desire to add my protest and objection to the continuance of that practice, which I understand was not authorized or approved by the remnant of this alleged Joint Committee, and*

I know that my hon. friend the minister (Mr. McCurdy), has no responsibility in the matter at all.

Mr. Louis Audet LAPOINTE (Lib.; St. James, Que.): Does my hon. friend know who is responsible for the inscriptions?

Mr. Samuel William JACOBS (Laurier Lib.; George-Étienne Cartier, Que.): I may inform the hon. gentleman; it is King David, of the Psalms.

Mr. MURPHY: Yes; but my knowledge of history leads me to the belief that the gentleman referred to by my hon. friend from George-Étienne Cartier (Mr. Jacobs), quit house building a great many centuries ago. He has nothing to do with the placing of these inscriptions on the building at the present time. I rather think it is the architect who is responsible, inasmuch as this building throughout exhales an overseas atmosphere, and in no particular breathes the air of Canada. I assume that it is the architect who is responsible for these mushy inscriptions, and I believe from what I have been told of the discussion yesterday, that such, in fact, was stated to this committee. In all seriousness I urge the Minister of Public Works to take such steps as will result in the removal of such of these inscriptions as can be removed without doing actual damage to the structure, and in any event, to prevent any more of them from being put up without competent authority.

That night King confided to his diary:

> *Pearson has made a mistake in inscriptions he is proposing to put on tower of main building – much objection to them by members – McCurdy Minister told me he wd likely ask him to change them. I suggested date of Confed'n or something of the kind instead.[sic]*[573]

On May 31, 1921 the *Ottawa Citizen* published an editorial titled *The Tower of Parliament*. Without mentioning the role he had played (a conflict of interest, perhaps?), Bowman praised architect John Pearson for conceiving "the splendid idea of adorning the tower around the windows of the memorial chamber with words of spiritual aspiration." He called the criticisms in the House of Commons petty and unhappy.[574]

Fortunately, the stone carvers were not stopped and the inscriptions were not changed. Most people think it was architect Pearson's idea to choose these verses from the Bible, but now you know what really happened.

GROTESQUES

About half way up to the flag is a group of beautifully ugly grotesques, three precariously perched on each buttress, each about a metre tall.

In stone carving jargon, *grotesques* are beasts, dragons, sea serpents or monsters that cling to the stonework with their sharp claws. Sometimes they are impish, distorted creatures that would be completely at home in a fantasy landscape like that in J.R.R. Tolkien's *The Lord of the Rings*; and sometimes they are chimeras: part man, part beast.

Several of our grotesques are musicians, it being a musical tower after all. We have one grotesque playing a mandolin, another playing a concertina, and one who is showing them just what he thinks of their playing because his face is scrunched up into a grimace, and his hands are cupped over his ears as if it is all too much to bear. Or perhaps it is because he is so near the bells which, as Pierre Guevremont knows, are incredibly loud from up close.[575]

We also have non-musical grotesques too. For example, there is an Indian complete with bow and arrow; a fellow I like to call *The Thinker* because he is posed with elbow on knee like Rodin's famous statue of the same name; another who has his hand cupped next to his mouth and is yelling something at the tourists on the ground over by the Library, and yet another who has his arms clasped tightly around his knees and is doing nothing but growling fiercely.

GARGOYLES

Gargoyles and grotesques are very similar, but real gargoyles are actually drain spouts. The old builders used gargoyles to throw rainwater that runs down the roof away from the masonry, to keep it from getting as wet. There is usually a channel or trough on the back of the gargoyle that leads to its mouth. When it rains, water runs down the roof, along the gargoyle's back and then spits out its mouth and falls straight down to the ground. You will see in Chapter 31 that constant wetting of masonry from rainwater can be very damaging to the stonework, especially if there are cracks and open mortar joints where water can soak into the stonework.

Our gargoyles are long and thin, projecting out from the Peace Tower. On the northeast corner of the tower, just below the glass-enclosed observation level, we have a winged dragon gargoyle. There is a bird gargoyle on the northwest, an Indian on the southeast and a lion on the southwest corner. All the gargoyles are carved in Stanstead Granite; axe finished, the job specifications tell us, "six to the inch,"[576] meaning six axe hits per inch, which results in a very smooth finish.

However, the gargoyles on the Peace Tower are not real - there are no troughs along their backs and they don't spit out water. They are not drain spouts.[577] They don't have the job of keeping the rainwater from washing down the stone, but they do have a small job holding up lightning rods. Each gargoyle has a short lightning rod mounted on the top of his head to protect the tower from lightning strikes. It can be seen in the photo at the end of this chapter, but it is completely invisible from the ground.

Many people get grotesques and gargoyles confused, including prime ministers. On August 12, 1921 the new Governor General Lord Byng and Lady Byng were visiting Parliament Hill for the first time. The day was fair and bright, and a large crowd had gathered to see the couple arrive. The workmen on the Peace Tower, which was still under construction at the time, had the best view of all. "The workmen on the tower sat on the edge looking down on the crowd," King wrote in his diary that night, "they were like so many of John Pearson's Gargoiles [*sic*]."[578] Of course it was a slip of the tongue. The Prime Minister meant to say Grotesques, not Gargoiles.

The Jail Cell

We learn from the *New York Times*[579] that there used to be a jail cell high up in the Peace Tower for members of the Senate and the House of Commons who defied parliamentary authority. Its furnishings were sparse; just one or two chairs and a couch. There were no bars on the windows, but then who would be crazy enough to climb down the outside of the tower?

The jail in the Peace Tower no longer exists. We know from the article that it wasn't used up until 1931, and may never have been used at all. However, the article goes on to tell us that in the 1880's one Hon. Member was incarcerated in a similar cell in the clock tower of the original Parliament Building. Unfortunately, we don't know what he did or even what his name was because the records were all destroyed when the building burned down the night of February 3, 1916.

Suicides

Today tourists take the elevator up to the observation level and look out at the surrounding countryside through strong Plexiglas windows. However, the tower wasn't always enclosed. Before 1970, the observation level was completely open to the outside. A balcony ran around the four sides of the tower and people stood outside on this balcony, looking out through a high parapet of stone and wrought iron.[580] I remember standing outside on this balcony with my mother as a young boy. We were right outside - if it had been raining we would have gotten wet.

Tragically, on April 1, 1970 Ronald Heatley, 21, climbed through the iron cage work and jumped 65 metres to his death. His girlfriend, 17-year-old Joyce Dunn said that they had been smoking hashish earlier that day in her apartment and that he had smoked again just before his leap. Before jumping, he handed her his pipe and said, "hold this for me."[581]

At the inquest, Ms. Dunn said they went to the cliff at the back first and talked about jumping, then went up the tower. They looked out the front of the tower, then the back, and then went back to the front where Mr. Heatly climbed through. She said he did not think he would hit the ground when he jumped. To this Crown Attorney Gordon Thompson asked, "Where did he think he was going? Was he going to fly, he must have thought this?" Miss Dunn said "He wasn't flying, he was going to another (inaudible)." The jury members were asked to decide whether it was a suicide, or not, but they said they were unable to reach a decision.[582]

After the incident workers attached wire mesh over the cagework to ensure no one else would jump, but a few months later on July 28 Himani Ghosh, 36, stood on a small stool, climbed through a hole in the east side of the tower and jumped. She was distraught because, although she had received a good education (a Bachelor of Science degree and a librarianship diploma from the University of Calcutta), she was unable to find a good job here. Her shoes and purse were found neatly placed on the floor by the stool.[583]

At the inquiry,[584] it was discovered that she had visited the tower three times before her fatal leap. On July 17th guard J. M. Derochers found her sitting on the west side wall with her head through the bars. She said she was very tired. On July 22, after being up in the tower for three-and-a-half-hours, she tried to climb through the bars feet first but was pulled back by guard Paul Desbiens. She said she wanted to climb up to one of the small towers that jut out above the clock so that she could get closer to God and pray. On July 24, she asked guard P. R. Prudhomme for a chair. After calling his sergeant, he told her the tower was closing. It was re-opened after she left.

Constable Albert Pieters said the largest opening in the east bars was only 170 mm wide by 325 mm high. Members of the jury were puzzled that anyone could fit through such a small opening. However, Detective John Aldrich said she pulled out a grounding cable and pulled on this to help her. He said the bars could flex slightly, and this helped her too.

The IIII on the Peace Tower clock. This unusual view of the clock was photographed from the roof of the Centre Block. The copper-clad structure in the foreground is the machine room roof for one of the elevators. Photographed by the author.

This is the south façade of the Peace Tower where the inscription over the stained glass window of the Memorial Chamber reads:

GIVE THE KING THY JUDGMENTS, O GOD, AND THY RIGHTEOUSNESS UNTO THE KING'S SON

It is from Psalm 72, verse 1 in the Old Testament. Photographed by the author.

220   *The Other Side of the Hill*

These grotesques are about two-thirds of the way up the east side of the tower. Keeping them company are some ducks, owls wearing reading glasses, and a World War One soldier. Photograph by the author.

Close-up of 'The Thinker' grotesque before it was conserved. This photograph was taken by my architect from inside the scaffold when we were conserving the Peace Tower from 1994-96. You can see places in the chest, but especially in his left thigh, where large amounts of stone have been damaged. The grotesques are carved in very soft sandstone from the Ohio Quarry. Sandstone is easy to carve, but it is also easily damaged by salt crystallization (see Chapter 31 for a description of how this damage occurs). Photograph reproduced by permission of Spencer R. Higgins Architect Inc.

Close-up of the concertina playing grotesque. Photograph by the author.

The mandolin player and over his left shoulder, the grotesque shouting to the tourists. Photograph by the author.

Peace Tower 223

Close-up of the lion gargoyle at the southwest corner. This photograph was taken by my architect from inside the scaffold when the Peace Tower was being conserved from 1994 to 1996. The gargoyles are made of granite, which is sometimes called the rock of ages because it lasts so long. They were in great shape and required very little work compared to the grotesques, which are in sandstone. The only problem this fellow had was a broken finger. Photograph reproduced by permission of Spencer R. Higgins Architect Inc.

I have always called her Bucky — for obvious reasons. When we were conserving the Peace Tower from 1994-1996, we found that the top part of her head had split off along a natural fault in the stone. To repair it we drilled a hole up into the broken piece and down into her head to fit a stainless steel dowel and then epoxy-glued the broken piece back into place. I'm pleased to report the operation was a complete success, leaving only a small scar that, while you can easily see it in the photograph, is completely invisible from the ground. Photographed by the author.

Chapter 21: The Inauguration of the Carillon (It was not William Lyon Mackenzie King's Best Day.)

Interwoven in a personal way was a thread of disorder and confusion not so perceptible to others, but sufficient to mar events considerably for myself.[585]

William Lyon Mackenzie King's diary entry for July 1, 1927

The carillon in the Peace Tower was played for the very first time on July 1, 1927, the Diamond Jubilee of Confederation.[586] Prime Minister King's day didn't start off very well. He didn't get a good sleep because it was so hot. That morning when he was on the toilet, the water overflowed. For a moment he thought the bathroom was going to be flooded and that the ceiling below would be ruined.

To make things worse, his flag was late being put up, and the new butler got his foot caught in the elevator. This caused a fuse to burn out with lots of smoke and, of course, July 1 was a holiday so no repair men were available. Finally, the General Electric man arrived at his house and took off the paneled door of the elevator. After being trapped for half an hour, the butler was released.[587]

At the ceremony, Viscount Willingdon, the Governor-General, arrived late and insisted on reviewing the guard. This made King late in beginning his speech. Fortunately, he had a printed copy in his pocket. He decided to read it while keeping an eye on his watch, but unfortunately his watch was faster than the tower clock. He cut out a part of his speech, only to finish nearly five minutes before the tower clock struck twelve. As a result, he had to fill in the time.[588]

A few seconds before noon, Viscount Willingdon pressed an electric button that had been given to him by the Minister of Public Works. This caused a number of things to happen.[589]

First there was a fanfare of twelve trumpets, the *Boom!* of the noon day gun, and then the carrilloneur, Mr. Percival Price, began to play; first *O Canada!*, then the *Maple Leaf* and after that *God save the King*.

To King's dismay, an airplane circled around the tower making a terrible noise, spoiling his first impression of the carillon. He thought *O Canada!* was very poorly played and was a little disappointed with the carillon generally. However, he thought it improved once the plane had left and quiet was restored.[590]

King need not have felt so bad. Everybody loved the music. The *Globe* reported: "A flood of carillon music of inexpressible beauty filled the air as, prefaced by a short scale, the strains of *O Canada!* poured from the throats of the whole bell family."[591]

In the crowd was Carol Fuller, a young woman of twenty-one. Her father was Thomas W. Fuller, Canada's Chief Architect between 1927 and 1936 and the son of Thomas Fuller, the architect who designed the original Parliament Building. It was he who hired the carillonneur, Percival Price. Carol's mother had asked Mr. Price if his first song – after *God save the King*, of course - could be *The Bells of St. Mary's*, and it was.[592] *Home Sweet Home*, *The Maple Leaf Forever* and other popular pieces followed. At 4:15 in the afternoon, following speeches, a second carillon performance was given.[593]

Mackenzie King wrote in his diary: "Ceremonies on the whole passed off very well – the day was beautiful, the turnout of people the largest ever on Parliament Hill, the decorations quite enough, the programs carried thro' without perceptible delays, the broadcasting a very great success. It will go down in history as a memorable occasion."

The broadcasting that Mackenzie King referred to was a radio broadcast of the speeches and carillon music all across Canada. In 1927 radio was in its infancy, and this was the very first time such a broadcast had ever been attempted. Now, can you guess what Canadian company made the broadcast? No, it wasn't the Canadian Broadcasting Corporation – its predecessor, the Canadian Radio Broadcasting Commission, wasn't created until 1932. It was the CNR, the Canadian National Railway, and the radio signal was broadcast across Canada on its telegraph wires.

Two days later, King heard the carillon again when funeral services were held on Parliament Hill for Lieutenant Johnson, an American flier who was killed while escorting Col. Charles A. Lindbergh to Ottawa to participate in the festivities.[594] "I ordered the flag on the main tower lowered during the service," King wrote in his diary, "and when the service itself commenced, the carillon began to play Chopin's funeral march. It was the first time the carillon had really been heard to advantage, in the silence of a Sunday afternoon. The music was like the skies opening and angels' harps sounding forth.- [*sic*] At moments the music seemed to come like sheets of flame out of the tower. It was the finest thing I have ever heard, and, it was the finest music from the finest carillon in the world."[595]

The large wooden keyboard (or 'clavier') is in a small room about two-thirds of the way up to the clock. It is played by striking small wooden handles, spaced about 50 mm apart, with the bottom of a closed fist. The feet also come into play on pedals. A system of wires, springs and pulleys transmits the movement of the key to the clapper, sounding the note. Counter weights are used to lighten the touch of the heavy bells and springs increase the tension with the lighter ones, evening out the touch across the whole keyboard, although that for the larger, deeper-toned bells is still somewhat heavier.[596]

I was project manager for the conservation of the Peace Tower between 1994 and 1996. We stopped the clock and the bells, and covered up the tower with scaffolding and tarpaulins for two years while skilled masons worked hard on the crumbling stonework. Our general contractor was Fuller Construction of Ottawa, and my day-to-day contact was Bill Fuller, great grandson of Thomas Fuller the architect. The scaffolding was subcontracted to another Fuller company run by Bill's brother Simon.

The Peace Tower was re-opened on December 2, 1996.[597] We had stopped the clock at noon, and Public Works Minister Diane Marleau restarted it at noon exactly two years later at a small ceremony on the central walkway.

The time to noon was counted down by the crowd, and exactly at noon the Minister restarted the clock by pressing a small electric button - or so it seemed. But the button was a fake. It was not connected to anything except a small green light on her podium that shone so it would seem like the button was doing something.

What actually happened was that one of our staff was in the crowd with a walky-talky - this was before cell-phones - and about ten seconds before the Minister pressed the button he radioed a worker in the tower who started the clock and chimes manually. It takes about ten seconds to get everything going. A push button couldn't really be used to start everything up because the technology of the clock and chime mechanisms are quite old, from 1927. However, it looked as if the Minister started it up and when the big bell struck the first of its twelve deep bongs the crowd broke out in applause, and everyone cheered!

Bill and Simon's Aunt Carol, now 90, was the guest of honour. As you know, her father hired the first Dominion Carillonneur, Percival Price, and she was there when her mother asked Mr. Price if the first song he played at the inauguration on July 1, 1927 could be *The Bells of St. Mary's*. Mr.Price played it then, and her request was the first song played by Gordon Slater at our ceremony too.

What did she think of the fine work done by her nephews on the Peace Tower? "It looks wonderful," she said, "I'm so glad it was repaired." [598]

The Inauguration of the Carillon (It was not...) 229

"Scene on Parliament Hill. Ottawa Garrison in position in front of Main Building for the Celebration of the Confederation Jubilee." July 1, 1927. Credit: William Lyon Mackenzie King / Library and Archives Canada / C-018068 / Acc. No. 1964-087 NPC.

Chapter 22: Thomas Ritchie Donates a Sundial

Let others tell of storms and showers. I'll only count your sunny hours.*

The Duke of Devonshire, May 19, 1921

**An inscription on a sundial belonging to the Queen Mother. At the unveiling of the Parliament Hill sundial on May 19 the Duke of Devonshire suggested it might be an appropriate motto for the sundial on Parliament Hill too.*[599]

The unveiling ceremony was supposed to take place at 2:30 p.m. on May 19, 1921. However, the Governor General, His Excellency the Duke of Devonshire, was delayed having lunch at the Chateau Laurier.

When he arrived on Parliament Hill, it was 3:10 p.m., but he had thought of a very clever way of apologizing to the crowd.

When he pulled off the Union Jack that was draped over the sundial, he pointed at the sundial's shadow and said with a wink and a smile that he wasn't really late at all; in fact, he was twenty minutes early! It was only ten past two by the sundial - standard time, that is.[600]

The sundial was donated by Thomas Ritchie who, as we saw earlier, was born on Barrack Hill in 1838. The inscription on the stone base says "on this spot a sundial was erected by the Royal Sappers and Miners under Lt.-Col. John By, R.E., about 1826-27, and restored in 1919 by the Historic Landmarks Association of Canada." This gives the impression that our sundial is the original one from Barrack Hill days, and that it was restored before being installed back on Parliament Hill. According to the newspaper coverage from 1921,[601] this is not correct. It is a new one from Messrs. Harrison and Company of Montreal, and was made in England. We don't know what happened to the original sundial.

The position of the dial was fixed by Thomas Ritchie, William H. Cluff, and other former residents of Bytown. It is very close to, if not exactly, where the original sundial was.[602]

Several hundred people attended the ceremony. In his speech, the Governor General mentioned that the dial was intended to replace the original one fixed there many years ago, recalled the distinguished service of Colonel By and asked his audience to try and imagine how different Parliament Hill must have been when his sundial stood on this same spot. His Excellency pictured the stone barracks, the series of low wooden buildings, the stockade made out of cedar posts sharpened at their ends, and the sentry who passed back and forth with his Brown Bess rifle slung over his shoulder at a time when Ottawa was just a clearing in the forest. The hill has witnessed many historic scenes since.

Several months after the ceremony, on December 7 1921, Thomas Ritchie passed away.[603]

CHAPTER 23: RATS AND ROACHES AND BATS, OH MY!

*little one said freddy im not
feeling well myself somebody poisoned some
cheese for me im as full of
death as a drug store ....*[604]

*freddy the rat**

*Stories about Freddy the rat, Archie the cockroach, Mehitabel the cat, Pete the Pup and other odd characters were written by newspaper man and humorist Don Marquis. They appeared first in a daily column called The Sun Dial in the Evening Sun (New York). The stories were very popular, and were carried in other newspapers across the United States and Canada, and later were collected into several books. All of the stories were in the odd typing style shown in the quotation at the top (no capitals, no punctuation).

RATS

1946 was a very bad year for rats. Old-timers couldn't remember there ever being so many. Rat expert Roy L. Twinn, in a characteristic bit of understatement, said the situation was "not good at all."[605] Mr. Twinn said the rats came up from the canal and spread out through the buildings along Elgin Street and Sparks Street.

It is well known that rats usually spread from cellar to cellar, but that year was so bad they actually jumped from roof to roof. Admittedly, the buildings along Sparks Street butt right up to each other, but how did they get across Wellington Street without being run over by all the cars and busses? The answer is simple. The Parliament Buildings are heated by high pressure steam pipes in an underground tunnel that starts off at the Cliff Street plant just west of the Supreme Court Building and goes over to Parliament Hill. From there it crosses underneath Wellington Street and carries on to the National Arts Centre and other government buildings. Apparently the rats went underground, taking this tunnel under Wellington Street to the Hill. The East Block was the first of the Parliament Buildings they came across, and so naturally most ended up there.

Here is a bit of rat nomenclature before we continue: male rats are called *bucks*; females are called *does*; baby rats without hair and whose eyes are not yet opened are called *pinkeys* and after that *pups* or *kittens*. A family of rats is called a *mischief*.

The largest mischief in the East Block was led by an old buck called Freddy, named after *Freddy the Rat* in the newspapers. Those in the know, like security guards and char ladies, said Freddy was "as big as a cat and three times as mean." His fur was greasy, but then all male rats have greasy fur unless they are bathed regularly or are neutered, and Freddy wasn't either of these. He and his mischief lived in the East Block behind the walls of room 240, which at that time was also the lunch room and private office of William Lyon Mackenzie King.[606]

In the old days, cats lived in the basements of the Parliament Buildings, and they took care of mice and rats, but in 1924 they were evicted. Without the cats, Hill workers tried setting traps. Once they even tried setting out poisoned cheese, but that was a big mistake. There were so many rats dying behind the walls that they couldn't rip out the baseboards fast enough. If you have ever smelled a rotting rat, you know how bad it must have been. One worker said "they had six carpenters doing nothing but ripping the building apart to find the bodies and they couldn't keep up with the death rate then."[607]

Excerpt from the House of Commons Debates
July 18, 1955, p. 6351

MR. *Harold Edward WINCH (C.C.F.; Vancouver East, B.C.): Before this house met in the first week of January, I understand that somebody exiled a number of cats from the House of Commons.*

May I suggest that you either bring back those cats or bring exterminators into the House of Commons between sessions and get rid of the mice on the fifth and sixth floors. We did not have them last session. I am amazed that the wives of M.P.'s have not raised particular hell. We now have the problem of mice in room 601. On the sixth floor you can see them going across the floor. There are not only mice in the House of Commons. There are cockroaches in the cafeteria and on the third, fifth and sixth floors of the House of Commons. As I say, it is only a small matter, but it means a great deal.

I suggest that you review the exile of the cats and bring them back or bring in exterminators – not while we are here, but in between sessions – and get rid of the cockroaches and the mice that are invading the building. It is not good advertising, and it is not even nice for the members of the House of Commons to see a mouse all of a sudden dashing across the marble corridors. Mice can do a great deal of damage in a building."

Fortunately the problem of *Mus Rattis* lasted only two years, and by 1948, for some unknown reason, the numbers were back down to normal. A spokesman for the health department said in May of that year that so far there were only ten complaints about rats, these being mainly from restaurants and private dwellings.[608]

... AND ROACHES

The Centre Block had rats, but the main problem there has always been cockroaches, maybe because of the food preparation in the cafeteria and dining room. In 1936, for reasons that are not completely understood, the cockroaches were not the normal kind, but albinos.[609] By 1939 the number of cockroaches had hit an all-time high, and in 1946 (the year Freddy was causing all that grief in the East Block) the situation was still pretty bad.[610] In 1955 and again in 1960, Mr. Winch, M.P. complained about the problem of bugs in the Parliament Buildings.

Excerpt from the House of Commons Debates
July 18, 1955, p. 6352

MR. Harold Edward WINCH (C.C.F.; Vancouver East, B.C.): My third point was that I hoped in between sessions exterminators would be brought in to get rid of the bugs which are in the House of Commons. As I was leaving the chamber at six o'clock I heard someone say there were no bugs in the House of Commons. Will a page boy come over here please? I spent exactly two minutes in one room catching these. Will you please take this envelope to the Minister of Public Works, to show him that there are bugs in the House of Commons.

MR. Robert Henry WINTERS (Lib.; Queens--Lunenburg, N.S; Minister of Public Works): On a point of order, Mr. Chairman, the Minister of Public Works is not responsible for bugs and mice in the House of Commons.

MR. WINCH: But he is responsible for getting rid of them.

MR. WINTERS: No, that is a matter of housekeeping; that is under the Sergeant-at-Arms.

MR. WINCH: Then call your wife; I imagine she is a good housekeeper. Just because someone said I could not find them, I wanted to show you what I could find in two minutes.

MR. WINTERS: Bring them to the attention of Mr. Speaker.

Excerpt from the House of Commons Debates
July 20, 1960, p. 6617-6618

MR. WINCH: What I have to raise at this moment is most picayune in comparison with that raised by the previous hon. member. If the minister is going to answer all questions at once I should like to draw a matter to his attention. I understand he is in charge of the centre block which houses the House of Commons and the Senate. It is my understanding that this building comes under the Department of Public Works. Although this matter is picayune, I want to raise it because it is the only chance I shall have. In *what I have to say I have no reference whatsoever to any member of this house or any party in the house.*

What I suggest to the minister is that he bring in somebody to do something about the advance of earwigs and cockroaches in this building. I raised this matter some five years ago, if I remember correctly, and about two days later a fumigation took place. That is the reason I said I am not referring either to members or to parties; but I do suggest to the Minister of Public Works, under whom this building comes, that there is need for fumigation of certain areas of the centre block because of the encroachment of earwigs and cockroaches. Conditions have reached such a state that if fumigation does not take place fairly soon you will not need a fumigator, you will need a big game hunter.

... AND BATS, OH MY!

1946 was also reported to be a bad year for bats in the Parliament Buildings,[611] and I was told that they were also bad in the 1950's, particularly in the southwest tower of the East Block, the one with the face in it.[612] In 1967, a bat caused havoc by circling the chandeliers in the Confederation Room of the West Block during a reception for the first performance of the National Capital Commission's popular Sound and Light show.[613]

CHAPTER 24: DEMOLITION OF THE LIBRARY

Many consider that the present library with its flying buttresses is a work of Gothic Architecture that should be preserved. However, it must be kept in mind that the retention of even a piece of work of this type, which has now reached a point that more than ordinary repairs will have to be made, should be viewed in the light of its usefulness towards the requirements of today.... Before making any recommendation, I feel we should give some study to a suggestion of removing the present building.[614]

Emmet Murphy, August 5, 1952

The source for this story is a book by Gordon Robertson titled *Memoirs of a Very Civil Servant*.[615] It was Mr. Robertson, along with Prime Minister Louis St.-Laurent, who saved the Library from demolition.

Early on the morning of August 4, 1952, a fire broke out high up in the roof of the library.[616] It was caused by an electrical failure, but it wasn't the fire that did the most damage to the building; it was the streams of water from the firemen's hoses to put out the blaze. At the time, Mr. Robertson was a senior advisor to Prime Minister St. Laurent.

On August 14, Emmet Murphy, Deputy Minister of Public Works, reported to the Cabinet on the damage and gave them options for repair. The Prime Minister was away at the time, and C.D. Howe was acting.

Murphy said there were two choices. The first was a reconstruction of the library for about $950,000; and the second, for which Murphy argued, was to demolish the library and construct a new building costing $6,000,000, a combined Parliamentary and National Library. At this time, a project to construct the National Library (which is now at 395 Wellington

Street) was in the planning stage, but a site had not been chosen, so the timing was good.

Cabinet decided to defer making a decision until the Prime Minister returned, but agreed with Murphy that the old building should go.[617] Mr. Robertson was asked to brief the Prime Minister on his return.

Howe thought the idea of a combined library would be "practical and efficient," but Robertson was becoming very nervous about the amount of support this bad idea seemed to be getting.

After first discussing it with the Prime Minister, he wrote in a follow-up memorandum:

> *Most other countries with more historic buildings and less wealth than Canada think it wise to spend large sums in the preservation of their historic structures, and I think that a great many people would regard it as something approaching a national scandal if we were to destroy the Parliamentary Library.*

On October 9, Cabinet met again but this time it was to tell Murphy that the library would be rehabilitated, not destroyed. Plans were to be developed that would see the conservation of the exterior façade. The Prime Minister directed Robertson to follow the progress of the work.

The Cabinet decision only dealt with saving the exterior, and Robertson soon learned that the woodwork inside was considered a fire hazard and was going to be ripped out. He argued it should be fireproofed using a chemical treatment and restored. The Prime Minister agreed.

A special committee was formed (the Prime Minister himself took the unusual step of sitting on this committee), and on February 18, 1953 Murphy presented to Cabinet the special committee's recommendations. These were to preserve the library, inside and out, including the woodwork.

In June 1953, Robertson learned that, despite the Cabinet decision, "they were not going to be able to save the paneling inside the library." Murphy told him he didn't realize it was a matter of any importance, but he said he would not let the contractor start ripping out the paneling right away, as they were about to do. However, he needed direction right away as it would affect the progress of the work.

Robertson had the matter raised to the Prime Minister, who at this time was in London. By now, the Prime Minister was completely convinced that it must be a full conservation, inside and out. This decision was passed back to Murphy, and Robertson continued to follow the work. It is thanks to this very civil servant and Prime Minister Louis St. Laurent that we have the Library of Parliament today.

THE MISSING PLAQUE THAT ALMOST BECAME SOMEONE'S COFFEE TABLE [618]

In 1860, when they were building the original Parliament Buildings, workers placed a six-pointed bronze star in the mortar on top of the cornerstone, sandwiching it between the cornerstone and the stone above. We don't know why they did this. It may have been hidden there as a kind of time capsule.[619]

After the building burned down in 1916, somebody found it in the ashes and put it for safekeeping in the library, which was the only part of the old Parliament Building left standing. Who this person was, where in the Library he put it, and why everybody forgot about it, is a complete mystery. Wherever it was, there it stayed for another 36 years.

After the library fire in 1952, a workman who was cleaning up found it buried in the mess on the ground and asked his foreman if he could have it. His boss told him he could and he brought it home. He didn't have a use for it right away so he leaned it up against the wall in his garage where it stayed for the next 18 years.

In 1970, the workman decided to clean up his garage. While he was doing this, he spotted the plaque and decided to mount it into the top of a coffee table he was building. As he was washing and scrubbing off the dirt he could see that there were names and words on it that appeared to be Latin.

Friends told him the plaque might be worth money so the workman showed it to experts at the Public Archives, the National Capital Commission, the Library of Parliament and Carleton University and asked if it was important. To his surprise, it was authenticated as the missing plaque from the cornerstone of the old Parliament Building.

A professor at Carleton University said the text was a very bad 'dog-Latin' which translated as: "He has thought it proper to set down that it is fortunate and happy to have built the building which will serve for the holding of the provincial assembly."[620]

Now that the government knew where the missing plaque was, they wanted it back. The National Capital Commission gave the workman $850 for it, which the Justice Department had said was a fair and reasonable price. The government was careful to say they weren't 'buying' it from him; they said it was theirs and the money was a 'reward' for finding it.

The NCC quietly held onto it for the next three years when somehow it became known that they had it. Then everyone wanted it. The Public Archives thought they should have it, and the National Museum and the Library of Parliament wanted it too. The Library said that since "their building is the only survivor of the original fire in 1916; the plaque belongs with the others above the Library door."

In the end, the Library won out. The plaque was restored, but it wasn't hung above the doorway. It was mounted on the wall near the entrance to the Library, and was unveiled by the Queen on August 1, 1973.

CHAPTER 25: DEMOLITION OF THE WEST BLOCK

MR.George Clyde NOWLAN (Prog. Cons.; Digby--Annapolis--Kings, N.S.): A hundred years from now, if this nation survives and develops in the way we are trying to develop it, people will be coming to Ottawa and looking around and asking, where is the west block? The answer will be that it was destroyed while Bob Winters was Minister of Public Works. If that happens it will not add greatly to his reputation. I say that as a friend. I ask him to study this very carefully and to weigh the aesthetic values against dollars and cents, if that is possible in this day and age. If he does that I am quite certain he will come to the decision that the west block should be preserved. If so, Canada will be the better because of it....

Excerpt from the House of Commons Debates, July 18, 1955 p. 6355-6356

When Robert Winters became Minister of Public Works on September 17, 1953, he inherited two big problems. The first problem was that Parliamentarians needed more space.

This problem had been around for a while. In 1949, MP's were housed in offices in all parts of the Centre Block, from the basement to the top storey, two to a room in most cases. Mr. Alphonse Fournier (Lib.; Hull, P.Q.; Minister of Public Works at the time) said when he first came here in 1930 that it was worse because there were three in a room. "I hope that eventually it will be possible for every Member of Parliament to have an office of his own," he added.[621]

Unlike today, in 1949 members' offices were only in the Centre Block. One of the suggestions Mr. Fournier had been looking at was to move some into either the East Block or the West Block. The East Block, which was then undergoing repairs, was not a good candidate as it was then being used for the Prime Minister's offices, the Privy Council Offices and the External Affairs Department. The Finance Department, which had been in the building for years, had been moved out to the Confederation Building to make more space.[622]

Another suggestion was the possibility of providing additional space in the Centre Block by erecting an addition in the central courtyard of the building.[623] (This idea was incorrectly reported[624,625] in the newspapers as building eighty rooms on two new floors.)

Yet another idea considered was to add wings on each side of the Library. Although this would provide 72 more rooms, Chief Architect E.A. Gardner didn't recommend it. "They will not add anything to the beauty of the Parliament Hill area," he said.[626]

Still another idea was to dig out a big hole behind the Library and build a building inside it, with windows poking out of the cliff. The hole would be covered up, putting back statues, roads, sidewalks and lawn on top. However, Gardner said he was "of the definite opinion that the appearance of the offices in the cliff face would be a decided detriment to the Parliament Hill area."[627]

The second problem facing Mr. Winters was the West Block. The heating and electrical services were old, requiring constant repair, and the elevators were always breaking down. In winter, the offices were cold and drafty, and staff had to wear heavy sweaters. They were miserably cold, complaining constantly.

The West Block was also unsafe in the event of a fire because it didn't even begin to meet the requirements of the fire code. Also, although the mortar joints had been recently repointed, workers had discovered huge voids in the walls that needed to be grouted.[628]

It soon became obvious that there was an opportunity to solve both problems by demolishing the West Block and replacing it with a bigger, better, brand new building.

The Minister was briefed on demolition of the West Block on February 2, 1954.[629] On April 10, he floated a trial balloon and told the newspapers they were considering rebuilding the old West Block.[630] Surprisingly, this didn't get a reaction. They then began a detailed study of what to do, keeping in mind the urgent need for more accommodation. This was completed in March 1955.[631] There were three options:

The first was to rehabilitate the West Block. This would solve the health and safety problems, but the number of offices would actually be reduced. There were 7,700 square metres of office space in the West Block, but in the rehabilitated building it would be reduced to 7,100 square metres because some of the floor space would need to be used for new stairs, washrooms and elevators. The life of the rehabilitated building was estimated at an additional 50 years. It would provide 273 offices at a cost of $2,000,000, which is $146 per office per year.

The second option was to rehabilitate the West Block and add a new wing at the northeast corner. The life of the building would still only be 50 years because of the old part, but it would provide 419 offices at a total cost of $3,550,000. This is a cost of $169 per office per year.

The third option was to demolish the West Block and build a new building. Since it was new construction, its lifetime was estimated at 100 years. It would provide 692 offices, cost $6,400,000, and with a cost per office per year of only $93 it was the cheapest of the three options. Committee rooms would be included and, if possible, the Mackenzie tower would be retained as a historical link with the past. Those currently in the West Block would be moved into rented offices until the work was complete.

The Accommodation Committee was briefed and agreed unanimously with the third option. On May 6, 1955 Minister Winters briefed the Cabinet and was authorized to make preliminary plans for the new building and for leasing temporary office space. The Minister was told that no announcement was to be made until preliminary plans had been drawn, and a sketch of the new building was ready for publication.[632]

However, the word was already out. Remember the trial balloon? The Ottawa Council of Women, representing some 100 women's organizations, led the charge,[633] followed in Parliament by the opposition party.

Excerpt from the House of Commons Debates,
July 18, 1955, p. 6354-6356

MR. George Clyde NOWLAN (Prog. Cons.; Digby--Annapolis--Kings, N.S.): The minister told us this afternoon that no decision has been made, as I understood him, with respect to the west block. He said he had asked for plans to be prepared and that there might be renovation, or that there might be reconstruction, or that there might be construction of a new building.

I noticed in one of the newspapers – I believe it was in the Montreal Gazette – that someone in his department said that so far there had been only one protest received respecting the demolition of the west block. If only one protest has been received up to now, I would like to increase the protests by 100 per cent by registering a second one....

Excerpt from the House of Commons Debates,
July 18, 1955, p. 6357-6359

MR. John Horace DICKEY (Lib.; Halifax, Nova Scotia): ...I think both this committee and the country must recognize that we are faced with a practical problem and it is the Minister of Public Works who has the responsibility of solving that problem....

Excerpt from the House of Commons Debates,
July 18, 1955, p. 6360

MR. Henry Alfred HOSKING (Lib.; Wellington South, Ontario):
...I think it would be a shame if we did anything to destroy the west block. It is a beautiful building. It is historic. It has tradition. If the members of the cabinet will just remember that no visitor who went through this building was not more thrilled by the old library that was not destroyed than by the new part of this building, they will not allow the west block to be altered....

Excerpt from the House of Commons Debates,
July 18, 1955, p. 6365-6366

MR. *George Alexander DREW (Prog. Cons.; Carleton, Ont.):*
There is need for modern accommodation here and I think we should have much more modern accommodation. Land is becoming increasingly expensive in Ottawa, but it is still relatively cheap as compared with land in the heart of London. Nevertheless they have preserved the buildings, some of them going back 600, 700 and 800 years. They have done this not simply as a reminder of the past but because they are part of the continuing love of British tradition. We in Canada should retain the opportunities we have to preserve the Canadian tradition of parliament. This is one unique opportunity. In many ways it is of more value from the historical point of view than this building itself....

Mr. *Herbert Wilfred HERRIDGE (Independent C.C.F; Kootenay West, B.C.):* Mr. Chairman, I wish to say that I support heartily the words of the Leader of the Opposition. I am sure if the people of Canada had an opportunity to express their opinions on this question 95 percent of them would say that we should retain this historic monument to Canadian tradition and Canadian history.

Hon. *George James McILRAITH (Lib.; Ottawa West, Ont.):* Mr. Chairman, I am afraid the second last speech was reactionarism rampant. The facts with respect to this building are that it has many architectural defects of a rather glaring nature. Notwithstanding what has been said by the hon. member for Digby-Annapolis-Kings, parts of it represent architectural garbage at its worst.... There is only a small part of the building that has historical significance. I do not want to get diverted, but there was the prime minister's office, a staircase, and so on. That should be preserved. But having done that, to go on to say that you must not modernize the building, that you must not make any changes, does not follow at all....

* * *

Mr. *McILRAITH: Surely we can make the proper decisions this time. I am perfectly well aware that a ramp has been organized for secondary purposes to prevent this step. I think those with local associations are familiar enough with that ramp and its method of working to consider the subject on its merits without being led into believing either that that represents the views of the members of the associations or that the subject matter was con-*

sidered by the members of these associations. This is a very important matter and it should be dealt with on its own merits, without relation to these other appeals to passion.

Mr. DREW: Mr. Chairman, if there had been any doubt about the necessity for emphasizing to the minister certain points in connection with this matter, that doubt would have been removed by the truly remarkable speech which has just been made. I doubt if there has been a more remarkable speech made in this house. It has been completely remarkable in the fact that it discloses a state of mind which calls for very careful emphasis upon the point we are trying to put forward. The member talks about a ramp. The desire to preserve the historic entities that are associated with the development of this country cannot be called a ramp and should not be so described. I fail to understand why such a term should be used.

Mr. McILRAITH: I was referring to the correspondence you received on the subject.

It is interesting to wonder what Mr. McIlraith was referring to when he spoke about local associations and correspondence that Mr. Drew had received. However, a search of the George Alexander Drew fonds[634] for a letter in the weeks before July 18th, 1955 concerning the demolition of the West Block did not reveal such a letter.

On November 24, 1955, Public Works announced the appointment of the architectural firm of Mathers & Haldenby from Toronto to find needed additional office space without upsetting the architectural balance on the hill.[635] Newspapers reported that the new West Block would probably contain a parliamentary swimming pool,[636] a lounge, and other recreational facilities.

The West Block was seen as the first project in a long-term plan for the hill. "The whole question of the rejuvenation of Parliament Hill is a long-term project with the rebuilding of the West Block as the first and major stage in its realization," a departmental spokesman said.[637]

There were those who agreed. Some architects called the West Block a monstrosity,[638] and Jacques Gréber, the famous French town planner responsible for planning the National Capital (the *Gréber Plan*, 1950), was in favor of a new building.[639]

Those who were in favour of tearing down the old building were careful to emphasize how nicely the new building would blend in. "The building will be designed to fit in with the architecture of the Centre Block and the same type of stone will be used," they said. "Thus, if at any time it is decided to demolish the East Block, a new building on that site following the architecture of the Centre Block and the proposed new West Block would result in three buildings fitting into a perfect architectural whole."[640]

However, most people liked the old building and didn't want to see it gone. The Parliament Buildings "seem quaintly beautiful to most Canadians," wrote the Editor of the *Ottawa Citizen*.[641] "Tearing down is easy," said the *Montreal Gazette*.[642]

Mathers & Haldenby made a visual inspection of the West Block, and on December 23, 1955 they submitted their report.[643] It was not possible to increase the height of the West Block by adding another story according to the report, nor was it possible to build an addition without a wholesale program of demolition and rebuilding. There were only two choices.

The West Block could be renovated without changing its size. This would please those who didn't want to see the traditional appearance of the hill changed from its original state, but would do nothing about solving the accommodation problem. The second choice was to demolish the building and build a new West Block.

There were no sketches or drawings in their report, but they described what the new building might have looked like. It would, of course, be planned for the function it must perform, permit maximum flexibility in internal arrangement, be of modern fireproof construction and have modern services and utilities. It would be in harmony and compatible with the Centre Block. It would have an interesting and lively skyline. The Mackenzie Tower would be retained if at all possible, but if it must be demolished then it would be replaced by another having the same general form and proportions. It would be one story higher than the present West Block, and its northerly end would be in line with the north end of the East Block.

The architects immediately began making drawings but they had only spent 200 hours on them before their work was put on hold because of opposition to any scheme for a new West Block. They had not had time to make any drawings ready for presentation.[644]

In November the *Citizen* published an article titled *Keep Your Hands off our Victorian Gothic*,[645] but in December 1956 came a huge push. A group of distinguished architects from all across Canada wrote an open letter titled *The West Block and its Future*, which was printed in the December 1956 issue of the prestigious Royal Architectural Institute of Canada journal.[646]

"The proposal to take down the West Block in order to rebuild it with a hundred or more additional rooms is opposed because the loss of such an important and handsome building in a country where history has left few monuments is deplorable," they said.

"If another wing were made in the general direction of the Central Block," they suggested, "the new accommodation would be convenient to the House of Commons, the old building would be preserved and one would hope, improved in interest as it could be expected that a new wing would be as splendidly designed as the most talented men in the field could make it."

"The old parliamentary buildings were built with vision and courage as physical evidence of a united Canada," they argued. "...the West and East Blocks remain from the mid-nineteenth century the original parliamentary buildings in Ottawa. Their accommodation may now be inadequate and shabby, but their poetic significance is no less and in the years to come their power to relate the spirit of their builders will be unparalleled." The letter concluded with, "The manner in which this problem is resolved is one of great significance and deserves the careful consideration of the people of Canada."

Despite these articles, on February 12, 1957 the Minister gave an interview which appeared the *Ottawa Citizen* the same day with the title *Old West Block Might Give way To Bigger $6,400,000 Building*.[647]

Demolition of the West Block 251

Excerpt from the House of Commons Debates
February 15, 1957, p. 1323

MR. Stanley Howard Knowles (C.C.F.; Winnipeg North Centre, Man.): Mr. Speaker, may I direct a question to the Minister of Public Works. Can the minister say whether the press report is correct that his department plans to tear down the west block and replace it with a new edifice?

MR. Robert Henry WINTERS (Lib.; Queens–Lunenburg, N.S; Minister of Public Works): The press report to which I presume the hon. member refers is the one appearing in the Ottawa Citizen of three days ago. This press report is not a correct interpretation of the writer's interview with me on the subject. I told him no decision had been made. That is the situation. How it appeared in the terms it did is beyond my knowledge.

A few weeks later the architects were asked to start again, but this time the idea of demolishing the old building was dropped. Instead, the idea was to fill in the lawn to the north with one large committee room, several smaller ones, a restaurant and kitchen, and make some alterations in the courtyard. No requirements were given for the interior of the West Block except "a general request that as much good space as possible be provided."

On October 10, 1957 E.A. Gardner wrote the architects saying the Deputy Minister had asked that the project be "picked up and put into process again." He asked to see their sketches, as they were. This was done in Gardner's office on November 19. Following this meeting the architects made changes he suggested and by April 16, 1958 were finished.

At this point the project was put on hold again.[648] Why, we don't know. Meanwhile, on June 21, 1957 the Conservatives won the Federal Election. Howard Charles Green became Minister of Public Works under Diefenbaker who, it may be remembered, had a great love of history and heritage. On June 16, Mr. Green put an end to any idea the West Block would be demolished.

> Excerpt from the House of Commons Debates
> June 16, 1958, p. 119
>
> *Mr. Herbert Wilfred HERRIDGE (Independent C.C.F; Kootenay West, B.C.):Mr. Chairman, I remember when the minister was in opposition he was very much concerned at that time about proposals to demolish the west block, I think because of some association his party has had with that building over a long period of time. Could the minister inform the committee now whether it is the policy of his government to decimate this block, to rehabilitate it, or to recreate it?*
> *Mr. Howard Charles GREEN (Cons.; Vancouver South, B.C.): I can assure the hon. member that as long as I am Minister of Public Works the west block will not be demolished.*

DEMOLITION OF THE EAST BLOCK

In the late 1940's, thought was briefly given to demolishing the East Block, but it would have been far too expensive. "To have torn down the old building and erected a completely new structure would have cost between $5 million and $7 million" the *Ottawa Citizen* reported.[649] Instead it was decided to do a complete modernization at a cost of $365,000.[650]

In the 1950's, Jacques Gréber believed the southwest tower of the East Block was too high and wanted to see a section of it removed.[651] He said it interfered with the view of the National War Memorial from the Peace Tower.[652]

Also, the government was still hinting at demolishing the East Block. The suggested compromise," the *Montreal Gazette* reported, "is that a replica might be built, at least as far as the exterior is concerned. It is a pitiful compromise...."[653]

Demolition of the West Block 253

The National Capital Commission guide in the middle left is orienting tourists who have just arrived on the Hill. When tourists come to Parliament Hill for the first time they have thousands of questions. "Which one is the Parliament Building?" they ask. "Where is the Prime Minister's office?" The NCC Guides are very experienced and are experts at answering all kinds of question, but happily they have never been asked "why was the West Block destroyed?" That's because it wasn't. It's right over there, behind the bus. Photograph by the author.

Chapter 26: Demolition of the old Supreme Court Building

MR.George Clyde NOWLAN (Prog. Cons.; Digby–Annapolis–Kings, N.S.): "Why is it going to be destroyed and what is going to be substituted therefore? A parking lot. It is proposed to replace this cherished building with a parking lot which could perhaps accommodate 20, 30 or 40 automobiles."

Excerpt from the House of Commons Debates,
August 3, 1956, p. 6937

Today, of course, there are three buildings on Parliament Hill. There is the Centre Block, the East Block and the West Block. You may not know this, but there used to be another building on Parliament Hill, down near Bank Street. It housed the government workshops that were built in 1874. H. Belden described them in his 1879 *Illustrated Historical Atlas of the County of Carleton Ont. (Including City of Ottawa)* as:

> "…a very fine block of buildings at the extreme west end of the grounds, just under the brow of Parliament Hill proper, facing Bank Street to the west, and extending from the great gates at the south-west entrance of Parliament Square to the entrance to the Lovers' Walk at the edge of the river precipice. These buildings are constructed principally of Nepean sandstone, with Ohio freestone trimmings – of the pointed Gothic style of architecture – two storeys and attic – roofed with slate and surmounted by wrought iron cresting. They are most complete in all

their details — such as steam engines, dryers, planers, etc., and within them is transacted all the blacksmithing, carpenter work, etc., always necessary in connection with the alterations and repairs which various parts of the Public Buildings are constantly undergoing."[654]

There were also the greenhouses behind the workshops which, Belden said, were "for the more tender variety of flowers and plants with which the various parts of the grounds are ornamented."[655] In the Victorian era, there were many flower beds on the grounds, many more than today. In some beds, the flowers were arranged to spell mottos like *Be Kind, Be True* and *God Save Our Queen*.

When the Supreme Court was created in 1876, it was held in the picture gallery in the Parliament Building. In 1880, it was decided that the Supreme Court would be moved out of the Parliament Building and into the workshops, which, of course, would be renovated first. The picture gallery was made into the reading room.[656]

Now, why do you think the Chief Justice of the Supreme Court would agree to move out? In 1956, MR. George Clyde NOWLAN (Prog. Cons.; Digby–Annapolis–Kings, N.S.) said: "It may be if tradition is justified — I presume prime ministers are often confronted with many problems — that the then prime minister had to placate people and it may be that the then chief justice of Canada did not like the then prime minister too well and the then prime minister did not like the then chief justice of Canada too well, and it may be that the chief justice was promised if he moved into this old building that shortly afterwards the new supreme court building would be built."[657]

The Court moved, but if Sir John A. actually promised the Chief Justice a new building, he didn't get it. Time passed, and perhaps the Supreme Court Building wasn't kept up as well as it should have been. In 1935, a health inspector was called in because someone had complained about bad air and noxious odors. The inspector found many infractions, but perhaps the worst was the women's washroom. "The toilet for the women," he wrote in his report, "consists of one bowl placed in a dark corner underneath the stairway. It should be condemned forthwith."[658]

This report undoubtedly helped expedite the building of the new edifice. It was completed in 1945, and in 1946 the Supreme Court of Canada left the old Supreme Court Building, as it was then called, and moved into their brand-new building at the end of Kent Street.

Over the next ten years, parts of the old Supreme Court Building were occupied sporadically. As is often the case with old buildings that aren't really needed any more, maintenance was cut back. The building fell further and further into disrepair.

In 1955, Minister Winters informed the *Citizen* that the old Supreme Court Building would be torn down the next summer.[659] Mr. Winters pointed out that the old building had been recommended for demolition by Jacques Gréber, the famous French town planner responsible for planning the National Capital (the Gréber Plan, 1950). It would take about $50,000 to repair the building, he said, and if it was going to be demolished anyway, it would be a waste of money. Mr. Winters said the cleared site would be used temporarily for parking and then later developed and terraced as an approach to the new West Block Public Works was going to build after the old one was demolished (see Chapter 25).

Excerpt from the House of Commons Debates
April 27, 1956, p. 3377-3378

Mr. George Clyde NOWLAN (Prog. Cons.; Digby–Annapolis–Kings, N.S.): Mr. George Clyde NOWLAN (Prog. Cons.; Digby–Annapolis–Kings, N.S.): I recall reading in the press that the minister's plans required the tearing down of the old supreme court building at the foot of the hill here and making a parking lot of it. One could spend ten minutes discussing that, but I am going to spend only one minute on it and say that I think the minister in his planning should look further ahead than the necessity of providing a parking lot for perhaps 15 or 20 cars.

Mr. Robert Henry WINTERS (Lib.; Queens–Lunenburg, N.S.; Minister of Public Works): That is a temporary arrangement. What we are doing will ultimately conform with the national capital plan.[660]

Mr. Nowlan: All I would like to say is that here we have one of the old historic buildings of the city, and one that means a great deal to this country. It is true that it was a stone carving shop at one time. Perhaps Sir John A. Macdonald's coachman went in there to warm his hands over the stove when he was waiting to drive home the boss. Afterwards it evolved into the Supreme Court building. Now, of course, we have a magnificent structure further down the street.

If this country grows as we hope and believe it will grow, perhaps in another 50 years there will be another Supreme Court of Canada building in some other place. Then everyone is going to be lamenting the fact that we did not have the foresight to preserve some of these earlier buildings and monuments.... I would urge the minister not to move too quickly in the demolition of that building.

Excerpt from the House of Commons Debates
July 4, 1956, p. 5657

Mr. John George DIEFENBAKER (Cons.; Lake Centre, Sask.): ...I should like to ask the minister whether this committee has made any report in connection with a structure on parliament hill which, I believe, more than anything else, is one of the great traditional buildings on the hill. I refer to the old Supreme Court of Canada building, for it was in that building that some of the great parliamentarians of Canada, including prime ministers, appeared as counsel. I think of Edward Blake –

Mr. Roch PINARD (Lib.; Chambly–Rouville, Que.??): Yes; but that would be under the Department of Public Works.

Mr. DIEFENBAKER: I will terminate my remarks. As I say, I think of Edward Blake, Sir John Thompson, Sir Robert Borden, Right Hon. R.B. Bennett and Louis St. Laurent, all prime ministers of Canada who appeared from time to time and made their distinguished names in that building. I should like to ask the minister whether or not the perpetuation or the preservation of that building, great in history – actually the place where our constitution received its major interpretation – should not be a matter of concern, and whether it should not be maintained as part and *parcel of those things worth preserving and deserving to be preserved as part of our history, our tradition, and our past.*

Indeed, in so far as the constitution is concerned all our future was made in that building. In that place these five outstanding lawyers, four of whom afterwards became prime ministers of Canada and Edward Blake, the leader of the Liberal Party in the 1880's and one of Canada's most outstanding lawyers if not the most outstanding one, made their reputation and shaped Canada's future. Has consideration been given by this committee to the need of preserving this building as one of our great and ancient heritages for the benefit of this and future generations?

It was a beautiful speech and someday Canada would have such a policy. However, it did not back in 1956, and plans to demolish the old building went ahead.

On September 6, 1956 it was photographed, and then handed over to the wreckers. A week later the windows were out and workers were busy on the roof, taking it apart board by board.[661] Soon after, a huge bulldozer, pushing and roaring and belching out clouds of dirty black smoke, crashed the building down.[662] A steam shovel loaded up dump trucks that hauled the mess away. By December most of it was gone and the steam shovel was just scraping here and there, smoothing and leveling the ground and cleaning up the last of the bits of broken stone and brick.

"Demolition of old Supreme Court Building December, 1956." The south wall was left standing to shield the ugliness of the parked cars from pedestrians on Wellington Street. As years passed by this wall became covered in ivy, like Mackenzie King's ruins at Kingsmere. Later, the part to the left of the entrance was knocked down, and today only the section on the right exists. Copyright: Copyright assigned to Library and Archives Canada by copyright owner Duncan Cameron. Acc. No. *1970-015 NPC.*

CHAPTER 27: DEMOLITION OF THE ABOMINABLE, OLD, WORN-OUT, UNPAINTED, SHABBY LOOKOUT

Mr. George Harris HEES (Prog. Cons.; Broadview, Ont.): Parliament Hill is literally swarming today with people who have come here to look at the capital of Canada. There are many of them in the galleries today and there will be more tomorrow and the next day. They come to see our beautiful buildings. They come to look at the handsome members of the R.C.M.P. on their horses. They look around the grounds and everything they see on parliament hill is attractive and in first class shape except the abominable, old, worn out, unpainted, shabby look-out on one of the most prominent parts of parliament hill.

Excerpt from the House of Commons Debates
July 19, 1955, p. 6390

Arthur James BATER (Lib.; The Battlefords, Sask.)

Well, we don't call it "the abominable, old, worn out, unpainted, shabby look-out." We call it the summer pavilion. However, the one we have on Parliament Hill today is not the original - it is a replica built in the early 1990's.

The original was built in 1877. It was made of wood, and as any home owner with an outside porch knows, wood must be painted regularly. For many years it was. However, sometime in the late 1930's or early 1940's, maintenance started to wane. By the early 1950's, the look-out was pretty shabby looking.

In 1951, Mr. Arthur James BATER (Lib.; The Battlefords, Sask.) stood up in the House: "Might I suggest to the Minister," he said, "that the little shelter at the northwest corner of the parliamentary grounds get two or three coats of paint. I consider the shelter is quite an eyesore when visitors are around the parliament buildings."

The Minister, Mr. Alphonse FOURNIER (Lib.; Hull, Que.) replied: "I am pleased that the hon. gentleman has called my attention to that because I can see that kiosk from my own window. I do not like it. I shall try to have it painted."[663]

However, despite what the Minister said, nothing was done. By 1955, it needed painting desperately.

Excerpt from the House of Commons Debates
May 31, 1955

Mr. George Harris HEES (Prog. Cons.; Broadview, Ont.): Mr. Speaker, I should like to address a question to the Minister of Public Works. Would the minister and his department give consideration to having the remains of what used to be a covered shelter, standing in a most prominent place on parliament hill overlooking the river, either painted so it will look respectable, or replaced by something more suitable?

Some hon. MEMBERS: Order.

An hon. MEMBER: A national emergency.

Mr. Robert Henry WINTERS (Lib.; Queens–Lunenburg, N.S.; Minister of Public Works): I shall be glad to look into the matter.

Excerpt from the House of Commons Debates
June 23, 1955, p. 4268

Mr. HEES: On a local issue, Mr. Speaker, may I address another question to the Minister of Public Works. When is his department going to do something about either repainting or replacing that monstrosity they have at the northwest corner of the grounds?

Mr. WINTERS: It will be repainted very soon.

Demolition of the Abominable, etc.

Excerpt from the House of Commons Debates
July 19, 1955, p. 6390

Mr. HEES: ...*I will move on to another question, and this, as they say in church, is the third time of asking. I brought it up several months ago. It involves something which the minister may not think is of too much importance –*

Mr. WINTERS: It is going to be done.

Mr. HEES: - but which concerns a most important part of parliament hill. I refer to the look-out on the northwest corner. Parliament Hill is literally swarming today with people who have come here to look at the capital of Canada. There are many of them in the galleries today and there will be more tomorrow and the next day. They come to see our beautiful buildings. They come to look at the handsome members of the R.C.M.P. on their horses. They look around the grounds and everything they see on parliament hill is attractive and in first class shape except the abominable, old, worn out, unpainted, shabby look-out on one of the most prominent parts of parliament hill. I suggest to the minister that he should stand out there, listen to the comments of these people, many of whom have come thousands of miles to see our capital city, and hear what they say about this really abominable looking monstrosity which I have been asking for several months now to have repaired, painted, or removed completely. Will the minister please give me an answer to that question and tell me what he plans to do and when?

Mr. WINTERS: It will be painted very shortly.

Mr. HEES: I have been getting that same answer for several months.

Mr. WINTERS: You have just had it once.

Mr. HEES: I have asked the minister twice, Mr. Chairman. Are you going to do it right away?

Mr. WINTERS: It will be done very shortly.

But it was not. Instead, the summer pavilion was demolished the next year.

"Summer House Pavillion, Parliament Hill, [Ottawa, Ontario]." This photograph of the summer pavillion was taken on August 17, 1950. It was one year after this photograph was taken that Mr. Bater made his complaint. © Government of Canada. Reproduced with the permission of the Minister of Public Works and Government Services Canada (2011). Source: Library and Archives Canada/Department of Public Works fonds/ PA-129642.

Chapter 28: Demolition of the Centennial Flame

I launched an editorial and write-in campaign to preserve the Flame in the early part of October, 1967 when it was announced that the Flame was to be dismantled at the end of 67. It is estimated that as many as 30,000 letters and petitions flooded into the offices of Prime Minister Pearson, Works Minister George McIlraith and Judy LaMarsh, the Minister in charge of Centennial projects.

Lowell Green, 2007[664]

On May 26, 1966, Cabinet met to discuss a May 5 memo from the Hon. George James McILRAITH (Lib.; Ottawa West, Ont.; Minister of Public Works) proposing a Centennial Flame on the centre walkway on Parliament Hill. It was suggested the Flame be lit at midnight on December 31, 1966, burn throughout the Centennial Year and continue burning in perpetuity as a memorial to the Centennial. Prime Minister Pearson supported the proposal for a Flame, but objections were raised to its maintenance in perpetuity. After discussing the matter, Cabinet decided it would be extinguished when the Centennial Year was over.[665]

On September 29, 1966 the *Ottawa Journal* reported that the Flame would burn for only one year.[666] This didn't cause any reaction at the time, but things would be very different one year later.

The purpose of the Flame and how long it should burn was discussed in the *Ottawa Citizen* a few weeks later.[667] If it is to represent Canada's 100th birthday party, and be blown out like candles on a birthday cake, that's one thing. But if it is to represent Canada, then surely it should be an eternal flame because Canada will still continue past the end of the year. Its purpose needs to be explained a lot better than it has, they said.

The Flame was constructed that fall and was lit at an official ceremony on New Year's Eve, 1966. It was still the government's intention to extinguish the Flame at the end of the year. For this reason, the structure was not designed to last.[668] For example, the provincial and territorial plaques around the flame were carved out of an olive or bluish-green sandstone from the Wallace Quarries in Nova Scotia. This particular stone, which is used extensively on the Peace Tower, is quite soft, very suitable for carving the plaques. However, while it would be perfectly adequate for one year, it would not be capable of withstanding years and years of the constant wetting and freeze-thaw.[669]

By October, 1967, the Centennial Flame had become tremendously popular with the over a million visitors to Parliament Hill. Lowell Green raised the issue of shutting down the Flame at the end of the year on his radio talk show *The Greenline*. He said the phone lines exploded.[670] If there had been e-mail in those days, the server would have crashed. The callers were absolutely furious.

Green then began an editorial and write-in campaign to preserve the Flame and urged his listeners to write to Prime Minister Pearson, Public Works Minister George McIlraith and Judy Lamarsh. Thousands upon thousands of letters and petitions flooded into their offices, and the pressure worked. "I am surprised by what has gone out in the news in the last days and weeks," McIlraith said. "It has got a little out of hand."[671]

On December 8, 1967, the Cabinet Committee noted that the Flame had become a significant symbol for the people of Canada and agreed to recommend to Cabinet that it should be maintained in perpetuity.[672] On December 11, Prime Minister Pearson agreed.

Excerpt from the House of Commons Debates
December 11, 1967, p. 5260

Mr. Herbert Wilfred HERRIDGE (Independent C.C.F; Kootenay West, B.C.): Mr. Speaker, I wish to address a question to the right hon. Prime Minister. In view of the fact that the centennial flame has caught the imagination of a great many people in Canada, has the Prime Minister received representations from people and organizations requesting that the centennial flame be maintained in perpetuity?

Right Hon. Lester Bowls Pearson (Lib.; Algoma East, Ont.; Prime Minister): Yes, Mr. Speaker. I have received representations, including representations from many member of the house on this side and others. I agree that the flame should become the symbol of our first centennial year and should not be extinguished. Perhaps it would be desirable to re-light it as we enter our second centennial year.

[Translation]

Mr. David Réal Caouette (Social Credit; Pontiac, Que.): Mr. Speaker, I should like to put a supplementary question to the Prime Minister.

When we look at that flame, we see a blue part. Would it be possible to put out only that part and maintain the other?

Cabinet approval (for keeping the Flame, not extinguishing only the blue part) came the next day.[673]

The monument is a large stainless steel pan built into the masonry structure depicting the Provinces and Territories of Canada at the time of our 100th birthday celebration in 1967. The pool is illuminated with coloured lights. There are pumps located below the flame in a crawl space, and the water is circulated to other pumps and filtration equipment in the East Block's mechanical room. Natural gas is supplied at approximately 5 psi pressure under the Centennial Emblem in the centre of the pool. The water is also pumped into the basin at the centre emblem. The gas bubbles out of a ring burner under the emblem cap into the water and is disbursed around the centre emblem to the atmosphere. With the exception of the gas bubbling through the water to escape, the flame burns like a gas stove or BBQ when it reaches the air.

PWGSC staff shut down the Flame several times a year for routine maintenance of the burner, the controls and pumps. The fountain is cleaned daily during the summer, and the coins are collected, cleaned and dried inside the Centre Block shops. The coins are counted and remitted to The House of Commons Controller's Office. The money is turned over to the Centennial Flame Foundation Award Committee, and used to fund research by and about Canadians with disabilities.

PART 5

MY OWN TIMES

CHAPTER 29: THE STATUES ON PARLIAMENT HILL

Mr. William Garland McQUARRIE (Unionist; New Westminster, B.C.): Do you say nothing can be done? They are in a disgraceful condition; surely something should be done to restore them.

Excerpt from the House of Commons Debates May 24, 1930, p. 2534.

When I started working on Parliament Hill back in the 1980's, statues everywhere were streaky green and black, not just on Parliament Hill but all around the world. People thought that's how outdoor bronzes were supposed to look. In 1951 Public Works' Building Superintendant W. L. Smith, and E.A. Gardner, then Public Works' Assistant Chief Architect, were giving an interview to an *Ottawa Citizen* reporter about cleaning the statues on Parliament Hill. [674] When asked about the verdigris, M. Smith replied, "Verdigris? The experts tell us not to disturb that." Mr. Gardner explained, "If you take off the green coating, then the statue would seem brand new and that wouldn't look right. The statue should take on age as it goes along. That appearance is probably what the sculptor envisaged it would look like.... And, incidentally, we don't call that deposit verdigris: it's known simply as a patina." However, Mr. Gardner, and everyone else in the world, was wrong. That green means trouble.

A car that is not maintained will rust. If you take a close look at rust on a car you will see that the surface of the metal is rough and pitted. In some places, the metal may have been corroded right through. This is called perforation corrosion. A similar kind of thing happens on a corroding statue, but it's slower. You won't see perforation corrosion because the metal on a statue is much thicker than on a car, about the thickness of your finger. When I gave media interviews, I used to say "Cars rust red, but statues rust green."[675]

But corrosion is corrosion. Over time, if nothing is done to stop it, the expressions on the face, the fine lines and detailing, will all be gone, and the metal will be horribly pitted and corroded.

So, in the 1970's when the experts saw the damage that was occurring on the famous *Horses of San Marco* in Venice, which were at that time streaky green and black, alarm bells started to go off. All around the world governments, conservators and scientists began to take an interest in conservation of outdoor monuments.[676]

Before I explain how we conserved the statues on Parliament Hill, let's first look at how statues are made, what causes them to corrode and what was done about it on Parliament Hill in the past.

How Statues are Made

There are many ways of casting a bronze statue. Statues can be made by sand casting, lost wax casting of which there are three methods (direct wax, solid investment core casting and ceramic shell casting), as well as lost Styrofoam casting and centrifugal casting.[677] Of all these, sand casting is the oldest. It was developed by the Egyptians and the Chinese some 5,000 years ago and is still used in foundries today.

This is a description of how sand casting was done in the latter part of the 19th and early 20th centuries. It is based on a lecture given by Prof. Weir in 1874, and an explanation in 1903 by a French workman who had been casting big figures all of his life.[678] This method, or something close to it, may have been how the Cartier (1885), Macdonald (1895) and Mackenzie (1901) statues on Parliament Hill were made.

After the sculptor completed his sculpture in clay the *formatore* cast it in plaster of Paris. The plaster was sawn into sections – head, body, arms and legs – which were taken to the foundry. The workers in the foundry included *porters, molders, mounters, chasers* and *patineurs*.

The first step was to make sand molds from the plaster casts. The plaster casts were brushed with shellac, and then finely ground potato dust was applied. After this came the sand, but it couldn't just be ordinary sand. "In order to get sand of the proper cohesiveness when worked, and stony hardness when dry," said the French workman, "it is necessary to send to France." This was reddish sand from Fontenay-aux-Roses, about twenty to twenty five kilometres from Paris. It had the proper workability when wet, and it dried stone hard.

The sand was fitted to the plaster in little chunks of various sizes – snugly, but not so snugly that they could not be easily taken apart when the mold was dry. In a big sculpture, there could be 2,000 or more of these little pieces. It took a lot of patience, but it had to be done right or the statue would be ruined!

When the blocks of sand were dry they were removed one by one and then fitted back together like giant three-dimensional jig-saw puzzles to make the molds. These molds were then filled with clay and when the clay had dried, the casts of the head, body, arms and legs were removed.

The next part of the work was very delicate. A small amount, about ten to fifteen millimetres, had to be scraped off the surface of the clay to make exact but slightly smaller copies of the plaster casts called 'cores'. The amount removed would be the thickness of the bronze in the final casting.

The cores were placed inside the sand molds, which by this time had been put back together again and lined with plumbago (graphite). Iron rods were used to steady the cores and to keep the distance all around the same ten to fifteen millimetres.

Molten bronze was then poured into the molds so that it completely filled the spaces. After the metal was cold (this took from two to four days), the sand molds were taken apart and the bronze casts removed. The sand was cleaned off with stiff brushes and hardwood tools. Then the casts were dipped in acid which cleaned off any impurities. This made the metal shine like a brand new penny.

Bronze is mostly copper, but with small amounts of tin, zinc and sometimes lead added. The Queen Victoria lion on Parliament Hill, for example, is about 90% copper, 2% tin and 8% zinc.[679] Bronzes like this with low zinc content (less than about 10%) are reddish. This colour can be seen in the beautiful burnished area on the lion's tail, caused by frequent human touching. On the other hand, those with higher zinc content (10% to 20%) are more orange-yellow. The Pearson statue, with the brassy burnished areas on the toe of his shoe and shoelaces, has higher zinc content.

The sculptor inspected the casts, and if he was pleased they were given to the chaser to take off the seams. The mounter welded the figure back together, and then the statue went back to the chaser to go over it again. The sculptor then went over the work one last time, and if any small changes were needed he had these done by the chaser.

The last step was for the patineur to *patinate* the statue. This involves warming the bright, shiny surface with a torch, and then spraying it with a chemical. Traditionally, 'liver of sulphur' (an impure form of potassium sulphide) was used. This immediately turned the metal shades of dark brown and black. As Prof. Weir explained in 1874, "the bronze is then darkened or toned, and so the work is done."

This dark appearance of statues can be clearly seen in early photographs of unveiling ceremonies on Parliament Hill, even though the pictures were taken in black and white. A colored postage stamp of the National War Memorial, issued when it was unveiled in 1939, shows its original appearance was dark brown or black.[680]

An idea of what newly installed statues might have looked like can be had by looking closely at the Queen Elizabeth II statue.[681] This statue, which was unveiled in 1992, has been regularly waxed every year and has never been corroded so you can still see the original colors. Although it looks brown from a distance, when you look at it closely you will see that it really consists of many rich, warm shades of browns and blacks, occasionally tinged with greens. The colors are lustrous and translucent, not solid, and very beautiful.

An exception is the statue of Sir Robert Borden by sculptor Frances Loring, which was unveiled in 1957. It was probably green when it was installed. According to Mr. Herridge, M.P., "a patina was made artificially to give this statue an appearance similar to those which had acquired a patina as a result of age."[682]

COAL BURNING, ACID RAIN AND THE CORROSION OF STATUES

In 1930, there were eight statues on Parliament Hill, some of which were in disgraceful condition.

Excerpt from the House of Commons Debates
May 24, 1930, p. 2534

Mr. William Garland McQUARRIE (Unionist; New Westminster, B.C.): I should like to ask the minister if he thinks treasury board would pass a little item for the cleaning and restoring of some of the statues on the grounds of this building. Some of them are getting into a very disgraceful condition, notably the statues of Sir Wilfrid Laurier and Sir John A. Macdonald. Something should be done to take care of them properly....

Mr. John Campbell ELLIOTT (Lib.; Middlesex West, Ont.; Minister of Public Works): What my hon. friend refers to is very largely the oxidation from the sulphur fumes which come from across the river, and there is no way of preventing that.

Mr. McQUARRIE: Surely they can be cleaned up and looked after.

Mr. ELLIOTT: No, it is the same as the action of the roofs of the buildings.

Mr. McQUARRIE: But you can get at them without much trouble. Do you say nothing can be done? They are in a disgraceful condition; surely something should be done to restore them.

The statues were cleaned in 1931,[683] and again in 1932.[684] In the 1932 cleaning, the statues of Queen Victoria and Sir John A. Macdonald were given a coating of a special varnish prepared by Dr. G. S. Whitby, director of the chemistry department at the National Research Council. So, for a few years afterwards, until the varnish wore off, these two statues would have been quite shiny.

The Minister was correct in saying the problem was caused by sulphur fumes from across the river because coal contains sulphur. He may have been aware of research by Vernon and Whitby a year earlier who said "atmospheric sulphuric acid must definitely originate from the combustion of coal and its products."[685] In speaking about copper roofs, he said "sulphur compounds, derived from products of combustion and disseminated by the wind, are the most potent agents in the development of patina."[686]

Coal started to be used in the Ottawa area in the early 1870's. Before that it was wood, but burning wood produces carbon dioxide, not sulphur dioxide. Wood smoke does not cause statues to corrode like coal because it does not contain sulphur.

In 1873, Alderman Pratt introduced a bylaw to require the weighing of coal on controlled scales because of the "increasing consumption of coal in this city of late." The bylaw was needed because the people had to take the coal dealers' word as to the weight. It was feared that there were some who "might be averse to the principle of honesty."[687]

It is surprising that the statue of Sir Wilfrid Laurier was in such bad shape when Mr. McQuarrie made those remarks in 1930, because it was only three years old at that time. It shows how quickly statues went green.

Parliament Hill is just downwind of the big smokestacks of the old E.B. Eddy Match Factory (now a heritage building) as well as many other plants and factories that used to burn coal. The Cliff Street power plant (which was built in 1920 to replace the old heating and ventilating system on Parliament Hill) burned coal up until 1960 when it was converted to use oil and natural gas.[688]

Homes and businesses in Ottawa and Hull were heated with coal as well, but sources far away (industries in Sudbury and the Ohio River Valley, for example) have also contributed to the corrosion of statues on Parliament Hill. Sulphur fumes from tall industrial smokestacks can be carried hundreds of kilometers, high in the atmosphere on the prevailing winds.

Table 6. Statues on Parliament Hill in 1930 (After Selwyn et. al.[689])

Monument	Sculptor	Installed
Sir George-Etienne Cartier	Louis-Philippe Hébert	1885
Sir John A. Macdonald	Louis-Philippe Hébert	1895
Alexander Mackenzie	Louis-Philippe Hébert & Hamilton MacCarthy	1901
Queen Victoria	Louis-Philippe Hébert	1901
George Brown	George William Hill	1913
Robert Baldwin & Sir Louis-Hippolyte Lafontaine	Walter Seymour Allward	1914
Thomas D'Arcy McGee	George William Hill	1922
Sir Wilfrid Laurier	Joseph-Emile Brunet	1927

Scientists now know that sulphur dioxide in the smoke combines with moisture in the clouds to make a weak sulphuric acid. This falls back to earth as *acid rain*. Acidity can also come back to earth dry, in the form of acidic gasses and particles blown about by the wind. It can even come back as acid snow or acid fog.

Consider a statue of any of the Prime Ministers. Acid rain coming straight down will land on the head and shoulders first and from there run off in tiny streams. One stream might, for example, run down his forehead to the end of his nose, drop off and hit his jacket, from there run down creases and folds in his jacket to his pants and from there down to the plinth. Another stream might wash down the side of his face and from there find its way down in smaller rivulets. Other streams will take different routes, but wherever they run the metal will become wet. Some parts will not get wet at all. For example, his armpits or the underside of folds in his clothing are sheltered and will stay nice and dry. Both the wet and dry areas will corrode. The wet areas corrode because of acid rain, and the dry areas because of windblown acidic gases and particles. The wet areas will corrode green. The sheltered areas will tend to be black because of dirt, and soot that collects and is not washed away by rain.

MacDonald's Pince-Nez Glasses

Excerpt from the House of Commons Debates
November 24, 1949, p. 2152

Mr. Jean-François POULIOT (Lib.; Témiscouata, Que.): I should like to direct the attention of the Minister of Public Works (Mr. Fournier) to the statue of Sir John A. Macdonald, one of the fathers of confederation, which is situated between this building and the east block. The other day the hon. member for Broadview (Mr. Church) referred to a conversation that had taken place before the monument, and it gave me the idea of going to look at it. I notice that the pince-nez which Sir John holds in his hand has become broken and is now a monocle. That is a historical error, and I hope it will be corrected as soon as possible.

Excerpt from the House of Commons Debates
June 28, 1950, p. 4255

Mr. POULIOT: Mr. Speaker, may I direct the attention of the Minister of Public Works (Mr. Fournier) to the fact that the historical error on the statue of Sir John A. Macdonald on these grounds has not yet been corrected in accordance with instructions that were given last year. The pince-nez of Sir John is still broken.

It was repaired in 1956. Workmen cast a replacement for the missing part, and then patinated it to match the original. At the same time, they gave all of the statues a good cleaning.[690]

BIRDS

In the 1950's the statues were being washed every spring, using a solution of water and mild detergent. It was Public Works' Building Superintendant W. L. Smith who gave them their annual bath.[691] Unfortunately, for some reason birds love to perch on the heads of statues, especially when they have just been washed.

Excerpt from the House of Commons Debates
June 28, 1950, p. 4255.

Mr. Jean-François POULIOT (Lib.; Témiscouata, Que.): May I also bring the attention of the minister to the fact that the statue of Sir Wilfrid Laurier, also on these grounds, has become a sanctuary for birds – a sanctuary for disrespectful and sacrilegious birds. I hope he will see to it that all the dirt on these statues is cleaned of at once.

Mr. Smith kept at it, but there were so many birds. In 1960, an unofficial war was declared in an attempt to force them to fly away somewhere else. Char ladies like Mrs. Mabbs, who for years had been in the habit of each morning tossing bread crumbs for the pigeons, were given strict orders to stop. However, it was not Public Works who gave the order. The Deputy Minister of Public Works, Maj.-Gen. H. A. Young, said in a newspaper interview that he personally liked pigeons, adding "perhaps you could say the Department of Public Works takes on the status of benevolent neutrality in respect to pigeons." He said the order may have come from some official in the Senate or the House of Commons, who perhaps thought that uneaten bread crumbs scattered about on the central walkway looked untidy.[692]

In any event, it was desecrating the statues that brought about, as General Young phrased it, "a problem of cleaning."[693]

Operation Lemon Juice

Cleaning began with the statue of D'Arcy McGee. McGee was a great orator. The statue behind the Centre Block depicts him standing up in the House of Commons the evening of April 7, 1868 speaking about the cause of Confederation. It was that night, on the way home to his residence on Sparks Street, that he was assassinated.[694]

The official name of the fair maiden seated at his feet, with her hand cupped to her ear as if to hear him better, is *Memory*.[695]

However, in the 1960's she was known affectionately to Public Works staff as *Molly*, perhaps after the character in the old comedy show *Fibber McGee and Molly* that was on the radio between 1935 and 1959.

Excerpt from the House of Commons Debates
May 10, 1960, p. 3727

Mr. Herbert Wilfrid HERRIDGE (Independent C.C.F; Kootenay West, B.C.): As somewhat of a conservative –

Some hon. MEMBERS: Hear, hear.

Mr. HERRIDGE: – so far as works of art and beauty are concerned, I want to ask the Minister of Public Works a question prompted by the shock I received on taking an after lunch constitutional around this building with a gentleman of the fourth estate. I wish to ask the minister this question. Who ordered the scouring and consequent desecration of the monuments on parliament hill, and what was the reason for this unusual and unique treatment of bronze monuments?

Mr. David James WALKER (Prog. Cons.; Rosedale, Ont.; Minister of Public Works): I cannot give the hon. gentleman the real answer to his question – it would not be polite – but may I thank him for his question and say that from one who calls himself a conservative it is delightful to have these examples of poetic license in which he usually indulges and in which he has indulged again today. Perhaps, some time, he could frame his question in blank verse.

Knowing that we have many connoisseurs in this house, before attempting the much needed cleaning of these monuments we sought the advice of the national research council, of which the hon. gentleman is a great admirer, and after considering many alternative methods we decided on this expert method of cleaning which, I am sure, work out to the satisfaction of even the hon. member for Kootenay West.

Excerpt from the House of Commons Debates
July 21, 1960, p. 6691

Mr. HERRIDGE: While I am on my feet I want to raise one other point. I have been very restrained during the last day or two. I want to refer to what I termed Operation Lemon Juice on the statues. I wish the minister would tell us why the statues are being cleaned with lemon juice and the purpose of the whole operation, as well as the approximate cost of cleaning each of the statues. I have looked at this thing very carefully, the one that has been cleaned, and it looks like a fairly new bronze without any patina. There seems to be no particular reason for this cleaning, and I wish the minister would explain it. I have done some reading on the subject and have not been able to discover any mention of the use of lemon juice to remove the patina of old statues. What is the purpose of this cleaning, and what will be the cost per statue?

Mr. WALKER: In so far as the monuments on parliament hill are concerned, we now have a lacquer coat which prevents patina growth in an attractive, natural manner. In the case of D'Arcy McGee, we have removed the lacquer by scrubbing and have darkened the bronze by an application of lemon oil. The lemon oil will not inhibit the patina growth and we expect in time the statue will return to an attractive colour.

This process was developed by the ministry of works in the United Kingdom and was also recommended to us by that celebrated sculptress, Miss Frances Loring.

The work on D'Arcy McGee has cost $120 so far. Until the effectiveness of the process has been established in the Ottawa climate no further work is scheduled. My friend will keep a watchful eye on it, and I will be very happy to have him serve, without salary, as the curator of monuments on parliament hill.

Mr. Herridge did keep a watchful eye on it, for almost a year, and then he reported back.

Excerpt from the House of Commons Debates
June 15th 1961, p. 6379

Mr. HERRIDGE: Mr. Chairman, I have made periodic visits along with other individuals interested in this project, and notice that only one statue has been tackled. I think anyone, in fairness, will say those which still retain their original patina are much more attractive than the statue of McGee and Mollie with the verdigris showing them in a most dilapidated condition. I think Mollie's complexion is really out of this world.

In view of the comments made last year and the information I received from the minister at that time as to the success of this very interesting project, and in view of the report appearing in the Globe and Mail in regard to the appearance of that lone statue in question which the department has scrubbed and rubbed, I should like the minister to inform me what is the policy of his department in respect to this operation.

At this point the Minister must have ordered Maj.-Gen. Young, to stop the work, because a few days later...

Excerpt from the House of Commons Debates
June 17, 1961, p. 6510

Mr. HERRIDGE: Mr. Chairman, in view of the fact that some general seems to have halted the attack on the patina covering the statues on parliament hill, would the minister inform the committee whether the attack is to be resumed or has it been definitely abandoned?

Mr. WALKER: It has been definitely abandoned. The hon. member for Kootenay West really has a point there. Although this chemical treatment is suitable in London, England, where there is salt in the air and different climactic conditions, it has not worked out too well here. It did not

do D'Arcy McGee too much harm but if some of the nudes who are looking up at D'Arcy McGee were treated in this way it might at times prove to be embarrassing.
Mr. HERRIDGE: *It was a bit damaging to Mollie.*
Mr. WALKER: *Damaging to modesty, yes.*

UNDERSTANDING THE PROBLEM

Before the 1970's nobody, not even the experts, knew that outdoor statues were being slowly destroyed. This was partly because research by Vernon and Whitby on copper roofs found the green patina was actually good. "The underlying metal," they said, "in all cases examined, representing various degrees of purity, and periods of exposure extending up to 300 years, has shown remarkable freedom from pitting."[696]

It was thought that this applied to bronze statues as well because, after all, bronze is about ninety percent copper. However, it wasn't until 1972 with *The Horses of S. Marco* that the experts realized that they were wrong. Over the next decade, researchers found that corrosion of a bronze statue is not the same as corrosion of a copper roof. A stable, protective green patina is never formed, and the metal will continue to be eaten away. Examination with a scanning electron microscope shows the greatest metal loss under the green areas, but even the top of the black areas are below the original patina.[697]

There are several reasons why copper roofs and bronze statues corrode differently.[698] One reason is that copper roofing pans are rolled, whereas a bronze statue is cast. Rolled copper sheet has a very fine, even grain structure, too small to be seen by the naked eye. In a bronze statue, the grain structure varies. Often individual grains are large enough on the surface to be visible.

Another difference is the composition of the metal. A copper roof is relatively pure copper, whereas a bronze statue is copper with tin, and zinc, and sometimes lead, added. The corrosion layer, therefore, has many different compounds with different solubility in rain.

One final point that makes bronze corrode differently is a 'galvanic effect.' When areas of slightly different composition are in contact with each other, (in this case, on a microscopic scale with different grains having slightly different compositions in a bronze statue), then some areas will corrode more quickly than other areas, making the corrosion a little uneven.

So, green copper roofs are good; green statues are bad.

WHAT WE DID

In the 1980's, armed with this increased knowledge and understanding, governments all over the world began to take an interest in conserving their outdoor monuments. In 1987, Canada began a five-year program to conserve sixteen outdoor monuments containing over fifty separate figures on and around Parliament Hill.

1987 was my first year as a project manager on Parliament Hill and the conservation of the statues was one of my first projects. A Curatorial Committee had already been set up that year by our Headquarters Fine Arts Expert. The Committee consisted of experts from the government and private sector in the fields of sculpture, art, history and conservation to provide advice on conservation and long-term maintenance. As the newly appointed project manager, I was invited to join.

Conservation began in 1988 with Sir John A. Macdonald. This statue shows our first Prime Minister pausing briefly in his reading, with his pince-nez glasses held in one hand. Seated at his feet is an allegorical figure, a young lady called *Glory*. Her tight blouse leaves little to the imagination, but by today's standards it wouldn't raise many eyebrows. However, back at the turn of the century it did. In 1911, Senator Laurent Olivier David said that the statue "has only one fault: the woman that he sculpted at the feet of Sir John to represent *Glory* is so pretty, so perfect, that she throws the great man of State a bit into the shadows, and distracts the young senators."[699]

Here is what we did.

First, because outdoor bronzes are works of art, we hired a professional art conservator who was experienced in the conservation of outdoor bronzes. Before starting, the conservator prepared two test areas for the committee to look at. The first test area was at the bottom of the flag pole held by the young lady. This area he hot waxed and then cold waxed it, right over the corrosion. With hot waxing the metal is first warmed with a torch. As soon as the wax touches the warm metal it melts and soaks right in. Cold waxing is done without applying heat.

The second test area was up on the flag pole a little, and over onto her left knee. However, on this test the conservator first toned the green areas to a darker color by spraying them with a dilute solution of ammonium sulphide (just the green areas; the black areas were not sprayed), and then the test area was hot waxed and cold waxed as before.

When the conservator had finished the test areas, the Curatorial Committee was called in to take a look and decide which it wanted. We unanimously preferred the second method because of its appearance. The dark colour was very close to what the patina would have looked like originally.

After erecting scaffolding around the MacDonald statue, the conservator gave it a good washing with an anionic detergent in water. Outdoor statues have all kinds of dirt on them. Bits of quartz, the main component of sand, iron compounds, gypsum, traces of waxes and drying oils from previous attempts at conservation.[700]

After the statue was washed the green areas were toned to a darker color, as described above, and then the entire statue was hot waxed and then cold waxed. This protected it from the weather and gave the bronze a rich, warm, lustrous appearance. We decided to keep the attractive, burnished areas on *Glory's* knees and toe nails, which is caused by frequent human touching.

Over the next five years, we completed all the statues, finishing with the National War Memorial in 1993. We left this until last because it was the largest and most complex.

MAINTENANCE

The statues on Parliament Hill are maintained by annual inspections and re-waxing each spring by a conservator. They are washed frequently during tourist season in the summer.

If you were to walk around Parliament Hill early in the springtime, before the maintenance work is done, you might see little white blisters on some of the statues. This is cold wax that has lifted away from the hot wax. In this case the blister would be removed, and cold wax reapplied.

Sometimes you might see a little green spot in the blister where the weather has gotten through the cold wax, through the hot wax, and is now corroding the metal. In this case, the conservator would tone the green spot using ammonium sulphide, and then the area would be hot and cold waxed, exactly as before.

They have been doing a great job. The statues on Parliament Hill look just as good today as they did when we conserved them originally.

Jerry's Tail

I was project manager of the Queen's statue on Parliament Hill, which is located in the treed area on the east side of the Centre Block. The statue, which has the Queen on horseback on a large granite plinth, was unveiled by Her Majesty on June 30, 1992 as part of the 125th anniversary of Confederation celebrations, and to celebrate the 40th anniversary of her accession to the Throne.

The horse was a gift to the Queen in our Centennial year. He was an RCMP horse, and when he was with the RCMP his name was Jerry, but the Queen named him 'Centenial...with one 'n' to distinguish Centenial the horse from Centennial the event.

The sculptor of the Queen's statue was Jack Harmon of Gibson's, British Columbia. After the statue was completed it was crated, loaded onto a flatbed truck and driven non-stop to Ottawa. The horse was standing backwards in the crate, facing west.

On the way, somewhere on this side of the Rockies, one of the tires had a blow-out and the truck came to a jarring stop in a ditch. The truck stopped safely but the statue didn't. It broke loose from its restraints, slid forward, and the tail of the horse bumped into the front of the crate. This bump bent the tail and caused it to crack at the top, where it meets the rear end.

Jack must have known about the accident, but none of us did. As soon as the truck arrived on Parliament Hill he jumped up on the flatbed and checked the statue out, but there was no more damage other than the cracked tail.

Later, after we put the statue on its granite plinth, hidden from view inside a big box we had built, Jack's son Steve climbed up and straddled the horse's rump. I can still see him up there, a welding helmet held up to his face in one hand, and a welding rod in the other, fixing the broken tail. So, if future conservators working on the statue spot the weld on the top part of the tail, they will know how it happened.

Only a handful of people have ever heard this story...up until now, that is!

This attractive young lady was affectionately known to DPW staff in the 1950's as "Mollie."

The Statues on Parliament Hill 289

It is impossible to appreciate the differences between test areas 1 and 2 in a black and white photograph, but if you visit Parliament Hill you can look for yourself. We retained the evidence as part of the history of this statue. The committee unanimously preferred the second method, and we used it on all the statues. Take a close look at the flag pole and the top of her left thigh. You can decide for yourself if we made the right choice!

This close-up of Macdonald's glasses shows his monocle turned back into a pince-nez. Apart from the weld where the glasses would fit over the bridge of his nose, which is quite visible when you know what to look for, the new part of his glasses (right) is almost indistinguishable from the original (left).

Sacrilegious bird! Very few people know this, but there are burnished areas surrounded by a ring of white bird droppings on the heads of every statue on Parliament Hill. The burnishing is caused by frequent touching of little bird feet. About the only way you can see this burnishing for yourself is to take a ladder to Parliament Hill, prop it up against one of the statues, climb up and take a look — of course this is completely not allowed!

Chapter 30: The X-Rated Story of Queen Victoria's Lion

On my tours I would always say this was an x-rated story, and asked if there was anyone under eighteen. Then, looking directly at someone my own age, or thereabouts, I would ask: "How about you ma'am (or sir)? You look under eighteen."

The Queen Victoria statue on Parliament Hill, with the impressive male lion at its base, is by Quebec sculptor Louis-Philippe Hébert. It was unveiled in 1901. As it happens, Louis-Philippe Hébert sculpted another statue of Queen Victoria, also with a lion, a few years later. It is located in Gore Park in Hamilton, Ontario and was unveiled in 1908. Both lions are fine beasts, but the one in Hamilton seems to have "a little something" between his hind legs that the one on Parliament Hill does not.

Before I retired, people at work would sometimes come up to me and ask, "Don, what's the story of the lion's *a-hem*?" I just winked and said that if they wanted to find out they would just have to take my tour! However, now that I'm retired, here is the story and how I used to tell it.

I would stand on the step at the granite plinth near the lion's side, and I would get my group up close, standing or sitting on the grass. I would arrange it so that someone with a sense of humor was on my left, near the lion's front legs, and had a clear view of its underside. In order to better impress on them just how manly this beast was, I would place a hand on the muscles of his front leg and say:

> "Now this lion is incredible...look at these muscles... and the mane...and that face...and look at those thigh muscles. This lion is incredibly male and macho, except, maybe, for one little thing.

At this point I would bend over and look at the lion's belly and then lean over to that person who I had set up and say:

> "*Can you guess what that one little thing might be? Oh, look! There's something missing! What's going on?*"

This would always get smiles and laughs, and people always came up close to have a look for themselves. When the hubbub died down I continued:

> "*Now the story goes that when the statue was unveiled on September 21, 1901 the lion was completely male, if you know what I mean. Now this was the Victorian era...*

Actually it wasn't, because Queen Victoria had died in January of that year, so we were now into the Edwardian era. However, I didn't let that stop me.

> *...and they didn't call it the Victorian era for nothing. Women had to wear long dresses that reached almost to the ground because they weren't allowed to expose their ankles. In Victorian parlors, even pianos, which have legs, had skirts around them. The skirts covered the legs of the pianos so you couldn't see them.*
>
> "*The day this statue was unveiled, the sun was shining; the weather perfect. Ten thousand people filled up the front lawns, down almost to Wellington Street, waiting for the arrival of their Royal Highnesses the Duke and Duchess of Cornwall and York. Their Excellencies the Governor General and the Countess of Minto had arrived some minutes previously, and stood in front of the statue which was covered over with a canvas. Standing with them were the Ministers and their wives and daughters, Major-General O'Grady Haly and his military staff.*
>
> "*Arranged in a semi-circle along the back and sides was the guard of honor of one hundred men from the Governor General's Foot Guards.*

> "At exactly 12:15 three mounted policemen galloped up the drive shouting to the crowd that the Duke and Duchess had arrived. They royal party was loudly cheered as their carriage drove up the grounds and they took their place on the platform in front of the statue. Without any formality at all, the Duke pulled the cord and the canvas, which had covered the statue, fell off. And can you imagine, when people were standing right where you're standing, and they saw this thing...oh my goodness gracious!
>
> "The story goes that the wife of one of the Ministers was so upset that she hired a contractor with a blowtorch to cut it off! Ouch! And for years it was used as a paperweight...

Here I pretended I had a hammer in my hand, and was hammering in a nail.

> ...in her husband's office which was...

(waving my hand in the general direction of the Centre Block)

> ...right over there on the first floor,

and everybody would look to see where his office was.

> "We conserved this statue in the summer of 1991. I heard this story the fall before, and I made up my mind to check into it and see if it was true, or not. And so I did.
>
> "Now, a statue is hollow. If you rap on its legs and chest...

(knocking on the lion's ribs with my knuckles)

> ...it sounds hollow. When you were kids, did you ever get a chocolate Easter bunny and when you broke an ear off you could see inside? It was hollow, unless you had a solid Easter bunny. This lion is hollow, except the metal

is thicker, about as thick as my finger. So when the contractor cut the lion's thingy off, it would have left a hole, and he would have had to weld in a patch.

"My background is engineering, and I know he would have had to use what's called a butt weld (no pun intended) and I'd recognize a butt weld when I saw it. So I made up my mind that when we cleaned off the dirt the next summer I was going to have a good look for the patch and the weld marks. I did, but if you come over here and look at the lion's belly there's no sign of a patch at all, absolutely nothing!

"As it happened, I had scientists on my team from the Canadian Conservation Institute who were taking small scrapings of metal from all of the statues and analyzing them for chemical composition. They took thirty-four samples from fifteen different monuments, six of which were from the Victoria statue. They took them from the left foot of the allegorical figure of the young woman at its base, the plaque, the wreath, the right shoulder of Victoria, and the base and belly of the lion. These samples had to be taken anyway, so I asked if one of them could be from the belly. If a patch had been put in, it would have to have been a different bronze because the monument was cast in Brussels. The contractor would probably have purchased a piece of bronze for the patch here in Ottawa, and it would not be the same. However, they found that the bronze at the base of the lion (90% copper, 2% tin and 8% zinc) was almost exactly the same as at the belly (89% copper, 3% tin and 8% zinc).[701] Also, there was no sign of any cutting and welding.

"I studied the photograph of the unveiling ceremony with a magnifying glass but saw nothing there. I also read newspaper accounts of the day (the September 22, 1901 *Ottawa Citizen*, for example) and looked for newspaper articles over the next few weeks to see if there anything untoward, but there was not. So after all this what we concluded is that it was just a story; a well-known story, but just a story. It never happened."

It's an old story though. At least 50 years old. Clyde Boehmer, who was an assistant librarian in the Library of Parliament, tells us that in the 1950's someone sent an angry letter to the government demanding to know why Victoria's lion had been castrated.

Mr. Boehmer should know; he was the one they asked to check it out. He said he went over to investigate, and there was no doubt the deed had been done. The file marks, he said, seemed fresh but could have been several years old. He also checked the *House of Commons Debates* to see if it had been discussed in Parliament, or if any order had been given to cut it off, but there was nothing.[702]

In 1992, one year after we did the conservation, the Chairman of *The Committee to Remasculate the Queen's Lion* wrote to then Governor General, Ray Hnatyshyn, accusing us of a cover-up. The Chairman said that there was no longer evidence such as file marks that showed there used to be something between the lion's hind legs. He said that before we had worked on the statue, there definitely had been.[703] I found this rather funny because, as I said, it's not true. It's just a story.

Post Script

There's a post script to my story, and it's a good joke on me. A few years ago I was giving a tour to my brother and his family who were visiting from the States. My mother was there and also my wife.

Now my wife is something of an animal expert, and while I was telling the story about the lion and pointing at his belly and saying "it's not there!" she had moved away and was at the back of the lion, having a close-up look at its rear end, just underneath the tail.

Later she told me that I was having everybody look in the wrong place. She said a lion is a member of the cat family and, as everyone with a tomcat knows, a cat's *ahem!* is not on its belly. This is where it is on a dog or a horse, but on a cat it's much further back, right under the tail. "And it's not as big as you think," she said.

Now I can understand why the sculptor didn't put one in when he did the lion on Parliament Hill. It was, after all, the Victorian era. The question is, when he did the lion in Hamilton a few years later he put something on the belly, but what? Have a look at the following pages.

The X-Rated Story of Queen Victoria's Lion 297

An unabashed view of the rear-end of the lion on Parliament Hill. Photograph by the author.

298 *The Other Side of the Hill*

Both lions are fine beasts, but this one in Hamilton seems to have a 'little something' the one on Parliament Hill does not. Photograph by Jean Hammell.

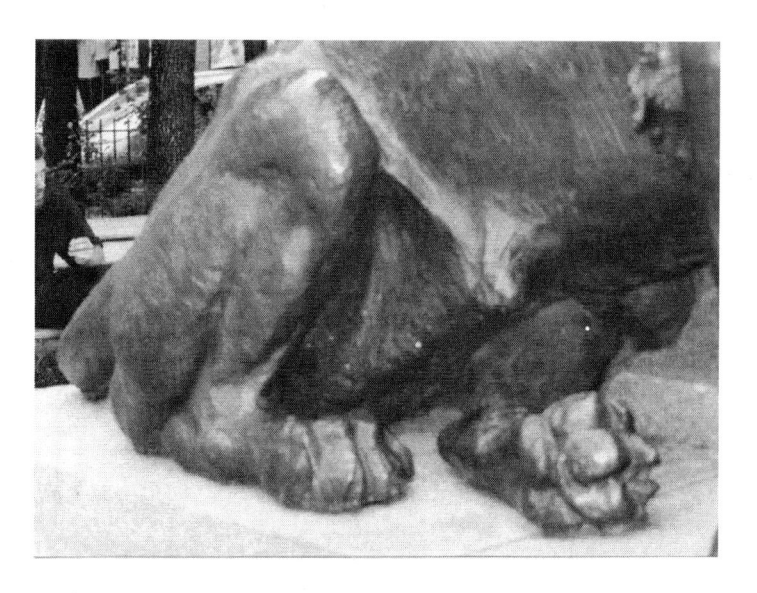

A close-up view between the lion's hind legs. So, what is it? A tuft of hair perhaps? A fold of loose skin? Photograph by Jean Hammell.

The X-Rated Story of Queen Victoria's Lion   299

"H.R.H. the Duke of Cornwall and York unveiling the statue of Queen Victoria, Parliament Hill. September 21, 1901" Credit: William James Topley/ Library and Archives Canada/ PA-011814/ Acc. No. 1936-270 NPC.

The author giving a 'goodbye tour' to Public Works staff in 2005 telling the post script and saying that, even on a big, macho lion like ours, his "thingy" would be very tiny. Photograph by Sybil Stymiest.

Chapter 31: Masonry Conservation 101

I used to tell my tour groups that this would be like part of a first year course at college or university. I call it Masonry Conservation 101.

In Masonry Conservation 101, you will learn about the different stones that were used to build the Parliament Buildings, the jargon that conservators and masons use, and two common masonry problems we found with the Parliament Buildings. You will learn what caused these problems and how they were repaired. Understanding what caused the problem is important – you can't fix something until you know why it broke.

THE BUILDING STONES

NEPEAN SANDSTONE

When you look at the Parliament Buildings most of the stone you see is Nepean sandstone. We talked in Chapter 6 about how this particular stone was chosen, and now we will learn more about it.

The pattern in which the stones are laid out in the Parliament Buildings is called *random coursing*. Because they are various sizes, they cannot be laid out in the regular pattern of coursing we find on a brick house, for example.[704]

In 1912 William Parks described three different types of Nepean sandstone – a white variety, a brown and yellow variety, and a hard, flinty white kind. Although it was commonly called white, the color could range from creamy white, to white with a slight cast of green, pink, grey or brown. The color is not always uniform; in some stone it appears in bands.

Back in the 1860's they didn't make any distinction between the three types, and mixed the white and colored with the hard flinty white kind. This is what you will see if you look at the Nepean stone on the Library and on the older parts of the East and West Blocks that face the front lawn. However, when they were constructing the Centre Block and Peace Tower, the builders only used the white and colored types, not the flinty white kind. These were much easier to chisel, and they hardened on exposure.[705]

In masonry, *patina* means the effects of years of accumulated dirt, staining, and weathering. The same applies for copper roofing. For statues, however, it is a little different. The patina is the dark colour given to the statue in the foundry.

Over time, Nepean sandstone patinates to beautiful shades of grey, rust, brown, yellow and black. The effect adds greatly to the quaintness and charm of the Parliament Buildings. J. D. Edgar (Speaker of the House of Commons from 1896 to 1899) said, "Its colouring is varied and beautiful, and grows in richness under the hand of time."[706]

It takes several decades for patina to form on freshly quarried stone. In 1867 when the Parliament Buildings were brand new the Nepean sandstone was cream-colored.[707] It was still cream-colored in 1879,[708] but by 1898, when Speaker Edgar made that comment, it had patinated nicely.[709]

When we conserved the Peace Tower from 1994 to 1996 we had to replace some of the stones in the gable over the main entrance because the original ones had deteriorated badly. The creamy white patch of the new stones is still (in 2008) quite visible, but over time these stones will patinate and blend in.

The black "dirt" on the stones is part of the patina. It's actually a gypsum crust (like the gypsum inside a sheet of drywall). Here is how it forms.

The mortar that holds the stonework together is made of lime, sand and water. When it rains, water runs down the wall, and as it passes over the mortar joints it dissolves calcium carbonate from the lime in the mortar, just a little. If there are cracks and open joints in the stonework, water can get inside the wall and while it is inside dissolve much more calcium carbonate. This water, now rich in dissolved calcium carbonate, washes back out through open joints further down the wall.

Water running down the wall tends to collect and stay longer on projecting stonework, such as surface roughness on the stones, horizontal bands, ledges, dormer roofs and heads of carvings. Gypsum forms when the dilute sulphuric acid that is in *acid rain* reacts with the calcium carbonate to produce calcium sulphate. This is the chemical name for gypsum.

Normally gypsum is white, but it is very good at trapping wind-blown bits of dirt, dust and soot, which make it turn it grey or black. In the coal-burning days, the soot used to come from smokestacks and chimneys, but nowadays it is from the exhaust fumes of cars and from the big busses and trucks that rumble up and down Wellington Street all day.

Other areas are rust colored. We're not used to thinking of stones as rusting, but in some stones the cementitious material that binds the small grains of sand together contains ferrous and ferric oxides.[710] If the ferrous oxides are exposed to water, they may dissolve and then when they run down the side of the building, they will be exposed to more oxygen, be oxidized (rusted) to ferric oxides which have low solubility. These will then precipitate as red rust stains. Ferric oxides are rust colored and are fully oxidized. They do not stain by rusting but by dissolving in acid rain and re-precipitating.

Dr. Van Cortland predicted rust staining in 1860, after he saw that some of the stone that was being selected contained ferrous and ferric oxides, but he thought it would ruin the buildings. In what must be one of the earliest references to acid rain he wrote to the Editor of the *Ottawa Citizen*, "as rain water and the atmosphere are more or less charged with acid, it is greatly to be feared from this cause alone, that the iron spots which permeate the stone will run, and not only irreparably disfigure the front of this otherwise magnificent structure, but as well, constitute a glaring and unsightly token of inexcusable ignorance."[711] He was right about the iron staining, but wrong about it ruining the appearance. It just makes it more quaint and beautiful.

We have talked about rust staining caused by the sandstone itself, but there is another way rust staining can form. There is a wonderful, very large area of rusty-colored patina on the south side of the East Block, near ground level, that was caused by run-off from an old iron roof.

Back in the 1860's, the high-pitched portions of the roof were covered with slates arranged in bands of different colors, and the decks, or the parts on top, were covered with galvanized iron laid on rolls.[712] Although nominally flat, these decks actually had a low slope towards the edges of the roof. When it rained, the water run-off from the roof produced these reddish-brown stains where it hit the wall below. So, this stain is very old, dating back to the time of Confederation. It tells a story about that old iron roof.

In some places the patina is green, caused by run-off from the copper roofs. Green staining can be seen all along the front of the Centre Block, about a metre above grade. Some of this was caused by run-off after we replaced the copper roof on the Centre Block South Façade Project in 1997. It has caused new patina on that section of stone that is now part of the history of the building, silent evidence of our roof replacement.

POTSDAM SANDSTONE

The reddish stone in the relieving arches over the windows of the Library, and the East and West Blocks, is Potsdam sandstone, from Potsdam in New York State. Except for color, it is identical to Nepean sandstone. In fact, it comes from the same rock formation. Its color ranges from white and buff to light shades of salmon, pink, purple, dark rose, and, less commonly, brick colored.[713] Potsdam was not used on the more modern Centre Block.

OHIO SANDSTONE

In 1867 John Page wrote: "The dressings, stairs, gablets, pinnacles, &c., are chiefly of a grayish colored freestone, from the State of Ohio...."[714] Ohio sandstone is soft, so it is easily carved and usually used for the moldings around windows and doors, and for stone sculpture such as the grotesques on the Peace Tower.

The quarry is in Amhurst, just outside of Cleveland, Ohio. It is still an active quarry and is used as a source of replacement stone today. Ohio sandstone is blue-grey in the lower parts of the quarry, but near the surface it is buff or beige. The quarrymen have made up their own name for the color of the stone that is in-between; it is '*greige.*'

The reason that it is buff at the top is because it is closer to the air. Over time, freshly quarried blue-grey stone gradually oxidizes to grey, and then to buff or beige.[715] For example, if you look at the stone around the windows in the East and West Blocks that John Page said in 1867 was grey, you will see that it is now buff. This color has a name: it is Birmingham Buff.

TEMPLETON SANDSTONE

Templeton sandstone is from the Templeton quarry just across the river in Quebec. It is used in the *quoins,* (pronounced 'coins'), which are the sawn blocks at the corners of the buildings laid with their faces alternately large and small.

WALLACE SANDSTONE

Wallace sandstone, which comes from the Wallace Quarry in Nova Scotia, is olive-green. The inscriptions over the Memorial Chamber, and the stone around the clock faces of the Peace Tower, for example, are Wallace sandstone. Only the Centre Block has Wallace stone in it. Wallace stone is not used anywhere else on the hill.

MORE JARGON YOU WILL NEED TO KNOW

Conservation is an umbrella term that includes *restoration, preservation,* and *rehabilitation.* It is the same kind of term as construction, which includes both renovation and building new. Conservation projects can include one, two or all three, just like a house construction project can include renovating the older part, and building on a new addition.

Restoration means turning back the clock, to make something look the way it did at some important time in its history.[716] In the 1980's East Block rehabilitation, for example, Sir John A. Macdonald's office was restored to what it looked like when he was Prime Minister, based on photographs and other evidence.[717]

Preservation means stopping the clock. The object is to prevent further damage, not to make it look the way it did when it was brand new. Preservation can be either short or long term.[718] Timber strapping at the corners of a badly cracked chimney or tower, held in place by closely spaced steel cables tightened with turnbuckles, is an example of short-term preservation. This strapping holds the structure together by giving it what amounts to a giant bear hug, until it can be given long-term attention. Many rooftop masonry elements were strapped in the early 1990's to await repair, and some of this strapping can still be seen. *Raking* and *repointing* (these terms are explained below), and repairing cracked stones, are examples of long-term preservation.

Rehablitation means turning the clock ahead, so that the building can continue to function into the future. Typically it involves replacing parts of the building that have reached the end of their service life, such as putting in a new heating and ventilating system, for example.[719] When we replaced the old copper roof on the south façade of the Centre Block with new copper, we rehabilitated the roof.

Mortar joints are called *pointing*. *Raking* a joint means scraping out deteriorated pointing, preferably using chisels and other hand tools to avoid damaging the stone. It is difficult to rake out very deeply because of the thickness of the joints. With Nepean sandstone, for example, raking is usually only to about 50 mm. *Repointing* means putting in new mortar. So if I were to say something like, "The pointing was so bad that we had to rake it all out and do 100% repointing," you will know exactly what I mean.

Two Common Problems

Rain will soak into a wall if there are cracks in the stone or if there are joints where mortar is missing. On sunny days the wall tends to dry out, but if more water goes in than comes out, after a while it will become saturated. A saturated wall leads to all kinds of problems, but in MASONRY CONSERVATION 101 we will look at just two.

FREEZE-THAW CRACKING

The first type of problem we will look at is called *freeze-thaw cracking*.

When we were in high school, we learned in science class that water expands when it freezes. Have you ever, on a hot summer day, wanted a soft drink but you forgot to put cans in the fridge? You might decide to put a can in the freezer so it will cool faster, but if you're like me you will probably forget about it, and when you finally remember it's too late. It's frozen and the can is bulging out all over. If you are very unlucky the tab has popped off, and frozen mush is all over the freezer, making a big mess for you to clean up!

On my tours I used to give a demonstration of what happens when a saturated wall freezes. I would have six or eight people stand in a row facing me, with their arms bent and the palms of their hands touching. They are blocks of Nepean sandstone, I tell them, and the spaces between them are mortar joints.

When I shout "freeze!" I tell them to expand by pushing against the person next to them. The person in the middle does not have any problem because the pressure on either side of him is balanced, but the persons on the end are pushed outwards.

When I shout "thaw!" they are to contract by staying in their displaced position and bringing just their hands back to where they were at the start. The person in the middle doesn't have to move his arms at all, but a "crack" occurs at the first joint in.

This is called one freeze-thaw cycle. In a typical Canadian winter there can be many freeze-thaw cycles. The temperature can drop below 0°C at night and rise above it in the day many times in a winter, especially in the spring thaws of February and March.

This demonstration suggests that the end stone moves out a considerable distance and that a big crack occurs after just one freeze-thaw cycle. However, in a real wall this doesn't happen.

The effects are very small but they occur every time the wall freezes and thaws and so they are cumulative. I have seen stones pushed out 25 to 50 mm.

We'll look at the repair after we look at the next problem because the same repair fixes both problems.

SALT CRYSTALLIZATION DAMAGE

Freeze-thaw occurs in the winter; but the problem we will look at now takes place in the summer. It is damage that comes from crystallization of salts that occur naturally in stone, such as potassium chloride, sodium sulphate, and others.

Permeability of a stone refers to how well water or water vapor can pass through it. If you hold a piece of stone in your hand it may seem solid enough, but it actually contains a large number of tiny holes, or pores. The pores in Nepean sandstone are not well interconnected so it is relatively impermeable. On the other hand the pores in Ohio sandstone are well connected. It is very permeable.

In a saturated wall, the pores in the stone are filled with water containing dissolved salts.[720] On a hot summer day this water can't evaporate through the hard Nepean sandstone (it is impermeable) so it travels along the interconnected pores, as well as voids and cracks in the stonework, to the permeable Ohio sandstone and evaporates out there. This might be at a window or a carving, for example, which are usually done in Ohio sandstone.

When the water evaporates, the salts crystallize and are left behind. The salt crystals left on the surface are called *efflorescence*. Efflorescence does not cause a problem; it is the salt crystals in the tiny pores about a millimetre below the surface, called *sub-flourescence,* that cause the damage. As these little holes fill up with salt crystals, stresses are built up in the thin walls of stone between the pores. When they get too great, these pore walls break, and the outside millimetre or so of stone pops off.

Each time stone flakes off, there's a little bit of damage done; not a lot at first, but over 30 or 40 years the surface can be taken back 75, 100 or even 150 mm.

WHAT WE DID

Both types of damage, freeze-thaw in the winter and salt crystallization in the summer, occur because the wall is saturated. So, the first thing is to dry the wall out.

Here is how it is done in major conservation projects like the Peace Tower or South Façade projects. First the masonry is scaffolded and roofed to keep out rain. In the summer the scaffold is covered with netting so that a breeze can come through. In winter the netting is replaced with insulated tarpaulins and heaters are turned on, so it is nice and warm inside year round.

The joints are then raked out (about 40 mm) so that the water can evaporate faster. While the wall is drying, the masons keep busy doing other types of work. On a big project, drying out can be for as long as a year.

Later the masons come back to repoint. The architect or engineer has designed the mortar so that it is very soft, and very permeable. It has to be softer and more permeable than the softest of the sandstones in the wall.

Repointing stops rainwater from getting in. However, realistically we have to assume that over time the mortar will crack and that rain water will get in. We have to have a safe way for it to evaporate back out.

It's amazing how many metres of joint there are in a wall. If you took a ruler and measured the length of each joint in the south façade of the Centre Block, for example, and added them up you would find there are 23 kilometres of joint. I did this one day by measuring the length of joint in a typical square metre and then multiplying it by the total area.

From the perspective of a water molecule, it is no longer necessary for it to migrate over to the Ohio sandstone to get out because it can simply travel to the nearest mortar joint and evaporate out there.

The mortar is also designed so that it is weaker than the stone. This way, if there is some freeze-thaw cracking it will follow the mortar joints and not take a short-cut through the stone. This approach forces salt crystallization damage and freeze-thaw cracking to occur in the joints, not in the stone. In a well-designed wall we expect the joints to fail, and they must be repointed as part of a regular maintenance program. We don't want the stones to fail. The stones that are the heritage fabric we want to preserve.[721]

Sandstone grotesques and other carved work can be *poulticed* to remove the salts. Poulticing is a very old technique that originated in medicine. When I was giving tours, I used to tell my group that when my grandpa had a boil, grandma used to use a mustard plaster to draw the infection out. This is very similar to what we do with stone, except instead of mustard we use a type of clay. Martin Weaver, one of Canada's early masonry conservators, described poulticing as "sucking the sulphur compounds out of the stone with mixtures of earth that would be smeared on the buildings like peanut butter on bread."[722]

Masonry Conservation 101 311

This strapping on the northwest tower of the East Block is an example of short term preservation. Photograph by the author.

Cracks and open joints in the east façade of the Centre Block allow water to get in the wall. Photograph by the author.

A demonstration of freeze-thaw cracking. Can you see how the 'stones' on the two ends are being pushed out? Photograph by the author.

This is a photograph of a freeze-thaw crack on the east façade of the Centre Block. The mortar is so hard that the crack goes right through the stones. In the old days builders thought that "stronger is better," but experts today know that mortar should be weaker than the stones so the crack follows along the joints and does not break the stones. Photograph by the author.

Damage from salt crystallization in the Ohio sandstone around a window on the West Block. Notice also in the top right how much the Nepean (dark) has been jacked outwards by freeze-thaw. There is a crack and then a mortar joint about 30 to 40 mm wide. When the wall was built, the joint would have been only about 5 mm wide. This wide joint is the result of several attempts in the past to repair the problem by simply filling the crack with mortar, but the real problem – water getting into the wall behind the stone – was not addressed. Photograph by the author.

You can find these black marks, shown on the right, at every entrance, on every building. Can you guess what they are? They are match strikes. In the old days, a Parliamentarian would come out of the building for a smoke, pack his pipe up with tobacco, reach into his pocket for his box of 'strike anywhere' E.B. Eddy wooden matches, take one out, strike it along the stonework and then light his pipe. This photograph is at the Peace Tower entrance. We cleaned the tower a little bit when we did the conservation, and we could have erased these marks. However, in a conservation project you don't do things like that! These match strikes tell part of the history of the tower. Photograph by the author.

CHAPTER 32: ALL I KNOW ABOUT COPPER ROOFS

When a young architect covers his roof with copper it will turn green when his hair turns grey.

A Danish saying[723]

THE LIFE-CYCLE OF A COPPER ROOF

The thickness of copper sheet is measured by its weight. Most copper roofs, including the Centre Block's, are 16 ounce copper. Imperial units are still used for copper, even in these days of metric. This means that a square foot of copper sheet weighs 16 ounces, or exactly one pound. The Peace Tower roof is thicker. It is 24 ounce copper.[724]

It is acid rain and wind-blown deposition of acidic gases and particles from burning coal that caused the copper roofs of the Parliament Buildings to turn green. It is the same mechanism that causes the statues to corrode (see Chapter 29).

A new copper roof is bright and shiny when it is first put on, just like a brand new copper penny. But it does not stay bright and shiny for long because the corrosion process begins immediately. After a few months the copper will turn brown, like a milk chocolate bar. This color gradually deepens and after about ten years it is like a dark, semi-sweet chocolate bar, almost black. Over the next decade it picks up hints of green in the black and when it is twenty-five to thirty years old it will be that wonderful shade of apple-green that is characteristic of the Parliament Buildings. (Excuse my mixed metaphors.)

The green patina is very thin, only 4 to 15 millionths of a metre,[725] but it adheres tenaciously to the metal. Samples cut from copper roofing can be bent back and forth through 90 degrees several times without cracking the patina. It is also stable to rubbing with abrasive pads.[726] However, unlike with statues, this green is actually good for the roof because it slows down the rate of corrosion and protects the underlying copper.

A copper roof can sometimes last a very long time. In 1929 researchers Vernon and Whitby examined the copper on the steeple of the North Mimms Church just north of London. After 300 years of exposure it showed remarkable freedom from pitting.[727]

The Peace Tower copper, which was installed in about 1925, is still in excellent shape. We carefully removed it as part of the 1994-1996 conservation project so that we could repair the concrete underneath. After we finished, we put it back on. The original Peace Tower copper may go on to have a very long life, perhaps as long as the steeple on the North Mimms Church.

Most copper roofs, however, don't last this long. We replaced the roof of the south façade of the Centre Block in 1997. It was installed in 1917, so it lasted 80 years. This explains why today the Peace Tower roof is green while the Centre Block roof lower down is brown.

The copper on the Centre Block was installed during World War I when there was a shortage of both men and materials. Many of the workers were learning on the job, and it was installed without allowing for expansion and contraction due to temperature changes. This caused the copper to buckle and tear.

It's surprising the temperature range that a roof experiences. On a hot summer day the temperature of a copper roof can be 40 to 45 degrees Celsius above the ambient temperature. The lowest temperature occurs approximately one hour before sunrise in the winter, when the copper temperature may be somewhat higher than ambient.[728]

In addition, maintenance workers sometimes used axes to break up ice buildups and this is not good for the copper.

The roof on the 1910 wing of the East Block was replaced in 1996 (it lasted 86 years), and the Library of Parliament roof, which was installed after the fire of 1952, was replaced in 2005. It lasted 53 years.[729]

How Long Does it take for the Copper to go Green?

The time it takes for a copper roof to go green depends on many factors, including geographic location, local and distant sources of air pollution and orientation of the copper with respect to the prevailing winds. Graedel *et. al.* graphed the time needed for the green patina to form on copper roofs in the northeast United States at different times between 1890 and 1978.[730]

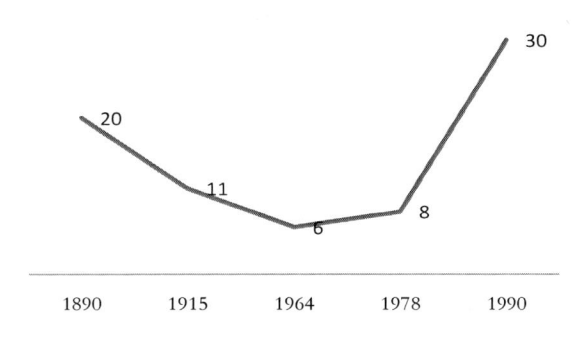

The number of years needed for development of the green patina on copper roofs over the last century.

Coal started to be used in Ottawa in the early 1870's, and its use continued up to the 1960's (Chapter 29). In 1890 it took, on average, about twenty years for a copper roof to go green, although the swing could be as much as plus or minus six years. As levels of air pollution increased, the time to go green decreased. It was the worst by the early 1960's, taking only about six years with a swing of three years. Graedel found that by 1978 there was a leveling off, or perhaps a slight increase in time required.

The original slate roof of the East Block was replaced with copper in the 1948-1951 rehabilitation[731] and took only 8 to 10 years to go green.[732] This fits reasonably well with Graedel's data for the northeastern United States, suggesting his graph would probably apply to Ottawa also.

There have been a number of copper roofing projects recently completed on or near Parliament Hill. The replacement of the copper roof on the south-west tower of the Chateau Laurier Hotel was completed in 1990, and is now (2008) almost green. The Langevin Building's copper roof, replaced in 1992, is now brown with a hint of green, especially on the west side. The new summer pavilion's copper roof (a 1993 replica of the one torn down in the 1950's) is beginning to turn green. The copper roof on the Supreme Court of Canada was replaced in 1994 and is now brown, but is starting to take on a bit of green. The roof on the south façade of the Centre Block, which was replaced in 1997, has a hint of green, and the Library of Parliament, replaced with copper in 2005, is still brown. All of this taken together suggests that it might take about 30 years for a roof to go green today.

Remembering that greenness is caused by air pollution, this is all good news! Clean air slows down corrosion tremendously. In 1932 Vernon reported copper spires on a roof in a remote part of Switzerland that were still bright and shiny after at least 30 years of exposure.[733] He also found that after 300 years, the south side of the steeple on the North Mimms Church was green, but the north side was still black. North Mimms had no coal-fired industries, and the supply of sulphate was almost entirely from pollution in London and other areas to the south, carried on the prevailing winds. These winds blew onto the south side of the steeple, which turned green, but the north side was shielded from the pollution and never progressed from black, even after 300 years![734]

It is interesting to think what might happen when air pollution is reduced further. It might be that the final stage of future copper roof replacements on the Parliament Buildings will be black, not green!

THEY USED TO DO WHAT?

One day when we were doing the south façade project I was walking up the central walkway towards the job site with Doug Pickard, the foreman of Heather and Little, my roofing subcontractor. He had completed the copper on the eastern third of the roof. It was bright and shiny, but the rest of the roof was still green. Doug pointed up at the new copper and told me this old roofer's tale.

Doug Pickard's Story

> *"You know, when they built the Centre Block back in 1916 they didn't have the dump trucks and gasoline powered construction equipment we have on job sites today. Back then they used real horsepower for hauling and other work. So there were a lot of horses at the jobsites, and of course, lots of horse urine.*
>
> *"Roofers used to mop horse urine on the new copper to make it go green faster. However, it couldn't be regular horse urine. It had to be from a mare-in-foal. I don't think it would have worked very well; it would have washed off in the rain."*

I looked in old architecture books to see if I could find more information on using horse urine to make the copper go green faster, without success. I did find out that the principal components of human urine (in mg per 100 ml of urine) are 1820 mg of urea, 53 mg of uric acid, 196 mg of creatinine, and small amounts of sodium, potassium, calcium, magnesium, chloride, bicarbonate, sulfate, and phosphate ions.[735] Pregnant mare's urine probably contains an even more complex mixture of compounds and is possibly potent at causing corrosion. After being wiped on copper, the corrosion products (a complex mixture of organic and inorganic salts) would most likely be green or blue-green, the typical colors of these compounds.[736]

Terry Sauve worked with our Realty group, and his work station was just down the corridor from mine. One day I was telling him about what Doug told me, and he told me this story.

Terry Sauve's Story

"My father, Roger Sauve, was a truck driver for Roy Braseau Cartage," he said. "I remember, when I was a small boy of about four or five, he was delivering sand to a construction site at the East Block. He would take me in the truck with him in the afternoons so my mom could rest. I remember very well the sand pit located on the north east corner of what are now the Hunt Club and River Roads. On entering the sand pit, my dad took me out of the truck and sat me on the sand bank. I watched in amazement as the big shovel loaded up my dad's truck. I still remember the shovel operator's name. It was Pete.

"When his truck was full, my dad drove it up to Parliament Hill. After each delivery, he and the others were asked to urinate in a pail so the roofers could use it. The roofers wiped the urine on the new copper. They said it made the copper go green faster."

This would have been in 1950.[737]

THE MISALIGNED PANS

Chris Borgal designed the copper roof that we put on in the Centre Block. When I told him I was writing a book, he asked me if I would include this story.

Chris Borgal's Story

"It is about half way along the roof between the east pavilion and the Peace Tower," he said. "When we took apart that section of roof, I was originally puzzled that the first cross seam down from the coping was misaligned at each "pan" (the flat part between each raised batten) in almost all of this length of the roof, while in all other locations the first cross-seams (which is the junction between lengths of copper pans) were pretty much aligned at a few inches below the coping (the rolled cap at the top of the roof slope). Concurrently with our work, there was some historical research underway which, in itself proved very interesting.... What was interesting was that the roof installation, including the copper, was initiated at the east end of the structure and, as far as I can recall, the first part of the roof to be re-coppered was the section between the east pavillion and what was to become the Peace Tower.

"Remembering that the building was constructed between 1916 and 1920 - an incredible feat that I am sure you are writing about - and that there was a war on during half this period, there was no question in my mind that the workers were being trained on the job (much in the manner that we had to train some 40 masons for the restoration work on the project). Their lack of skill, probably up to the forman's level, was to my mind the cause of the uneven seams. It seemed appropriate to provide a small memorial of this fact in the final result. So I asked the forman of Heather and Little to misalign the pan near the centre of the roof – being a perfectionist himself, I had to take a bit of time to explain why! But it was done in such a manner that it took me a bit of time to find it when looking for it later— which is just right in my mind as the memorial to those wartime workers is there but only visible to those who take the time to seek it out."

FINIALS AND CRESTINGS

Along the tops of the older buildings (the East and West Blocks, and the Library), where the roofs meet the skyline, are knee-high ornamental crestings, or fences, made of wrought iron with flowers and leaves. Long spear-like finials, also of wrought iron, stick up from the peaks of all the dormers, towers and turrets.

In 1949 Joe (or Robert?[738]) Swartman, a steeplejack with Public Works, drew large crowds when he was spotted clinging onto a finial on top of one of the East Block's highest towers. His job of repairing and replacing the decorations was never ending. At any one time about 50 of the more than 800 wrought iron spikes, with their flowers and leaves, needed work. High winds would bend them over, and sometimes they even fell to the ground, endangering tourists. So that, and shoveling snow off the green copper roofs, kept him outside all year long, even in winter.[739]

It was a healthy life-style...except for the day he fell of the roof of the Mackenzie Tower.

CLEARING ICE AND SNOW OFF THE ROOFS

In 1950 Joe and two other men were cleaning ice from the eaves of the roof high up at the top of the Mackenzie tower of the West Block, when his safety rope broke, and he fell 56 metres to the ground. Fortunately he landed in a deep snow bank, breaking only a leg and several ribs. The newspaper article in the *Globe and Mail* shows a photograph of the three workers waving happily at the camera a few minutes before the accident.[740]

I don't know if they were using axes to chop off the ice (the newspaper account doesn't say), but they shouldn't have. An axe can cut into the copper. You wouldn't use an axe to chop the ice off your roof at home, would you?

Public Works used to get help from the Ottawa Fire Department. They used hoses, working from the tall ladders on their fire trucks, to melt the ice off the roofs with steam. Unfortunately, the steam sometimes mixed with the smoke from nearby chimneys. When this occurred it could achieve considerable volume, and it looked like the building was on fire. In 1938 someone turned in a fire alarm,[741] and it happened again in 1958. "The building isn't on fire," said a House of Commons security guard. "There are four fire trucks here to clear off the ice."[742]

THE STORY OF THE COPPER PINS

One summer day in August 1994, I was on the roof of the East Block with Dianne Brydon and her boss Bob Desramaux. They were with the House of Commons Guide Program, which at that time was responsible for the tours inside the Centre Block. Today it is the Library of Parliament.

I had them on the roof so that I could show them the badly deteriorated chimneys and towers and other masonry close up. I wanted them to see the kind of damage that was going on, so their guides could explain the importance of what we were doing to the tourists.

At that time, the Peace Tower was being scaffolded. As we were watching the cranes hoisting huge pre-assembled sections of scaffolding up to ironworkers who bolted them into position around the tower, I said that next year we would be scaffolding the entire south façade of the Centre Block to do conservation there too. I told them we would be replacing the copper roof, because it was installed in 1917 and had reached the end of its service life.

Bob asked me what we were going to do with the old copper. My reply was that there was a standard clause in the specifications that required the general contractor to dispose of all waste, and that he would probably sell it as scrap. In those days, scrap copper was worth about 75 cents a pound and this would be reflected in lower tender prices. Bob's thought was that was too bad, because surely a better use could be found than to sell it as scrap.

A few weeks later I was in a jewelry store and saw a woman's brooch made of green copper with a certificate of authenticity in the box that said it was guaranteed to have come from a genuine heritage building. I remembered what Bob had said. If they could sell jewelry made from the copper roof of some unnamed heritage building, how much better it would be if the copper was from the Parliament Building!

Over the next four or five months, as we were completing the design and getting ready to tender the south façade, I spoke to many people around the office about doing something different with the copper roof, without success. One day my boss said to me that I shouldn't be spending so much time on it - it wasn't my job. By this time I just wanted to forget all about it. I told Chris to put a clause in the specs about giving the copper to the contractor.

A month later we got a new Director General, Glenn Duncan. One day (I don't know why) I mentioned to Glenn the idea of doing something different with the copper, and I told him about the brooch I had seen in the jewelry store. He said this was a great idea and told me, "do it." Well, this put me in an awkward situation because my boss had already told me to stop. In the end, I was able to explain to Glenn that I would be too busy now that the south façade was almost ready for tender.

I asked Chris to re-write that clause so that the contractor would give us the old copper. Glenn assigned the task of figuring out what to do with the copper to another fellow in the office, Vassily Sakalarides.

It was Vassily who came up with the wonderful idea of pins, plaques, paperweights, coasters and key chains being made out of the copper by persons with developmental disabilities. He made arrangements with two such organizations, one in Ontario and the other in Quebec,[743] and the contractor began to remove the old copper in November of 1996.

An unhappy incident occurred while some of the copper was in temporary storage in a warehouse on Villebois Street in Hull. During the night, thieves climbed a chain link fence and loaded two tons of the copper onto a truck. This represented about $1.5 million and three years of work for over 100 developmentally handicapped people.[744] Fortunately the Gatineau police were right on top of it. Within days they had captured the thieves and recovered the stolen copper.[745]

A few months, later Vassily came up to me and said that we had been nominated for the Minister's Award for the pins. I was shocked, and said to Vas that I didn't have very much to do with it; that the work was all his. He said it was too late. The decision had already been made, and I was being credited with the idea. Vas and I won the Minister's award for 1997.

You can buy this jewelry as a souvenir at the Centre Block gift shop, and I believe they are also sold in stores across Canada. The maple leaf pins are especially popular with tourists on Parliament Hill because of their low cost, about $8 dollars.

Speaking of cost, if you look at a pin you will see that the size of the green copper maple leaf is really quite tiny. I would think that many hundreds could be stamped out of a square foot of copper. At eight dollars a pin, that's a lot of money. If that same square foot of copper had been sold as scrap the contractor would have gotten only about 75 cents. The cost savings, passed on to the Crown in the form of a reduced tender, might even have been less.

The *Ottawa Citizen* called it "a recycling tale with a Canadian unity twist" and gave full credit to Public Works Canada for starting it all off.[746]

Chapter 33: Time Capsules

This was a tradition that started as early as the 11th century. As the largest of these buildings were religious, the client was usually the local bishop or cardinal. When told that the masons had completed the foundations and the corner stone was ready to be laid, or the sanctuary was being completed, or the nave, the bishop would declare a feast day known as a holy day, or holiday, to celebrate the event. Corner stones were always set at the north east corner of the building if proper masonry practice and superstition was being observed. Of course the greatest feast was held when the last stone on the building, the cap stone, was set into place. And they nearly always had a time capsule of some sort buried beneath them in the masonry wall.[747]

Bobby Watt 2006

I don't know how many time capsules are buried in the walls, chimneys and turrets of the Parliament Buildings. Probably, since the 1860's, there have been hundreds. As Bobby Watt states above, time capsules are usually buried at the north-east corner of the building, under the corner stone. When there is no cornerstone, like with a chimney, it is still buried at the north-east corner. You will never find a time capsule at, for example, the north-west corner.

Some time capsules were placed as part of a grand ceremony that was reported in the newspapers of the day. I've noticed (although I don't know if it a rule or not) that these ceremonies are usually held on September 1, at about 11 o'clock in the morning. Although these ceremonies were public knowledge at the time, they have been forgotten over the years, and most people today don't know that time capsules on Parliament Hill even exist.

The corner stone at the northeast corner of the Centre Block has had two time capsules under it. The first time capsule was put in at eleven o'clock in the morning on September 1, 1860 when the cornerstone for the original Parliament Building was laid by the Prince of Wales. "It [the cornerstone] was suspended from the centre of the huge ornamental crown by a large pulley, which ran around a gilt block. Under this was a cavity in which was placed a glass bottle containing a collection of coins of the present day, and a parchment-scroll...."[748] Of course, this time capsule was totally consumed in the fire of February 3, 1916.

However, the cornerstone itself survived and was removed from the ruins and cleaned. New text was added below the original, and it was re-laid at the northeast corner of the new Centre Block by the Duke of Connaught, the Governor General of Canada. A time capsule was again placed below it with the following contents: a $10 gold piece and a $5 gold coin dated 1912, the first issue of gold coins minted in Canada; the Canadian coins of 1916; die-proofs and Canadian postage stamps; local newspapers.[749] This time capsule is still buried there.

The cornerstone at the northeast corner of the Peace Tower was laid by His Royal Highness Edward, Prince of Wales at 11:30 a.m., September 1, 1919. The time capsule is in a sealed copper box in the stone below the corner stone. Inside is a history of the Parliament Buildings, a set of gold, silver and copper coins, postage stamps of the day, current issues of the Ottawa daily newspapers, a message of greeting, and other items.[750]

These time capsules were installed officially, as part of a grand and public ceremony. More often than not, though, time capsules were buried informally; just one mason leaving a simple message for the future that will only be found by another mason. It is a tradition that has been going on for centuries.

Bobby Watt is a Scottish Master Mason. He is President and General Manager of *RJW Stonemasons*, who were subcontractors on my Peace Tower and Centre Block South Façade projects. Bobby is also a talented singer with several CD's to his credit. He is a great guy and a good friend. He gave me this story for my book.

Bobby Watt's Story

"In ancient times the time capsule could be a wooden or metal box and would usually contain the names of the master mason, his masons, and apprentices, as well as the name of the official who had ordered the works. There were quite often artifacts included in the time capsule such as coins, articles of clothing and curios.

"On Parliament Hill, any job that RJW Stonemasons have been involved with has had a time capsule built into the wall. Ours are airtight cylinders that are sometimes as simple as masons jars put inside a metal single malt scotch container. They always include my name and a brief history of the company, the names of the masons, apprentices, and labourers working on the project, the front page of the Globe and Mail and The Citizen, any coins of the realm that can be rustled and something quirky to provide some enjoyment for whoever finds the time capsule. It could be a can of pop or old masons' chisel, a CD or tape. Just something that would be neat to find a century or more from now.

"For the Centre Block South façade project [1997] the capsule is buried in the chimney closest to the west side of the Peace Tower. It is two courses [i.e., two stones] down from the cap behind the large quoin on the northeast corner. There are some fine pictures of the ceremony that day, and although I had asked for, and was offered, the whole City of Ottawa Police Pipe Band, we had to settle for retired Deputy Chief Sandy Mackie who did an admiral job of piping up the flag-festooned cap stone. Also on hand was my (then) Member of Parliament, Alex Shepherd Esq.

"In the East Block Ventilation Shafts project [late 1990's] the capsule is buried beneath the cap stone on the eastern-most tower. In the Library Project [2005], it is buried two courses beneath the cap stone of the Stair Tower roof. That capsule also contains two letters as well as the usual stuff. One was written by Lothar Von Dannenburg, in German. Lothar is my most experienced

mason, and the Library was to be his last project before he retired and moved back to Germany with his wife after nearly fifty years in Canada. The other was written by my son Douglas, who outlines his hopes for the future and best wishes for whoever opens the time capsule. He also included a flag from the Toronto Maple Leafs 2002 playoff run that he had taken off his car, and added his most fervent hopes that the Leafs would win the Stanley Cup at some time prior to the capsule being found!"

A Post Script

A funny thing is that the ceremony with the flag-festooned cap stone wasn't supposed to have happened. A few weeks earlier, Bobby brought up the question of a ceremony to mark the last stone at one of our construction meetings. He explained that it was a tradition that went back to the 11th century.

I passed the request up the line and said I thought this was a good idea, but for whatever reason management's answer was no. I told the rest of the project team the bad news at our next meeting. "However we could have our own little celebration in private," I said, "but no media event."

On the day the cap stone was to be lifted, the sun was shining and the sky was blue. When I got to the construction site, much to my surprise Bobby's M.P., Alex Shepherd (Lib.; Durham, Ont.), was there. There was a Scottish piper, a Rabbi and an Anglican Priest. Bobby appeared to be both surprised and delighted, and he asked them if they would mind blessing the stone. Very curiously, they seemed to have come already prepared to do so.

Some members of the media were also there, and I knew the story would be on television that evening and in the newspapers the next day. The other media would complain about being left out as this would be perceived as an official event.

As the stone rose up in the air the wind caught the flag, the crowd applauded, and spontaneously broke into an emotional rendition of *O Canada!* I just stood there, overcome with pride at being part of that wonderful project, but at the same time embarrassed and nervous because I was the one who was going to have to explain all this when I got back to the office.

ANOTHER POST SCRIPT

That's not the only time Bobby wanted to organize an event on the Hill. It's kind of funny looking back on it, but I didn't find it very funny at the time.

At one of our construction meetings on the south façade I mentioned to no one in particular that my birthday was coming up. Bobby asked me if I would like it if he got a pipe band to line up along the edge of the roof of the Centre Block and play *Happy Birthday* for me.

Joking along I replied "sure, Bobby, that would be nice." Then I forgot all about it. But he was serious! He interpreted what I said as approval for him to go ahead. At the next meeting, he reported back that he was making good progress in arrangements for the pipers! I was stunned and cancelled the whole thing then and there.

"Bobby," I said, "I thought you were joking."

"Don," he replied in his best Scottish burr, "I never-r-r joke."

It was a very nice thought, but can you imagine if it had actually happened? A dozen Scottish pipers in kilts standing on the edge of the Centre Block roof playing *Happy Birthday?* Talk about a media event, and I would have been caught right in the middle of it! They would have been playing *Happy Birthday* to me, and my name would have been in all the coverage. Can you imagine all the explaining I would have had to do? I'm glad it didn't happen, but, like I said, it was a nice thought.

THE INSCRIPTIONS ON THE CORNER STONE OF THE CENTRE BLOCK

The Centre Block cornerstone was laid twice, so there are two inscriptions on it; one from 1860 and the other from 1916. By 1928 the original inscription was becoming very difficult to read (it was, after all, 68 years old), and the question of renewing it came up in the House of Commons.

Excerpt from the House of Commons Debates
May 11, 1928, p. 2931

Mr. William Garland McQUARRIE (Unionist, New Westminster, B.C.): I would like to call the attention of the minister to the cornerstone tablet at the northeast corner of the parliament buildings. Part of the lettering on this tablet has become almost entirely obliterated; I have seen a number of visitors looking at this tablet, and I think it would be a good thing to have that attended to and the lettering renewed so that anyone might be able to read the inscription.

Mr. John Campbell ELLIOTT (Lib.; Middlesex West, Ont.; Minister of Public Works): I have not had my attention particularly brought to this matter and I have not noticed it myself, but I will be glad to look into it. Certainly the corner stone and inscription should be kept in proper condition.

Excerpt from the House of Commons Debates
May 24, 1930, p. 2534

Mr. McQUARRIE: Last session I drew the attention of the minister to the cornerstone of the building, and he had the inscription renewed, which made a great improvement.

Cornerstones, Capstones and Time Capsules 333

The "flag-festooned cap stone" being hoisted with the Peace Tower in the background to the admirable piping of retired Deputy Chief Sandy Mackie. The crowd applauded and spontaneously broke into an emotional rendition of O Canada! Photograph by Bobby Watt.

Chapter 34: The Cats

*You would be surprised at the things which are allowed to go on for seven years, even in this department.**

General H. A. Young, 1954[751]

*This was the General's answer to why the cats were allowed to live under the steps in front of the Peace Tower for seven years, capturing the hearts and emotions of kindly old ladies. From this we know that Peregrine must have showed up on Parliament Hill in 1947.

The Early History of the Cats

A lot is known about the cats from 1924 on, but before that information is rather sparse, just a few scratches here and there.

I knew René Chartrand, the cat man of Parliament Hill. When I was giving tours, I used to stop with my group when we got to the cat colony. He would always take time from whatever he was doing to talk. I remember one day, he remarked that the cats had been on Parliament Hill longer than he had, and that they were there even before the Parliament Buildings had been built. "They came over with the soldiers when they built the Rideau Canal," he said.

René was probably right. The soldiers on Barrack Hill would have had cats, but the local hang-out for cats was not Barrack Hill. It was at Lavois' butcher shop on George Street down in Lower Town. We know this because William Pittman Lett wrote about it in his *Recollections of Bytown and its Old Inhabitants*:

> *J.B. Lavois, with thee I close*
> *My lengthy memories of those*
> *I knew of old in Lower Town,*
> *Though last, not least in size, I own.*
> *A butcher of the olden time,*
> *Who furnished roasts and steaks most prime,*
> *In the old George Street Market House,*
> *Where cats held many a grand carouse,*
> *Ere rats to Bytown emigrated*
> *In swarms pestiferous and hated.*[752]

Cats would have been used as mousers in the barracks and around the cookhouses and stables on Barrack Hill. However, Barrack Hill wasn't famous for its cats, not like Parliament Hill would later be. William Pittman Lett didn't say anything about the cats on Barrack Hill, nor did Thomas Ritchie, Mr. White, George R. Blyth, James Stevenson, William H. Cluff, Mr. H.P. Hill, and George C. Holland who we met in Chapter 2. They would have if Barracks Hill had been famous for them.

We can trace the history of cats on Parliament Hill back to 1924 when there was a mild plague of rats and mice in the basement of the then brand-new Centre Block.[753,754] Nobody knew where the rats and mice came from, but it is speculated that they might have come in through the steam tunnel from the Cliff Street Power Plant, or perhaps from the sewers.

Workers brought in cats to deal with the problem. They were fearless hunters, and the number of rats and mice soon fell to the point where they were no longer a problem. At night, the cats patrolled along the white marble corridors of the Centre Block, and kept the building safe and sound for our hard-working Members of Parliament.[755]

However, you can't mix boy cats and girl cats together and not expect anything to happen. The number of cats began to multiply rapidly, and a complaint was soon registered about the number of cats in the building. The 'higher ups' said they had to go. The workers in the basement protested because, in the first place, they had become fond of the cats and, in the second place, they said the cats were essential to keep the number of rats and mice down. However, the authorities were adamant.

The cats were banished to the outside, and it was not very long before the rats and mice took over again.

At 8:08 a.m. on Sunday, January 20, 1924, firemen were called to put out a small fire that broke out in some waste papers that had been collected from the offices and were being stored in the basement. However, it was only a small blaze, and by the time the firemen arrived it had been put out by enginemen, watchmen and so on. According to these fellows, it was very likely started by mice chewing on matches that may have been in the refuse, and it would not have occurred if the cats had still been inside.[756]

From 1924, up to perhaps the mid-1940s, the cats were outside cats. René Chartrand said that when he was a little boy (this would have been sometime in the late 1920's or early 1930's[757]) he would come to Parliament Hill and see cats everywhere. Animal control officers from the city had no jurisdiction on the Hill, and since there was no position of 'Parliamentary Dog and Cat Catcher' the cats lived without fear of being caught. No one looked after them, and René supposed that they ate birds, pigeons, and mice, which were in plentiful supply along the wooded cliff.[758]

There were also wild rabbits back then. In 1932 Captain George Black (Cons.; Yukon, Yukon), Speaker of the House of Commons, and a well-known figure from the Yukon Gold Rush of 1898, shot a half-dozen nibbling on the bark of evergreens on Parliament Hill. He spotted them from a window of his apartment at the back of the Centre Block. "You can go out and see the damage they had done before I bagged them with my 22-caliber target pistol," he said. He hung them up for a few days so they could properly ripen, and then had his chef make them into rabbit stew[759] (or possibly rabbit pie).[760]

Mrs. Mabbs

When René said that nobody looked after the cats in the 1930's, he was mistaken. Mrs. Mabbs worked almost 40 years for the House of Commons as a char lady, retiring in the late 1950's or early 1960's.[761]

There were about forty char ladies for the Senate, and sixty for the House of Commons.[762] The char ladies dusted and cleaned, but there were also men who did the heavier work like garbage collection, moving furniture, and washing floors. Their cleaning shift started at 5:30 a.m. and ended at 8:30 a.m., so they were gone before the Parliamentarians arrived for work.

They arrived on Parliament Hill quite early, between 4:00 am and 5:00 in the morning, and had to wait on the central walkway for the doors of the Parliament Buildings to open. In those days, people were not allowed on the grass as they are today. This was strictly enforced, and everybody had to keep to the walkways and paths. There were benches along the central walkway to sit on, more than there are today, and they used the stairs at the end of the walkway too.

Some of the char ladies would bring bags of food for the cats and birds. Two cats lived under the steps, and cats would come up from the escarpment too, where they lived in hideouts along the abandoned Lovers' Walk.

The char ladies wanted to bring the unused food into the Parliament Buildings and keep it fresh in the ice coolers. Back then there were ice coolers in every corridor where the Parliamentarians would go to get ice for their glasses of water. The char ladies were very upset when they were told they couldn't use the coolers because the smell of the tuna fish might taint the ice.

After their work shift was over, the char ladies would feed the cats again while waiting for their rides or the tram.

PEREGRINE AND POPPETT

Peregrine (aka Perry[763] or – but only to the char ladies – Queenie[764]) was a tame, very quiet, grey and white cat. She showed up on Parliament Hill in 1947, and by 1951 was one of the hill regulars.[765] In the spring of 1953, she gave birth to her daughter, Poppett.[766] Poppett was also a grey and white, the spitting image of her mother. However, while her mother was very quiet and calm, Poppett was a bit on the wild side – rambunctious and full of energy.[767]

The Cats   339

Peregrine and Poppett lived under the stairs at the end of the walkway in front of the Peace Tower. Their home was not heated by the steam that keeps the honourable members so nice and warm in the winter. On sunny days, Peregrine and Poppett could usually be found outside, warming themselves on the granite steps. There were two holes in the sandstone walls of the stairs, through which the cats could come and go, and which also let in fresh air. They shared their home with Charles Saunders the groundskeeper, who used it to store his wheel barrows and rakes and shovels when he was not busy working on the tulip beds. Mr. Saunders used a side door, and although it could be locked with a heavy chain and padlock, it was usually kept ajar, and the cats used it too.[768]

We know that rats invaded the Parliament Buildings in 1946,[769] and workers may have brought cats back in the buildings to deal with the problem then. By the 1950's there were cats in the East Block.[770] There was also Tobermory, the West Block's cat, a tough, male tabby cat whose skills as a ratter were the stuff of legends.[771] But the cats in the East and West Blocks were not known as the Parliamentary Cats. This was an honour enjoyed only by Peregrine and Poppett.[772]

Some of the out-of-town newspapers called Tobermory Punky[773,774] but in the *Ottawa Citizen* and the *Ottawa Journal* he was always referred to as Tobermory. Since these papers are local, they were probably correct.

We don't know who Poppet's father was. It was not Tobermory; at least, this was never mentioned in any historical accounts. It may have been one of the numerous feral cats who came and went on the forested escarpment, and who lived nearby in the abandoned ventilation shafts along Lovers' Walk.

Peregrine and Poppett were the favorites of the thousands of tourists who visited Parliament Hill each year, who loved to stop on the steps to stroke their fur. Of course, they were also the favourites of the char ladies,[775] Charles Saunders the groundskeeper,[776] the parliamentary stenographers,[777] Members of Parliament (especially Herbert Wilfred HERRIDGE, Independent C.C.F; Kootenay West, B.C.), Mounties, untold numbers of amateur photographers[778] and reporters like Special Correspondent John Bird.

Special Correspondent Bird wrote that for years Mrs. Mabbs[779] fed the cats a bowl of milk every morning, summer and winter, and even though cats and birds are natural enemies she fed the parliamentary pigeons too.

You know, the pigeons on Parliament Hill are very smart. A mother pigeon used to call the inside of that huge, octagonal chandelier that hangs down from the arch of the Peace Tower home, and on cold nights she and her *squeakers* (young pigeons still in the nest) happily enjoyed the heat inside from its many lighted electric bulbs. Their front door was a shattered pane of glass in the side of the bronze fixture through which they could come and go, flying down to get bread crumbs from Mrs. Mabbs, or to do other pigeonly things. Parliament Hill staff called them *The Happy Breed*. Unfortunately, they were evicted when the chandelier was taken down for refurbishment in 1947, and a new piece of glass was put in.[780]

But getting back to the cats, life was good for Peregrine and Poppet until suddenly, late in November of 1953 and without any warning or explanation whatsoever, their two entrances under the stairs were blocked up with steel grills.[781]

Excerpt from the House of Commons Debates
December 1, 1953, p. 491

Mr. Herbert Wilfred HERRIDGE (Independent C.C.F; Kootenay West, B.C.): I am sorry to rise a second time, but I have been approached by a number of dear old ladies in Ottawa asking me to put a question to the Minister of Public Works. Will the Minister of Public Works investigate reports that our well-known and popular cats are likely to starve to death owing to the blocking of certain apertures in the steps in front of the parliament buildings?

Mr. Herridge said that it was the dear old ladies of Ottawa who had approached him. However it's a pretty safe bet that it was not these ladies at all, but Special Correspondent John Bird because in the *Ottawa Citizen* the next day he told his readers the whole story.[782]

He provided a history of the cats and a description of their residence under the steps, and described how workers had blocked up their holes with steel plates. Moreover, he said that the real peril – of which Mr. Herridge had not been informed, was the groundskeeper's side door. Peregrine and Poppett were still living under the steps, even as Mr. Herridge was addressing the House, because they could still get in through this side door. It was usually left open, but if it were ever closed while the cats were inside, they would be trapped with absolutely no way out. No one would ever hear their heart-breaking meowing through the thick stone steps, and they would surely freeze or starve to death.

Mr. Herridge's question in the House of Commons and John Bird's newspaper report raised a caterwaul of protest from parliamentarians and public alike. The result was that the steel plates were taken off!

However, a year later, in November of 1954, they tried again. This time, the Humane Society was called in to trap the cats, but it was done on a weekend when the char ladies were not around to interfere. The traps were live traps that would not harm the animals, and they were inspected every hour on the hour, round the clock, to make sure the cats were not imprisoned any longer than necessary.[783]

It was Tobermory's bad luck that he was feeling a bit frisky that particular weekend. He had just come over from the West Block, and was visiting the girls when he got caught too. Mrs. Mabbs knew something was terribly wrong Monday morning when she went to feed the cats and discovered that they were gone. Once again, Special Correspondent John Bird discovered what had happened and rallied the char ladies and Mr. Herridge. He wrote a flurry of newspaper articles that resulted in a national furor.[784]

This time the department was firm. General Young, the Deputy Minister of Public Works, told reporter Bird it was for humanitarian reasons. They were chewing the electrical wiring underneath the steps, and could easily be electrocuted. He said that they were being fed too much during the summer, when all the tourists were about, and too little in winter, forcing them to hunt and kill pigeons. Lastly, he said, "That is no place for cats anyway."[785]

Mrs. E.S. Sherwood of 2 Crescent Road in Rockliffe wrote to the Editors of *The Ottawa Journal*:

> *What's the charge against them anyway? If the chars don't mind them and the gardener sticks up for them, who's complaining?"*
> *They've made the front page now, let's keep them!*[786]

But the decision was final.[787]

Now, under normal circumstances the policy of the Humane Society was to keep stray cats for thirty-six hours, and if homes couldn't be found they were put painlessly to sleep. However, Kenneth Switzer, the Director of the Humane Society, said they wouldn't dare put Peregrine, Poppett and Tobermory to sleep because they had "too much influence." He said that they were prepared to wait indefinitely, if need be, until good homes were found.[788]

It didn't take very long. Thanks to all the publicity, new homes were found within days.[789] Mrs. Hubert Spratt of 384 Sunnyside Avenue adopted Peregrine, who was perhaps the most easily placed because of her docile temperament. Having lived under the Parliament Hill steps most of her life, Peregrine liked sleeping in Mrs. Spratt's basement, but not as much as she enjoyed lying on Mrs. Spratt's lap and having her fur stroked and her ears rubbed.

Now, you would think that Tobermory and Poppett, being a bit on the rough side, would be more difficult to place, but they weren't! A good home was found for both of them. It was with farmer Allan Healy in Carp who, as it happened, was looking for two good mousers for his barn at that very time.[790]

Mrs. Mabbs died in 1963 at the age of 73. In a touching obituary reporter Win Mills of the *Ottawa Citizen* called her the hill's cat lady.[791]

The Cats Came Back

In June of 1968, a mother cat gave birth to five little kittens in a stump near the top of the escarpment. House of Commons messenger Donald Connell discovered them when he was out walking one day. He began setting down bowls of milk and cans of tuna fish for them. He figured that it cost him about $10 weekly.

By September, Connell was getting concerned about winter coming on and began seeking shelter for the cats. The newspaper article gives no details, but it seems that his compassionate nature had got him in some kind of trouble with his superiors; something about "a public servant who might have transgressed his oath of allegiance." [792]

Sgt. Hull

Another fan of the cats was Sgt. Hull. Frank Foran worked as a Senate Page until 1964, at which time he joined Senate Security. He retired in 1995 as a Sergeant. Foran knew Sgt. Hull well, and told me about him. [793]

Frank Foran's Description of Sgt. Hull

"Sgt. Lorne Hull lived on Woodroffe Street and was a doorman at the Lord Elgin hotel before he joined Senate Security as a constable in 1966. He eventually made Sergeant.

"He was a tall, tall gentleman, very polite and had cats of his own. At noon he would drive to the market and maybe the Lord Elgin and come back with scraps of food for the cats. He would feed them on the east side of Parliament Hill, behind the Sir John A. Macdonald statue. When he drove up, fourteen or fifteen cats would just appear. It wasn't that they were waiting for him, but they would just appear. He fed the cats from 1966 to when he retired, about 1982 or 1984."

Irène Desormeaux

Modern history of the cats begins with Irène Desormeaux. In 1976, she started the cat colony at the edge of the cliff behind the statue of Queen Victoria.[794] She fed the cats for 11 years until her death in 1987.

It all started when a man who worked in the Centre Block brought a cat to work. He had taken it home at first, but his wife didn't like it, so he brought it to Parliament Hill. Irène began taking care of it.[795]

She was known as the cat lady,[796] the bag lady, the pigeon lady[797] and, oddly enough, the 'go-to-hell' lady. Frank Foran remembered her well.[798]

> *"She was medium height and build for a woman,"* he said, *"a little heavy, and she always wore a long, red coat with a tam hat and a white pom-pom for as long as I knew her.*
>
> *"When she arrived on the hill each morning, it was with at least three large brown paper bags with handles in each hand, filled with scraps of food from the market. These were not paper bags like we have today, but about 3 feet long, with handles, and were double bagged for strength. Whenever anyone criticized her for feeding the cats she would say 'go to hell, go to hell, go to hell' repeating this 5 or 6 times. We used to call her the go-to-hell lady."*

Irène made the first cat shelter on Parliament Hill out of a cardboard box, with green plastic garbage bags for waterproofing held together by tape. It didn't last very long. When it fell apart in the fall of 1986,[799] the man who had given her that first cat built new shelters for her out of plywood.[800, 801] They were about the size of a large breadbox, lined with rugs that she would change when they got soaked.[802] In the summer, she fetched water for the cats from the Centennial Flame. In the winter, she would get water from the women's washroom in the House of Commons[803]

She went to Parliament Hill every day until she became sick. Then her neighbor, René Chartrand, who lived in the same apartment building on Charlotte Street, helped out. At first it was a favor, but she was getting sicker and sicker, and every day she would ask him to promise to take care of her cats if anything happened to her.[804] Finally he told her that he would, and the next day he and his wife Rita found her dead in her apartment.[805, 806]

She died August 13, 1987 at the age of 74. Sadly, her obituary does not mention her being the cat lady of Parliament Hill.[807] At the time of her death, there were five cats on the hill: two orange tabbies, a couple of black and whites and a grey.[808]

RENÉ CHARTRAND

At first René came to Parliament Hill twice a day to feed the cats, but by December 1987 he was being helped by Jean Marc Joubarne, a messenger in New Democratic Party leader Ed Broadbent's office, and Ed LaFranchaise the head groundskeeper.[809,810,811]

Joubarne fed the cats weekday mornings, while René came in the afternoons and twice on weekends. They paid for most of the cat food themselves, but were helped by other hill workers who contributed to a cat fund.[812]

The plywood shelters used by Irene were enlarged in 1988. The two men built insulated housing units, one with wall-to-wall carpeting. Joubarne called it Hotel California while Chartrand called it Parliament Zoo. It had twelve little doors, and the cats were housed in two's, so there was room inside for twenty-four cats.[813]

Later on Joubarne left, and René took over completely, but coming just once a day. Each morning René and Rita cooked chicken, beef and pork liver, mixed in some tuna, and packed everything into margarine tins to take to the hill. Do you know why they did that? They mixed in tuna because then the chicken, beef and pork liver wouldn't freeze as quickly, a fact most people don't know! Milk was carried in soft drink bottles and empty spice jars. With this mixture for the cats and raccoons, plus peeled carrots for the ground hogs, and peanuts for the squirrels, pigeons, chickadees, blue jays and sparrows, they were soon spending more than half their combined pension of $12,000 on the animals and birds. They couldn't afford the cost and were going broke.[814]

Many came forward to help out when they heard about their predicament. At Christmas, 1989, Bob Hicks (Prog. Cons.; Scarborough East, Ont.) set up a fund and collected money from around the hill. Ritchie Feed and Seed and an embassy donated food and people mailed money to René at home.[815]

Sadly, Rita Chartrand died in the spring of 1990.[816] However, René continued to look after the cats after her death. He used to name the cats after politicians. In 1995, for example, there was Brian, a big orange tabby, as well as Mila, Kim Campbell, Petit Jean and Joe Clark.[817] However, that was a long time ago, and more recently René was using normal names for cats, like Blackie, Brownie and Fluffy.

July 1997 started off badly. René announced that he was going to retire and was looking for a replacement. It was just too cold in the winter, and the work was too hard and too expensive. René's story was widely reported in the newspapers and on television. This generated a lot of interest, and the kindness of people really astonished and touched him. *Ralston-Purina Canada Inc.* offered to help by providing food. *The Alta Vista Animal Hospital* said it would spay and neuter the cats.[818]

In February of 1998 Hotel California came down and was replaced with the insulated, two-story cat apartment complex we have today.[819] The wood was donated by one of our contractors working on the CBUS project, an underground extension to the basement of the Centre Block.

It was at this time that Glenn Duncan, our Director General decided to make official what René had been doing unofficially all these years. René was granted a five-year license of occupancy for one dollar. Brian Cooke and Bob Louisseize each chipped in 50 cents to make up the dollar and Dan King drew up the license. This made René the *official* cat man of Parliament Hill.

About that time, Brian Caines began helping René, and in 2003 Klaus Gerken joined him. The two decided to put together a support team of eight to ten caregivers, including a veteri-

narian, to help René and ensure the cats are always well provided for. Brian was responsible for the cats' health and welfare. Klaus was the Official Photographer and created the Cats of Parliament Hill Blog at
 http://www.synapse.net/kgerken/CatsBlog.HTM.

I retired on my sixtieth birthday. My last day on the job was July 24, 2006. That afternoon I handed in all my passes which for years I had carried on a chain around my neck. They included the powerful blue House of Commons pass that allowed me to go almost anywhere in the Parliament Buildings. The Prime Minister's area on the third floor was about the only place that was out-of-bounds. In the last few hours I had before my bus came to take me home to Carleton Place, I decided to walk around the hill and say good-by. When I got to the cat colony, I saw René working away. I told him that I wouldn't be seeing him anymore. I told him that this was my last day, that I was retiring, and I asked him how much longer he was going to be around.

"Me?" he said. "I'll be here forever."

Author's Note: I wrote this chapter in 2006. Since that time there have been a number of developments. René retired at the end of 2008, and Klaus retired in 2010, at which point Brian took over full responsibility for the colony. Brian also manages the Cats of Parliament Hill Mailing List. Klaus still maintains the Blog and, along with Dan Taurozzi, developed and maintains the Cats of Parliament Hill Facebook Page. If you visit facebook at http://www.facebook.com/pages/The-Cats-of-Parliament-Hill/10150154879045652 you can follow the cats' adventures every day!

This may be one of Irene Desormeaux's original cat shelters, and it is still being used. The cat is Bugsy. At the start Bugsy was Betty, but his first physical at the vet's sorted out this little mistake! Bugsy is pretty easy-going though; he didn't mind the mistake! Photograph by the author.

The Cats 349

René always kept the area clean and tidy. On this cold December day, he had it nicely decorated with a Christmas wreath, hanging ornaments and strings. There are two cats in the lower right, but the attention of the young girl is captured by another off camera. Photographed by the author.

René and Blackie, 2006. Photograph by the author.

BIBLIOGRAPHY

A family story told by Lauren Moline, January 31, 1999. http://www.rideau-info.com/canal/feedback99.html.

A few lines of recent American history. [Providence]: Providence Journal, [1917], Harvard University Library Page Delivery Service, http://pds.lib.harvard.edu/pds/view/11221806?n=3&s=4&imagesize=1200&jp2Res=0.5&rotation=0

"A Death in Ottawa." *The Montreal Gazette*, July 4, 1911, p. 1.

"A Fortune in Opium Burned at Ottawa." *The Globe,* April 4, 1911, p. 2.

"A Partial Record Alien Enemy Activities 1915-1917: A Compelling Appeal for a War Policy for Aliens to be Adopted by the Government and Citizens of the United States", Reprinted from Data Prepared by the Providence Journal by the National Americanization Committee, Harvard University Library, http://pds.lib.harvard.edu/pds/view/12014464?n=3&imagesize=1200&jp2Res=.25

"Air Drafts Through Commons Endanger Health of Members." *The Globe and Mail,* May 17, 1944, p. 9.

Allison, Catherine. "Stray cats Strut for Birthday: Parliament Hill's Feline Friend Turns 80, vowing to give food 'til I'm 100'." *The Montreal Gazette*, December 29, 2001, p. A.8.

"Amateure Performance."*The Bytown Gazette,* February 16, 1837.

"An Historic Sundial." *The Citizen,* May 19, 1921, p. 1.

"Architects Plead for the West Block." *The Gazette,* Montreal, January 24, 1957.

"Are Opposed To Idea Silencing 'Big Ben'." The *Ottawa Citizen*, July 20, 1927, p. 2.

Arthur, E.R., *et. al.*. "The West Block and its Future." *Journal of the Royal Architectural Institute of Canada,* December (1956): 485.

Ashurst, Nicola. "Air/Water Abrasive Cleaning of Stone and Brickwork," http://www.buildingconservation.com/articles/masonry/abrasive.html. This article is reproduced from *The Building Conservation Directory*, 1996.

"Artistic License Bows to Biology in decoration of the Peace Tower." *The Globe and Mail,* June 7, 1938, p. 3.

"At the Capital," *The Globe,* February 16, 1897.

"Bared Teuton Plots, Means Testifies," The New York Times, December 7, 1917, p. 9.

Barmazel, Steven. "Keeping the Cats Fat on Parliament Hill; Pensioner Keeps Promise to Dying Friend to Aid Strays." The *Ottawa Citizen,* December 18, 1987, p. A.1.FRO.

Baptista-Neto, José A., Bernard J. Smith, John J. McAllister, Maria Augusta M. Silva, and Fabio S. Castanheira. "Surface modification of a granite building stone in central Rio de Janeiro." *Anais da Academia Brasileira de Ciências, Print ISSN 0001-376, An. Acad. Bras. Ciênc.,* 78 no.2, (2006), http://www.scielo.br/scielo.php?script=sci_arttext&pid=S0001-37652006000200011.

"Battalion on guard on the Hill." *The Citizen,* February 4, 1916, p. 3.

Beauchesne, Arthur. Canada's Parliament Building – The Senate and House of Commons, Ottawa. Ottawa, published by the author, 1946.

"Beaver Receives Position of Honor in Carved Doorway of Peace Tower." *The Globe and Mail,* January 10, 1938, p. 15.

Belden, H. *Illustrated Historical Atlas of the County of Carleton Ont. (Including City of Ottawa).* Toronto: H. Belden & Co., 1879.

Bilkey, Paul. *Persons, Papers and Things.* Toronto: The Ryerson Press, 1940.

Binnie, Nancy E. "Color Monitoring on Outdoor Bronze Statues in Ottawa, Canada". *From Marble to Chocolate, The Conservation of Modern Sculpture,* Tate Gallery Conference 18-20 September 1995, editor: Jackie Heuman (London: Archetype Publications), p. 73-81.

Bishop, Charles (Senator). "Years Around Parliament: Thoughts, Men, Memories. Chapter 3: Atmosphere of Parliament". The *Ottawa Citizen,* September 29, 1945, p. 1.

Bird, John. "A Bird Of A Yarn Tells About 'Hill' Pigeons." The *Ottawa Citizen,* March 5, 1949, p. 16.

Bird, John. "No longer 'backscratchworthy': Peregrine And Poppett The Hill cats Being Evicted From Cosy Quarters." The *Ottawa Citizen,* December 2, 1963, p. 23.

Bird, John. "Peregrine and Poppett Escape Death by a Cat's Whisker." *The Ottawa Journal*, November 23, 1954, p. 1. See also "West Block's Tobermory Arrested Too As Found-In." November 23, p. 18, and "General Young is Sympathetic but Firm on Cats' Eviction," November 25, p. 1.

"Blaze in Commons is Blamed on Rats," *The Ottawa Journal*, January 21, 1924, p. 4.

"Blaze in West Block." *The Globe*, June 15, 1910, p. 2.

Blyth, George R.. "Bytown, 1834, to Ottawa, 1854." *Women's Canadian Historical Society of Ottawa,* Transactions, Vol. IX (1925): 5-15.

"Bomb or no Bomb, Ottawa is Alert." *The Globe*, February 5, 1916, p. 1.

Bond, Courtney C.J.. *Where Rivers meet: An Illustrated History of Ottawa*. Windsor: Windsor Publications (Canada Ltd.), 1984.

Bourrie, Mark. "Parliamentary Cat Keeper." *The Toronto Star*, February 11, 1996, p. C2.

Bourrie, Mark. *Canada's Parliament Buildings*. Toronto, Ontario: Hounslow Press, 1996.

Bowman, Charles. O*ttawa Editor, the Memoirs of Charles A. Bowman. S*idney, British Columbia: Gray's Publishing Ltd., 1966.

Bowman, Charles. "The Tower of Parliament." *The Citizen*, May 31, 1921. In *Each Morning Bright, 160 Years of Selected Readings from the Ottawa Citizen 1845-2005*, Doug Fischer, editor, Ralph Willsey, editor/designer, 223-225.

"Boy Friend Took Drug before Leap, Girl Says." *The Globe and Mail*, June 25, 1970, p. 4.

"Boy Injured On Parliament Hill." The *Ottawa Citizen*, March 27, 1933, p. 5.

Bower, V.A. "Bronze Penthouse Pigeons Thrown Out By Landlord. The *Ottawa Citizen*, October 22, 1947, p. 12.

Brault, Lucien. *Ottawa Old & New*, Ottawa: Ottawa Historical Information Institute, 1946.

Brault, Lucien. *Parliament Hill.* 2nd ed. Ottawa: The National Capital Commission, 1979.

"Brighten up Statues on Hill in view of Coming Conference," The *Ottawa Citizen*, June 28, 1932, p. 1.

"Bronze Bigwigs on Parliament Hill to Get Bath in Harmless Detergent." The *Ottawa Citizen*, September 19, 1951, p. 21.

Brown, Craig (Ed.). T*he Illustrated History of Canada*, Toronto: Lester & Dennys Limited, 1987.

Brown, Dave. "Brown's Beat (Final Edition) - Jewels of the Hill." The *Ottawa Citizen*, August 21, 1986, p. B.1.

Brown, Karen. "Memorial to Slain Officers Dedicated on Parliament Hill." The *Ottawa Citizen*, (final edition), March 23, 1994, p. A.4.

Burgess, Beth. "He Helped Save the PM From 1916 Parliament Fire." *The Local Citizen*, February 3, 1984, p. 17.

Ottawa: Ottawa Citizen Group Inc., 2005.

Canada. Cabinet Conclusions database at Library and Archives Canada website www.collectionscanada.gc.ca. Meeting date: December 12, 1967, RG2, Privy Council Office, Series A-5-a, Vol. 6323, Access Code: 90, p. 2. See also meeting date: May 26, 1966, RG2, Privy Council Office, Series A-5-a, Vol. 6321, Access Code: 90, p. 8.

Canada. E*nvironment Canada, Atmospheric Science Division - Acid Rain FAQ*, http://www.atl.ec.gc.ca/msc/as/acidfaq.html

Canada. *A Treasure to Explore, Parliament Hill, Ottawa, Ontario, Canada*, http://www.parliamenthill.gc.ca.

Canada. B*uilding the Future – House of Commons Requirements for the Parliamentary Precinct*, http://www.parl.gc.ca/common/AboutParl_Building.asp?Language=E

Canada. *Contract between His Majesty the King and P. Lyall & Sons Construction Company Limited, Reconstruction of the Parliament Buildings at Ottawa*, September 29, 1916, P.W. No. 11132.

Canada. H*ouse of Commons Debates,* June 6, 1887, 13 June 13, 1895, March 17, 1904, July 4, 1905, April 6, 1906, January27, 1911, February 4, 1916, April 12, 1916, May 27, 1921, May 28, 1921, June 13, 1924, May 11, 1928, May 24, 1930, May 11, 1932, May 8, 1936, June 6, 1938, June 11, 1941, August 12, 1946., November 24, 1949, June 28, 1950, June 28, 1951, December 1, 1953, June 23, 1955, July 1, 1955, July 18, 1955, July 19, 1955, April 27, 1956, August 3, 1956, July 4, 1956, February 15, 1957, June 16, 1958, May 10, 1960, July 18, 1960, July 20, 1960, July 21, 1960, June 15, 1961, June 17, 1961, February 28, 1966, October 24, 1966, December 11, 1967, December 12, 1967, June 28, 1972, February 12, 1976.

Canada. *Report on Collapse of Tower*, 5-6 Edward VII, Sessional Papers (No. 161), A. 1906, 6p.

Canada. *Report of the Commissioner of Public Works for the Year Ending 30th June, 1867*, 31 Victoria, Sessional Papers (No. 8), 1867, Appendix No. 21, "Report on the Public Buildings at Ottawa", by John Page, August 29, 1867 p. 201-243.

Canada. *Royal Commission Re. Parliament Buildings Fire at Ottawa, February 3, 1916: Report of Commissioners and Evidence*. Sessional Paper No. 72a. Ottawa: J. de L. Taché, 1916.

Canada. *Standards and Guidelines for the Conservation of Historic Places in Canada*. Parks Canada, 2003.

Canada, Province of. *Documents Relating to the Construction of the Parliamentary and Departmental Buildings at Ottawa*. Quebec: 1862.

Canada, Province of. *Report of the Commission Appointed to Inquire Into Matters Connected With the Public Buildings at Ottawa*. Quebec: Hunter, Rose & Co., 1863.

Canada. *Scrapbook Debates*, 8 June to 27 July, 1866, National Archives of Canada, AMICUS No. 3445729.

Canada, Province of. *Contract, Specification, Questions and Answers, and Schedule of prices of Parliament Buildings, Ottawa City, C.W.*. Quebec: Printed by Augustin Coté, 1861.

Canada, Province of. *Specification of Departmental Buildings Ottawa*. Quebec: Printed by Rollo Campell, October 1859. National Archives of Canada, RG 11, Vol. 183, File: Specification of Departmental Buildings/Ottawa.

Canada, Province of. *Contract, Specifications and Schedule of Prices of Departmental Buildings, Ottawa City, C.W.*. Quebec: Printed by Stewart Derbishire & George Desbarats, 1859.

Canada, *Specification for the Completion of Tower and memorial Chamber, Parliament Buildings, Ottawa*, J.O. Marchand and John A. Pearson, January, 1924.

"Champlain Sea", *Wikipedia, the free encyclopedia*, http://en.wikipedia.org/wiki/Champlain_Sea

"Candles Light Commons – All MP's in the dark During Power Break." *The Globe and Mail*, July 5, 1961, p. 8.

Carroll, Bill. "The Disneyesque conspiracy." The *Ottawa Citizen*, September 26, 1968, p. 25.

"Carved Stone of Commons, Passes at 72 (Anthony Borysink)." The *Ottawa Citizen*, July 30, 1957, p. 7.

Centennial Flame Research Award Act (1991, c.17), http://laws.justice.gc.ca/en/C-27.5/text.html.

Centennial Flame Research Award Act (1991, c.17), http://cmte.parl.gc.ca/HOC/committee/372sper/webdoc/wd.

"Chapter I: History Without Hansard." *Debates of the Legislative Assembly of United Canada*, edited by Elizabeth Nish, XI. Montreal: Presses de L'Ecole des hautes études commerciales, 1970.

Chapman, Gladys. "Ottawa's Famed Noon-Day Gun." *The Globe and Mail*, December 15, 1956, p. 21.

Clippings related to the design and construction of the Parliament and Departmental Buildings (from the *Daily Globe*, page 2, unless noted otherwise) - May 10, 1859, May 21, 1859, June 1, 1859, July 25, 1859, August 31, 1859, September 16, 1859, September 19, 1859, October 28, 1859, November 19, 1859, November 21, 1859, November 25, 1859, December 15, 1859, December 17, 1859, December 23, 1859, December 24, 1859 (two articles), March 10, 1860, March 16, 1860, September 3,1860, December 24, 1860, April 11, 1861, May 11, 1861, June 18, 1861, February 21, 1862, March 26, 1862, April 2, 1862, April 12, 1862, April 16, 1862, May 6, 1862, May 8, 1862, May 9, 1862, May 10, 1862, May 12, 1862, May 13, 1862, p. 1, May 14, 1862, May 16, 1862, May 17, 1862, May 21, 1862, p. 1, May 21, 1862, p. 2, May 22, 1862, June 4, 1862, June 12, 1862, p. 1, June 21, 1862, July 2, 1862, August 6, 1862, August 21, 1862, August 25, 1862, August 29, 1862, October 2, 1862, October 2, 1862, p.1, November 24, 1862, p. 1, December 11, 1862, December 16, 1862, December 17, 1862, January 31, 1863, February 28, 1863, March 2, 1863, p. 1, March 2, 1863, March 3, 1863, March 10, 1863, March 24, 1863, April 20, 1863, April 21, 1863, April 30, 1863, May 26, 1863, September 10, 1863, September 18, 1863, February 20, 1864, February 27, 1866, March 31, 1868.

Cluff, W.H. "Memories of Bytown." *Women's Canadian Historical Society of Ottawa*, Transactions – Vol. VIII (1922): 63-76.

Commonwealth Historic Resource Management Limited, *The Landscape of Parliament Hill: A Collection of Illustrations*, Architectural and Engineering Services, National Capital region, Public Works and Government Services Canada, Revised June 1992.

Connolley, Greg. "Unofficial war On Hill: Cut Off Pigeons' Food." The *Ottawa Citizen*, December 20, 1960, p. 40.

Contract, Specification, Questions and Answers, and Schedule of Prices, Parliament Buildings, Ottawa City, C.W. Quebec: Printed by Augustin Coté, 1861.

Copper Development Association, Architecture Design Handbook: Section 4 Architectural Details: Roofing Systems, http://www.copper.org/applications/architecture/arch_dhb/roofing/long_pan.html

"Copper Recovered: Theft of Roofing threatened Project for Disabled People." *The Gazette*, November 8, 1996, p. A.5.

Cragg, Kenneth C.. "Ottawa rats – East Block Main Scene of Invasion." *The Globe and Mail*, November 9, 1946, p. 17.

Crerar, J.P. "All-Night Clock Chimes." The *Ottawa Citizen*, July 19, 1927, p. 9.

Cross, Austin F.. "Dead Statesmen Stand On Parliament Hill." The *Ottawa Citizen*, June 27, 1949, p. 2.

Cross, Austin F.. "Old West Block Might Give way to Bigger $6,400,000 Building." The *Ottawa Citizen*, February 12, 1957, p. 1.

"Crowds Thronged the City Streets." *The Citizen*, February 4, 1916, p. 2.

"Date Concealed In Stone." *The Montreal Gazette*, September 1, 1919, p. 12.

"Date There, Though Hidden." *The Evening Herald*, Rock Hill, S.C., December 20, 1919, p. 31.

David, L. O. *Souvenirs et Biographies.* Montreal: Librairie Beauchemin Limitée, 1911.

"Death of Dr. Vancourtland." *The Citizen*, March 25, 1875. In *Each Morning Bright, 160 Years of Selected Readings from the Ottawa Citizen 1845-2005*, Doug Fischer, editor, Ralph Willsey, editor/designer, 86-87. Ottawa: Ottawa Citizen Group Inc., 2005.

"Departmental Buildings" *The Globe,* December 3, 1875, p. 3.

"Departmental Buildings at Ottawa." *The Globe*, September 13, 1877, p. 2.

Deputy Minister of the Public Archives. *Letter to Mr. R.C. Wright, Chief Architect of Public Works*, September 2, 1926.

Deputy Minister of Public Works. M*emorandum to the Minister,* August 5, 1952. National Archives of Canada, RG11, Vol. 5028, file 822-419.

National Archives of Canada, RG11, B1(a), Vol. 399, Subject 1025, p.349-355.

De Jonge, James A. T*he Military Establishment at Bytown, 1826-1856.* Parks Canada, 1983.

Dickason, Anthony. " 'Walk Of The Lovers' Gone To Weeds." The *Ottawa Citizen*, June 20, 1953, p. 13.

Dictionary of Canadian Biography Online, Library and Archives Canada, http://www.biographi.ca/EN/

"Dominion Parliament Buildings." *The Globe,* April 8, 1893.

Drew, George Alexander. George Drew fonds (MG32-C3), Federal Political Career series, vol. 248, file 334.1 "House of Commons – The Opposition – Material for Questions in the House 1954-1956"; and George Drew fonds (MG32-C3), Federal Political career series, vol. 255, file 352, DPW.1 "Federal Departments – Public Works."

"Drinks Down Stairs." *The Globe,* May 23, 1888. See also *The Globe*, June 18, 1896, p. 5 and September 16, 1896, p. 4.

"Drowned in the Ottawa." *The Globe,* December 7, 1901, p. 1.

Dugas, Dan. "Queen's Bronze Lion: Did it Used to be a He?; Restored Statue Has no Scars From the Testicular Tampering." *The Gazette,* July 25, 1992, p. A.7.

Dyer, Trish. "Pensioner the Santa of Parliament." *Toronto Star (final edition),* December 9, 1988, p.E13.

Eade, Ron. "Putting Our House in Order." The *Ottawa Citizen (Valley Edition),* March 18, 1995, p. A1.

"East Block Will Be Renovated." The *Ottawa Citizen*, December 19, 1949, p. 8.

Edgar, J.D.. *Canada and its Capital.* Toronto: George N. Morang, 1898.

Eighty Years' Progress of British North America. Toronto: Published by L. Nichols, 1865.

Bibliography 361

Egan, Kelly. "NRC's Talking Clock Keeps Canada on Time: Official Timekeeper Improves Public Access to Precise System." The *Ottawa Citizen*, December 26, 1999, p. C8.

"1870's Grandeur Returns to East Block." *The Globe and Mail*, October 12, 1981, p. 12.

"Explosion in the House of Commons," *The Globe*, July 1, 1886.

"Fall of the Great Tower is Watched by Many Thousands." *The Citizen*, February 4, 1916, p. 1.

"Fatal Delay in Handling Fire: Could it Have Been Stopped?" *The Citizen*, February 16, 1916, p. 10.

Fetterley, Norman. *Renovations at Parliament Buildings*. CTV-TV, Sunday Edition, July 7, 1996, 12:52, MH Media Monitoring Limited, Ref. 12270.17.

"51st State?" *The Citizen*, February 6, 1976, p. 3.

"Fire", *The Packet*, September 4, 1847. In *Each Morning Bright, 160 Years of Selected Readings from the Ottawa Citizen 1845-2005*, Doug Fischer, editor, Ralph Willsey, editor/designer, 13-14. Ottawa: Ottawa Citizen Group Inc., 2005.

"Fire Chief Graham is Certain Parliament Fire was Incendiary." *The Citizen*, February 16, 1916, p.3.

"Fire the Act of Alien Foes?" *The Globe*, February 4, 1916, p. 1.

"Firemen Thaw Commons Ice." *The Globe and Mail*, December 24, 1958, p. 2.

"Firemen Tried to Save Women." *The Citizen*, February 4, 1916, p. 2.

"Fire Protection. *The Globe*, February 17, 1897, p. 2.

"Five are Lost in Great Fire." *The Citizen*, February 4, 1916, p. 3.

Fortin, Lynn. *Parliament Building Facelift*. CBC Radio, The House, April 6, 1996, 9:33am, MH Media Monitoring Limited, Ref. 56040.5.

Gardner, E.A.. Memo to the Deputy Minister, Public Works, from the Chief Architect titled "Rehabilitation and/or Reconstruction – West Block – Ottawa, Ontario", March 10, 1955. National Archives RG 11, Vol. 5032, File 822-421 (volume 3), 5 pages.

"German U.S. Ambassador Responsible for the Fire," *The Globe*, February 4, 1916, p. 1.

Grams, Grant W., Department of History, University of Alberta. "Karl Respa and German Espionage in Canada During World War One." Journal of Military and Strategic Studies, Fall 2005, Vol. 8, Issue 1. www.jmss.org/2005/fall/articles/grams.pdf

Franey, J.P., and M.E. Davis. "Metallographic Studies of the Copper Patina Formed in the Atmosphere." *Corrosion Science*, 27, no.7 (1987): 659-668.

Fraser, John. "Scandals, Illusion Make East Block Symbol of Canada." *The Globe and Mail*, July 1, 1980.

Friel, M.A. "Some Account of Bytown," *Women's Canadian Historical Society of Ottawa*, Transactions, Vol. 1, 1901, pp. 22-35.

"Future of the West Block." The *Ottawa Citizen*, June 24, 1957, p. 6.

"Gaston Means," Wikipedia, the free encyclopedia, http://en.wikipedia.org/wiki/Gaston_Means

Gerken, Klaus J. "The Cats of Parliament Hill Blog," http://www.synapse.net/kgerken/CatsBlog.HTM.

"German U.S. Ambassador Responsible for the Fire." *The Globe,* February 4, 1916, p. 1.

Gillan, Michael. "Parliament Hill Fence Widens to Smooth Route for Traffic." *The Ottawa Journal,* September 29, 1966.

"Gossip from the Capital", *New York Times*, January 13, 1895, Wednesday, Page 19.

"Gov't Publishing Information For Carillon Lovers." The *Ottawa Citizen*, July 12, 1928, p. 19.

Gradel, T.E., K. Nassau, and J.P. Franey. "Copper Patinas Formed in the Atmosphere – I. Introduction." *Corrosion Science*, 27, no.7 (1987): 639-657.

Gray, Walter. "Test on McGee, Mollie satisfactory to Ottawa." *The Globe and Mail*, June 3, 1960, p. 13.

Gray, Walter. "Parliament's West Block, Now 99, is Given an Up-to-Date Interior." *The Globe and Mail*, July 21, 1961, p. 13.

Green, Lowell. I*t's Hard to Say Goodby.* Ottawa: Creative Bound International Inc., 2007.

Gwyn, Sandra. *The Private Capital*. Toronto: McClelland and Stewart Limited, 1984.

Haig, Robert. *Ottawa, City of the Big Ears*. Ottawa: Haig & Haig Publishing Company, 1969.

Hain, George. "Ottawa Letter." *The Globe and Mail*, June 20, 1956, p. 6.

Hand Book to the Parliamentary and Departmental Buildings, Canada. Ottawa: Printed by G.E. Desbarats, 1867.

Hardy, Reginald, H. "Piper-Member Recalls When He Defied Police." The *Ottawa Citizen*, May 22, 1943, p. 24.

Hardy, Reg. "Architects at Work: 700 Rooms in Plans for New West Block." The *Ottawa Citizen*, November 22, 1955, p. 1.

"Healthier Working Conditions Sought for Civil Servants." *The Globe and Mail*, July 15, 1944, p. 5.

Heeney, A.D.P. M*emorandum for the Prime Minister re: Inscription on Bell from Old Parliament Buildings*, August 24, 1939, King's Paper reel c-4277.

Holland, George. "Recollections of Bytown, Reminiscences of Ottawa," Ottawa History Vol. VII, p. 30.

"House Recess Due to Storm." *The Globe and Mail*, May 22, 1941, p. 20.

"How One Fire Started From Lighted Cigar." *The Globe*, February 24, 1916.

Hickey, Harvey. "Face of Parliament Hill Due for Plastic Surgery." *The Globe and Mail*, November 25, 1955, p. 1.

Hill, H.P. "Before and After Colonel By. Beginnings of the Dominion Capital And The Men Who Guided It's Destinies in Early Years." *The Maple Leaf*, August, 1923, p. 11.

Hodge, Harry. "Bells Ring Again as Peace Tower Reopens: Carillon and Clock Running Once More After Two-Year Silence". The *Ottawa Citizen* (final edition), December 3, 1996, p. B.2.

Holland, George C. "My Ottawa Memories." *Macleans Magazine, May 15, 1922*.

"Hose Burst Drenches Crowd." *The Citizen*, February 4, 1916, p. 1.

"House Carvings Called Inartistic." *The Globe*, May 9, 1936, p. 1.

"How Statues are Made: The Sculptor's Art as Practiced Here and Abroad." *New York Times,* January 25, 1891, p. 14.

Hume, J. A. "Federal Buildings Unclean, Says M.P." The *Ottawa Citizen,* June 21, 1947, p. 2.

Hume, J. A. "Old Supreme Court Building to be Demolished Next Year." The *Ottawa Citizen,* December 28, 1955, p. 15.

Hume, J. A. "West Block Saved." The *Ottawa Citizen,* June 19, 1957, p. 43.

Hunter, C.B. Deputy Minister of Public Works. *Letter to Mr. H.R.L. Henry, Private Secretary to the Right Honorable the Prime Minister,* November 9, 1938, Kings Paper V. 252, reel c-3734.

Hutchison, Bruce. "The Empty Tower." The *Ottawa Citizen,* January 31, 1932, p. 34.

Illustrated Guide to the House of Commons and Senate of Canada. Ottawa: Published by F.R.E. Campeau; Printed by A. Bureau, Sparks Street, 1879.

"In the West Block." *The Globe,* February 12, 1897, p. 1.

Jackman, Peter. "100-Year Reprieve for Centennial Flame?" *The Ottawa Journal,* December 12, 1967.

Jackson, Richard. "Historic Hill Plaque Found," *The Ottawa Journal,* July 5, 1973.

James, M.E.. "Jubilant Message of Glorious Music Comes From Bells" *The Globe,* Saturday, July 2, 1927, p. 1.

Jenkins, Charles, C. "Huge Broadcast is Great Success." *The Globe,* Saturday, July 2, 1927, p. 1.

Kenny, F. Gertrude. *Some Account of Bytown.* Read to the Women's Canadian Historical Society of Ottawa in December, 1898. *Women's Canadian Historical Society of Ottawa,* Transactions, Vol. I, 1901, p. 24.

King, William Lyon Mackenzie. M*emorandum for Mr. Heeney,* December 1, 1939, King's Paper, reel c-4277.

Kirby, Jason. "New Hill Cat Keeper Ditched." *Centretown News,* February 6, 1998, p.1.

Korski, Tom. "Burning down the House: A modern analysis of the 1916 Centre Block fire poses intriguing new questions," the *Ottawa Citizen,* January 29, 2011.

Kritzwiser, Kay. "Peace Tower and Carillon Get $4.6 Million Overhaul: Ottawa Rings in the New." *The Globe and Mail*, September 2, 1982, p. 19.

Landau, Henry (Captain). *The Enemy Within: The Inside Story of German Sabotage in America.* New York: G.B. Putnam's Sons, 1937.

"Laplante Lost Life by Fear of Jumping." *The Globe*, February 5, 1916, p. 1.

"Latest From Ottawa." *The Daily Globe,* September 1, 1877, p. 8.

Lawrence, D.E. "Building Stones of Canada's Federal Parliament Buildings." *Geoscience Canada,* 28, no.1 (2001):13-30.

"Lays Bare German Plots," New York Times, December 7, 1918, p. 1

"Leadership Since Last war Scored By Colonel Steacy." The *Ottawa Citizen*, November 12, 1941, p. 7.

"Let the Senators Go to Hull, Knowles urges in Commons." *The Globe and Mail,* February 9, 1949, p. 1.

Lett, William Pittman. *Recollections of Bytown and its Old Inhabitants.* Ottawa: "Citizen" Printing and Publishing Company, 1874.

Lett, William Pittman. *A Short Panoramic view of Ottawa's History Written in its Jubilee Year 1877.* The Historical Society of Ottawa: Bytown Pamphlet Series No. 45, 1993.

Lett, William Pittman. *The Transition of Bytown to Ottawa, 1827-1877*, The Historical Society of Ottawa: Bytown Pamphlet Series No. 45, 1993.

"Light On The East And West Blocks." The *Ottawa Citizen*, March 13, 1950, p. 6.

Livermore, J.D. *A History of Parliamentary Accommodation in Canada, 1841-1974.* Ottawa: Advisory Committee on Parliamentary Accommodation, 1975.

Lofaro, Tony. "The Height of National Pride." The *Ottawa Citizen,* final edition, October 9, 1996 p. C.1.

London, Mark. *Masonry: How to Care for Old and Historic Brick and Stone.* Washington: The Preservation Press, 1988.

"Lovers' Walk Benches." The *Ottawa Citizen*, September 3, 1930, p. 31.

"Lovers' Walk Will Be Closed For Duration." The *Ottawa Citizen*, July 29, 1932, p. 49.

Macdonnell, John. "Parliament Hill rabbits. The *Ottawa Citizen*, April 20, 1932, p. 11.

MacGregor, Kerry. "Catman Gets Corporate Help." The *Ottawa Citizen*, July 30, 1997.

MacGregor, Roy. "While Great Men Meet, Hill Lady Cares for Cats." The *Ottawa Citizen*, April 7, 1987, p. A.3.

MacGregor, Roy "Parliament Hill's 'Cat Man' Doesn't Count Cost of Helping Animals (final edition)." The *Ottawa Citizen*, June 23, 1989, p. A.3.

MacGregor, Roy. "Keeping the Faith; Robbed by Death of his Partner in Life, the Cat Man of Parliament Hill Soldiers on Alone." The *Ottawa Citizen (Final Edition)*, November 30, 1990, p. A.1.FRO.

Mack, Robert C., and John P. Speweik, "Repointing Mortar Joints in Historic Masonry Buildings." Preservation Briefs, Technical Preservation Services, National Park Service, US Dept. of the Interior http://www.cr.nps.gov/hps/tps/briefs/brief02.htm#Properties%20of%20 Mortar.

"Magnificent Public Buildings Crowning Glory of the Capital." The *Ottawa Citizen*, May 16, 1939, p. 4.

Maintaining Eternal Flame, CBC Radio, CBO Morning, May 4, 1990, 5:55am., Media Tapes and Transcripts Ltd.

"Making Bronze Statues: Difficulty in Preparing for Casting the Big Figures." *New York Times*, November 15, 1903, p. 22.

Malloy, Katie. *Peace Tower Needs a Facelift*. The Hill Times, September 13, 1990, p. 11.

Mathers, A.S. *Letter to Mr. E.A. Gardner, Chief Architect of Public Works, Regarding The West Block*, April 1, 1960. National Archives RG 11, Vol. 4793, File 744-1013 (volume 1), 2 pages.

Mathers & Haldenby, Architects, and Edouard Fiset, Associate Architect. *Report to the Deputy Minister of Public Works of Canada on the Present Condition and Future Disposition of the Building on Parliament Hill in Ottawa Known as the West Block*. This is an 8 page attachment to a letter to Maj.-Gen. H.A. Young, Deputy Minister of Public Works, Regarding the West Block of the Parliament

Buildings, December 23, 1955. Library and Archives Canada, RG 11, Series B4a, Vol. 4800, File 752-1013, pt.1, 1955-60.

Mathers, A.S. *Letter to Mr. E.A. Gardner, Chief Architect of Public Works, Regarding The West Block*, June 29, 1960. Library and Archives Canada, RG 11, Series B4a, Vol. 4800, File 752-1013, pt.1, 2 p. with floor plan of Scheme #3, June 27, 1960, attached.

Maurenbrecher, A.H.P., K. Trischuk, M.Z. Rousseau, and M.I. Subercaseaux. "Key Considerations for Repointing Mortars for the Conservation of Older Masonry", National Research Council of Canada, Institute for Research in Construction, IRC-RR-225, January 2007. http://irc.nrc-cnrc.gc.ca/pubs/rr/rr225/rr225.pdf

Maytor. "To the Editor of the Bytown Gazette." *The Bytown Gazette and Ottawa Advertiser*, December 7, 1843.

McCabe, Aileen. "Showpiece of the Hill About to Open." *The Citizen*, June 20, 1980, p. 37.

McCabe, Aileen. "It's Squatters' Rights as Ministers Rush In." *The Citizen*, June 20, 1980, p. 37.

McGovern Heritage Archaeological Associate. *Stage 3/4 Archaeological Assessment of the Bank Street Building Site Zones A, C, E. and F, Parliament Hill, City of Ottawa*. Ottawa: Public Works and Government Services Canada, Parliamentary Precinct, 2004.

"Means Admits Acting as German Agent." The New York Times, July 18, 1918, p. 5.

"Members Slid Down Rope of Towels; One Fell Twenty Feet." *The Citizen*, February 4, 1916, p. 2.

"Memorandum to Cabinet – Centennial Flame," Cab. Doc. No. 818/67, December 8, 1967, National Archives of Canada, RG 2, Vol. 6329.

Meredith, C.P., Lieutenant-Colonel, "Ottawa in the Seventies", *Women's Canadian Historical Society of Ottawa,* Transactions – Vol. 11 (1954): 44.

Mica, Nick and Helma. B*ytown – The Early Days of Ottawa*. Belleville: Mika Publishing Company, 1982.

Mills, Win. "Hill's cat lady goes to reward." The *Ottawa Citizen*, February 21, 1963.

"Miss Blair Drowned. In Bravely Attempting to Rescue Her, Mr. H.A. Harper Perishes." *The Citizen*, December 7, 1901, p. 1.

"Mmes Bray and Morin Died Trying to Save Their Furs." *The Citizen*, February 5, 1916, p. 7.

"More Room for MP's." *The Globe and Mail*, April 10, 1954, p. 4.

"More Room Needed." *The Globe*, April 28, 1901, p. 1.

Mullington, Dave. "Parliament Hill Cats Cope Well With Construction." The *Ottawa Citizen*, April 17, 1997, p. B7.

Munro, Margaret. "Acid Rainfall Ravaging Parliament Buildings." The *Ottawa Citizen*, January 10, 1981, P. 1.

Murray, Henry A. *Lands of the Slave and the Free, or, Cuba, the United States, and Canada*. London: 1857.

"New Copper Roof for East Block," *The Windsor Daily Star*, April 11, 1950, p. 16.

New York Times, February 5, 1916, p.2
http://query.nytimes.com/mem/archive-free/pdf?_r=1&res=9506E5D61E38E633A25756C0A9649C946796D6CF

"Night and day Work Among The Debris Recovers Two Bodies of Flame Victims." The *Ottawa Citizen*, February 7, 1916, p. 1.

"Ninety Tons Of Steel In Tower Where Carillon Now holds Sway." The *Ottawa Citizen*, Huly 2, 1927, p. 7.

"No Dice." *The Maple Leaf*, January 25, 1945, p. 5.

" 'No Pets' Remain To Warm Official Hearts on Parliament Hill," *The Globe*, May 16, 1936, p. 1.

"No warning of a German Plot." *The Citizen*, February 11, 1916, p. 3.

"Noon Gun will Boom Again." The *Ottawa Citizen*, final edition, May 6, 1992, p. C.5.

"Notes and Comments." *The Globe*, June 4, 1895, p. 4.

"Notes and Comments." *The Globe*, April 18, 1906, p. 6.

"Now These Really are the Fat Cats of Ottawa." *The Vancouver Sun (3* edition)*, December 21, 1987, p. F6.

Obituary. Samuel Keefer," *Transactions of the Canadian Society of Civil Engineers*, Vol. IV, January-December, 1890, p. 332-7.

Obituary. Irène Desormeaux. *Le Droit*, August 15, 1987, p. 41.

"Old Peregrine, Poppett and Punky To Be Missed on Parliament Hill." *The Montreal Gazette*, November 23, 1954, p. 2.

"Ohio Gangster," *Time Magazine*, U.S., May 31, 1930, http://www.time.com/time/magazine/article/0,9171,738946,00.html

"One Jail Never Occupied – Room in Canadian Parliament Building Reserved for Defiant Members," *The New York Times*, December 26, 1931, p. 14.

"One of Our Most Historic Buildings." The Montreal Gazette, July 11, 1955, p. 6.

"Only PM Can Predict Future of West Block." The *Ottawa Citizen*, October 8, 1958, p. 4.

"Ottawa Buzz." The *Ottawa Citizen*, June 26, 2000, p. D3.

"Ottawa Firemen Are Fooled Again." *The Globe and Mail*, February 19, 1938, p. 15.

"Ottawa's Chiming Clock." The *Ottawa Citizen*, August 24, 1928, p. 12.

Owram, Douglas. *Building for Canadians: A History of the Department of Public Works, 1840-1960*. Ottawa: Public Relations and Information Services, Public Works Canada, 1979.

Ottawa History, a scrapbook in the Ottawa Room of the Ottawa Public Library. Vol. I, II(a), III(a), III(b), IV(a), V, VI, VII.

"Ottawa's 'Crown of Towers.'" *The Globe*, February 4, 1916, p. 2.

"Our Civilian Destruction Program." The *Ottawa Citizen*, April 15, 1957, p. 3.

"Our National Carillon in the Peace Tower." *The Globe*, September 3, 1927, p. 17.

"Political Neutrality." *The Montreal Gazette*, March 17, 1951, p. 7.

Padovano, Anthony. *The Process of Sculpture*. New York: Doubleday & Company, Inc., 1981.

Page, John. "Report on the Public Buildings at Ottawa," August 29, 1867. In *Report of the Commissioner of Public Works for the Year Ending 30th June, 1867*, 31 Victoria, Sessional Papers (No. 8), 1867, Appendix No. 21, p. 201-43.

Parks, Wm. A.. *Report on the Building and Ornamental Stones of Canada*, v.1 Ottawa: Government Printing Bureau, 1912.

Parley, Graham Parley. "The Gun Falls Silent; NCC quietly muzzles the noon-hour cannon on Parliament Hill." The *Ottawa Citizen*, final edition, April 27, 1991, pg. A.1.FRO.

"Parliament Hill Cats Are Justified by Fire." *The Globe*, January 21, 1924, p. 1. See also "Automatic Fire Alarm Gives Warning and Outbreak is Speedily Checked." *The Globe*, February 1, 1924, p. 2.

"Parliament Hill Fire Brought Into King Murder Case." The Montreal Gazette, December 7, 1917, p. 5.

"Parliament's West Block, Now 99, is Given an Up-to-Date Interior," *The Globe and Mail*, July 21, 1961, p. 13.

"Parliament Buildings Plans are Exhibited." *The Globe*, March 22, 1916, p. 7.

"Parliament Buildings Today Represent $2,000,000 Asset. Present Walls Can Be Reused." *The Citizen*, February 18, 1916, p.2.

Passfield, Robert W.. *Building the Rideau Canal: A Pictorial History*. Markham: Fitzhenry & Whiteside in association with Parks Canada, 1982.

"Peace Tower Back in Business after Facelift." *The Times Colonist (Victoria, BC)*, December 3, 1996, p. A8.

"Peace Tower is Reopened for Visitors." *The Globe and Mail*, July 30, 1970, p. 31.

"Peace Tower Struck by Lightning Bolt; Near Panic Ensues." *The Globe*, March 26, 1929, p. 1.

Phillips, R.A.J. *The East Block of the Parliament Buildings of Canada*. Ottawa: Queen's Printer, 1967.

Phillips, R.A.J.. *The House of History: The East Block of the Parliament Buildings*. The Historical Society of Ottawa Bytown Pamphlet Series No. 11, 1984.

Photograph caption. *The Globe and Mail*, April 2, 1949, p. 17.

Photograph caption. *The Globe and Mail*, October 3, 1952, p. 1.

"Plans By Greber Tabled In Commons Urge New Office For Prime Minister." The *Ottawa Citizen*, October 19, 1945, p. 20.

"Plexiglass Cover Planned for Peace Tower Lookout." *The Globe and Mail*, April 4, 1970, p. 3.

"Policeman Gave Life in Saving Mr. Nesbitt." *The Globe,* February 5, 1916, p. 3.

Pope, Joseph, C.M.G.. T*he Tour of Their Royal Highnesses the Duke and Duchess of Cornwall and York through The Dominion of Canada in the Year 1901*, 52-53. Ottawa: Printed by S.E. Dawson, Printer to the King's Most Excellent Majesty, 1903.

Pope, Joseph. M*emoirs of The Right Honorable Sir John Alexander MacDonald*, Vol. 1. Ottawa: J. Durie & Son, 1894.

"Premier Escaped Without Hat or Coat and With Difficulty." *The Citizen,* February 4, 1916, p. 1.

"Prince May Lay The Corner Stone Of Peace Tower." The *Ottawa Citizen*, July 29, 1919, p. 2.

Programme for the Laying of the Corner Stone of the Main Tower by His Royal Highness Edward, Prince of Wales, K.G. etc. etc. at 11:30 o'clock a.m. Monday the first day of September, 1919, Public Works and Government Services Canada Record Room.

"Progress of the Public Buildings", *The Citizen*, February 17, 1860. In *Each Morning Bright 160 Years of Selected Readings from* The *Ottawa Citizen 1845-2005*, Doug Fischer, editor, Ralph Willsey, editor/designer, 37. Ottawa: Ottawa Citizen Group Inc., 2005.

"Protesters Disrupt Peace Tower Ceremony."*Ottawa Global News,* 6:54 p.m., December 2, 1996, Mediascan.

"Public Works Estimates." *The Globe,* May 20, 1897.

Pullen, Derek and Jackie Heuman, "Outdoor Sculpture: Challenges and Advances." *Conservation,* the Getty Conservation Institute, v. 22, n. 2, 2007. www.getty.edu/conservation/publications/newsletters/pdf/v22n2.pdf .

"RCMP Haul Down New Flag Flying in Ottawa." *The Globe and Mail,* August 6, 1957, p. 18.

"Reading Room Paper Found in Blaze Two Days Before Big Fire was Extinguished." *The Citizen,* February 24, 1916, p. 10.

"Reading Room Stands Burned in an Instant." *The Citizen,* February 4, 1916, p. 3.

"Rebuilding Capitol in Hon. 'Bob's' Hands." *The Globe,* July 1, 1916.

"Repairs Aloft on Parliament Hill." *The Globe and Mail,* August 8, 1964, p. 3.

"Rescue." *The Montreal Gazette,* January 28, 1954, p. 2.

"Restoration Work on the Peace Tower," *Ottawa CBO Radio,* 7:40 CBO Morning., July 28, 1995, Mediascan.

RG2, Privy Council Office, Series A-5-a, Volume 2657, Reel T-12184, Access code: 12.

Ricker, Angus. "Jury can't find reason for jump from tower." The *Ottawa Citizen*, September 18, 1970, p. 3.

Ricker, Angus. "Jump from Peace Tower was second attempt inquest told." The *Ottawa Citizen*, October 2, 1970, p. 6.

Robert Laird Borden: His Memoirs, edited and with a preface by Henry Borden. Toronto: The Macmillan Company of Canada Limited, 1938.

Roberts, Arthur G. "Quietly Thumps Clay Into Carving Models." The *Ottawa Citizen,* January 10, 1947, p. 9.

Roberts, Siobhan. "The Wild Side of Parliament Hill: Ottawa's Catman is Looking to Retire. 'I put an ad in the Newspaper. Nobody Showed Up.' " *National Post,* May 30, 2000, p. B.2.

Roe, James. "Careful Vigilance Eliminating Mr. Rat." The *Ottawa Citizen*, May 26, 1948, p. 18.

Roger, Charles. *Ottawa Past and Present.* Ottawa: The Times Printing and Publishing Company, 1871.

Rogers, Dave. "Copper Stolen Within Sight of Police Station: BIG LOSS: The Two Tonnes of Scrap From the Roof of the Centre Block Was to Have Been Used by Developmentally Handicapped Group to Make Souvenirs to Help Finance Their Programs." The *Ottawa Citizen,* November 7, 1996, p. B.3.

Bibliography 373

Rogers, Dave. "Police Recover Stolen Copper at Metal Dealer." The *Ottawa Citizen*, November 8, 1996.

"Saving Something That Couldn't Be Bought." *The Montreal Gazette*, May 12, 1961, p. 6.

Selwyn, L.S, *et. al.*. "Outdoor Bronze Statues: Analysis of Metal and Surface Samples." *Studies in Conservation, The Journal of the International Institute for Conservation of Historic and Artistic Works*, 41 (1996): 205-228.

"Statue of Queen Victoria Unveiled on Parliament Hill." *The Citizen*, September 22, 1901.

Scott, David. *Copper and Bronze in Art: Corrosion, Colorants, Conservation*. Los Angeles: The Getty Conservation Institute, 2002.

"Sculptor Scooped Government By 11 Years on Tenth Province." *The Globe and Mail*, July 31, 1948, p. 13.

Selwyn, Lyndsie. M*etals and Corrosion: A Handbook for the Conservation Professional*, Ottawa: The Canadian Conservation Institute, 2004.

Sherwood, E.S. "Those Cats." *The Ottawa Journal*, November 26, 1954, p. 6.

Simms, Henry Augustus. H*enry Augustus Simms Papers,* diary entry for October 18, 1863. Library and Archives Canada, MG29, B36.

Simpson, Jenny Russell. "Some Reminiscences of Bytown." *Women's Canadian Historical Society of Ottawa,* Transactions, Vol. VII (1917): 5-11.

"Small Blaze Occurs in Parl't. Buildings," *The Citizen*, January 21, 1924, p. 12.

"Speaker of Commons Shoots Wild Rabbits On Parliament Hill." The *Ottawa Citizen*, April 11, 1932, p. 29.

"Spookiest Spot In Capital Right In Parliament Hill." The *Ottawa Citizen*, March 29, 1955, p. 30.

Statues of Parliament Hill. Ottawa-Hull: the Visual Arts Programme, National Capital Commission, 1986.

Stevens, Geoffrey. "Audience Interest Flickers like the Lights at Ottawa Centennial Pageant Premiere." *The Globe and Mail,* May 15, 1967. p. 8.

"Stone Ledge Loose; Close Peace Tower." *The Globe and Mail,* October 28, 1955, p. 3.

"Stonemason Inscribing Date On Peace Tower Base." The *Ottawa Citizen*, September 10, 1946, p. 25.

"Stop Smoking in Office Hours." *The Citizen*, February 23, 1916, p. 10.

"Sun-Dial Unveiled by His Excellency Historic Function." *The Citizen*, May 20, 1921, p. 3.

Suter, G.T., C.P. Borgal and K. Blades. "Overview of mortars for Canadian historic structures." Proceedings of the 9th Canadian Masonry Symposium, University of New Brunswick (2001), http://irc.nrc-cnrc.gc.ca/bes/hmpe/masonry/mortar/pubs_e.html

Sutherland, C.D. Chief Architect of Public Works. *Memo to Mr. Wiley*, July 16, 1938.

Swanson, Frank. "Eighty Rooms Might Be Added To Parliament Building." The *Ottawa Citizen*, April 8, 1949, p. 32.

Swanson, Frank. "Face-Lifting For All Of Buildings On Hill." The *Ottawa Citizen*, November 24, 1955, p. 1.

Taber, Jane. "Parliament Hill; Big Bang for Less Bucks; Commons Officially Revives Tradition of Firing Noonday Gun." The *Ottawa Citizen*, final edition, June 18, 1992, p.A.5.

"Takeover on the Hill Was a Prank." *The Globe and Mail*, February 7, 1976, p. 10.

Tammemagi, Hans. E*xploring the Hill: A guide to Canada's Parliament past and present*. Markam, Ontario: Fitzhenry and Whiteside Limited, 2002.

Taylor, John H. *The History of Canadian Cities/Ottawa: An Illustrated History*. Toronto: James Lorimer & Co. Publishers and Canadian Museum of Civilization, National Museums of Canada, 1986.

"Tearing Down is Easy." *The Montreal Gazette*, November 25, 1955, p. 6.

"Tenders Called for Rebuilding West Block." *The Globe and Mail*, December 9, 1960, p. 8.

The Arms, Flags and Emblems of Canada, 2nd ed. Deneau Publishers, 1981.

The Bytown Gazette, June 20, 1838.

The Canadian Press. "What Time is It? This Guy Knows for Sure." *Daily News, Halifax NS*, October 27, 2002, p. 12.

"The Capital in Mourning." *The Globe,* December 10, 1901, p. 2.

"The Clock Bells At Night." The *Ottawa Citizen,* July 13, 1928, p. 12.

The Daily Globe, September 3, 1860, p. 2.

The Evening Citizen, August 5, 1952, p. 15.

"The Fine Arts. Sculpture. Third Lecture by Prof. Weir at the Yale School of Arts." *New York Times,* November 19, 1874, p. 3.

The Globe, June 28, 1898, p. 9.

The Globe and Mail. March 15, 1950, p. 1.

"The Ottawa Scene." *The Globe and Mail,* July 7, 1980, p. 8.

"The River's Victims." *The Globe,* December 9, 1901, p. 1.

The Tour of H.R.H. The Prince of Wales through British America and The United States, A British Canadian (Henry Morgan), Montreal, Printed for the compiler by John Lovell, St. Nicholas Street, 1860.

"The Tower Came Down With a terrific Crash." *The Ottawa Evening Journal,* April 5, 1906, p. 9.

"The Wildly Improbable West Block." The *Ottawa Citizen,* editorial, November 24, 1955.

"3 Ottawa Cats Find New Homes." The Montreal Gazette, November 26, 1954, p. 22.

"Thomas Ritchie Passes to Rest." *The Globe,* December 8, 1921, p. 3.

Thompson, Chris, "Turning Back the Clock," *The Ottawa Sunday Sun,* February 25, 1996, p. 22

"Thousands View the Pathetic Spectacle on Parliament Hill." *The Citizen,* February 5, 1916, p. 1.

"Thrilling Escapes as Building Burned." *The Globe,* February 5, 1916, p. 1.

"To Investigate Tower Collapse." *The Globe,* April 6, 1906, p. 9.

"Tower Closed After Woman Leaps to Death." *The Globe and Mail,* July 29, 1970, p. 23.

"Tower's Fall No Surprise." *The Citizen*, April 7, 1906, p. 2.

"True and Unaltered." *The Montreal Gazette*, June 25, 1956, p. 6.

"Trying to Clean the Statues on Parliament Hill." The *Ottawa Citizen*, August 7, 1931, p. 1.

"Unveiling the Statue." *The Globe*, September 23, 1901, p.1.

Varkaris , Jane and Lucile Finsten. *Fire on Parliament Hill!* Ontario: The Boston Mills Press, 1988.

Vernon, W.H.J., and L. Whitby. "The Open Air Corrosion of Copper. A Chemical Study of the Surface Patina." *J. Inst. Metals*, 42, (1929): 181-195.

Vernon, W.H.J. "The Open-Air Corrosion of Copper. Part III – Artificial Production of Green Patina." *J. Inst. Metals*, 49, (1932): 153-161.

Walker, Harry J.. *The Ottawa Story*. Ottawa: The Journal, 1953.

Ward, John. "Heading for the Hill; Parliament Hill is a Mountain of History." *Daily News*, Halifax, N.S., January 12, 1992, p. 37.

Warner, Michael. "The Kaiser Sows Destruction," *Studies in Intelligence* 46, no. 1 (2002), 7. This paper is also published electronically on the Central Intelligence Agency's website at https://www.cia.gov/library/center-for-the-study-of-intelligence/csi-publications/csi-studies/studies/vol46no1/article02.html

Weil, Phoebe Dent. "Patina on bronze sculpture from the historical-artistic point of view." Lecture: BMC2004 Genoa 2 December, 2004.
http://www.northernlightstudio.com/new/patinalec.php.

Weil, Phoebe Dent. "The Conservation of Outdoor Bronze Sculpture: A Review of Modern Theory and Practice." *The American Institute for Conservation of Historic and Artistic Works.* Preprints of papers presented at the eighth annual meeting, San Francisco, California, 22-25 May 1980. Published by The American Institute for Conservation of Historic and Artistic Works, 1522 K Street N.W., Suite 804, Washington, D.C., 20005, p. 129-140.

Weil, Phoebe Dent with Peter Gaspar, Leonard Gulbransen, Ray Lindberg and, *in memoriam*, David Zimmerman. "The Corrosive Deterioration of Outdoor Bronze Sculpture." Preprints of the contributions to the Washington Congress, 3-9 September, 1982, *Science and Technology in the Service of Conservation*,

Published by The International Institute for Conservation of Historic and Artistic Works, 6 Buckingham Street, London, WC2N 6BA, p. 130-134.

Weil, Pheobe Dent. "Patina from the Historical-Artistic Point of View," Northern Light Studio, www.northernlightstudio.com/new/patina.php , n.d.

Weiselberger, Carl. "Keep Your Hands Off Our 'Victorian Gothic'." The *Ottawa Citizen*, November 10, 1956, p. 17.

"West Block New Tower Piled in a Heap." *The Evening Citizen*, April 6, 1906, p. 1.

West, Bruce. "Churchill Didn't, FDR Didn't; Bruce Did." *The Globe and Mail*, December 17, 1949, p. 17.

"Why Will the Flame Burn?" The *Ottawa Citizen*, October 5, 1966.

Wiley, W., Assistant Superintendent of Dominion Buildings at Ottawa. *Memo to the Chief Architect of Public Works*. May 25, 1924.

Willett, Carolyn. "Statues of Great Men Ring Parliament Hill." The *Ottawa Citizen*, January 29, 1957, p. 28.

"Wiring Fault Suspected in Parliament Hill Fire." *The Globe and Mail*, October 6, 1986, p. A5.

"Wonderful Escape." *The Montreal Daily Witness*, February 4, 1878, p. 2.

"Work under way at the Peace Tower," *Ottawa CBO Radio*, 7:48 CBO Morning., October 31, 1994, Mediascan.

Woolfitt, Catherine and Graham Abrey, "Poultices: The true or Plain Poultice and the Cleaning and Desalination of Historic Masonry and Sculpture." http://www.buildingconservation.com/articles/poultices/poultice.htm. This article is reproduced from *The Building Directory*, 2000.

Woolfitt, Catherine. "Soluble Salts in Masonry," http://www.buildingconservation.com/articles/salts/salts.htm. This article is reproduced from *The Building Conservation Directory*, 2000.

"World Worried About the Tower." *The Globe*, April 10, 1906, p. 5.

"Would They Swim in It?" Editorial in the *Peterborough Examiner* reprinted in *the Globe and Mail*, December 1, 1955.

Wright, Ashley. *Use of Copper Roofing*. CBC Radio, CBO Morning, June 25, 1996, 6:48am, MH Media Monitoring Limited, Ref. 5666.12.

Wright, R.C. Chief Architect of Public Works. M*emo to the Secretary of the Ottawa Improvement Commission*, August 30, 1926.

Wuorio, Eva-Lis. "Chimes Voice of Ottawa, Peace Tower is its Heart." *The Globe and Mail,* April 2, 1947, p. 12.

Young, Carolyn A. T*he Glory of Ottawa: Canada's First Parliament Buildings.* Montreal & Kingston, London, Buffalo: McGill-Queen's University Press, 1995.

Young, Ronald D.. *Contemporary Patination.* 5th ed.: Sculpt Nouveau, 2000, p. 2.

End Notes

[1] William Pittman Lett, *Recollections of Bytown and its Old Inhabitants,* (Ottawa: "Citizen" Printing and Publishing Company, 1874).

[2] See, for example, http://en.wikipedia.org/wiki/Champlain_Sea; http://geoscape.nrcan.gc.ca/ottawa/pdf/theme7_3a_e.pdf and Ice Age http://en.wikipedia.org/wiki/Ice_age

[3] Whale Bones Tell Sandpits Antiquity," *The Citizen,* July 2, 1948.

[4] Charles Roger, *Ottawa Past and Present* (Ottawa: The Times Printing and Publishing Company, 1871), 12 to 33.

[5] James Corbett, Clerk of Works, Royal Engineers Dept., "Sketch of the Rise and Progress of Bytown, Canada West, and Physical Aspect," January 23, 1849, Library and Archives Canada, MG13, W.O. 55, Vol. 883, p. 354-362; cited in James A. De Jonge, *The Military Establishment at Bytown, 1826-1856,* (Parks Canada, 1983): 65.

[6] F. Gertrude Kenny, *Some Account of Bytown,* read to the Women's Canadian Historical Society of Ottawa in December, 1898. W*omen's Canadian Historical Society of Ottawa,* Transactions, Vol. I (1901): 24.

[7] Named after Lady Ashburnham, a daughter of Col. By.

[8] William Pittman Lett, *A Short Panoramic view of Ottawa's History Written in its Jubilee Year 1877* (The Historical Society of Ottawa: Bytown Pamphlet Series No. 45, 1993), 1.

[9] William Pittman Lett, *Lines Recited by the Author in "Her Majesty's Theatre," at a Festival of the Mechanics' Institute in March, 1868. A*nnex to William Pittman Lett, *Recollections of Bytown and its Old Inhabitants,* (Ottawa: "Citizen" Printing and Publishing Company, 1874).

[10] We know this from early maps of the area, for example National Library and Archives NMC 25633 which is an 1858 copy of an 1831 map (C-029286) signed by Col. By. Kenny has it between Lyon and O'Connor (*Women's Canadian Historical Society of Ottawa,* Transactions, Vol. I (1901): 24), but none of the maps support this.

[11] F. Gertrude Kenny, *Some Account of Bytown*, read to the Women's Canadian Historical Society of Ottawa in December, 1898. *Women's Canadian Historical Society of Ottawa,* Transactions, Vol. I (1901): 24.

[12] Col. By would make this pond into the "canal basin", a feature that no longer exists on today's canal. The canal basin was a turn-around that allowed boats to turn around so they could return back up the canal to Kingston.

[13] F. Gertrude Kenny, *Some Account of Bytown*, read to the Women's Canadian Historical Society of Ottawa in December, 1898. *Women's Canadian Historical Society of Ottawa,* Transactions, Vol. I (1901): 24. See also Library and Archives Canada NMC 025633.

[14] F. Gertrude Kenny, *Some Account of Bytown*, read to the Women's Canadian Historical Society of Ottawa in December, 1898. *Women's Canadian Historical Society of Ottawa,* Transactions, Vol. I (1901): 24.

[15] William Pittman Lett, *Recollections of Bytown and its Old Inhabitants,* (Ottawa: "Citizen" Printing and Publishing Company, 1874).

[16] F. Gertrude Kenny, *Some Account of Bytown*, read to the Women's Canadian Historical Society of Ottawa in December, 1898. *Women's Canadian Historical Society of Ottawa,* Transactions, Vol. I (1901): 26.

[17] William Pittman Lett, *Recollections of Bytown and its Old Inhabitants,* (Ottawa: "Citizen" Printing and Publishing Company, 1874).

[18] Robert Haig, *Ottawa, City of the Big Ears* (Ottawa: Haig & Haig Publishing Company, 1969), 50.

[19] F. Gertrude Kenny, *Some Account of Bytown*, read to the Women's Canadian Historical Society of Ottawa in December, 1898. *Women's Canadian Historical Society of Ottawa,* Transactions, Vol. I (1901): 26.

[20] James Corbett, Clerk of Works, Royal Engineers Dept., "Sketch of the Rise and Progress of Bytown, Canada West, and Physical Aspect," January 23, 1849, Public Archives of Canada, MG13, W.O. 55, Vol. 883, p. 354-362; in James A. De Jonge, *The Military Establishment at Bytown, 1826-1856,* (Parks Canada, 1983): 64-70.

[21] Henry A. Murray, Lands of the Slave and the Free, or, Cuba, the United States, and Canada. London: 1857.

[22] William Pittman Lett, *Recollections of Bytown and its Old Inhabitants*, (Ottawa: "Citizen" Printing and Publishing Company, 1874).

[23] Henry A. Murray, Lands of the Slave and the Free, or, Cuba, the United States, and Canada. London: 1857.

[24] M.J. Hickey, "The Capital of the Canadas," *Harpers Magazine*, September, 1861, reproduced in part in an article by Harry J. Walker in *The Journal*, October 31, 1959; in *Ottawa History*, a scrapbook in the Ottawa Room of the Ottawa Public Library Vol. I, p. 19.

[25] A family story told by Lauren Moline, January 31, 1999. Http://www.rideau-info.com/canal/feedback99.html.

[26] George R. Blyth, "Bytown, 1834, to Ottawa, 1854," *Women's Canadian Historical Society of Ottawa*, Transactions, Vol. IX (1925): 14.

[27] "Village Laid Out On Instructions of the Earl of Dalhousie," in *Ottawa History*, a scrapbook in the Ottawa Room of the Ottawa Public Library, Vol. VI, p. 45. See also "The Begley Dower Suits," Vol. V, p. 28; and "First Holders of Ottawa Real Estate," Vol. V, 36.

[28] James Corbett, Clerk of Works, Royal Engineers Dept., "Sketch of the Rise and Progress of Bytown, Canada West, and Physical Aspect," January 23, 1849, Public Archives of Canada, MG13, W.O. 55, Vol. 883, p. 354-362; in James A. De Jonge, *The Military Establishment at Bytown, 1826-1856*, (Parks Canada, 1983): 64-65.

[29] *Ibid.*

[30] How it got the name "sleigh bay" is interesting. The closest Justice of the Peace in those days was in Perth, which was in Upper Canada. This caused a problem when a young man and woman in Wrightsville wished to marry because, as they lived in Lower Canada, he could not perform marriages there. The problem was solved (in winter, anyway) by the wedding party and guests crossing the river in their sleighs, forming them into a circle, and the young couple took their vows outside, on the ice.

[31] James Corbett, Clerk of Works, Royal Engineers Dept., "Sketch of the Rise and Progress of Bytown, Canada West, and Physical Aspect," January 23, 1849, Public Archives of Canada, MG13, W.O. 55, Vol. 883, p. 354-362; in James A. De Jonge, *The Military Establishment at Bytown, 1826-1856,* (Parks Canada, 1983): 23.

[32] *Ottawa History,* a scrapbook in the Ottawa Room of the Ottawa Public Library, Vol. V, p.11.

[33] *The Perth Independent Examiner, November 26, 1830,* in *Ottawa History,* a scrapbook in the Ottawa Room of the Ottawa Public Library, Vol. V, p. 14.

[34] James Corbett, Clerk of Works, Royal Engineers Dept., "Sketch of the Rise and Progress of Bytown, Canada West, and Physical Aspect," January 23, 1849, Public Archives of Canada, MG13, W.O. 55, Vol. 883, p. 354-362; in James A. De Jonge, *The Military Establishment at Bytown, 1826-1856,* (Parks Canada, 1983): 13.

[35] H.P. Hill, "Before and After Colonel By. Beginnings of the Dominion Capital And The Men Who Guided It's Destinies in Early Years," *The Maple Leaf,* August, 1923, p. 10.

[36] See figure on p. 10 of H.P. Hill, "Before and After Colonel By. Beginnings of the Dominion Capital and the Men Who Guided its Destinies in Early Years," *The Maple Leaf,* August, 1923. See also National Library and Archives C-021558, C-021559, C-002367. A short while later these trees were cut down too. See, for example, National Library and Archives C-001201, C-011048, C-011864, C-092930.

[37] Harry J. Walker, *The Ottawa Story* (Ottawa: The Journal, 1953), 9.

[38] H.P. Hill, "Before and After Colonel By. Beginnings of the Dominion Capital and the Men Who Guided its Destinies in Early Years," *The Maple Leaf,* August, 1923, 11.

[39] James A. De Jonge, *The Military Establishment at Bytown, 1826-1856,* (Parks Canada, 1983): 52.

[40] Library and Archives Canada, NMC 020054 and NMC 122352

[41] Jenny Russell Simpson, "Some Reminiscences of Bytown," *Women's Canadian Historical Society of Ottawa,* Transactions, Vol. VII (1917): 7.

[42] "Thomas Ritchie Passes to Rest," *The Globe,* December 8, 1921, p. 3.

[43] "Soldiers Had Gardens on the Barracks Hill," in *Ottawa History,* a scrapbook collection in the Ottawa Room of the Ottawa Public Library Vol. V, p. 95.

[44] George R. Blyth, "Bytown, 1834, to Ottawa, 1854," *Women's Canadian Historical Society of Ottawa,* Transactions, Vol. IX (1925): 14.

[45] *Ottawa History,* a scrapbook in the Ottawa Room of the Ottawa Public Library, Vol. V, p. 10.

[46] W.H. Cluff, "Memories of Bytown," *Women's Canadian Historical Society of Ottawa,* Transactions – Vol VIII (1922): 67-8.

[47] H.P. Hill, "Before and After Colonel By. Beginnings of the Dominion Capital And The Men Who Guided It's Destinies in Early Years," *The Maple Leaf,* August, 1923, p. 11.

[48] "Recollections of Bytown; Reminiscences of Ottawa - Looking Backwards over Fifty Years of Life in the Capital City of Canada, Mr. George Holland Tells The Citizen Readers What He Sees," in *Ottawa History,* a scrapbook in the Ottawa Room of the Ottawa Public Library Vol. VII, p. 31-32.

[49] Jenny Russell Simpson, "Some Reminiscences of Bytown," *Women's Canadian Historical Society of Ottawa,* Transactions, Vol. VII (1917): 7.

[50] "Thomas Ritchie Passes to Rest," *The Globe,* December 8, 1921, p. 3.

[51] W.H. Cluff, "Memories of Bytown," *Women's Canadian Historical Society of Ottawa,* Transactions – Vol VIII (1922): 68.

[52] George R. Blyth, "Bytown, 1834, to Ottawa, 1854," *Women's Canadian Historical Society of Ottawa,* Transactions, Vol. IX (1925): 14. Although Mr. Blyth, Mr. White and the others are consistent in their description of where the stockade, guard house, etc. were in relation to the Parliament Buildings and statues, Mr. Slater's 1959 map suggests Barrack Hill proper may have been about 100 feet (30 metres) further

north than they describe. If Slater's map is correct the stockade would have been about in line with the statue of Alexander Mackenzie.

[53] "Soldiers Had Gardens on the Barracks Hill," in *Ottawa History*, a scrapbook collection in the Ottawa Room of the Ottawa Public Library Vol. V, p. 95.

[54] H.P. Hill, "Before and After Colonel By. Beginnings of the Dominion Capital And The Men Who Guided It's Destinies in Early Years," *The Maple Leaf,* August, 1923, p. 11.

[55] James A. De Jonge, *The Military Establishment at Bytown, 1826-1856,* (Parks Canada, 1983): 15.

[56] "Soldiers Had Gardens on the Barracks Hill," in *Ottawa History*, a scrapbook collection in the Ottawa Room of the Ottawa Public Library Vol. V, p. 95.

[57] Lucien Brault, *Parliament Hill,* 2nd ed. (Ottawa: The National Capital Commission, 1979), 10-12.

[58] James A. De Jonge, *The Military Establishment at Bytown, 1826-1856,* (Parks Canada, 1983): 37.

[59] *Ottawa History*, a scrapbook in the Ottawa Room of the Ottawa Public Library, Vol. V, p. 17.

[60] An 1840 map (Library and Archives Canada NMC 021868 shows a stockade but it is gone in an 1842 map (NMC 020054).

[61] James A. De Jonge, *The Military Establishment at Bytown, 1826-1856,* (Parks Canada, 1983): 17.

[62] Lucien Brault, *Parliament Hill,* 2nd ed. (Ottawa: The National Capital Commission, 1979), 10.

[63] "Soldiers Had Gardens on the Barracks Hill," in *Ottawa History*, a scrapbook collection in the Ottawa Room of the Ottawa Public Library Vol. V, p. 95.

[64] George Holland, "Recollections of Bytown, Reminiscences of Ottawa," Ottawa History Vol VII, p. 30.

[65] "The Fraser Private School Was an Institution Here; It Flourished in the Fifties," in *Ottawa History*, a scrapbook in the Ottawa Room of the Ottawa Public Library Vol. V, p. 74. See also Vol VII, p. 30.

[66] William Pittman Lett, *Recollections of Bytown and its Old Inhabitants*, (Ottawa: "Citizen" Printing and Publishing Company, 1874).

[67] For example Library and Archives Canada NMC 20054.

[68] Harry J. Walker, *The Ottawa Story* (Ottawa: The Journal, 1953), 10.

[69] W.H. Cluff, "Memories of Bytown," *Women's Canadian Historical Society of Ottawa*, Transactions – Vol VIII (1922): 66-7.

[70] *Ibid.*, p. 66.

[71] *Ibid.*, p. 66-7.

[72] *Ibid.*, p.71.

[73] "Made Wild Slide on Barracks Hill on a Hand Sleigh," in *Ottawa History*, a scrapbook in the Ottawa Room of the Ottawa Public Library Vol. VII, p. 62.

[74] "Fire", *The Packet*, September 4, 1847. In *Each Morning Bright 160 Years of Selected Readings from the Ottawa Citizen 1845-2005*, Doug Fischer, editor, Ralph Willsey, editor/designer, 14, (Ottawa: Ottawa Citizen Group Inc., 2005.)

[75] W. H. Cluff. "Memories of Bytown," *Women's Canadian Historical Society of Ottawa*, Transactions – Vol VIII (1922): 67-8.

[76] William Pittman Lett, *Recollections of Bytown and its Old Inhabitants*, (Ottawa: "Citizen" Printing and Publishing Company, 1874).

[77] Madge Macbeth, "Our History Lives Among Those Who Have Passed Away", *The Citizen*, July 2, 1955, in *Ottawa History*, a scrapbook in the Ottawa Room of the Ottawa Public Library Vol. I, p. 262.

[78] W. H. Cluff. "Memories of Bytown," *Women's Canadian Historical Society of Ottawa*, Transactions – Vol VIII (1922): 69, 74.

[79] Mator, "Letter to the Editor," *The Bytown Gazette and Ottawa Advertiser*, December 7, 1843.

[80] Harry J. Walker, *The Ottawa Story* (Ottawa: The Journal, 1953), 20.

[81] "The Fraser Private School Was an Institution Here; It Flourished in the Fifties," in *Ottawa History*, a scrapbook in the Ottawa Room of the Ottawa Public Library Vol. V, p. 74. See also Vol VII, p. 30.

[82] *Ottawa History*, a scrapbook in the Ottawa Room of the Ottawa Public Library, Vol. V, p. 59.

[83] W. H. Cluff. "Memories of Bytown," *Women's Canadian Historical Society of Ottawa*, Transactions – Vol VIII (1922): 69, 74.

[84] "Recollections of Bytown; Reminiscences of Ottawa - Looking Backwards over Fifty Years of Life in the Capital City of Canada, Mr. George Holland Tells The Citizen Readers What He Sees," in *Ottawa History*, a scrapbook in the Ottawa Room of the Ottawa Public Library Vol. VII, p. 30.

[85] Madge Macbeth, "Our History Lives Among Those Who Have Passed Away", *The Citizen*, July 2, 1955, in *Ottawa History*, a scrapbook in the Ottawa Room of the Ottawa Public Library Vol. I, p. 262.

[86] H.P. Hill, "Before and After Colonel By. Beginnings of the Dominion Capital And The Men Who Guided It's Destinies in Early Years," *The Maple Leaf*, August, 1923, p. 11.

[87] "Amateure Performance," *The Bytown Gazette*, February 16, 1837.

[88] Lucien Brault, *Parliament Hill*, 2nd ed. (Ottawa: The National Capital Commission, 1979), 10.

[89] The Bytown Gazette, June 20, 1838.

[90] James A. De Jonge, *The Military Establishment at Bytown, 1826-1856*, (Parks Canada, 1983): 42-44.

[91] "Thomas Ritchie Passes to Rest," *The Globe*, December 8, 1921, p. 3.

[92] James A. De Jonge, *The Military Establishment at Bytown, 1826-1856*, (Parks Canada, 1983): 44.

[93] W. H. Cluff. "Memories of Bytown," *Women's Canadian Historical Society of Ottawa*, Transactions – Vol VIII (1922): 67-68.

[94] William Pittman Lett, *Recollections of Bytown and its Old Inhabitants*, (Ottawa: "Citizen" Printing and Publishing Company, 1874).

[95] George C. Holland, "My Ottawa Memories," *Macleans Magazine, May 15, 1922*.

[96] Lucien Brault, *Parliament Hill*, 2nd ed. (Ottawa: The National Capital Commission, 1979), 12.

[97] Robert Haig, *Ottawa, City of the Big Ears* (Ottawa: Haig & Haig Publishing Company, 1969), 86.

[98] Craig Brown (Ed.), *The Illustrated History of Canada* (Toronto: Lester & Dennys Limited, 1987), 290.

[99] Government of Canada, *1871 - Uniform Currency Act*, http://canadianeconomy.gc.ca/english/economy/1871Uniform_Currency_Act.html

[100] Province of Canada, *Documents Relating to the Construction of the Parliamentary and Departmental Buildings at Ottawa*, (Quebec: 1862), No. 1, pp. 3-4

[101] *Ibid.*, No. 1½ , p. 5, F.P. Rubidge, to Thomas A. Begly, March 29, 1856.

[102] Canada, *Report of the Commissioner of Public Works for the Year Ending 30th June, 1867*, 31 Victoria, Sessional Papers (No. 8), 1867, Appendix No. 21, "Report on the Public Buildings at Ottawa", by John Page, August 29, 1867 p. 201.

[103] M.J. Hickey, "The Capital of the Canadas," *Harpers Magazine*, September, 1861, reproduced in part in an article by Harry J. Walker in *The Journal*, October 31, 1959, in *Ottawa History*, a scrapbook in the Ottawa Room of the Ottawa Public Library Vol. I, p. 19.

[104] Canada, *Report of the Commissioner of Public Works for the Year Ending 30th June, 1867*, 31 Victoria, Sessional Papers (No. 8), 1867, Appendix No.

21, "Report on the Public Buildings at Ottawa", by John Page, August 29, 1867 p. 201.

[105] "The Choice of the Capital," in *Ottawa History,* a scrapbook in the Ottawa Room of the Ottawa Public Library Vol. V, p. 27.

[106] *Ibid.*

[107] *Ibid.*

[108] *Ibid.*

[109] *Ibid.*

[110] David M.L. Farr, "Sir John Rose", *Dictionary of Canadian Biography Online*, Library and Archives Canada, http://www.biographi.ca/EN/

[111] Province of Canada, Province of Canada, *Documents Relating to the Construction of the Parliamentary and Departmental Buildings at Ottawa,* (Quebec: 1862), No. 2 , p. 8.

[112] Province of Canada, *Report of the Commission Appointed to Inquire Into Matters Connected With the Public Buildings at Ottawa.* Quebec: Hunter, Rose & Co., 1863, Testimony of Samuel Keefer, September 5, 1862.

[113] *Ibid.*, Testimony of Frederick Preston Rubidge, September 9, 1862.

[114] An undated draft "Notice to Architects" shows a total of only $480,000. Ref.: Carolyn A.Young, *The Glory of Ottawa: Canada's First Parliament Buildings,* (Montreal & Kingston, London, Buffalo: McGill-Queen's University Press, 1995), 19.

[115] Michèle Brassard and Jean Hamelin, "Thomas McGreevy", *Dictionary of Canadian Biography Online*, Library and Archives Canada, http://www.biographi.ca/EN/

[116] Province of Canada, *Report of the Commission Appointed to Inquire Into Matters Connected With the Public Buildings at Ottawa.* Quebec: Hunter, Rose & Co., 1863, Testimony of Thomas Fuller, August 14, 1862.

[117] *Ibid.*, Testimony of Thomas Fuller, August 12, 1862.

[118] "As We Supposed," *The Daily Globe,* May 10, 1859, p. 2.

[119] Province of Canada, *Report of the Commission Appointed to Inquire Into Matters Connected With the Public Buildings at Ottawa.* Quebec: Hunter, Rose & Co., 1863, Testimony of Samuel Keefer, September 4, 1862.

[120] *Ibid.*, Testimony of Samuel Keefer, September 3, 1862.

[121] Province of Canada, *Documents Relating to the Construction of the Parliamentary and Departmental Buildings at Ottawa,* (Quebec: 1862), No. 4, p. 11.

[122] *Transactions of the Canadian Society of Civil Engineers,* Vol. IV, January-December, 1890, p. 332-7.

[123] Province of Canada, *Report of the Commission Appointed to Inquire Into Matters Connected With the Public Buildings at Ottawa.* Quebec: Hunter, Rose & Co., 1863, Testimony of Samuel Keefer, September 3, 1862.

[124] "As We Supposed," *The Daily Globe,* May 10, 1859, p. 2.

[125] Province of Canada, *Report of the Commission Appointed to Inquire Into Matters Connected With the Public Buildings at Ottawa.* Quebec: Hunter, Rose & Co., 1863, Testimony of Samuel Keefer, September 3, 1862.

[126] *Ibid.*, Testimony of John Morris, August 9, 1862.

[127] *Ibid.*, Testimony of Samuel Keefer, September 5, 1862.

[128] *Ibid.*, Testimony of Frederick Preston Rubidge, September 9, 1862.

[129] *Ibid.*, Testimony of Alexander Mackenzie, August 23, 1862.

[130] Province of Canada, *Documents Relating to the Construction of the Parliamentary and Departmental Buildings at Ottawa,* (Quebec: 1862), No. 6, p. 15 ½ .

[131] Pro Bono Publico, "The New Parliament Buildings at Ottawa." *The Daily Globe,* September 19, 1859, p.2.

[132] Cited by Pro Bono Publico, "The New Parliament Buildings at Ottawa." *The Daily Globe,* September 19, 1859, p.2.

[133] Pro Bono Publico, "The New Parliament Buildings at Ottawa." *The Daily Globe,* September 19, 1859, p.2.

[134] Province of Canada, *Report of the Commission Appointed to Inquire Into Matters Connected With the Public Buildings at Ottawa.* Quebec: Hunter, Rose & Co., 1863, Testimony of Samuel Keefer, September 3, 1862.

[135] *Ibid.,* Testimony of Samuel Keefer, September 4, 1862.

[136] *Ibid.,* Testimony of Thomas Fuller, August 12, 1862.

[137] *Ibid.,* Testimony of Thomas Stent, August 15, 1862.

[138] *Ibid.,* Testimony of Samuel Keefer, September 5, 1862.

[139] Library and Archives Canada, NMC-118810. Mr. Slater's map of Barrack Hill done on a fifty foot grid. The grid with the Barrack Hill buildings was drawn in June, 1859 and the government building outlines were added sometime in January, 1860 after their locations were approved [139] and after the decision was made that same month to "turn the east Block around" from how it was originally designed. Originally the long side faced south and the short side faced west instead of vice-versa.

[140] Province of Canada, *Report of the Commission Appointed to Inquire Into Matters Connected With the Public Buildings at Ottawa.* Quebec: Hunter, Rose & Co., 1863, Testimony of Thomas Fuller, August 12, 1862.

[141] *Ibid.,* Testimony of Samuel Keefer, September 3, 1862.

[142] *Ibid.,* Testimony of Thomas Fuller, August 12, 1862.

[143] *Ibid.,* Testimony of Thomas Fuller, August 12, 1862.

[144] *Ibid.,* Testimony of Thomas Stent, August 16, 1862.

[145] *Ibid.,* Testimony of Samuel Keefer, September 4, 1862.

[146] *Ibid.,* Testimony of Alexander MacKenzie, August 23, 1862.

[147] *Ibid.,* Testimony of Samuel Keefer, September 3, 1862.

148 Canada, *Report of the Commissioner of Public Works for the Year Ending 30th June, 1867*, 31 Victoria, Sessional Papers (No. 8), 1867, Appendix No. 21, "Report on the Public Buildings at Ottawa", by John Page, August 29, 1867 p. 201.

149 Province of Canada, *Report of the Commission Appointed to Inquire Into Matters Connected With the Public Buildings at Ottawa*. Quebec: Hunter, Rose & Co., 1863, Testimony of Thomas Fuller, August 12, 1862.

150 Province of Canada, *Documents Relating to the Construction of the Parliamentary and Departmental Buildings at Ottawa*, (Quebec: 1862), No. 15 , p. 25.

151 This can sometimes happen, but it is very rare. Tie bids today are sometimes resolved (with the agreement of all parties) by a coin toss.

152 Michèle Brassard and Jean Hamelin, "Thomas McGreevy", *Dictionary of Canadian Biography Online*, Library and Archives Canada, http://www.biographi.ca/EN/

153 "Ottawa Buildings," *The Daily Globe*, March 3, 1863, p. 2.

154 Canada, Province of. Contract, Specification, Questions and Answers, and Schedule of prices of Parliament Buildings, Ottawa City, C.W.. Quebec: Printed by Augustin Coté, 1861.

155 Fuller explained the difference this way: "I apply the term extra," he said, "as applicable to work done, which has been erroneously omitted to be specified, and the term additional to work done beyond the work shown, or intended to be specified." Ref. Province of Canada, *Report of the Commission Appointed to Inquire Into Matters Connected With the Public Buildings at Ottawa*. Quebec: Hunter, Rose & Co., 1863, Testimony of Thomas Fuller, August 12, 1862.

156 Province of Canada, *Report of the Commission Appointed to Inquire Into Matters Connected With the Public Buildings at Ottawa*. Quebec: Hunter, Rose & Co., 1863, Testimony of Thomas McGreevy, September 17, 1862.

157 *Ibid.*, Testimony of Samuel Keefer, September 10, 1862.

158 *Ibid.*, Testimony of the Hon. John Rose, September 9, 1862.

159 *Ibid.*, Testimony of Samuel Keefer, September 11, 1862.

[160] *Ibid.*, Testimony of Alexander MacKenzie, August 23, 1862.

[161] *Ibid.*, Testimony of Samuel Keefer, September 4, 1862.

[162] Province of Canada, *Documents Relating to the Construction of the Parliamentary and Departmental Buildings at Ottawa,* (Quebec: 1862), No. 20 , p. 29.

[163] "Ottawa Buildings," *The Daily Globe,* March 3, 1863, p. 2.

[164] Province of Canada, *Report of the Commission Appointed to Inquire Into Matters Connected With the Public Buildings at Ottawa.* Quebec: Hunter, Rose & Co., 1863, Testimony of Alexander MacKenzie, August 23, 1862.

[165] *Hand Book to the Parliamentary and Departmental Buildings, Canada* (Ottawa: Printed by G.E. Desbarats, 1867), 13.

[166] "First Parliament Buildings Under Construction, Aug. 1865," in *Ottawa History,* a scrapbook in the Ottawa Room of the Ottawa Public Library Vol. III(a), p. 37.

[167] *The Daily Globe,* December 24, 1859, p. 2.

[168] "Saw Barracks Hill Cedar Bush Cleared," in *Ottawa History,* a scrapbook in the Ottawa Room of the Ottawa Public Library Vol. V.

[169] J.D. Livermore, *A History of Parliamentary Accommodation in Canada, 1841-1974* (Ottawa: Advisory Committee on Parliamentary Accommodation, 1975), 8.

[170] "Progress of the Public Buildings," *The Citizen*, February 17, 1860. In *Each Morning Bright 160 Years of Selected Readings from the Ottawa Citizen 1845-2005*, Doug Fischer, editor, Ralph Willsey, editor/designer, 37, (Ottawa: Ottawa Citizen Group Inc., 2005.)

[171] "First Parliament Buildings Under Construction, Aug. 1865," in *Ottawa History,* a scrapbook in the Ottawa Room of the Ottawa Public Library Vol. III(a), p. 37.

[172] Harry J. Walker, *The Ottawa Story* (Ottawa: The Journal, 1953), 22.

[173] Province of Canada, *Report of the Commission Appointed to Inquire Into Matters Connected With the Public Buildings at Ottawa.* Quebec: Hunter, Rose & Co., 1863, "Boiler houses and size of extra excavation in them".

[174] *Ibid.*

[175] Province of Canada, *Report of the Commission Appointed to Inquire Into Matters Connected With the Public Buildings at Ottawa.* Quebec: Hunter, Rose & Co., 1863, Testimony of Samuel Keefer, September 5, 1862.

[176] "Death of Dr. Vancourtland*", the Citizen*, March 25, 1875. In *Each Morning Bright 160 Years of Selected Readings from the Ottawa Citizen 1845-2005*, Doug Fischer, editor, Ralph Willsey, editor/designer, 86-87, (Ottawa: Ottawa Citizen Group Inc., 2005.)

[177] "A Pen Sketch of the Late Dr. Van Courtland," in *Ottawa History*, a scrapbook in the Ottawa Room of the Ottawa Public Library Vol. V, p. 71.

[178] Archaeological Mysteries in the Ottawa Area, Canadian Museum of Civilization, http://www.civilization.ca/cmc/archeo/ossuary/ossuary-2e.html

[179] "The Corner Stone of the Parliament Buildings", in *Ottawa History*, a scrapbook collection in the Ottawa Room of the Ottawa Public Library Vol. I, p. 132.

[180] A British Canadian (Henry Morgan), *The Tour of H.R.H. The Prince of Wales through British America and The United States,* Montreal, Printed for the compiler by John Lovell, St. Nicholas Street, 1860, p. 135.

[181] Province of Canada, *Report of the Commission Appointed to Inquire Into Matters Connected With the Public Buildings at Ottawa.* Quebec: Hunter, Rose & Co., 1863, "in allowing Mr. Morris to assume too much."

[182] *Hand Book to the Parliamentary and Departmental Buildings, Canada* (Ottawa: Printed by G.E. Desbarats, 1867), 13.

[183] "The Stone Cutters of Ottawa," *The Daily Globe*, December 24, 1860, p. 2.

[184] Robert Haig, *Ottawa, City of the Big Ears* (Ottawa: Haig & Haig Publishing Company, 1969), 121.

[185] Province of Canada, Documents Related to the Construction of the Parliamentary and Departmental Buildings at Ottawa, No. 90, p. 317, Report by S. Keefer, May 3, 1861.

[186] Province of Canada, *Report of the Commission Appointed to Inquire Into Matters Connected With the Public Buildings at Ottawa.* Quebec: Hunter, Rose & Co., 1863, Testimony of the Hon. Joseph Cauchon, September 18, 1862.

[187] Robert Haig, *Ottawa, City of the Big Ears* (Ottawa: Haig & Haig Publishing Company, 1969), 121.

[188] "Ottawa Buildings", *The Daily Globe,* March 26, 1862, p.2.

[189] *Daily Globe* of May 9, 1862, p. 2.

[190] S. Lynn Campbell and Susan L. Bennett, "Eliza Maria Harvey", *Dictionary of Canadian Biography Online*, Library and Archives Canada, http://www.biographi.ca/EN/

[191] J.D. Livermore, *A History of Parliamentary Accommodation in Canada, 1841-1974* (Ottawa: Advisory Committee on Parliamentary Accommodation, 1975), 18.

[192] Christina Cameron, "Charles Baillairgé, *Dictionary of Canadian Biography Online*, Library and Archives Canada, http://www.biographi.ca/EN/

[193] Joseph Pope, *Memoirs of The Right Honourable Sir John Alexander MacDonald*, Vol. 1 (Ottawa: J. Durie & Son, 1894), 266.

[194] J.D. Livermore, *A History of Parliamentary Accommodation in Canada, 1841-1974* (Ottawa: Advisory Committee on Parliamentary Accommodation, 1975), 18.

[195] Douglas Owram, *Building for Canadians: A History of the Department of Public Works, 1840-1960* (Ottawa: Public Relations and Information Services, Public Works Canada, 1979), 87.

[196] Christina Cameron, "Charles Baillairgé", *Dictionary of Canadian Biography Online*, Library and Archives Canada, http://www.biographi.ca/EN/

[197] George C. Holland, "My Ottawa Memories," *Macleans Magazine, May 15, 1922.*

[198] *Eighty Years' Progress of British North America,* (Toronto: Published by L. Nichols, 1865), p. 98.

[199] Michèle Brassard and Jean Hamelin, "Thomas McGreevy", *Dictionary of Canadian Biography Online*, Library and Archives Canada, http://www.biographi.ca/EN/

[200] Canada, *Report of the Commissioner of Public Works for the Year Ending 30th June, 1867*, 31 Victoria, Sessional Papers (No. 8), 1867, Appendix No. 21, "Report on the Public Buildings at Ottawa", by John Page, August 29, 1867, p. 239-240.

[201] Canada, *Expenditure on Public Works Canada prior to and since Confederation*, Sessional Paper 9, Appendix #222, p. 251-253; cited in D.E.Lawrence, "Building Stones of Canada's Federal Parliament Buildings," *Geoscience Canada,* 28, no.1 (2001): 15.

[202] Lieutenant-Colonel C.P. Meredith, "Otawa in the Seventies", *Women's Canadian Historical Society of Ottawa,* Transactions – Vol 11 (1954): 44.

[203] The man who carved these additional letters was Anthony Borysink, a Public Works stone carver. Ref. "Carved Stone of Commons, Passes at 72," The Citizen, July 30, 1957, p. 7.

[204] From Wikipedia, http://en.wikipedia.org/wiki/Geep.

[205] Province of Canada, *Report of the Commission Appointed to Inquire Into Matters Connected With the Public Buildings at Ottawa.* Quebec: Hunter, Rose & Co., 1863, Testimony of Samuel Keefer, September 5, 1862

[206] Hon. J.D. Edgar, *Canada and its Capital* (Toronto: George N. Morang, 1898), 57-59, 66.

[207] Province of Canada, *Documents Relating to the Construction of the Parliamentary and Departmental Buildings at Ottawa,* (Quebec: 1862), No. 63 , p. 253.

[208] Edward Van Cortland, "To the Editor of the *Ottawa Citizen,"* August 6, 1860, in *Ottawa History,* a scrapbook collection in the Ottawa Room of the Ottawa Public Library Vol. I, p. 132.

[209] "Dr. Van Cortland's Lecture," *The Bytown Gazette*, November 21, 1859, in *Ottawa History*, a scrapbook collection in the Ottawa Room of the Ottawa Public Library Vol. I, p. 126.

[210] Province of Canada, Province of Canada, *Documents Relating to the Construction of the Parliamentary and Departmental Buildings at Ottawa*, (Quebec: 1862), No. 63, p. 253.

[211] *Ibid.*, No. 64, p. 255.

[212] *Ibid.*, No. 68, p. 265.

[213] Province of Canada, *Report of the Commission Appointed to Inquire Into Matters Connected With the Public Buildings at Ottawa.* Quebec: Hunter, Rose & Co., 1863, Testimony of John Morris, August 7, 1862.

[214] Ibid., Testimony of Thomas Stent, August 18, 1862.

[215] In 1867 John Page was the Chief Engineer of Public Works. The descriptions in his 1867 "Report on the Public Buildings at Ottawa" and in the 1867 *Hand Book to the Parliamentary and Departmental Buildings* gives us a pretty good idea of what it must have been like. Ref: Canada, *Report of the Commissioner of Public Works for the Year Ending 30th June, 1867*, 31 Victoria, Sessional Papers (No. 8), 1867, Appendix No. 21, "Report on the Public Buildings at Ottawa", by John Page, August 29, 1867 and *Hand Book to the Parliamentary and Departmental Buildings, Canada* (Ottawa: Printed by G.E. Desbarats, 1867).

[216] Canada, *Report of the Commissioner of Public Works for the Year Ending 30th June, 1867*, 31 Victoria, Sessional Papers (No. 8), 1867, Appendix No. 21, "Report on the Public Buildings at Ottawa", by John Page, August 29, 1867 p. 205.

[217] See the photograph at the end of Chapter 5.

[218] George C. Holland, "My Ottawa Memories," *Macleans Magazine, May 15, 1922*.

[219] *Hand Book to the Parliamentary and Departmental Buildings, Canada* (Ottawa: Printed by G.E. Desbarats, 1867), 14.

[220] Canada, *Report of the Commissioner of Public Works for the Year Ending 30th June, 1867*, 31 Victoria, Sessional Papers (No. 8), 1867, Appendix No. 21, "Report on the Public Buildings at Ottawa", by John Page, August 29, 1867 p. 215.

[221] Marcel called it this one day when we were looking at the West Block masonry in the late 1990's.

[222] It remained at that spot until 1874 when it burned down. James A. De Jonge, *The Military Establishment at Bytown, 1826-1856*, (Parks Canada, 1983): 44.

[223] Robert Haig, *Ottawa, City of the Big Ears* (Ottawa: Haig & Haig Publishing Company, 1969), 65.

[224] William Pittman Lett, *A Short Panoramic view of Ottawa's History Written in its Jubilee Year 1877* (The Historical Society of Ottawa: Bytown Pamphlet Series No. 45, 1993), 3.

[225] Canada, *Report of the Commissioner of Public Works for the Year Ending 30th June, 1867*, 31 Victoria, Sessional Papers (No. 8), 1867, Appendix No. 21, "Report on the Public Buildings at Ottawa", by John Page, August 29, 1867 p. 208.

[226] *Ibid.*

[227] *Hand Book to the Parliamentary and Departmental Buildings, Canada* (Ottawa: Printed by G.E. Desbarats, 1867), 15.

[228] For example, Library and Archives Canada CB-M-016.

[229] By 1898 the Ladies gallery was carefully regulated and tickets had to be obtained from the Sergeant-at-Arms. Ref. Hon. J.D. Edgar, *Canada and its Capital* (Toronto: George N. Morang, 1898), 62.

[230] Senator Charles Bishop, "Years Around Parliament: Thoughts, Men, Memories. Chapter 3: Atmosphere of Parliament", the *Ottawa Citizen*, September 29, 1945, p. 3.

[231] *Ibid.*

[232] "Dominion Parliament Buildings," *The Globe*, April 8, 1893.

[233] Craig Brown (Ed.), *The Illustrated History of Canada* (Toronto: Lester & Dennys Limited, 1987), 324.

[234] "Dominion Parliament Buildings," *The Globe,* April 8, 1893.

[235] Charles Roger, *Ottawa Past and Present* (Ottawa: The Times Printing and Publishing Company, 1871), 61.

[236] Canada, *Report of the Commissioner of Public Works for the Year Ending 30th June, 1867*, 31 Victoria, Sessional Papers (No. 8), 1867, Appendix No. 21, "Report on the Public Buildings at Ottawa", by John Page, August 29, 1867 p. 205.

[237] Lucien Brault, *Parliament Hill*, 2nd ed. (Ottawa: The National Capital Commission, 1979), 27.

[238] William Pittman Lett, *Recollections of Bytown and its Old Inhabitants,* (Ottawa: "Citizen" Printing and Publishing Company, 1874).

[239] W.H. Cluff, "Memories of Bytown," *Women's Canadian Historical Society of Ottawa,* Transactions – Vol VIII (1922): 65-66.

[240] Annual Report of the Chief Architect, DPW, 1870, p.96-97; cited in McGovern Heritage Archaeological Associates, *Stage 3/4 Archaeological Assessment of the Bank Street Building Site Zones A, C, E. and F, Parliament Hill, City of Ottawa*, 2004, pp. 22-23.

[241] Canada, *House of Commons Debates* May 11, 1932, p. 2839.

[242] Charles Roger, *Ottawa Past and Present* (Ottawa: The Times Printing and Publishing Company, 1871), 62.

[243] *Illustrated Guide to the House of Commons and Senate of Canada* (Ottawa: Published by F.R.E. Campeau; Printed by A. Bureau, Sparks Street, 1879), 121.

[244] Library and Archives Canada, RG11, B1(b), Vol. 699, p.2736. Cited in McGovern Heritage Archaeological Associates, *Stage 3/4 Archaeological Assessment of the Bank Street Building Site Zones A, C, E. and F, Parliament Hill, City of Ottawa*, 2004, p. 45.

[245] H. Belden, Illustrated Historical Atlas of the County of Carleton Ont. (Including City of Ottawa), (Toronto: H. Belden & Co., 1879), p.xxiii. Cited in McGovern Heritage Archaeological Associates, Stage 3/4 Archaeological Assessment of the Bank Street Building Site Zones A, C, E. and F, Parliament Hill, City of Ottawa, 2004, p. 45.

[246] *The Globe*, June 28, 1898, p. 5

[247] The Diaries of William Lyon Mackenzie King, July 24, 1900, National Archives of Canada, http://king.collectionscanada.ca/EN/Default.asp.

[248] *Ibid.*, August 22, 1900.

[249] Annual Report of the Chief Architect, DPW, 1905, Part 3, p.20.

[250] Bill Neddow, "A Walk in the Past", *The Citizen*, October 14, 1967, in *Ottawa History*, a scrapbook collection in the Ottawa Room of the Ottawa Public Library Vol. IV (a), p. 64.

[251] R.A.J. Phillips, *The East Block of the Parliament Buildings of Canada*, (Ottawa: Queen's Printer, 1967), 23.

[252] The Diaries of William Lyon Mackenzie King, May 19, 1921, National Archives of Canada, http://king.collectionscanada.ca/EN/Default.asp.

[253] "Lovers' Walk Benches," the *Ottawa Citizen*, September 3, 1930, p. 31.

[254] "Piper-Member Recalls When he Defied Police," the *Ottawa Citizen*, May 22, 1943, p. 23.

[255] "Boy Injured on Parliament Hill," the *Ottawa Citizen*, March 27, 1933.

[256] Bill Neddow, "A Walk in the Past", the *Citizen*, October 14, 1967, in *Ottawa History*, a scrapbook collection in the Ottawa Room of the Ottawa Public Library Vol. IV (a), p. 64.

[257] Anthony Dickason, " 'Walk of the Lovers' Gone to Weeds," the *Ottawa Citizen*, June 20, 1963, p. 13.

[258] Canada, House of Commons Debates, July 21, 1960, p. 6691.

[259] "Lovers' Walk Will Be Closed for Duration," the *Ottawa Citizen*, July 29, 1942, p. 49.

[260] "No Dice," *The Maple Leaf*, January 25, 1945, p. 5.

[261] John Bird, "A Bird of a Yarn Tells About 'Hill' Pigeons," the *Ottawa Citizen*, March 5, 1949, p. 16.

[262] He later died. Ref: Bill Neddow, "A Walk in the Past", *The Citizen*, October 14, 1967, in *Ottawa History*, a scrapbook collection in the Ottawa Room of the Ottawa Public Library Vol. IV (a), p. 64.

[263] Canada, House of Commons Debates, June 15, 1961, p. 6378-6379 and June 17, 1961, p. 6511.

[264] *Ibid.*, February 28, 1966, p. 1847 and October 24, 1966, p. 9016.

[265] *Ibid.*, June 28, 1972, p. 3591

[266] "Wonderful Escape," The *Montreal Daily Witness*, February 4, 1878, p. 2.

[267] *Illustrated Guide to the House of Commons and Senate of Canada* (Ottawa: Published by F.R.E. Campeau; Printed by A. Bureau, Sparks Street, 1879), 120.

[268] Victoria Tower is used, for example, in the *Illustrated Guide to the House of Commons and Senate of Canada* (Ottawa: Published by F.R.E. Campeau; Printed by A. Bureau, Sparks Street, 1879), 120.

[269] Canada, *Report of the Commissioner of Public Works for the Year Ending 30th June, 1867*, 31 Victoria, Sessional Papers (No. 8), 1867, Appendix No. 21, "Report on the Public Buildings at Ottawa", by John Page, August 29, 1867 p. 205-206.

[270] *Ibid.*, p. 206.

[271] Hon. J.D. Edgar, *Canada and its Capital* (Toronto: George N. Morang, 1898), 57.

[272] *Illustrated Guide to the House of Commons and Senate of Canada* (Ottawa: Published by F.R.E. Campeau; Printed by A. Bureau, Sparks Street, 1879), 120.

[273] *Illustrated Guide to the House of Commons and Senate of Canada* (Ottawa: Published by F.R.E. Campeau; Printed by A. Bureau, Sparks Street, 1879), 120.

[274] Hon. J.D. Edgar, *Canada and its Capital* (Toronto: George N. Morang, 1898), 56.

[275] *Ottawa History*, a scrapbook in the Ottawa Room of the Ottawa Public Library Vol. V, p. 55.

[276] Harry J. Walker, "Noon 'Boom' is Most Reliable Institution in the Capital" *The Journal*, in *Ottawa History*, a scrapbook collection in the Ottawa Room of the Ottawa Public Library Vol. I, p. 236.

[277] *Ibid.*

[278] *Ottawa History*, a scrapbook in the Ottawa Room of the Ottawa Public Library Vol. V, p. 55.

[279] "RCMP Recover Stolen Cannon", *The Citizen*, January 29, 1966, in *Ottawa History*, a scrapbook collection in the Ottawa Room of the Ottawa Public Library Vol. IV (a), p. 76.

[280] "Cannon Booms at Noon for Ottawans" *The Citizen*, October 27, 1948, in *Ottawa History*, a scrapbook collection in the Ottawa Room of the Ottawa Public Library Vol. I, p. 238.

[281] "Ottawa's Faithful Noon Gun", *The Journal*, May 4, 1967, in *Ottawa History*, a scrapbook collection in the Ottawa Room of the Ottawa Public Library Vol. IV (a), p. 91.

[282] *Ibid.*

[283] Harry J. Walker, "Noon 'Boom' is Most Reliable Institution in the Capital" *The Journal*, in *Ottawa History*, a scrapbook collection in the Ottawa Room of the Ottawa Public Library Vol. I, p. 236.

[284] "No Noon Boom in Ottawa … 'Old Chum' Chokes Up" *The Journal*, August 2, 1963, in *Ottawa History*, a scrapbook collection in the Ottawa Room of the Ottawa Public Library Vol. II(a), p. 71.

[285] *Ottawa History*, a scrapbook in the Ottawa Room of the Ottawa Public Library Vol. V, p. 55.

[286] "Ottawa's Faithful Noon Gun", *The Journal*, May 4, 1967, in *Ottawa History*, a scrapbook collection in the Ottawa Room of the Ottawa Public Library Vol. IV (a), p. 91.

[287] *Ottawa History*, a scrapbook in the Ottawa Room of the Ottawa Public Library Vol. V, p. 55.

[288] *Ibid.*

[289] *Ibid.*

[290] *Ibid.*

[291] *Ibid.*

[292] "Fires Noon-Day Gun on Second and Ottawa Sets Watch by Him" *The Journal*, June 14, 1941, in *Ottawa History*, a scrapbook collection in the Ottawa Room of the Ottawa Public Library Vol. I, p. 232.

[293] *Ottawa History*, a scrapbook in the Ottawa Room of the Ottawa Public Library Vol. V, p. 55.

[294] "Fires Noon-Day Gun on Second and Ottawa Sets Watch by Him" *The Journal*, June 14, 1941, in *Ottawa History*, a scrapbook collection in the Ottawa Room of the Ottawa Public Library Vol. I, p. 232.

[295] *Ibid.*

[296] "Cannon Booms at Noon for Ottawans" *The Citizen*, October 27, 1948, in *Ottawa History*, a scrapbook collection in the Ottawa Room of the Ottawa Public Library Vol. I, p. 238.

[297] "Ottawa's Faithful Noon Gun", *The Journal*, May 4, 1967, in *Ottawa History*, a scrapbook collection in the Ottawa Room of the Ottawa Public Library Vol. IV (a), p. 91.

[298] "Fires Noon-Day Gun on Second and Ottawa Sets Watch by Him" *The Journal*, June 14, 1941, in *Ottawa History*, a scrapbook collection in the Ottawa Room of the Ottawa Public Library Vol. I, p. 232.

[299] "No Noon Boom in Ottawa ... 'Old Chum' Chokes Up" *The Journal,* August 2, 1963, in *Ottawa History,* a scrapbook collection in the Ottawa Room of the Ottawa Public Library Vol. II(a), p. 71.

[300] "Ottawa's Faithful Noon Gun", *The Journal,* May 4, 1967, in *Ottawa History,* a scrapbook collection in the Ottawa Room of the Ottawa Public Library Vol. IV (a), p. 91.

[301] *Ibid.*

[302] Harry J. Walker, "Noon 'Boom' is Most Reliable Institution in the Capital" *The Journal,* in *Ottawa History,* a scrapbook collection in the Ottawa Room of the Ottawa Public Library Vol. I, p. 236.

[303] "No Noon Boom in Ottawa ... 'Old Chum' Chokes Up" *The Journal,* August 2, 1963, in *Ottawa History,* a scrapbook collection in the Ottawa Room of the Ottawa Public Library Vol. II(a), p. 71.

[304] Bruce West, "Churchill Didn't, FDR Didn't; Bruce Did," *The Globe and Mail,* December 17, 1949, p. 17.

[305] Gladys Chapman, "Ottawa's Famed Noon-Day Gun," *The Globe and Mail,* December 15, 1956, p. 21.

[306] "Ottawa's Faithful Noon Gun", *The Journal,* May 4, 1967, in *Ottawa History,* a scrapbook collection in the Ottawa Room of the Ottawa Public Library Vol. IV (a), p. 91.

[307] Harriet Hill, "Facts and Fancies," *The Gazette,* January 31, 1958, in *Ottawa History,* a scrapbook collection in the Ottawa Room of the Ottawa Public Library Vol. I, p. 233.

[308] Frank Swanson, "Modern Six-Pounder Gun Replacing Majors Hill Park Ancient Cannon," *The Citizen,* in *Ottawa History,* a scrapbook collection in the Ottawa Room of the Ottawa Public Library Vol. I, p. 235.

[309] ___ Bell, "Ancient Cannon on Parliament Hill Still Bang on Time," *The Citizen,* June 7, 1963, in *Ottawa History,* a scrapbook collection in the Ottawa Room of the Ottawa Public Library Vol. I, p. 233.

[310] Walford Reeves, "Noon – but no 'Boom'!", *The Citizen,* January 28, 1966, in *Ottawa History,* a scrapbook collection in the Ottawa Room of the Ottawa Public Library Vol. III (b), p. 230.

[311] "RCMP Recover Stolen Cannon", *The Citizen,* January 29, 1966, in *Ottawa History,* a scrapbook collection in the Ottawa Room of the Ottawa Public Library Vol. IV (a), p. 76.

[312] "Ottawa's Faithful Noon Gun", *The Journal,* May 4, 1967, in *Ottawa History,* a scrapbook collection in the Ottawa Room of the Ottawa Public Library Vol. IV (a), p. 91.

[313] Ibid.

[314] Graham Parley, "The Gun falls Silent; NCC quietly muzzles the noon-hour cannon on Parliament Hill," the *Ottawa Citizen,* final edition, April 27, 1991, pg. A.1.FRO.

[315] "Noon Gun will Boom Again," the *Ottawa Citizen,* final edition, May 6, 1992, p. C.5.

[316] I played a small role in this move. My job as project manager was to make the changes needed inside the old Lovers' Walk washroom on the cliff so that the squibs and gunpowder could be stored inside, and to install posts and a chain that would keep people safely away when the gun was being fired.

[317] Jane Taber, "Parliament Hill; Big Bang for Less Bucks; Commons Officially Revives Tradition of Firing Noonday Gun," the *Ottawa Citizen,* final edition, June 18, 1992, p.A.5.

[318] "Noon Gun will Boom Again," the *Ottawa Citizen,* final edition, May 6, 1992, p. C.5.

[319] "Ottawa Buzz," the *Ottawa Citizen,* June 26, 2000, p. D3.

[320] Paul Bilkey, *Persons, Papers and Things* (Toronto: The Ryerson Press, 1940), 62.

[321] *Ibid.*

[322] *The Globe,* May 23, 1888

[323] *Ibid.*, June 18, 1896, p. 5.

[324] *Ibid.*, September 16, 1896, p. 4.

[325] Senator Charles Bishop, "Years Around Parliament: Thoughts, Men, Memories. Chapter 3: Atmosphere of Parliament", the *Ottawa Citizen*, September 29, 1945, p. 1.

[326] "World Worried About the Tower," *The Globe*, April 10, 1906, p. 5.

[327] "The Tower Came Down With a terrific Crash," the *Ottawa Evening Journal*, April 5, 1906, p. 9.

[328] "West Block New Tower Piled in a Heap," *The Evening Citizen*, April 6, 1906, p. 1.

[329] *Ibid.*, p.9.

[330] *Ibid.*, p.1.

[331] "The Tower Came Down With a Terrific Crash," *The Ottawa Evening Journal*, April 5, 1906, p. 9.

[332] "Notes and Comments," *The Globe*, April 18, 1906, p. 6.

[333] Canada. *Report on Collapse of Tower*, 5-6 Edward VII, Sessional Papers (No. 161), A. 1906, 6p.

[334] Paul Bilkey, *Persons, Papers and Things* (Toronto: The Ryerson Press, 1940), 64-66.

[335] *Ibid*.

[336] "Latest From Ottawa," *The Daily Globe*, September 1, 1877, p. 8.

[337] "Departmental Buildings at Ottawa," *the Globe*, September 13, 1877, p. 2.

[338] "Light on the East and West Blocks," The *Ottawa Citizen*, March 13, 1958, p. 6.

[339] "In the West Block," the *Globe,* February 12, 1897, p. 1.

[340] "At the Capital," *the Globe,* February 16, 1897.

[341] "A Fortune in Opium Burned at Ottawa," *The Globe,* April 4, 1911, p. 2.

[342] "Notes and Comments," *The Globe,* June 4, 1895, p. 4.

[343] Canada, *Report of the Commissioner of Public Works for the Year Ending 30th June, 1867,* 31 Victoria, Sessional Papers (No. 8), 1867, Appendix No. 21, "Report on the Public Buildings at Ottawa", by John Page, August 29, 1867 p. 211.

[344] *Ibid.,* p. 222 to 229.

[345] "Boiler houses, and size of extra excavation in them," in *Report of the Commission Appointed to Inquire Into Matters Connected With the Public Buildings at Ottawa.* Quebec: Hunter, Rose & Co., 1863

[346] "The Ottawa Buildings," *The Daily Globe,* October 2, 1862, p.1.

[347] "The Ottawa Arbitration," *The Daily Globe,* February 27, 1866, p.2.

[348] Province of Canada, *Report of the Commission Appointed to Inquire Into Matters Connected With the Public Buildings at Ottawa.* Quebec: Hunter, Rose & Co., 1863, Testimony of Thomas Fuller, August 13, 1862.

[349] "Coal Weighing Began in Ottawa in Year 1873", in *Ottawa History,* a scrapbook collection in the Ottawa Room of the Ottawa Public Library Vol. V, p. 90.

[350] Canada, *Scrapbook Debates,* June 14, 1866, Library and Archives Canada, AMICUS No. 3445729.

[351] *Ibid.,* July 27, 1866

[352] R.A.J. Phillips, *The House of History: The East Block of the Parliament Buildings* (The Historical Society of Ottawa Bytown Pamphlet Series No. 11, 1984), 4.

[353] Canada, *Scrapbook Debates,* June 14, 1866, Library and Archives Canada, AMICUS No. 3445729.

[354] Canada, House of Commons Debates, April 12, 1889, p. 1228

[355] Province of Canada, *Specification of Departmental Buildings Ottawa* (Quebec: Printed by Rollo Campell, October 1859), 11 and 14. Library and Archives Canada, RG 11, Vol. 183.

[356] Province of Canada, Contract, Specification, Questions and Answers, and Schedule of prices of Parliament Buildings, Ottawa City, C.W., (Quebec: Printed by Augustin Coté, 1861), 24,36, 37, 43, 48 and 49.

[357] Canada, *Report of the Commissioner of Public Works for the Year Ending 30th June, 1867*, 31 Victoria, Sessional Papers (No. 8), 1867, Appendix No. 21, "Report on the Public Buildings at Ottawa", by John Page, August 29, 1867, p. 229.

[358] "Explosion in the House of Commons, "The *Globe*, July 1, 1886.

[359] Sandra Gwyn, *The Private Capital* (Toronto: McClelland and Stewart Limited, 1984), 229.

[360] *Ibid.*

[361] Canada, *House of Commons Debates* (27 January 1911), p. 2583.

[362] Lucien Brault, *Ottawa Old & New*, (Ottawa: Ottawa Historical Information Institute, 1946), 113.

[363] Canada, *Report of the Commissioner of Public Works for the Year Ending 30th June, 1867*, 31 Victoria, Sessional Papers (No. 8), 1867, Appendix No. 21, "Report on the Public Buildings at Ottawa", by John Page, August 29, 1867 p. 234-236.

[364] *Ibid.*, p. 235-236.

[365] Scrapbook debates for July 27, 1866, Library and Archives Canada, AMICUS No. 3445729.

[366] *Ottawa History*, a scrapbook in the Ottawa Room of the Ottawa Public Library, Vol. V, "Old Oaken Bucket Stood by the Well", p. 77.

[367] *Ottawa History*, a scrapbook in the Ottawa Room of the Ottawa Public Library, Vol. V, "Ottawa in Year Sixty-Four", p. 60.

[368] *Ottawa History*, a scrapbook in the Ottawa Room of the Ottawa Public Library, Vol. V, "Had to Argue in Favor Waterworks", p. 58.

[369] *Ibid.*

[370] Lucien Brault, *Ottawa Old & New*, (Ottawa: Ottawa Historical Information Institute, 1946), 116-7.

[371] *Ibid.*

[372] Canada, *Royal Commission Re. Parliament Buildings Fire at Ottawa, February 3, 1916: Report of Commissioners and Evidence*, Sessional Paper No. 72a (Ottawa: J. de L. Taché, 1916), 65-72.

[373] *Ibid.*

[374] *Ibid.*

[375] "Ottawa's 'Crown of Towers,'" *The Globe*, February 4, 1916, p. 2.

[376] "Battalion on guard on the Hill," *The Citizen*, February 4, 1916, p. 3.

[377] "Fire the Act of Alien Foes?" *The Globe*, February 4, 1916, p. 1.

[378] Canada, *Royal Commission Re. Parliament Buildings Fire at Ottawa, February 3, 1916: Report of Commissioners and Evidence*, Sessional Paper No. 72a (Ottawa: J. de L. Taché, 1916), 37.

[379] "Ottawa's 'Crown of Towers,'" *The Globe*, February 4, 1916, p. 2.

[380] "Hose Burst Drenches Crowd," *The Citizen*, February 4, 1916, p. 1.

[381] "Mysterious Fire Wrecks the Imposing Central Structure; Several fatalities Result" *The Citizen*, February 4, 1916, p. 1.

[382] Canada, *House of Commons Debates* (4 February 1916), p. 578.

[383] "Bomb or no Bomb, Ottawa is Alert," *The Globe*, February 5, 1916, p. 1.

[384] "Battalion on guard on the Hill," *The Citizen*, February 4, 1916, p. 3.

[385] "Field Kitchens Useful," *The Citizen,* February 4, 1916, p. 1.

[386] "Bomb or no Bomb, Ottawa is Alert," *The Globe,* February 5, 1916, p. 1.

[387] "Fall of Great Tower is watched by Many Thousands," *The Citizen,* February 4, 1916, p. 1.

[388] "Peace Tower Back in Business after Facelift,"*The Times Colonist (Victoria, BC),* December 3, 1996, p. A8.

[389] "Protesters Disrupt Peace Tower Ceremony," *Ottawa Global News,* 6:54 p.m., December 2, 1996, Mediascan.

[390] "Crowds Thronged the City Streets," *The Citizen,* February 4, 1916, p. 2.

[391] "Bomb or no Bomb, Ottawa is Alert," *The Globe,* February 5, 1916, p. 1.

[392] John Fraser, "Scandals, Illusion Make East Block Symbol of Canada," *The Globe and Mail,* July 1, 1980.

[393] "Thousands View the Pathetic Spectacle on Parliament Hill," *The Citizen,* February 5, 1916, p. 1.

[394] After the book was written I learned of another document called *Minutes of Evidence*, which was an inquest into the death of Mable Morin, Records Group 11 (records of the Department of Public Works), RG11, Volume 2650, file 1575-18.

[395] "Two Guests of Mme. Sevigny Died in Fire," *The Citizen,* February 4, 1916, p. 1.

[396] Hon. J.D. Edgar, *Canada and its Capital* (Toronto: George N. Morang, 1898), 61-62.

[397] Canada, *Royal Commission Re. Parliament Buildings Fire at Ottawa, February 3, 1916: Report of Commissioners and Evidence*, Sessional Paper No. 72a (Ottawa: J. de L. Taché, 1916), 108.

[398] *Ibid.,* 156-7.

[399] "Mmes. Bray and Morin Died Trying to Save Their Furs," *The Citizen,* February 5, 1916, p. 7.

[400] Canada, *Royal Commission Re. Parliament Buildings Fire at Ottawa, February 3, 1916: Report of Commissioners and Evidence*, Sessional Paper No. 72a (Ottawa: J. de L. Taché, 1916), 155-156.

[401] "Mmes. Bray and Morin Died Trying to Save Their Furs," *The Citizen*, February 5, 1916, p. 7.

[402] *Ibid.*

[403] Canada, *Royal Commission Re. Parliament Buildings Fire at Ottawa, February 3, 1916: Report of Commissioners and Evidence*, Sessional Paper No. 72a (Ottawa: J. de L. Taché, 1916), 157.

[404] *Ibid.*, 129-130.

[405] *Ibid.*, 131.

[406] "Mmes. Bray and Morin Died Trying to Save Their Furs," *The Citizen*, February 5, 1916, p. 7.

[407] *Ibid.*

[408] Canada, *Royal Commission Re. Parliament Buildings Fire at Ottawa, February 3, 1916: Report of Commissioners and Evidence*, Sessional Paper No. 72a (Ottawa: J. de L. Taché, 1916), 65-66.

[409] *Ibid.*, 155-156.

[410] "Mmes. Bray and Morin Died Trying to Save Their Furs," *The Citizen*, February 5, 1916, p. 7.

[411] Canada, *Royal Commission Re. Parliament Buildings Fire at Ottawa, February 3, 1916: Report of Commissioners and Evidence*, Sessional Paper No. 72a (Ottawa: J. de L. Taché, 1916), 134-135.

[412] *Ibid.*, 58, 130.

[413] *Ibid.*, 58.

[414] Jane Varkaris and Lucile Finsten, *Fire on Parliament Hill!* (Erin, Ontario: The Boston Mills Press, 1988), 33.

[415] "Two Guests of Mme. Sevigny Died in Fire," *The Citizen*, February 5, 1916, p. 1

[416] Canada, *Royal Commission Re. Parliament Buildings Fire at Ottawa, February 3, 1916: Report of Commissioners and Evidence*, Sessional Paper No. 72a (Ottawa: J. de L. Taché, 1916), 16.

[417] Canada, *Royal Commission Re. Parliament Buildings Fire at Ottawa, February 3, 1916: Report of Commissioners and Evidence*, Sessional Paper No. 72a (Ottawa: J. de L. Taché, 1916).

[418] *Ibid.*, 211.

[419] *Ibid.*, 34.

[420] *Ibid.*, 5.

[421] *Ibid.*, 107.

[422] *Ibid.*, 22.

[423] *Ibid.*, 25.

[424] *Ibid.*, 36.

[425] *Ibid.*, 107.

[426] *Ibid.*, 23.

[427] *Ibid.*, 16-19.

[428] *Ibid.*, 19.

[429] *Ibid.*, 16-19.

[430] *Ibid.*, 16-19.

[431] *Ibid.*, 19-20.

[432] *Ibid.*, 23.

[433] *Ibid.*, 26-28.

[434] *Ibid.*, 30-31.

[435] *Ibid.*, 30-31, 150.

[436] *Ibid.*, 16-19.

[437] *Ibid.*, 44.

[438] *Ibid.*, 46.

[439] Canada, *Report of the Commissioner of Public Works for the Year Ending 30th June, 1867*, 31 Victoria, Sessional Papers (No. 8), 1867, Appendix No. 21, "Report on the Public Buildings at Ottawa", by John Page, August 29, 1867 p. 209.

[440] Canada, *Royal Commission Re. Parliament Buildings Fire at Ottawa, February 3, 1916: Report of Commissioners and Evidence*, Sessional Paper No. 72a (Ottawa: J. de L. Taché, 1916), 23-25.

[441] *Ibid.*, 23.

[442] *Ibid.*, 20.

[443] *Ibid.*, 27, 31, 78.

[444] *Ibid.*, 105.

[445] *Ibid.*, 23.

[446] "Policeman Gave Life in Saving Mr. Nesbitt," *The Globe,* February 5, 1916, p. 3.

[447] Canada, *Royal Commission Re. Parliament Buildings Fire at Ottawa, February 3, 1916: Report of Commissioners and Evidence*, Sessional Paper No. 72a (Ottawa: J. de L. Taché, 1916), 106.

[448] *Ibid.*, 114.

[449] John R. Rathom, "Three Years of Germany's War on the United States", *The Empire Club of Canada Speeches 1916-1917* (Toronto, Canada: The Empire Club of Canada, 1917), June 15, 1917, 570-587.

[450] *Robert Laird Borden: His Memoirs,* edited and with a preface by Henry Borden, (Toronto: The Macmillan Company of Canada Limited, 1938), 549.

[451] Canada, *Royal Commission Re. Parliament Buildings Fire at Ottawa, February 3, 1916: Report of Commissioners and Evidence*, Sessional Paper No. 72a (Ottawa: J. de L. Taché, 1916), 34.

[452] *Ibid.*, 137.

[453] *Ibid.*, 55-56.

[454] *Ibid.*, 76.

[455] *Ibid.*, 21.

[456] *Ibid.*, 32.

[457] *Ibid.*, 55-56.

[458] Canada, *Royal Commission Re. Parliament Buildings Fire at Ottawa, February 3, 1916: Report of Commissioners and Evidence*, Sessional Paper No. 72a (Ottawa: J. de L. Taché, 1916), 18.

[459] *Ibid.*, 112.

[460] *Ibid.*, 18, 21, 42, 44, 45, 46 and 138.

[461] *Ibid.*, 132.

[462] Tom Korski, "Burning down the House: A modern analysis of the 1916 Centre Block fire poses intriguing new questions," the *Ottawa Citizen*, January 29, 2011.

[463] "Gossip from the Capital", New York Times, January 13, 1895, Wednesday, Page 19. See also http://www.adolf-

cluss.de/index.php?lang=en&topSub=washington&content=h&sub=3.5.49

[464] Captain Henry Landau, "The Enemy Within: The Inside Story of German Sabotage in America", (New York: G.B. Putnam's Sons, 1937).

[465] *Ibid.*, Introduction.

[466] *Ibid.*, 4.

[467] *Ibid.*, 9.

[468] *Ibid.*, 35.

[469] *Ibid.*, 263.

[470] "A Partial Record Alien Enemy Activities 1915-1917: A Compelling Appeal for a War Policy for Aliens to be Adopted by the Government and Citizens of the United States", Reprinted from Data Prepared by the Providence Journal by the National Americanization Committee, Harvard University Library, http://pds.lib.harvard.edu/pds/view/12014464?n=3&imagesize=1200&jp2Res=.25

[471] *A few lines of recent American history.* [Providence]: Providence Journal, [1917], Harvard University Library Page Delivery Service, http://pds.lib.harvard.edu/pds/view/11221806?n=3&s=4&imagesize=1200&jp2Res=0.5&rotation=0

[472] "Caffey Reveals Rathom Admissions", New York Times, October 28, 1920, p. 10.

[473] *Ibid.*

[474] Captain Henry Landau, "The Enemy Within: The Inside Story of German Sabotage in America", (New York: G.B. Putnam's Sons, 1937).

[475] Under Secretary of State in the German Foreign Office. See http://en.wikipedia.org/wiki/Arthur_Zimmermann

[476] "Ohio Gangster," Time, U.S., May 31, 1930, http://www.time.com/time/magazine/article/0,9171,738946,00.html

[477] Wikipedia, the free encyclopedia, http://en.wikipedia.org/wiki/Gaston_Means

[478] "Lays Bare German Plots," New York Times, December 7, 1918, p. 1

[479] "Ohio Gangster," Time, U.S., May 31, 1930, http://www.time.com/time/magazine/article/0,9171,738946,00.html

[480] "Says Boy-Ed Hid Gold at Trinity Grave," The New York Times, July 9, 1920, p. 5.

[481] "Means Admits Acting as German Agent," The New York Times, July 18, 1918, p. 5.

[482] "Says Boy-Ed Hid Gold at Trinity Grave," The New York Times, July 9, 1920, p. 5.

[483] *Ibid.*

[484] "Means Admits Acting as German Agent," The New York Times, July 18, 1918, p. 5.

[485] "Says Boy-Ed Hid Gold at Trinity Grave," The New York Times, July 9, 1920, p. 5.

[486] "Bared Teuton Plots, Means Testifies," The New York Times, December 7, 1917, p. 9.

[487] *Ibid.*

[488] "Parliament Hill Fire Brought Into King Murder Case," The Montreal Gazette, December 7, 1917, p. 5.

[489] "Caffey Reveals Rathom Admissions", New York Times, October 28, 1920, p. 10.

[490] Untitled, The New York Times, February 5, 1916, p. 2

[491] Reprinted in "German U.S. Ambassador Responsible for the Fire," *The Globe,* February 4, 1916, p. 1.

[492] Untitled, The New York Times, February 5, 1916, p. 2

[493] "Caffey Reveals Rathom Admissions", New York Times, October 28, 1920, p. 10.

[494] Canada, Royal Commission Re. Parliament Buildings Fire at Ottawa, February 3, 1916: Report of Commissioners and Evidence, Sessional Paper No. 72a (Ottawa: J. de L. Taché, 1916), 7.

[495] Untitled, The New York Times, February 5, 1916, p. 2

[496] "Fire Chief Graham is Certain Parliament Fire was Incendiary," *The Citizen*, February 16, 1916, p. 3.

[497] Canada, *Royal Commission Re. Parliament Buildings Fire at Ottawa, February 3, 1916: Report of Commissioners and Evidence*, Sessional Paper No. 72a (Ottawa: J. de L. Taché, 1916), 38-41.

[498] *Ibid.*, 7 to 9.

[499] *Ibid.*, 68.

[500] *Ibid.*, 152.

[501] *Ibid.*, 61.

[502] *Ibid.*, 62.

[503] *Ibid.*, 149.

[504] Charles A. Bowman, *Ottawa Editor, the Memoirs of Charles A. Bowman*, (Sidney, British Columbia: Gray's Publishing Ltd., 1966), 34.

[505] Canada, *Royal Commission Re. Parliament Buildings Fire at Ottawa, February 3, 1916: Report of Commissioners and Evidence*, Sessional Paper No. 72a (Ottawa: J. de L. Taché, 1916), 149.

[506] *Ibid.*, 156.

[507] *Ibid.*, 9.

[508] *Ibid.*, 42, 157.

[509] Charles A. Bowman, *Ottawa Editor, the Memoirs of Charles A. Bowman*, (Sidney, British Columbia: Gray's Publishing Ltd., 1966), 32-35.

[510] Canada, *Royal Commission Re. Parliament Buildings Fire at Ottawa, February 3, 1916: Report of Commissioners and Evidence*, Sessional Paper No. 72a (Ottawa: J. de L. Taché, 1916), 140.

[511] Canada, *Royal Commission Re. Parliament Buildings Fire at Ottawa, February 3, 1916: Report of Commissioners and Evidence*, Sessional Paper No. 72a (Ottawa: J. de L. Taché, 1916), 58, 9.

[512] There are two reports on file, but they are the same one. The published report is in Sessional Paper 72a (Vol. LI, No. 28, 1916), Library and Archives Canada. There is also an unpublished, typewritten version of this report in RG11, Volume 2650, file 1575-18 that is identical except for page numbering.

[513] Personal communication with Christopher Andrew. Dr. Andrew is Professor of History at Cambridge University and was former Official Historian of the Security Service (MI5).

[514] Douglas Owram, *Building for Canadians: A History of the Department of Public Works, 1840-1960* (Ottawa: Public Relations and Information Services, Public Works Canada, 1979), 202-203.

[515] *Robert Laird Borden: His Memoirs*, edited and with a preface by Henry Borden, (Toronto: The Macmillan Company of Canada Limited, 1938), 548-549.

[516] "Parliament Buildings Today Represent $2,000,000 Asset. Present Walls Can Be Reused," *The Citizen*, February 18, 1916, p.2.

[517] "Parliament Buildings Plans are Exhibited," *The Globe*, March 22, 1916, p. 7.

[518] "Public Works Estimates," *The Globe*, May 20, 1897.

[519] "More Room Needed," *The Globe*, April 28, 1901, p. 1.

[520] Douglas Owram, *Building for Canadians: A History of the Department of Public Works, 1840-1960* (Ottawa: Public Relations and Information Services, Public Works Canada, 1979), 204-205.

[521] Jane Varkaris and Lucile Finsten, *Fire on Parliament Hill!* (Erin, Ontario: The Boston Mills Press, 1988), 61.

[522] From Pearson Mand Marchand's July 29, 1916 report. Cited in Jane Varkaris and Lucile Finsten, *Fire on Parliament Hill!* (Erin, Ontario: The Boston Mills Press, 1988), 62 to 63.

[523] Jane Varkaris and Lucile Finsten, *Fire on Parliament Hill!* (Erin, Ontario: The Boston Mills Press, 1988), 62.

[524] Jane Varkaris and Lucile Finsten, *Fire on Parliament Hill!* (Ontario: The Boston Mills Press, 1988), 68.

[525] Douglas Owram, *Building for Canadians: A History of the Department of Public Works, 1840-1960* (Ottawa: Public Relations and Information Services, Public Works Canada, 1979), 201.

[526] Jane Varkaris and Lucile Finsten, *Fire on Parliament Hill!* (Erin, Ontario: The Boston Mills Press, 1988), 62.

[527] *Ibid.*

[528] Harry Hodge, "Bells Ring Again as Peace Tower Reopens: Carillon and Clock Running Once More After Two-Year Silence", the *Ottawa Citizen* (final edition), December 3, 1996, p. B.2.

[529] The Diaries of William Lyon Mackenzie King, May 19, 1921, National Archives of Canada, http://king.collectionscanada.ca/EN/Default.asp.

[530] D.E.Lawrence, "Building Stones of Canada's Federal Parliament Buildings," *Geoscience Canada*, 28, no.1 (2001): 18.

[531] *Ibid.* 24-25.

[532] Canada, *Contract between His Majesty the King and P. Lyall & Sons Construction Company Limited, Reconstruction of the Parliament Buildings at Ottawa*, September 29, 1916, P.W. No. 11132.

[533] Douglas Owram, *Building for Canadians: A History of the Department of Public Works, 1840-1960* (Ottawa: Public Relations and Information Services, Public Works Canada, 1979), 203 to 205.

[534] *Ibid.*, 204.

[535] D.E.Lawrence, "Building Stones of Canada's Federal Parliament Buildings," *Geoscience Canada,* 28, no.1 (2001): 25.

[536] Douglas Owram, *Building for Canadians: A History of the Department of Public Works, 1840-1960* (Ottawa: Public Relations and Information Services, Public Works Canada, 1979), 204.

[537] D.E.Lawrence, "Building Stones of Canada's Federal Parliament Buildings," *Geoscience Canada,* 28, no.1 (2001): 25.

[538] Jane Varkaris and Lucile Finsten, *Fire on Parliament Hill!* (Ontario: The Boston Mills Press, 1988), 70.

[539] The Diaries of William Lyon Mackenzie King, November 9, 1924, National Archives of Canada, http://king.collectionscanada.ca/EN/Default.asp.

[540] *Ibid.*, March 2, 1925.

[541] Jane Varkaris and Lucile Finsten, *Fire on Parliament Hill!* (Ontario: The Boston Mills Press, 1988), 70.

[542] D.E.Lawrence, "Building Stones of Canada's Federal Parliament Buildings," *Geoscience Canada,* 28, no.1 (2001): 26.

[543] Jane Varkaris and Lucile Finsten, *Fire on Parliament Hill!* (Ontario: The Boston Mills Press, 1988), 70.

[544] "Prince May Lay The Corner Stone of Peace Tower," the *Ottawa Citizen,* July 29, 1919, p. 2.

[545] The Diaries of William Lyon Mackenzie King, November 9, 1924, National Archives of Canada, http://king.collectionscanada.ca/EN/Default.asp.

[546] *Ibid.*

[547] "Gov't. Publishing Information for carillon Lovers," the *Ottawa Citizen*, July 12, 1928, p. 19.

[548] "Magnificent Public Buildings Crowning Glory of the Capital," the *Ottawa Citizen*, May 18, 1939, p. 4.

[549] "Leadership Since Last war Scored by Colonel Steacy," The Ottawa Citizen, November 12, 1941, p. 7.

[550] Bruce Hutchison, "The Empty Tower," the *Ottawa Citizen*, January 31, 1952, p. 34.

[551] http://en.wikipedia.org/wiki/Canadian_2_dollar_coin

[552] Arthur Beauchesne, Canada's Parliament Building – The Senate and House of Commons, Ottawa, (Ottawa, published by the author, 1946), 25.

[553] J.P. Crerar, "All-Night Clock Chimes," the *Ottawa Citizen*, July 19, 1927, p. 9.

[554] "Are Opposed to Idea Silencing 'Big Ben'," the *Ottawa Citizen*, July 20, 1927, p. 2.

[555] Excerpt from the House of Commons Debates, October 1, 1945, p. 593.

[556] "51st State?" *The Citizen,* February 6, 1976, p. 3.; " 'Takeover' on the Hill was a Prank," *The Globe and Mail,* February 7, 1976, p. 10.

[557] "A Treasure to Explore," Frequently Asked Questions - Carvings. http:/www.parliamenthill.gc.ca/text/faq_e.html

[558] Canada, *Specification for the Completion of Tower and memorial Chamber, Parliament Buildings, Ottawa,* J.O. Marchand and John A. Pearson, January, 1924.

[559] Arthur G. Roberts, "Quietly Thumps Clay into carving Models," the *Ottawa Citizen*, January 10, 1947, p. 9.

[560] "Sculptor Scooped Government By 11 Years on Tenth Province," the *Globe and Mail,* July 31, 1948, p. 13.

[561] "Prime Minister St. Laurent mounted scaffold erected in the archway of the Peace Tower to strike the first chips for carving of Newfoundland heraldic shield, left blank when buildings were constructed," photograph caption, *The Globe and Mail,* April 2, 1949, p. 17.

[562] Excerpt from the House of Commons Debates, May 8, 1936, p. 2656.

[563] "House Carvings Called Inartistic," *The Globe,* May 9, 1936, p. 1.

[564] "Beaver Receives Position of Honor in Carved Doorway of Peace Tower," *The Globe and Mail,* January 10, 1938, p. 15.

[565] "Artistic License Bows to Biology in decoration of the Peace Tower," *The Globe and Mail,* June 7, 1938, p. 3.

[566] "Stonemason Inscribing date on Peace Tower Base," the *Ottawa Citizen,* September 10, 1946, p. 25.

[567] "Date Concealed in Stone," the Montreal Gazette, September 1, 1919, p. 12.

[568] The Evening Herald, Rock Hill, S.C., December 20, 1919, p. 31 (quoted from the Christian Science Moinitor).

[569] Charles A. Bowman, *Ottawa Editor, the Memoirs of Charles A. Bowman,* (Sidney, British Columbia: Gray's Publishing Ltd., 1966), 272.

[570] *Ibid.*, 270.

[571] *Ibid.*, 270-273.

[572] *Ibid.*

[573] The Diaries of William Lyon Mackenzie King, entry for May 28, 1921, National Archives of Canada, http://king.collectionscanada.ca/EN/Default.asp.

[574] "The Tower of Parliament", editorial in the *Ottawa Citizen,* May 31, 1921. In *Each Morning Bright 160 Years of Selected Readings from the Ottawa Citizen 1845-2005,* Doug Fischer, editor, Ralph Willsey, editor/designer, 14, (Ottawa: Ottawa Citizen Group Inc., 2005.)

[575] Actually, this is the reason we stopped the clock for two years while we repaired the crumbling stonework of the tower. Can you imagine what it would have been like if our masons were up there on the scaffolding, behind the tarpaulins, and that big Bourdon bell went off?

[576] Canada, *Specification for the Completion of Tower and memorial Chamber, Parliament Buildings, Ottawa,* J.O. Marchand and John A. Pearson, January, 1924.

[577] There are two real gargoyles (and as far as I know these are the only real ones) on the north side of the south west tower of the East Block, at the level of the main roof of the building. However they have been capped off and haven't worked for decades. The caps are made of sheet lead and look like hats or caps placed on their heads so the water doesn't run inside and out their open mouths.

[578] The Diaries of William Lyon Mackenzie King, entry for August 12, 1921, National Archives of Canada, http://king.collectionscanada.ca/EN/Default.asp.

[579] "One Jail Never Occupied – Room in Canadian Parliament Building Reserved for Defiant Members," The New York Times, December 26, 1931, p. 14.

[580] Eva-Lis Wuorio, "Chimes Voice of Ottawa, Peace Tower is its Heart," *The Globe and Mail,* April 2, 1947, p. 12.

[581] "Plexiglass Cover Planned for Peace Tower Lookout," *The Globe and Mail,* April 4, 1970, p. 3; "Boy Friend Took Drug before Leap, Girl Says," *The Globe and Mail,* June 25, 1970, p. 4.).

[582] Angus Riker, "Heatley inquest: Jury can't find reason for jump from tower," the *Ottawa Citizen,* September 18, 1970, p. 3.

[583] "Tower Closed after Woman Leaps to Death," *The Globe and Mail,* July 29, 1970, p. 23; "Peace Tower is Reopened for Visitors," the *Globe and Mail,* July 30, 1970, p. 31.

[584] Angus Ricker, "Jump from Peace Tower was second attempt inquest told," the *Ottawa Citizen,* October 2, 1970, p. 6.

[585] The Diaries of William Lyon Mackenzie King, July 1, 1927, National Archives of Canada, http://king.collectionscanada.ca/EN/Default.asp.

[586] "Our national Carillon in the Peace Tower," *The Globe*, September 3, 1927, p. 17.

[587] The Diaries of William Lyon Mackenzie King, July 1, 1927, National Archives of Canada, http://king.collectionscanada.ca/EN/Default.asp.

[588] *Ibid.*

[589] Kay Kritzwiser, "Peace Tower and Carillon Get $4.6 Million Overhaul: Ottawa Rings in the New," *The Globe and Mail*, September 2, 1982, p. 19.

[590] The Diaries of William Lyon Mackenzie King, July 1, 1927, National Archives of Canada, http://king.collectionscanada.ca/EN/Default.asp.

[591] M. E. James. "Jubilant Message of Glorious Music Comes From Bells" *The Globe*, Saturday, July 2, 1927, p. 1.

[592] Harry Hodge, "Bells Ring Again as Peace Tower Reopens: Carillon and Clock Running Once More After Two-Year Silence," the *Ottawa Citizen* (final edition), December 3, 1996, p. B.2.

[593] M. E. James. "Jubilant Message of Glorious Music Comes From Bells" the *Globe*, Saturday, July 2, 1927, p. 6.

[594] "Canada in Mourning for American Flier," New York Times, July 4, 1927, p. 16.

[595] The Diaries of William Lyon Mackenzie King, July 3, 1927, National Archives of Canada, http://king.collectionscanada.ca/EN/Default.asp.

[596] Arthur Beauchesne, Canada's Parliament Building – The Senate and House of Commons, Ottawa, (Ottawa, published by the author, 1946), 28.

[597] Harry Hodge, "Bells Ring Again as Peace Tower Reopens: Carillon and Clock Running Once More After Two-Year Silence," the *Ottawa Citizen* (final edition), December 3, 1996, p. B.2.

[598] *Ibid.*

[599] "Sun-Dial Unveiled by His Excellency Historic Function," *The Citizen*, May 20, 1921, p. 3.

[600] *Ibid.*

[601] *Ibid.*

[602] *Ibid.*

[603] "Thomas Ritchie Passes to Rest," *The Globe*, December 8, 1921, p. 3.

[604] http://www.donmarquis.org/freddy.htm

[605] Kenneth C. Cragg, "Ottawa rats – East Block Main Scene of Invasion," *The Globe and Mail,* November 9, 1946, p. 17.

[606] J.D. Livermore, *A History of Parliamentary Accommodation in Canada, 1841-1974* (Ottawa: Advisory Committee on Parliamentary Accommodation, 1975), 67.

[607] Kenneth C. Cragg, "Ottawa rats – East Block Main Scene of Invasion," *The Globe and Mail,* November 9, 1946, p. 17.

[608] James Roe, "Careful Vigilance Eliminating Mr. Rat," the *Ottawa Citizen*, May 26, 1948, p. 18.

[609] " 'No Pets' Remain To Warm Official Hearts on Parliament Hill," the *Globe,* May 16, 1936, p. 1.

[610] Kenneth C. Cragg, "Ottawa rats – East Block Main Scene of Invasion," *The Globe and Mail,* November 9, 1946, p. 17.

[611] *Ibid.*

[612] I was told this by Frank Foran who had been around Parliament Hill a long, long time. He began working on Parliament Hill in 1950 as a Senate page and in 1964 joined Senate Security, retiring in 1995 as a Sergeant.

[613] Geoffrey Stevens, "Audience Interest Flickers like the Lights at Ottawa Centennial Pageant Premiere," *Globe and Mail,* May 15, 1967. p. 8.

[614] Deputy Minister to Minister of Public Works, Memorandum dated August 5, 1952, Library and Archives Canada, RG11, Vol. 5028, file 822-419.

[615] Gordon Robertson, *Memoirs of a Very Civil Servant – Mackenzie King to Pierre Trudeau,* (Toronto Buffalo London: University of Toronto Press, 2000), p. 89-93.

[616] *The Evening Citizen,* August 5, 1952, p. 15.

[617] National Archives and Library Canada, Record of Cabinet Decision No. 204, August 14, 1952. Cited by Gordon Robertson, *Memoirs of a Very Civil Servant – Mackenzie King to Pierre Trudeau,* (Toronto Buffalo London: University of Toronto Press, 2000), p. 90.

[618] Richard Jackson, "Historic Hill Plaque Found," *The Ottawa Journal,* July 5, 1973. (Jackson writes that the star was mounted on the cornerstone on the afternoon of September 24, 1860, suggesting the Prince came back after unveiling the cornerstone on September 1. This is incorrect. It was there when H.R.H. unveiled it - see next reference.)

[619] A British Canadian (Henry Morgan), *The Tour of H.R.H. The Prince of Wales through British America and The United States,* Montreal, Printed for the compiler by John Lovell, St. Nicholas Street, 1860, p. 135.

[620] The text has been officially translated as: "May it be happy and fortunate! Albert Edward, Prince of Wales, has deigned to lay this cornerstone of the building that will serve to hold the Assemblies of the Province, in the year 1860, the First day of September, the twenty-fourth year of Victoria's reign."

[621] Frank Swanson, "Eighty Rooms Might be added to Parliament Building," the *Ottawa Citizen,* April 8, 1949.

[622] *Ibid.*

[623] Cabinet Conclusions, RG2, Privy Council Office, Series A-5-a, Volume 2643, Reel T-2366, Access code: 20, p. 1b and 2.

[624] Frank Swanson, "Eighty Rooms Might be addedto Parliament Building," the *Ottawa Citizen,* April 8, 1949.

[625] "More Space for M.P.'s," the *Ottawa Citizen*, April 8, 1949, p. 69.

[626] E.A. Gardner, Memo to the Deputy Minister, Public Works, from the Chief Architect titled "Rehabilitation and/or Reconstruction – West Block – Ottawa, Ontario", March 10, 1955, p. 4. Library and Archives Canada, RG 11, Vol. 5032, File 822-421 (volume 3).

[627] *Ibid.*

[628] *Ibid.*

[629] Library and Archives Canada, RG 11, Vol. 5032, File 822-421 (volume 3). See handwritten note on the routing slip that was attached to a letter sent from the Deputy Minister to the Minister on February 2, 1954 (unfortunately the letter itself is not in the file); a Ministerial query about fees for demolition on February 5, and the Deputy Minister's reply on February 8.

[630] "More Room for MP's," *The Globe and Mail,* April 10, 1954, p. 4.

[631] E.A. Gardner, Memo to the Deputy Minister, Public Works, from the Chief Architect titled "Rehabilitation and/or Reconstruction – West Block – Ottawa, Ontario", March 10, 1955, p. 3. Library and Archives Canada, RG 11, Vol. 5032, File 822-421 (volume 3).

[632] Cabinet Conclusions, RG2, Privy Council Office, Series A-5-a, Volume 2657, Reel T-12184, Access code: 12.

[633] "One of our most historic buildings," the Montreal Gazette, July 11, 1955, p. 6.

[634] George Drew fonds (MG32-C3), Federal Political Career series, vol 248, file 334.1 "House of Commons – The Oppposition – Material for Questions in the House 1954-1956"; and George Drew fonds (MG32-C3), Federal Political career series, vol 255, file 352, DPW.1 "Federal Departments – Public Works."

[635] Harvey Hickey, "Face of Parliament Hill Due for Plastic Surgery," *The Globe and Mail,* November 25, 1955, p. 1; Reg Hardy, "Architects at Work: 700 Rooms in Plans for New West Block," the *Ottawa Citizen,* November 22, 1955, p. 1.

[636] "Would They Swim in It?" Editorial in the *Peterborough Examiner* reprinted in *the Globe and Mail*, December 1, 1955.

[637] Frank Swanson, "Face-Lifting For All Of Buildings On Hill," the *Ottawa Citizen*, November 24, 1955

[638] Harvey Hickey, "Face of Parliament Hill Due for Plastic Surgery," *The Globe and Mail*, November 25, 1955, p. 1.

[639] Reg Hardy, "Architects at Work: 700 Rooms in Plans for New West Block," the *Ottawa Citizen*, November 22, 1955, p. 1.

[640] *Ibid.*

[641] "The Wildly Improbable West Block," the *Ottawa Citizen*, editorial, November 24, 1955.

[642] "Tearing down is easy," the Montreal Gazette, November 25, 1955, p. 6.

[643] Mathers & Haldenby, Architects, and Edouard Fiset, Associate Architect, *Report to the Deputy Minister of Public Works of Canada on the Present Condition and Future Disposition of the Building on Parliament Hill in Ottawa Known as the West Block*. An 8 page attachment to a letter to Maj.-Gen. H.A. Young, Deputy Minister of Public Works, Regarding the West Block of the Parliament Buildings, December 23, 1955, Library and Archives Canada, RG 11, Series B4a, Vol. 4800, File 752-1013, pt.1, 1955-60.

[644] A.S. Mathers, *Letter to Mr. E.A. Gardner, Chief Architect of Public Works, Regarding The West Block*, April 1, 1960. Library and Archives Canada, RG 11, Vol. 4793, File 744-1013 (volume 1), 2 pages.

[645] Carl Weiselberger, "Keep Your Hands Off Our 'Victorian Gothic'," the *Ottawa Citizen*, November 10, 1956, p. 17.

[646] E.R. Arthur, John Bland, Fred Lasserre, H.H. Madill and John Russell, "The West Block and its Future," *Journal of the Royal Architectural Institute of Canada*, December (1956): 485. See also "Architects Plead for the West Block" which appeared on the editorial page of *The Gazette*, Montreal, on January 24, 1957.

[647] Austin F. Cross, "Old West Block Might Give way to Bigger $6,400,000 Building", the *Ottawa Citizen*, February 12, 1957, p. 1.

[648] A.S. Mathers of Mathers & Haldenby Architects, *Letter to Mr. E.A. Gardner, Chief Architect of Public Works, Regarding The West Block*, April 1, 1960. Library and Archives Canada, RG 11, Vol. 4793, File 744-1013 (volume 1), 2 pages.

[649] "East Block Will Be Renovated," the *Ottawa Citizen*, December 19, 1949, p. 8.

[650] "East Block Will Be Renovated," the *Ottawa Citizen*, December 19, 1949, p. 8.

[651] R.A.J. Phillips, *The East Block of the Parliament Buildings of Canada*, (Ottawa: Queen's Printer, 1967), 28.

[652] "Rescue," The Montreal Gazette, January 28, 1954, p. 2.

[653] The Montreal Gazette, November 25, 1955, p. 6.

[654] H. Belden, *Illustrated Historical Atlas of the County of Carleton Ont. (Including City of Ottawa)*, (Toronto: H. Belden & Co., 1879), xiii. Cited in McGovern Heritage Archaeological Associates, *Stage 3/4 Archaeological Assessment of the Bank Street Building Site Zones A, C, E. and F, Parliament Hill, City of Ottawa*, 2004, p.43.

[655] *Ibid.*

[656] Canada, *Royal Commission Re. Parliament Buildings Fire at Ottawa, February 3, 1916: Report of Commissioners and Evidence*, Sessional Paper No. 72a (Ottawa: J. de L. Taché, 1916), 24.

[657] Excerpt from the House of Commons Debates, August 3, 1956, p. 6937

[658] NAC, RG11, B3(a), Vol. 4327, File 2994-1-C. Cited in McGovern Heritage Archaeological Associates, Stage 3/4 Archaeological Assessment of the Bank Street Building Site Zones A, C, E. and F, Parliament Hill, City of Ottawa, 2004, p.74.

[659] J. A. Hume, "Old Supreme Court Building to be Demolished Next Year," the *Ottawa Citizen*, December 28, 1955, p. 15.

[660] A year later Mr. Winters revealed plans to build a three-storey underground parking garage, capable of holding 1,000 cars (ref. Austin

F. Cross, "Old West Block Might Give way to Bigger $6,400,000 Building", the *Ottawa Citizen,* February 12, 1957, p. 1). However this idea, which was linked to the demolition of the West Block, never went ahead.

[661] "Government Tears Down Historic Ottawa Landmark," *Ottawa Journal,* September 13, 1956.

[662] "A Ruin to Remain Among Ottawa's Souvenirs," *Ottawa Journal,* October 17, 1956.

[663] Excerpt from the House of Commons Debates, June 28, 1951, p. 4829.

[664] Personal communication, Lowell Green, 2007.

[665] Cabinet Conclusions database at Library and Archives Canada website www.collectionscanada.gc.ca. Meeting date: May 26, 1966, RG2, Privy Council Office, Series A-5-a, Vol. 6321, Access Code: 90, p. 8.

[666] "Parliament Hill fence widens to smooth route for traffic", *The Ottawa Journal,* September 29, 1966.

[667] "Why Will the Flame Burn?" the *Ottawa Citizen,* October 5, 1966.

[668] Excerpt from the House of Commons Debates, December 12, 1967, p. 5359

[669] These stones deteriorated very rapidly. In the early 1980's they were recarved using a durable red Canadian granite from the Grenville region in Quebec. Ref: Canada, *A Treasure to Explore, Parliament Hill, Ottawa, Ontario, Canada, in Frequently Asked Questions.* http://www.parliamenthill.gc.ca.

[670] Lowell Green, *It's Hard to Say Goodby* (Ottawa: Creative Bound International Inc., 2007), 73-81.

[671] Excerpt from the House of Commons Debates, December 12, 1967, p. 5359

[672] "Memorandum to Cabinet – Centennial Flame," Cab. Doc. No. 818/67, December 8, 1967, National Arcjives of Canada, RG 2, Vol. 6329.

[673] Cabinet Conclusions database at Library and Archives Canada website www.collectionscanada.gc.ca. Meeting date: December 12, 1967, RG2, Privy Council Office, Series A-5-a, Vol. 6323, Access Code: 90, p. 2.

[674] "Bronze Bigwigs on Parliament Hill to Get Bath in Harmless Detergent," the *Ottawa Citizen*, September 19, 1951, p. 21.

[675] Strictly speaking, bronze statues don't rust. Rusting is associated with iron. Cars rust because the steel they are made of contains iron. Nepean sandstone rusts because it contains iron. But bronze doesn't rust; it corrodes.

[676] Phoebe Dent Weil with Peter Gaspar, Leonard Gulbransen, Ray Lindberg and, *in memoriam,* David Zimmerman, "The Corrosive Deterioration of Outdoor Bronze Sculpture." Preprints of the contributions to the Washington Congress, 3-9 September, 1982, *Science and Technology in the Service of Conservation.* Published by The International Institute for Conservation of Historic and Artistic Works, 6 Buckingham Street, London, WC2N 6BA, p. 130-133.

[677] Anthony Padovano, *The Process of Sculpture* (New York: Doubleday & Company, Inc., 1981), 211.

[678] "The Fine Arts – Sculpture - Third Lecture by Prof. Weir at the Yale School of Arts," *New York Times,* November 19, 1874, p. 3; "How Statues are Made: The Sculptor's Art as Practiced Here and Abroad," *New York Times,* January 25, 1891, p. 14; and "Making Bronze Statues: Difficulty in Preparing for Casting the Big Figures," *New York Times,* November 15, 1903, p. 22.

[679] L.S. Selwyn, N.E. Binnie, J. Poitras, M.E. Laver, and D.A. Downham, "Outdoor Bronze Statues: Analysis of Metal and Surface Samples," *Studies in Conservation,* 41 (1996): 208.

[680] Nancy E. Binnie, "Colour Monitoring on Outdoor Bronze Statues in Ottawa, Canada", *From Marble to Chocolate, The Conservation of Modern Sculpture,* Tate Gallery Conference 18-20 September 1995, editor: Jackie Heuman (London: Archetype Publications), p. 74.

[681] This horse was a gift to the Queen in 1967. When he was with the RCMP his name was "Jerry" but the Queen changed his name to "Centenial" with one "n" to distinguish it from "Centennial", the year.

[682] Canada, House of Commons Debates, July 18, 1960, p. 6458

[683] "Trying to Clean the Statues on Parliament Hill," the *Ottawa Citizen,* August 7, 1931, p. 1.

[684] "Brighten up Statues on Hill in view of Coming Conference," the *Ottawa Citizen*, June 28, 1932, p. 1.

[685] W.H.J. Vernon and L. Whitby, "The Open Air Corrosion of Copper. A Chemical Study of the Surface Patina," *J. Inst. Metals,* 42, (1929): 188.

[686] W.H.J. Vernon and L. Whitby, "The Open Air Corrosion of Copper. A Chemical Study of the Surface Patina," *J. Inst. Metals,* 42, (1929): 181.

[687] "Coal Weighing Began in Ottawa in Year 1873", in *Ottawa History,* a scrapbook collection in the Ottawa Room of the Ottawa Public Library Vol. V, p. 90.

[688] *Ibid.*, 205-6.

[689] L.S. Selwyn, N.E. Binnie, J. Poitras, M.E. Laver, and D.A. Downham, "Outdoor Bronze Statues: Analysis of Metal and Surface Samples," *Studies in Conservation*, 41 (1996): 207.

[690] Carolyn Willett, "Statues of Great Men Ring Parliament Hill," the *Ottawa Citizen,* January 29, 1957, p. 28.

[691] "Bronze Bigwigs on Parliament Hill to Get Bath in Harmless Detergent," the *Ottawa Citizen*, September 19, 1951, p. 21.

[692] Greg Connolley, "Unofficial War on Hill – Cut Off Pigeons' Food," the *Ottawa Citizen,* December 29, 1960, p. 40.

[693] *Ibid.*

[694] *Statues of Parliament Hill* (Ottawa-Hull: the Visual Arts Programme, National Capital Commission, 1986), 77-87.

[695] *Ibid.*

[696] W.H.J. Vernon and L. Whitby, "The Open Air Corrosion of Copper. A Chemical Study of the Surface Patina," *J. Inst. Metals,* 42, (1929): 194.

[697] Phoebe Dent Weil with Peter Gaspar, Leonard Gulbransen, Ray Lindberg and, *in memoriam,* David Zimmerman, "The Corrosive Deterioration of Outdoor Bronze Sculpture." Preprints of the contributions to the Washington Congress, 3-9 September, 1982, *Science and Technology in the Service of Conservation.* Published by The International Institute for Conservation of Historic and Artistic Works, 6 Buckingham Street, London, WC2N 6BA, p. 130-133.

[698] Personal communication, Dr. Lyndsie Selwyn, Canadian Conservation Institute, Ottawa, 2005.

[699] L. O. David, *Souvenirs et Biographies* (Montreal: Librairie Beauchemin Limitée, 1911), 248.

[700] L.S. Selwyn, N.E. Binnie, J. Poitras, M.E. Laver, and D.A. Downham, "Outdoor Bronze Statues: Analysis of Metal and Surface Samples," *Studies in Conservation,* 41 (1996): 216-219.

[701] L.S. Selwyn, N.E. Binnie, J. Poitras, M.E. Laver, and D.A. Downham, "Outdoor Bronze Statues: Analysis of Metal and Surface Samples," *Studies in Conservation,* 41 (1996): 208.

[702] Dave Brown, "Brown's Beat (Final Edition) - Jewels of the Hill," the *Ottawa Citizen,* August 21, 1986, p. B.1.

[703] Dan Dugas, "Queen's Bronze Lion: Did it Used to be a He?; Restored Statue Has no Scars From the Testicular Tampering" *The Gazette,* July 25, 1992, p. A.7.

[704] Wm. A. Parks, *Report on the Building and Ornamental Stones of Canada,* v.1 (Ottawa: Government Printing Bureau, 1912), 111.

[705] *Ibid.,* p. 133-136.

[706] Hon. J.D. Edgar, *Canada and its Capital* (Toronto: George N. Morang, 1898), 57-59, 66.

[707] *Hand Book to the Parliamentary and Departmental Buildings, Canada* (Ottawa: Printed by G.E. Desbarats, 1867), 14.

[708] *Illustrated Guide to the House of Commons and Senate of Canada* (Ottawa: Published by F.R.E. Campeau; Printed by A. Bureau, Sparks Street, 1879), 116.

[709] Hon. J.D. Edgar, *Canada and its Capital* (Toronto: George N. Morang, 1898), 57-59, 66.

[710] Wm. A. Parks, *Report on the Building and Ornamental Stones of Canada*, v.1 (Ottawa: Government Printing Bureau, 1912), 136.

[711] Edward Van Cortland, "To the Editor of the *Ottawa Citizen*," August 6, 1860, in *Ottawa History*, a scrapbook collection in the Ottawa Room of the Ottawa Public Library Vol. I, p. 132.

[712] Canada, *Report of the Commissioner of Public Works for the Year Ending 30th June, 1867*, 31 Victoria, Sessional Papers (No. 8), 1867, Appendix No. 21, "Report on the Public Buildings at Ottawa", by John Page, August 29, 1867 p. 222.

[713] D.E.Lawrence, "Building Stones of Canada's Federal Parliament Buildings," *Geoscience Canada*, 28, no.1 (2001): 18.

[714] Canada, *Report of the Commissioner of Public Works for the Year Ending 30th June, 1867*, 31 Victoria, Sessional Papers (No. 8), 1867, Appendix No. 21, "Report on the Public Buildings at Ottawa", by John Page, August 29, 1867 p. 205.

[715] D.E.Lawrence, "Building Stones of Canada's Federal Parliament Buildings," *Geoscience Canada*, 28, no.1 (2001): 19.

[716] *Ibid.*

[717] "1870's Grandeur Returns to East Block," *The Globe and Mail*, October 12, 1981, p. 12.

[718] Standards and Guidelines for the Conservation of Historic Places in Canada, Parks Canada, 2003, p. 2-3.

[719] *Ibid.*

[720] Catherine Woolfitt, "Soluble Salts in Masonry," http://www.buildingconservation.com/articles/salts/salts.htm. This article is reproduced from *The Building Conservation Directory*, 2000.

[721] A.H.P. Maurenbrecher, K. Trischuk, M.Z. Rousseau, and M.I. Subercaseaux, "Key Considerations for Repointing Mortars for the Conservation of Older Masonry", National Research Council of Canada, Institute for Research in Construction, IRC-RR-225, January 2007, p. 7-9. http://irc.nrc-cnrc.gc.ca/pubs/rr/rr225/rr225.pdf

[722] Margaret Munro, "Acid Rainfall Ravaging Parliament Buildings", the *Ottawa Citizen*, January 10, 1981, P. 1.

[723] T.E. Gradel, K. Nassau, and J.P. Franey, "Copper Patinas Formed in the Atmosphere – I. Introduction," *Corrosion Science*, 27, no.7 (1987): 639.

[724] Canada, *Specification for the Completion of Tower and memorial Chamber, Parliament Buildings, Ottawa*, J.O. Marchand and John A. Pearson, January, 1924.

[725] J.P. Franey and M.E. Davis "Metallographic Studies of the Copper Patina Formed in the Atmosphere," *Corrosion Science*, 27, no.7 (1987): 659.

[726] T.E. Gradel, K. Nassau, and J.P. Franey, "Copper Patinas Formed in the Atmosphere – I. Introduction," *Corrosion Science*, 27, no.7 (1987): 644.

[727] W.H.J. Vernon and L. Whitby, "The Open Air Corrosion of Copper. A Chemical Study of the Surface Patina," *J. Inst. Metals*, 42, (1929): 194.

[728] Copper Development Association, Architecture Design Handbook: Section 4, Architectural Details: Roofing Systems, http://www.copper.org/applications/architecture/arch_dhb/roofing/long_pan.html

[729] Part of the Library of Parliament's new roof is copper, which will go brown, green, etc.. Part is terne-plated copper (terne is an alloy of lead and tin) which will always stay a shiny lead-grey colour.

[730] T.E. Gradel, K. Nassau, and J.P. Franey, "Copper Patinas Formed in the Atmosphere – I. Introduction," *Corrosion Science*, 27, no.7 (1987): 640.

[731] J.D. Livermore, *A History of Parliamentary Accommodation in Canada, 1841-1974* (Ottawa: Advisory Committee on Parliamentary Accommodation, 1975), 55.

[732] R.A.J. Phillips, *The East Block of the Parliament Buildings of Canada,* (Ottawa: Queen's Printer, 1967), 31.

[733] W.H.J. Vernon, "The Open-Air Corrosion of Copper. Part III – Artificial Production of Green Patina," *J. Inst. Metals,* 49, (1932): 154.

[734] W.H.J. Vernon and L. Whitby, "The Open Air Corrosion of Copper. A Chemical Study of the Surface Patina," *J. Inst. Metals,* 42, (1929): 191.

[735] David Scott, *Copper and Bronze in Art: Corrosion, Colorants, Conservation,* (Los Angeles: The Getty Conservation Institute, 2002), 280.

[736] Personal communication, Dr. Lyndsie Selwyn, Canadian Conservation Institute, Ottawa, Ontario, Canada, 2005.

[737] "New Copper Roof for East Block," *The Windsor Daily Star,* April 11, 1950, p. 16.

[738] The *Globe and Mail,* March 15, 1950, p. 1.

[739] The *Calgary Herald,* July 13, 1949, p. 3.

[740] The *Globe and Mail,* March 15, 1950, p. 1.

[741] "Ottawa Firemen Are Fooled Again," *The Globe and Mail,* February 19, 1938, p. 15.

[742] "Firemen Thaw Commons Ice," *The Globe and Mail,* December 24, 1958, p. 2.

[743] Tony Lofaro, "The Height of National Pride", the *Ottawa Citizen,* final edition, October 9, 1996 p. C.1.

[744] Dave Rogers, "Copper Stolen Within Sight of Police Station: BIG LOSS: The Two Tonnes of Scrap From the Roof of the Centre Block Was to Have Been Used by Developmentally Handicapped Group to Make Souvenirs to Help Finance Their Programs, " the *Ottawa Citizen,* final edition, November 7, 1996, p. B.3.

[745] Dave Rogers, "Police Recover Stolen Copper at Metal Dealer", *The Citizen,* November 8, 1996.

[746] Tony Lofaro, "The Height of National Pride", the *Ottawa Citizen,* final edition, October 9, 1996 p. C.1.

[747] Personal communication, 2006.

[748] A British Canadian (Henry Morgan), *The Tour of H.R.H. The Prince of Wales through British America and The United States,* Montreal, Printed for the compiler by John Lovell, St. Nicholas Street, 1860, p. 135.

[749] Jane Varkaris and Lucile Finsten, *Fire on Parliament Hill!* (Ontario: The Boston Mills Press, 1988), 68.

[750] *Programme for the Laying of the Corner Stone of the Main Tower by His Royal Highness Edward, Prince of Wlales, K.G. etc. etc. at 11:30 o'clock a.m. Monday the first day of September, 1919,* Public Works and Government Services Canada Record Room.

[751] "General Young is Sympathetic but Firm on Cats' Eviction," November 25, 1954, p. 1.

[752] William Pittman Lett, *Recollections of Bytown and its Old Inhabitants,* (Ottawa: "Citizen" Printing and Publishing Company, 1874).

[753] "Small Blaze Occurs in Parl't. Buildings," *The Citizen,* January 21, 1924, p. 12.

[754] Blaze in Commons is Blamed on Rats," *The Ottawa Journal,* January 21, 1924, p. 4.

[755] " 'No Pets' Remain To Warm Official Hearts on Parliament Hill," *The Globe,* May 16, 1936, p. 1.

[756] "Parliament Hill Cats Are Justified by Fire," *The Globe,* January 21, 1924, p. 1. See also "Automatic Fire Alarm Gives Warning and Outbreak is Speedily Checked," *The Globe,* February 1, 1924, p. 2.

[757] Catherine Allison, "Stray cats Strut for Birthday: Parliament Hill's Feline Friend Turns 80, vowing to give food 'til I'm 100'", *The Gazette,* December 29, 2001, p. A.8.

[758] Mark Bourrie, "Parliamentary Cat Keeper," *The Toronto Star,* February 11, 1996, p. C2.

[759] "Speaker of Commons Shoots Wild Rabbits on Parliament Hill," the *Ottawa Citizen*, April 11, 1932, p. 29.

[760] John Macdonnell, "Parliament Hill rabbits, the *Ottawa Citizen*, April 20, 1932, p. 11.

[761] Win Mills, "Hill's cat lady goes to reward" the *Ottawa Citizen,* February 21, 1963, p. 2.

[762] Personal communication, Frank Foran, 2006. This description of the char ladies and the cats was told to me by Frank Foran. Frank started working on Parliament Hill in 1950 as a Senate Page. In 1964 he joined Senate Security, retiring in 1995 as a Sergeant.

[763] John Bird, "West Block's Tobermory Arrested Too As Found-In," *The Ottawa Journal,* November 23, 1954, p. 18.

[764] John Bird, "Our Man Bird Finds Homes for Evicted Parliament Cats", *The Ottawa Journal,* November 26, 1954, p. 3.

[765] "Political Neutrality," the *Ottawa Citizen*, March 17, 1951, p. 7.

[766] John Bird, "No longer "Backscratchworthy" - Peregrine and Poppett The Hill Cats Being Evicted From Cosy Quarters," the *Ottawa Citizen,* December 2, 1953, p. 23.

[767] John Bird, "Peregrine and Poppett Escape Death by a Cat's Whisker," *The Ottawa Journal,* November 23, 1954, p. 1.

[768] John Bird, "No longer "Backscratchworthy" - Peregrine and Poppett The Hill Cats Being Evicted From Cosy Quarters," the *Ottawa Citizen,* December 2, 1953, p. 23.

[769] Kenneth C. Cragg, "Ottawa rats – East Block Main Scene of Invasion," *The Globe and Mail,* November 9, 1946, p. 17.

[770] *The Windsor Daily Star*, March 20, 1959, p. 4.

[771] John Bird, "Our Man Bird Finds Homes for Evicted Parliament Cats", *The Ottawa Journal,* November 26, 1954, p. 3.

[772] John Bird, "West Block's Tobermory Arrested Too As Found-In," *The Ottawa Journal,* November 23, 1954, p. 18.

[773] "Old Peregrine, Poppett and Punky To Be Missed on Parliament Hill," *The Montreal Gazette*, November 23, 1954, p. 2.

[774] "Three Ottawa Cats Find New Homes," The Montreal Gazette, November 26, 1954, p. 22.

[775] John Bird, "No longer "Backscratchworthy" - Peregrine and Poppett The Hill Cats Being Evicted From Cosy Quarters," the *Ottawa Citizen,* December 2, 1953, p. 23.

[776] John Bird, "West Block's Tobermory Arrested Too As Found-In," *The Ottawa Journal,* November 23, 1954, p. 18.

[777] John Bird, "West Block's Tobermory Arrested Too As Found-In," *The Ottawa Journal,* November 23, 1954, p. 18.

[778] John Bird, "No longer "Backscratchworthy" - Peregrine and Poppett The Hill Cats Being Evicted From Cosy Quarters," the *Ottawa Citizen,* December 2, 1953, p. 23.

[779] A note on her death (Win Mills, "Hill's cat lady goes to reward" the *Ottawa Citizen,* February 21, 1963, p. 2.) says Maggs, but Special Correspondent Bird used Maggs. Ref: -John Bird, "No longer "Backscratchworthy" - Peregrine and Poppett The Hill Cats Being Evicted From Cosy Quarters," the *Ottawa Citizen,* December 2, 1953, p. 23.

[780] V.A. Bower, "Bronze Penthouse Pigeons Thrown Out by Landlord," the *Ottawa Citizen*, October 22, 1947, p. 12.

[781] John Bird, "No longer "Backscratchworthy" - Peregrine and Poppett The Hill Cats Being Evicted From Cosy Quarters," the *Ottawa Citizen,* December 2, 1953, p. 23.

[782] *Ibid.*

[783] John Bird, "Peregrine and Poppett Escape Death by a Cat's Whisker," *The Ottawa Journal,* November 23, 1954, p. 1.

[784] Greg Connolley, "Unofficial War on Hill – Cut Off Pigeons' Food," the *Ottawa Citizen,* December 29, 1960, p. 40.

[785] John Bird, "General Young is Sympathetic but Firm on Cats' Eviction," *The Ottawa Journal,* November 25, 1954, p. 1.

[786] E.S. Sherwood, "Those Cats," *The Ottawa Journal,* November 26, 1954, p. 6.

[787] John Bird, "General Young is Sympathetic but Firm on Cats' Eviction," *The Ottawa Journal,* November 25, 1954, p. 1.

[788] John Bird, "Peregrine and Poppett Escape Death by a Cat's Whisker," *The Ottawa Journal,* November 23, 1954, p. 1.

[789] John Bird, "Our Man Bird Finds Homes for Evicted Parliament Cats", *The Ottawa Journal,* November 26, 1954, p. 3.

[790] *Ibid.*

[791] Win Mills, "Hill's cat lady goes to reward" the *Ottawa Citizen,* February 21, 1963, p. 2.

[792] Bill Carroll, "The Disneyesque conspiracy," the *Ottawa Citizen,* September 26, 1968, p. 25.

[793] Personal communication, Frank Foran, 2006.

[794] Steven Barmazel, "Keeping the Cats Fat on Parliament Hill; Pensioner Keeps Promise to Dying Friend to Aid Strays," the *Ottawa Citizen,* December 18, 1987, p. A.1.FRO. This reference says that when she died in 1987 she had been caring for the cats 11 years, so she started in 1976.

[795] Klaus J. Gerken, "The Cats of Parliament Hill Blog," http://www.synapse.net/kgerken/CatsBlog.HTM, April 14 and 15, 2006.

[796] Steven Barmazel, "Keeping the Cats Fat on Parliament Hill; Pensioner Keeps Promise to Dying Friend to Aid Strays," the *Ottawa Citizen*, December 18, 1987, p. A.1.FRO.

[797] Roy MacGregor, "While Great Men Meet, Hill Lady Cares for Cats," the *Ottawa Citizen*, April 7, 1987, p. A.3.

[798] Personal communication, Frank Foran, 2006 and 2007.

[799] Roy MacGregor, "While Great Men Meet, Hill Lady Cares for Cats," the *Ottawa Citizen*, April 7, 1987, p. A.3.

[800] Klaus J. Gerken, "The Cats of Parliament Hill Blog," http://www.synapse.net/kgerken/CatsBlog.HTM, April 14 and 15, 2006.

[801] An article in *The Vancouver Sun* puts the date for construction of the first cat house about four years earlier. Ref. "Now These Really are the Fat Cats of Ottawa," *The Vancouver Sun (3* edition)*, December 21, 1987, p. F6.

[802] Steven Barmazel, "Keeping the Cats Fat on Parliament Hill; Pensioner Keeps Promise to Dying Friend to Aid Strays," the *Ottawa Citizen*, December 18, 1987, p. A.1.FRO.

[803] "Now These Really are the Fat Cats of Ottawa," *The Vancouver Sun (3* edition)*, December 21, 1987, p. F6.

[804] Roy MacGregor, "Parliament Hill's 'Cat Man' Doesn't Count Cost of Helping Animals (final edition)," the *Ottawa Citizen*, June 23, 1989, p. A.3.

[805] *Ibid.*

[806] Trish Dyer, "Pensioner the Santa of Parliament," *Toronto Star (final edition)*, December 9, 1988, p.E13.

[807] Obituary, *Le Droit*, August 15, 1987, p. 41.

[808] "Now These Really are the Fat Cats of Ottawa," *The Vancouver Sun (3* edition)*, December 21, 1987, p. F6.

[809] Steven Barmazel, "Keeping the Cats Fat on Parliament Hill; Pensioner Keeps Promise to Dying Friend to Aid Strays," the *Ottawa Citizen*, December 18, 1987, p. A.1.FRO. This reference says that when she died in 1987 she had been caring for the cats 11 years, so she started in 1976.

[810] Trish Dyer, "Pensioner the Santa of Parliament," *Toronto Star (final edition)*, December 9, 1988, p.E13.

[811] "Now These Really are the Fat Cats of Ottawa," *The Vancouver Sun (3* edition)*, December 21, 1987, p. F6.

[812] The earliest mention of a cat fund is Steven Barmazel, "Keeping the Cats Fat on Parliament Hill; Pensioner Keeps Promise to Dying Friend to Aid Strays," the *Ottawa Citizen*, December 18, 1987, p. A.1.FRO.

[813] Trish Dyer, "Pensioner the Santa of Parliament," *Toronto Star (final edition)*, December 9, 1988, p.E13.

[814] Roy MacGregor, "Keeping the Faith; Robbed by Death of his Partner in Life, the Cat Man of Parliament Hill Soldiers on Alone," the *Ottawa Citizen (Final Edition)*, November 30, 1990, p. A.1.FRO.

[815] *Ibid.*

[816] *Ibid.*

[817] Mark Bourrie, "Parliamentary Cat Keeper," *The Toronto Star*, February 11, 1996, p. C2.

[818] Kerry MacGregor, "Catman Gets Corporate Help," the *Ottawa Citizen*, July 30, 1997.

[819] Jason Kirby, "New Hill Cat Keeper Ditched," *Centretown News*, February 6, 1998, p.1.